A STUDENT'S GUIDE TO ACADEMIC
Writing

A STUDENT'S GUIDE TO ACADEMIC

Writing

MICHAEL O'BRIEN MORAN

University of Manitoba

L. KAREN SOIFERMAN

University of Manitoba
and University of Winnipeg

PEARSON

Toronto

Vice-President, Editorial Director: Gary Bennett
Editor-in-Chief: Michelle Sartor
Acquisitions Editor: David S. Le Gallais
Signing Representative: Duncan MacKinnon
Marketing Manager: Jennifer Sutton
Senior Developmental Editor: Darryl Kamo
Project Manager: Marissa Lok
Project Coordination, Editorial Services, and Text Design: Electronic Publishing Services, Inc., NYC
Art Rendering and Electronic Page Makeup: Jouve
Proofreaders: Cy Strom, Nina Taylor
Art Director: Julia Hall
Cover and Interior Designer: Anthony Leung
Cover Image: Fotolia

---

10 9 8 7 6 5 4 3 2   EB

Library and Archives Canada Cataloguing in Publication

O'Brien Moran, Michael, 1958–

A student's guide to academic writing / Michael O'Brien Moran, and L. Karen Soiferman.

Includes bibliographical references and index.

ISBN 978-0-13-257204-0

   1. Academic writing.   2. Report writing.   3. English language—Rhetoric.
   I. Soiferman, Lisa Karen, 1955–   II. Title.

PE1408.O27 2013   808'.042   C2012-905479-8

ISBN 978-0-13-257204-0

*We dedicate this book to the
first-year students from whom
we have learned so much.*

BRIEF CONTENTS

CONTENTS

Chapter 6   The Importance of Authoritative Sources   135

REFLECTING ON THE TEXT I: THE PLANNING STAGE

The Planning Stage

SECTION II: WRITING AND REVISION

Chapter 9   Transitions   234

REFLECTING ON THE TEXT II: THE WRITING AND REVISION STAGE

The Writing and Revision Stage

SECTION III: REVIEWING

Chapter 14   Templates for Common Academic Writing Styles   385

REFLECTING ON THE TEXT III:
THE REVIEWING STAGE

Preface

We'll begin by recognizing the limited claim that we make for this first edition of *A Student's Guide to Academic Writing*. We cannot make you a great writer or artist of vision whose deft touch with words and phrases brings tears to the eyes of strong men and women. We cannot teach you to recast tired images in fresh new ways or to frame original and sometimes risky metaphors in the style of E. E. Cummings. We're not entirely sure that anyone else can do that either. Writing as art is, to some extent at least, a gift. Those who have it can thank the Muses, genetics, and the lives they've lived. Genius is born in a mysterious blend of the three.

We can, however, make this much smaller promise: we can show you the things you need to do to make yourself a more effective writer. That is, we teach concepts that will help you make the decisions you need to make in order to write an essay that fulfills your purpose or intention. We base our method on teaching practices that we've used in the classroom for a number of years. Often working with students who insist that they cannot write, we developed strategies that return the authority of the writing process to the writers themselves, encouraging them to think of writing as a problem-solving exercise. Those strategies are based on a writing process theory that has been popular for decades: (1) identify the writing purpose, (2) identify the audience, and (3) think of the things that must be done to realize the writing purpose in a way that satisfies the audience. All we've added to the process is an emphasis on decision making: *What decisions do you, as the writer, have to make to achieve the goal of realizing the writing purpose in a way that satisfies the audience?*

The conversational tone of the book is intentional. We have found that, for many students, moments of insight occur in conferences in response to questions from instructors or teaching assistants. We have tried to simulate that environment with what is, admittedly, a one-sided conversation-sort-of-thing between the reader and the authors. In a further attempt to simulate the writing conference environment, we have, wherever possible, phrased writing challenges as questions.

This book is designed for use by college and university students as they navigate the challenges of learning to write an academic essay in a new writing environment. It's written with a focus on writing decisions and arranged with a number of recurring features designed to help with decision making.

UNDERSTANDING THE DIFFERENCE BETWEEN THE PRACTICE OF THE NOVICE WRITER AND THE PRACTICE OF THE EXPERIENCED WRITER

Each chapter of the text begins with a section aimed at helping you understand the difference between the practice of the novice writer and the practice of the experienced writer. The section includes a brief discussion of the ways in which the writing practices of a novice writer differ from those of an experienced writer at a particular point in the writing process. Those differences are important. It often appears that writing instruction begins and ends with a review of the sorts of things that effective writers do well, a review that experienced writers might find interesting if they were the kind of people who bought introductory textbooks on writing. In most cases, they don't. They don't need to. They're experienced writers. You, on the other hand, do buy introductory textbooks on writing (or, at least, have bought this one) and, while you may find the discussions of the practices of effective writers vaguely interesting, you may not find those discussions, in and of themselves, entirely useful. What you need to know is not simply *what* experienced writers do but *why*, and perhaps more importantly, *how* they do it. The initial discussion of the differences in writing practice, therefore, always leads to a more general discussion of the decisions you have to wrestle with in order to achieve the effects an experienced writer achieves.

METACOGNITION

To help the novice writer learn, this textbook employs a principle of educational psychology known as *metacognition*. Metacognition refers to the process of monitoring your own thinking to determine whether the steps you're taking to solve a problem produce the desired effect. As you work through the composition of your essay, you will need to make decisions about the best way to organize and express your ideas. You will also need to consider the effect your decisions will have on the reader. Metacognition allows you (1) to identify a writing goal, (2) to reflect on the decisions you need to make to achieve that goal, and (3) to evaluate the degree to which those decisions are successful by examining the effect they have on the essay you're writing. Metacognition puts you in a position of control as a writer, permitting you to monitor your writing process and adjust your writing decisions in accordance with the new challenges the text presents to you.

THE IDDL MODEL

We organized this book around a writing model, the IDDL model, which guides you in the process of drafting and revising your essay. IDDL is an acronym for a four-stage essay-writing process:

1. **I**nscribe the writing space.
   - In this stage, you create a structure for the essay by using your thesis statement to identify the beginning of the essay (i.e., the introduction, with a statement of the claim you intend to explore), the body (i.e., the individual reasons you've offered in support of your claim or the individual themes you intend to explore), and the end of the essay (i.e., the conclusion, with its discussion of the ways in which you've satisfied your writing purpose).
   - When you start with a structure that maps the beginning and end of the essay and the path you will follow to get from one to the other, you escape the mind-numbing experience of staring at a blank page, trying to find a way to get started. The model tells you where you are (i.e., the beginning, or introduction), where you're going (i.e., the end, or conclusion), and the problems you have to solve along the way.
2. **D**efine the rhetorical problems locally.
   - In the second stage, you use the thesis statement again to define the individual elements in the thesis that need to be either supported by evidence or explored. These will become paragraphs or thematically linked groups of paragraphs in your essay.
   - One problem we all face as writers is a limited working memory. By looking at each rhetorical problem individually, you're better able to devote your full attention to it. The rest of the essay will wait patiently while you do so. It's not going anywhere. The use of the model ensures that the essay remains where it is, each of its other themes exactly as you left them, while you attend to the problem that lies before you. In the fourth stage, you will return again to the essay as a whole, revising as necessary to link the individual pieces together.
3. **D**iscover the information necessary to solve the local rhetorical problems.
   - The third stage of the process is one in which you seek out the information you need to fully explore each of the rhetorical problems you identified in the second stage. You're looking for information that is specific to the particular problem. As you find it, you attach it to the theme to which it belongs (remembering to include the information you need for citations).
   - At this point, you're able to write the individual paragraphs of your essay, using your own critical analysis of the rhetorical problem and the information you discovered in this stage.
4. **L**ink the individual units of the essay logically.
   - In this final stage, you return again to the thesis statement. You will need to ensure that each paragraph has been organized around a single key theme, that groups of paragraphs have been arranged logically, and that the reader is being led from the introduction to the conclusion in a way that makes sense.

The IDDL model is a visual representation of the writing process (which makes it easier to manage the process). It breaks the process down into manageable steps, and a series of embedded questions helps to guide you through your decision making. The IDDL model is featured in most chapters of the text.

CHARTS AND TABLES

In each chapter, you will notice that we've included a series of charts and tables. Some of these are designed to facilitate comparisons between different strategies or categories and some are meant to guide you as your write your essay. The decision-making charts appear at various points in the text to help with the decision-making process.

PRACTICE EXERCISES

We've included practice exercises throughout the text. These are designed to provide you with an opportunity to integrate the concepts and practices being discussed into your own writing process. Writing, unfortunately, is one of those skills that you can only master through practice. Reading about writing, like reading about playing the piano, will only get you so far. Try booking a concert in Carnegie Hall after leafing through volumes I and II of *Concert Piano for Beginners*. Certain skills can only be acquired through the application of your knowledge. Writing is one of them.

EVALUATION WORKSHEETS

Most chapters conclude with self-evaluation worksheets. While these can be used to conduct last-minute assessments of individual aspects of your essay, they also serve a larger function. They are designed to enhance your understanding of the processes you followed when making the decisions you made. As you work through the worksheets, you will revisit the earlier decisions you made, asking yourself whether those decisions had the intended effect. Like the peer-evaluation checklists discussed below, the evaluation worksheets encourage you to look at your work from the perspective of the reader.

PEER-EVALUATION CHECKLISTS

We've included peer-evaluation worksheets at the end of most chapters, to enable student writers to examine one another's work from the reader's perspective, assessing the degree to which an essay is coherent and logical. The peer reviewer serves as a surrogate for the reader, speaking on the reader's behalf, identifying points at which the phrasing of a sentence is confusing, the organization of a paragraph doesn't seem to work, the ordering of the paragraphs might be reconsidered, or the reasoning of the essay seems flawed. The peer reviewer is not a proofreader. He or she is looking at larger questions of meaning. Does the essay say what it means to say and does it say it effectively?

ORGANIZATION OF CHAPTERS

The book is organized to reflect stages in the writing process.

Section I: Planning

- Chapter 1 identifies some the problems students experience in making the transition from high school writing to college or university writing. It also includes a discussion of some of the thinking processes involved in writing and an introduction to the concept of metacognition (i.e., the process of monitoring one's own thinking).

- Chapter 2 includes a discussion of the nature of academic writing, with a specific focus on the argumentative essay. It also includes a discussion of the process needed to develop an effective thesis statement and an arguable proposition.

- Chapter 3 introduces the IDDL writing model and includes a step-by-step demonstration of the way in which you can use it to create a draft of an essay.

- Chapter 4 guides you through the research process, identifying some of the decisions you need to make to find relevant and reliable evidence.

- Chapter 5 introduces the annotated bibliography, identifying its purpose and the process you can follow to create one. The chapter includes a discussion of the format for the annotated bibliography and provides samples for you to study. It also provides a discussion of the ways in which you might use the annotated bibliography as a writing tool.

- Chapter 6 provides a discussion of the importance of authoritative sources, including strategies for reading sources critically, selecting evidence, assessing the authority of information, and introducing evidence to your paper. There is also a section on evaluating the quality and reliability of information you find on the internet.

Section II: Writing and Revision

- In Chapter 7, we discuss the importance of crafting sentences and paragraphs purposefully, so that you make decisions about each on the basis of the effect you mean to create.

- Chapter 8 includes a discussion of the purpose of the introductory paragraph and the considerations that ought to inform your decisions when you write an introduction. It also provides both a list of strategies that might prove useful when you write introductions and a list of strategies you might want to avoid.

- In Chapter 9, we identify the value of using transitions to create intentional connections between ideas. We discuss the way in which transitions work between sentences, within paragraphs, and between paragraphs to establish logical connections. We also provide a list of transitional words and phrases that will assist you in choosing the word that suits your purposes.

- Chapter 10 provides an exploration of the purpose of conclusions, and includes some of the considerations that ought to inform your decision making when you write conclusions. The chapter includes a list of strategies for writing effective conclusions and a second list of strategies to avoid.

- The final chapter of Section II is Chapter 11. In it, we discuss the complementary concepts of recursivity (i.e., circling back to an earlier point in the text) and revision. Recursivity and revision are characteristic practices of experienced writers who understand that, during the writing process, the best-laid plans often go awry. We provide a discussion of the principles involved in revision and some strategies for making the process more efficient.

Section III: Reviewing

- In Chapter 12, we discuss the three most common types of formatting used in colleges and universities (APA, MLA, *Chicago* style), providing guidelines for addressing the most significant features of each format. We also supply strategies for learning to work with the different formats and practice exercises for you to improve your understanding of the process of formatting.
- Chapter 13 provides a discussion of strategies for editing. It also includes practice exercises to allow you to familiarize yourself with the process of editing systematically.
- In Chapter 14, we provide templates for writing essays in the humanities, social sciences, and natural sciences, and review the way in which you can adapt the IDDL model for use in the different disciplines. The chapter is by no means exhaustive, but it will give you a general sense of the differences between essays in different fields of study.

MyCompLab®

The moment you know.
Educators know it. Students know it. It's that inspired moment when something that was difficult to understand suddenly makes perfect sense. Our MyLab products have been designed and refined with a single purpose in mind—to help educators create that moment of understanding with their students.

MyCompLab delivers **proven results** in helping individual students succeed. It provides **engaging experiences** that personalize, stimulate, and measure learning for each student. And it comes from a **trusted partner** with educational expertise and an eye on the future.

You can use MyCompLab by itself or by linking it to any learning management system. To learn more about how MyCompLab combines proven learning applications with powerful assessment, visit **www.mycomplab.com.**

Visit **www.mycomplab.com** to access diverse resources for composition in one easy-to-use place:

1. Sections on **writing, research,** and **grammar** cover all the key topics in the text, providing additional instruction, examples, and practice. **Exercises**

offer the opportunity to practise the skills you've learned in class and include both self-grading quizzes and writing activities. **Writing samples** provide examples of different types of writing and different documentation styles; some are annotated to highlight key aspects or to stimulate reflection and discussion. **Videos** illustrate aspects of the writing process through scenarios, or provide grammar and editing tutorials through on-screen revision.

2. **Pearson eText** gives you access to the text whenever and wherever you have access to the internet. The eText pages look exactly like the printed text, offering powerful new functionality for students and instructors. Users can create notes, highlight text in different colours, create bookmarks, zoom, click hyperlinked words and phrases to view definitions, and view in single- or two-page view. Pearson eText allows for quick navigation to key parts of the eText using a table of contents and provides full-text search. Icons in the eText are hotlinked to related material within MyCompLab:
    - ■ Practice icons link to practice exercises and evaluation worksheets   ✓●─ Practice

3. An online **composing** space includes tools such as writing tips and editing FAQs, so you can get the help you need when you need it, without ever leaving the writing environment. Within this space, you'll find access to **EBSCO's ContentSelect,** a database of articles from academic journals that you can use for research and reference.

4. The **portfolio** feature allows you to create an e-portfolio of your work that you can easily share with your instructor and peers. Use the access code packaged with new copies of this textbook to log on to MyCompLab, or purchase separate access through your campus bookstore or directly through the website.

Study on the Go

Featured at the end of each chapter, you will find a unique QR code providing access to Study on the Go, an unprecedented mobile integration between text and online content. Students link to Pearson's unique Study on the Go content directly from their smartphones, allowing them to study whenever and wherever they wish! Go to one of the sites below to see how you can download an app to your smartphone for free. Once the app is installed, your phone will scan the visual applications, as well as quizzes, all of which can be accessed at any time.

ScanLife
http://getscanlife.com/

NeoReader
http://get.neoreader.com/

QuickMark
http://www.quickmark.com.tw/

SUPPLEMENTS

Pearson Custom Library

For enrolments of at least twenty-five students, you can create your own textbook by choosing the chapters that best suit your own course needs. To begin building your custom text, visit **www.pearsoncustomlibrary.com**. You may also work with a dedicated Pearson custom editor to create your ideal text—publishing your own original content or mixing and matching Pearson content. Contact your local Pearson representative to get started.

CourseSmart for Instructors

CourseSmart goes beyond traditional expectations—providing instant, online access to the textbooks and course materials you need at a lower cost for students. While students save money, you can save time and avoid hassles with a digital eTextbook that allows you to search for the most relevant content at the very moment you need it. Whether it's evaluating textbooks or creating lecture notes to help students with difficult concepts, CourseSmart can make life a little easier. See how when you visit **www.coursesmart.com/instructors**.

Technology Specialists

Pearson's technology specialists work with faculty and campus course designers to ensure that Pearson technology products, assessment tools, and online course materials are tailored to meet your specific needs. This highly qualified team is dedicated to helping schools take full advantage of a wide range of educational resources, by assisting you to integrate a variety of instructional materials and media formats. Your local Pearson sales representative can provide you with more details on this service program.

ACKNOWLEDGMENTS

Michael's Acknowledgments

I would like to acknowledge my co-author, Karen Soiferman, without whom the text could not have been completed. I am, I'm told, a little temperamental. She wrote chapters knowing I would change them, watched as I cut and slashed our work in revisions, and endured my endlessly annoying practice of scrapping entire chapters when I thought I had come up with a better idea. She coaxed me to work when I didn't want to do so, dragged me to work when coaxing failed, and shielded me from our wonderful editor, Darryl, whenever she feared that his advice or criticism might send me into a rant that would cost us weeks of valuable writing time. Thank you.

I would also like to acknowledge the many people who have supported me through this endeavour: my friends and family, especially my sister, Louise, and, my partner, Leslie, who, for the past year, has patiently endured my absence. I would like to acknowledge and thank my wonderful children, Zachariah, Seamus, and Flannery, for learning to live with a quick dinner and a wave as I rushed home from work, dropped plates on the table, and rushed away. I love you, my babies, and, for good or for ill, I'm back now. Somebody had better do the dishes and vacuum the living room. We're going to start living like a normal family again.

Michael O'Brien Moran, 2012

Karen's Acknowledgments

I want to acknowledge Michael, my co-author, who provided me with the opportunity to share in his vision of this book. Together, we have been on a wild and crazy ride for the past four years that has culminated both in our individual Ph.D.'s and in this book. I will be forever grateful for his continuous support, endless encouragement, and fierce loyalty. The mere fact that we have completed the book still speaking to one another is a testament to our enduring friendship. That friendship was sorely tested on many occasions, but I believe we have emerged stronger than ever. Thanks, Michael.

I want to thank my children, Heather and Marc, who make everything I do worthwhile. Their love has sustained me through this whole process and provided me with the incentive to continue. Love to you both.

L. Karen Soiferman, 2012

Reviewers

We would like to extend thanks to the following reviewers, whose feedback played a key role in the development of this text:

Stephen Ahern, *Acadia University*
Marc Alcock, *Conestoga College*
Steve Bennett, *University of Waterloo*
Brent Cottle, *Lethbridge College*
Aurelea Mahood, *Capilano University*
Karen Selesky, *University of the Fraser Valley*
Jaffer Sheyholislami, *Carleton University*
Joanne Valin, *Nipissing University*
Kent Walker, *Brock University*
David West, *Douglas College*

We also extend thanks to the team at Pearson Canada for their expertise and guidance, as well as their efforts in bringing this project forward: David Le Gallais, Acquisitions Editor; Jennifer Sutton, Marketing Manager; Darryl Kamo, Senior Developmental Editor; Marissa Lok, Project Manager; and Cy Strom and Nina Taylor, Proofreaders.

A STUDENT'S GUIDE TO ACADEMIC

Writing

SECTION I: PLANNING

CHAPTER 1

Making the Transition to Writing at College or University

Learning Objectives

At the completion of this chapter, you will be able to:

1. Illustrate differences in the writing practices of novice and experienced writers.

2. Explain the importance of using metacognition to monitor the decisions you make while writing.

3. Distinguish between the process of writing and the written product.

4. Summarize the difference between writing in high school and writing at college or university.

1.1 INTRODUCTION

What's the difference between you and writers who tear off one work of genius after another, apparently without effort, seemingly transcribing words of inspiration from beyond, barely working up a sweat?

They write better?

Maybe.

They certainly write differently. Thirty years ago, researchers began looking at the differences between the ways in which novice and experienced writers compose text and found that the two groups follow distinctly different writing processes. In this chapter, we discuss a new way of looking at both the writing process and the manner in which people acquire writing skills. We identify some of the differences between the ways in which novice and experienced writers compose text, highlighting the importance of decision making. We also introduce you to some of the recurring features of this textbook, explaining their purpose and their significance. Most importantly, perhaps, we will discuss the importance of learning through **metacognition,** which is a process that allows you to reflect on both your writing behaviours and the decisions that guide those behaviours. The aim of focusing on metacognition is to encourage you to recognize the effect of the decisions you make on the essay you are trying to produce. We believe that, once you come to see the relationship between your decisions and the essay that emerges, you will be better able to develop your ideas in text purposefully and intentionally.

One of the challenges you face when entering university studies is how to adjust to the new expectations for your written work. University faculty members widely assume that students ought to have been taught to write before they enter university. Those of us who study first-year learning have argued for years that students *have* been taught to write. They were simply taught to write in a different setting, in answer to different expectations, and in accordance with different writing protocols. (*Protocols* is a term that refers to a particular set of rules.) In this chapter, we look at some of the significant differences between writing in high school and in university.

You will see this word throughout this text. **Metacognition** refers to the process of monitoring your own thinking. Since the text is based on the assumption that good writing comes from good decision making, the ability to reflect on your thinking process while writing is essential. As you work through the composition of your essay, you will need to make decisions about the best way to organize your ideas and about the expression of those ideas. You will also need to consider the effect your decisions will have on the reader. In effect, that is metacognition. Thinking about your thinking.

1.2 DIFFERENCES BETWEEN NOVICE WRITERS AND EXPERIENCED WRITERS

LO 1

Examining the differences between novice and experienced writers is a recurring feature of this textbook. You might wonder why we use the terms, and why they are important. The term *novice* is not meant to be insulting. There's nothing wrong with being a novice. Every time a person enters a new writing environment, he or she becomes a novice again. There is a value to knowing that. If you understand that different writing environments call for different writing practices, and you also understand that one of the best ways to understand those practices is for you to compare what you are doing to the practices of those who are more experienced in that writing environment, then you can modify your own writing procedures by emulating, or imitating, the practices of others. As we are about to discuss, this does not excuse you from the obligation of making your own decisions. Instead, it foregrounds the decisions that you need to make and allows you to adapt to the new environment by focusing only on the aspects of the writing processes that are different.

Near the beginning of most chapters in this textbook, you will find a chart like the one that follows. We'll use each chart to identify differences between novice and experienced writers that are relevant to the subject discussed in that particular chapter. At this point, however, we are discussing the entire spectrum of significant differences in a general way.

Novice Writers	Experienced Writers
■ Require thought for procedural, or "mechanical," writing functions.	■ Have, to a significant degree, automated procedural functions.
■ Focus on error avoidance rather than meaning.	■ Focus on developing or refining meaning.
■ Begin writing without planning, and edit, if at all, for grammatical errors.	■ Invest time and energy in planning and reviewing.
■ Focus on "knowledge telling" (i.e., relating all the information they have and can find on a topic, rather than exercising critical judgment to determine relevance).	■ Organize, and reorganize, essay structure to allow individual ideas to serve the overall purpose of the essay.

The differences between the two kinds of writers fall into two categories:

1. The first category refers to the degree to which a writer has internalized, and automated, procedural knowledge. That means that some writers are able to operate without having to think about the steps they need to follow. *Novice writers tend to require thought for procedural, or "mechanical," writing functions, while more experienced writers have, to a significant degree, automated procedural functions.*

If you've learned to drive, you will know that at first you had to pay attention to the difference between the accelerator and the brake (this is an important distinction—many a fencepost has been lost due to confusion about the two). Similarly, at first you needed to think about the dangers of over-turning a steering wheel or following the driver in front of you too closely. In short, in order to drive safely as a novice, you had to concentrate actively on the physical operation of the vehicle. In time, however, those skills became automatic and you were better able to focus on driving decisions.

Writing is like that. Once you have mastered the procedures, you are in a better position to think about the decisions you need to make. Unfortunately, automatization takes time and practice. However, if you follow the advice we provide in this and subsequent chapters, the strategies you learn should make it possible for you to write effectively even before you acquire that procedural mastery.

2. The second category of differences is connected to the ways that novice and experienced writers make decisions about writing. *Novice writers tend to focus on error avoidance rather than meaning; begin writing without planning; edit, if at all, for grammatical errors; and focus on "knowledge telling." More experienced writers focus on developing or refining meaning, invest time and energy in planning and reviewing, and organize (and reorganize) essay structure to allow individual ideas to serve the overall purpose of the essay.*

You'll notice that the list of differences in the second category is characterized by a common interest in the development of meaning. There is some good news here. It is easier to acquire an understanding of decision-making strategies than it is to automatize procedural skills. Much of the focus of this text addresses ways in which you can learn to make more effective writing decisions by identifying the purpose of your writing exercise and thinking about the decisions that will lead to the fulfillment of that purpose.

1.3 METACOGNITION AND LEARNING LO 1, 2

In the introduction to the chapter, we suggested that we would introduce you to a different way of thinking about writing. Metacognition—which is commonly defined as thinking about thinking—is a cognitive practice that allows you to make changes to a strategy that is not working by reflecting on the differences between a strategy that isn't working and another strategy that might work. Metacognition, in short, allows you to adjust intentionally.

It's particularly useful when applied to skills like writing. What is the difference between the essay you meant to write and the one you ended up with? If you don't know, it will be difficult to move from the first essay to the second one. It's much more difficult to alter an intellectual or cognitive practice if you don't know what, or why, you are changing. Metacognition allows you (1) to identify the differences between the work you are doing and the work you want to do, and (2) to consciously search for a process you can follow to make the first essay (the one you aren't satisfied with) more like the second (the essay you want to write). The box on the following page explains the way in which the metacognitive perspective allows you to make intentional changes in your thinking and writing.

Since the concept of metacognition is one we mention repeatedly, it's important that you understand the concept and the ways in which it can be applied to writing. Think of metacognition as your own personal tool box. The strategies you have in your metacognitive tool box will determine which skills you can use when it comes time to make writing decisions. Expert and novice learners differ in the way they make use of their metacognitive abilities. Experienced writers consider their goals, plan accordingly, and monitor their own progress as they carry out their plans. Novice writers, in contrast, often fail to articulate a goal or fail to develop a plan for meeting that goal. In some cases, novice writers rely on a single writing strategy, which they apply without thinking about the degree to which it is appropriate to the situation. Many students fail to set explicit writing goals for themselves, or fail to make plans to meet the goals they have set.

What does metacognition mean for you as a writer? It means you will think about (1) your thinking processes, (2) the effect of writing decisions on your essay, and (3) the effect of your writing decisions on the reader. That sounds like a lot of work, doesn't it? The good news is that metacognitive skills can be learned. More good news? Once learned, metacognitive skills tend to become automatic, operating in the background without requiring the degree of conscious effort they seem to demand now.

Throughout the textbook, we apply metacognitive learning principles to our discussions of the differences between novice and experienced writers in particular and to the writing decisions you must make in general. The chart below is one of the recurring features of the textbook. These charts appear at various points in the text to draw your attention back to the decisions you make while writing.

METACOGNITION AND LEARNING

Imagine that you've been asked to operate a vintage cannon and to hit a target that's hidden behind a screen. Though you have never used a cannon before, you attempt to aim and fire it. When you go around the screen to check, you discover that the cannonball flew off to the left and fell far short of the target. You adjust the cannon, though again you are not entirely sure what you're doing, and fire again. This time, the cannonball misses to the right, but you're getting a better feel for the range. For the third shot, you adjust to the left and raise the angle of the cannon. It's bound to work this time, right? Sadly, when you go around the screen, you find that you've overshot the target altogether.

The difficulty, of course, is that you don't understand how to operate a cannon and so you don't really know how to manipulate it to get the result you want. You work by trial and error and you never entirely understand the effect of any action you take. In addition, because you're only vaguely aware of the location of the target, you're shooting in a general direction rather than aiming at something specific.

Imagine now that somebody instructed you briefly on how to operate the cannon. The person explained the effect that each of the adjustments would have and described how to load and charge the cannon to ensure that its operation would be relatively predictable. You're given an opportunity to practise, and your guide explains, after each shot, why the cannonball flew the way it did. In short, you're provided with the sort of instruction that allows you to use the cannon for a specific purpose with a reasonable expectation that the cannon will operate the way you expect it to. Next, your guide removes the screen, revealing the target. With your operational knowledge of the cannon and your clear view of the target, you're able to independently adjust your firing practice to increase the likelihood that you will hit the target.

That's the kind of advantage metacognition provides. Metacognition is a psychological principle that asks you to think about your own intellectual practices. It allows or encourages you to look at the difference between what you intend to do and what you actually do and to understand the differences between the two. Metacognition also encourages you to understand both your practice and your goal. Only then can you begin to move toward your desired outcome.

In the case of developing writing skills, metacognition allows you to identify the different elements in the process of writing and to specifically address those aspects of the process that are problematic. You are better able to grasp the way in which abstract concepts function when those concepts are contextualized, or put into context. You can also see the specific areas in which an essay has succeeded and the ways in which the essay can be improved.

Making Writing Decisions   Using the Metacognitive Perspective

What is the purpose of this writing decision?

The intent of a metacognitive approach is to allow you to see differences in both the purposes and processes that are followed by novice and experienced writers, and by writers in high school and writers in university.

What is the effect of this writing decision?

By identifying the specific differences between the way in which you composed your essay and the way in which an experienced writer might compose an essay, you're better able to acquire writing practices that make your essays succeed. Metacognition also allows you to see the ways in which your essay has succeeded and the ways in which the essay can be improved.

What considerations inform this decision?

You will learn to write more easily if you have a model of a successful essay. However, in order to use the metacognitive approach effectively, you need to be able to identify *significant* similarities and differences between the essay you're writing and the one you perceive to be more successful.

Suggested strategy for making this decision.

Identify the five most important differences between your work and the work you're emulating. To help make that decision, ask yourself which five of the differences you've identified are the most important and why. You will make your selections on the basis of the difference in the *effect* on the text. Attempting to address all of the differences in a single step tends to cause confusion.

Questions to guide your use of metacognition for decision making in your own essay.

1. Look at the chart to identify the differences between the novice writer and the experienced writer. Do the characteristics listed for the novice writer accurately describe your writing practices?
2. What are the differences between your writing practices and the writing practices of the experienced writer? What changes do you need to make to your own writing process to bring it closer to that of the experienced writer? What specific changes should you make?
3. What changes should you make in the planning stage? What changes should you make in the composing, or translating, stage? What changes should you make during the revising stage?
4. What effect do you think the proposed changes will have on your planning process?
5. What effect do you think the proposed changes will have on your composing process?
6. What effect do you think the proposed changes will have on your revising process?

1.4 WRITING INTENTIONALLY, OR UNDERSTANDING THE EFFECT OF THE DECISIONS YOU MAKE WHEN YOU ARE WRITING

LO 1, 2

One of the principal differences we identified between novice and experienced writers is the degree to which experienced writers focus on the planning, and revision, of their text—in other words, making informed decisions that are guided by clear intentions. It's true that experienced writers have also internalized rules of grammar and standard language usage, and that this provides them with a number of advantages. Writing effectively does not, however, require you to memorize the thousands of rules and recommendations you find in textbooks and writing guides. It certainly helps to know the rules, of course, but neither you nor anyone else can acquire all the information there is to know about grammar and essay structure over the course of one or two semesters. Don't blame yourself. It can't be done. It's not your fault.

That's the good news.

Unfortunately, there's some bad news too (there's always bad news too). There is no universal formula for essay writing that allows you to insert information into a specific slot without thinking about the effect the information may have. Writing effectively requires that you make decisions about the development of meaning, carefully organizing content in accordance with your writing purpose and constantly attending to the effect of the decisions you're making. Writing effectively also demands that you think about your reader as you are writing, understanding that you are governed by a kind of contract that obliges you to observe the conventions that the reader expects. You could choose to violate those conventions, we suppose, but you run the risk of creating a text that no one will understand. It's hard to see the logic in that.

In writing this textbook we set out to offer a different kind of writing instruction, one that focuses less on the rules of grammar and rhetoric and more on the strategies that you can use to express your ideas effectively. We don't mean to suggest that the rules are unimportant. They are important. However, you cannot compose by looking at an instructor or writing guide any more easily than you can drive by surrendering control of the car to someone in the back seat. You need to think in advance about the kind of essay you will write, reflecting on the conventions that govern that kind of essay and planning in accordance with those conventions. Once you start to write, however, you need to think about the development of meaning, concentrating on the decisions that will allow you to move from a thesis at the beginning of the text, through an exploration of the ideas that support that thesis, to a conclusion that is—within the context of the essay you're writing, at least—reasonable. You need to focus on the decisions that allow you to make sense within the parameters of the essay you are writing.

A thesis statement summarizes your argument in one or two sentences. It introduces the reader to the argument and provides the writer with a concise statement of the writing purpose.

We can't make those decisions for you. Unfortunately, neither can anyone else. In order to learn to write effectively, you need to learn to manage the decisions that will drive the text forward, linking the individual ideas together to create a coherent whole. The bad news? You're in charge. The writing process demands that you work from within the text, thinking about the purpose of the essay, and ensuring that your decisions are serving that purpose. The good news? It's more or less the same as the bad news. You don't need anyone else to produce writing that is clear and coherent. You can do it. We have designed this textbook in such a way as to provide you with the information you need when you find yourself at a decision-making crossroad. We can't tell you what to do. We can, however, help you identify the decisions you need to make, and provide you with some strategies for making them.

LO 1, 2　1.5　WRITING AND DECISION MAKING

One of the difficulties you will face as you begin to write an essay is the total number of decisions you need to address. There are a lot of them. In addition you will find that, once you've made one decision, the decisions that follow have a tendency to shift and change. The first decision can alter all of the others. It's a little like playing three-shell Monte with a con man in a New York alleyway. You're trying to keep track of the small ball under the walnut shells but things keep moving.

That's what writing is like. You begin with an airtight plan (that's your outline). You know what you mean to say. In your head, you've planned the piece from beginning to end, with rigorous logic at every turn, and a number of ingenious asides tossed in for good measure. How is it, then, that the essay that emerges veers from one idea to another, failing to demonstrate the clarity of your intention, and arrives, limping, at a conclusion that seems to have been pasted on to the essay rather than deriving organically from the essay's argument? Good question. Though there is a structure that allows writers to operate with a pre-existing organizational strategy, that strategy does not excuse the writer from the obligation to make contextual decisions as he or she moves through the composition process. That is, we can tell you that certain organizational strategies are generally more effective than others. We cannot, however, free you from the obligation to make the decisions that will allow you to express your ideas in the way that you intend (even though we will provide you with strategies that can help you identify and isolate your intentions).

We can also suggest the order in which you might want to consider the series of decisions that you have to make. Novice writers often have trouble managing the complex series of decisions that essay writing requires. In many cases, the novice attempts to orchestrate all, or many, of the decisions simultaneously. Bad idea. The fact is that experienced writers are not better able to juggle all those decisions, but rather have come to understand that the decisions need to be made in sequence. Certain questions have to be asked, and answered, first. When the writer has made the first decision, a new series of decisions presents itself. One of the advantages of this textbook is that it includes a model (the IDDL model, discussed in Chapter 3) that allows you to isolate the decisions and deal with them one at a time. The model ensures that the order in which you address the decisions makes sense, and that, if one changed decision forces you to backtrack to correct the text, you will be able to identify—without excessive pain—all the elements that are related to the change. Don't thank us. You paid for this book. It's the least we can do.

1.6   MAKING WRITING DECISIONS   LO 2

In many ways, the understanding of writing as a series of related decisions may seem more difficult than other strategies. It's not. Or, more precisely, it won't be. Once you get used to the process, in fact, it ought to make the writing process much easier. If you divide the decisions you must make into the following two categories, you might even find that the process of writing an essay becomes more manageable:

1. Decisions about the essay as a complete document
2. Decisions about some smaller aspect of the essay

Here's why. The first decisions you make will reflect the purpose of your essay: What topic will you write about? What aspect of that topic will you address? What position will you take? What specific argument will you make? What are the limits to your claim? These decisions will determine the shape of your essay. Essentially, these first decisions will transform writing from a complicated, ambiguous process of filling space on a blank page to a practical series of related steps.

The second series of decisions emerges from the first. The first category of decisions you make (discussed in the paragraph above) defines the goals of your essay. The second category allows you to achieve those goals. How will I convince the reader that my topic is worthwhile? How will I clearly articulate the position I'm taking? What things need to be discussed or proven to satisfy my reader? How will I prove those things?

Seems like a bit of challenge? Again, making writing decisions in an essay is not as difficult a process as it appears to be. You just need to do it systematically. The first decisions will frame the ones that follow. The logic of the essay structure will emerge from the decisions you make. The individual sections of the essay will emerge from that logic.

And then, as if by magic, you will find that the unruly cluster of vague notions with which you began is now performing in perfect harmony—a symphony of ideas, pleasing to both the ear and the mind.

1.6.1 Steps to Consider When Making Writing Decisions about the Essay on Which You Are Working

You should consider the following points as you make your decisions:

1. Determine your purpose. Clarify your position on the issue you are addressing and decide which way you will approach it. Having trouble? It's easier than it appears. Answer this question: Why are you writing the paper?
2. Evaluate the purpose. Evaluation requires that you explore the topic you want to discuss and make decisions about the nature of the essay you're about to write.
3. Develop a plan to put your decision into action. The IDDL writing model to which you will be introduced in Chapter 3 will help make these decisions easier.
4. Monitor the effects of your decisions. As you write, you need to constantly evaluate the degree to which the decisions you make are delivering the results you intend. Again, this capacity to monitor the effect of decisions comes from the metacognitive perspective we spoke of earlier. It is the ability to make judgments based on your understanding of decisions that are working well and those that are not working.

The ability to make decisions may appear to be easier for some people than it is for others. It is. The good news is that this ability is not simply natural or innate. People who make good decisions in any particular field are generally those who have an understanding of the factors that must be considered. You can acquire that understanding. If you follow the guidelines of decision making we've outlined, your ability to make good writing decisions will improve.

There will, however, be obstacles along the road. Developing the ability to work through writing problems takes time. Sometimes, when you encounter a new problem or have to make a decision in a situation you have not previously encountered, you will react by resorting to a strategy that worked for you before. That's natural enough. After all, it worked once. The problem with this approach is that you force solutions on problems rather than adapt a solution that is specific to the problem. That is, sometimes the old solution doesn't fit the new problem. That's why we're suggesting that you use an organized approach to problem solving and decision making. We recognize that we are not going to be able to identify every single way that you could approach each of the decisions you face. If, however, you are armed with a unified strategy for decision making, you will, at least, be in a position to narrow down the options available to you.

The next chart features a series of questions and answers that are designed to focus your attention on the decisions you need to make at various points in the writing process. This is a recurring feature of the textbook, which is meant to (1) make you aware of the kinds of decisions you need to make at any particular point in the process, and (2) provide some of the information you require to guide those decisions.

Making Writing Decisions About Making Writing Decisions

What is the purpose of this writing decision?

You will learn to exercise greater control over your writing when you recognize that effective writing derives less from a magical facility with language (though that certainly doesn't hurt) and more from an understanding of the relationship between the decisions you make and the essay that emerges from those decisions.

What is the effect of this writing decision?

You will learn that you can compose and revise your essay intentionally (i.e., you will see that modifying a specific section of your essay alters the meaning of that section). But first you have to learn to monitor your writing by examining the relationship between the decisions you make as a writer and the effect of those decisions on the essay you are writing.

What considerations inform this decision?

The purpose of writing is to develop an idea, using content or reference material, and shape that idea until it emerges finally as a coherent expression of your position. Novice writers may be under the mistaken impression that the aim is to simply insert content and then try, mechanically, to shuffle things around until the essay has the form, more or less, of an essay.

Suggested strategy for making this decision.

If you learn to monitor the effect of the writing decisions you make, you will come to see that your decisions have effects. Sometimes these effects are the effects you intended. Sometimes they are not. By attending to the effect of your individual writing decisions (i.e., noticing what happens when you take a particular action), you will discover the degree to which your decisions drive the writing process.

Questions to guide decision making in your own essay.

1. When you prepare an outline for your essay, use questions to guide you rather than statements (we'll talk more of this in Chapters 2 and 3). Reflect on the thesis statement for your essay. What are you attempting to prove or demonstrate?
2. Break that thesis statement into its subordinate themes. What do you need to prove or demonstrate for the first theme? The second theme? For each succeeding theme?
3. Looking at each paragraph unit, or series of related paragraph units, ask yourself what unifying idea links all the ideas in the paragraph or series of related paragraphs. What is the relationship between each of the ideas in the respective paragraphs and the controlling idea?
4. What pattern of reasoning is reflected in the order of the paragraphs? Does that pattern make sense?

LO 1, 3   1.7   THE DIFFERENCES BETWEEN WRITING AND THE WRITTEN TEXT

An advantage that experienced writers enjoy is that they have come to terms with the subtle differences between the act of writing and the actual written text. The act of writing is a dynamic and recursive process, often characterized by false starts and dead ends, and the written text, which—if it corresponds to the usual conventions for written text—generally lies still and behaves itself. Once again, it's easy to understand the confusion. Writing and the product of writing (i.e., the written text) are very different things. The act of writing (the writing process) is active. You have to put down what you want to say in a logical, coherent manner so that your reader will understand what it is you are attempting to say. The written product, on the other hand, is static.

To continue this discussion, we are going to discuss two important characteristics of written text and identify some of the differences between the *writing process* and the *written text*.

1.7.1 Writing and the Imposition of Order

Writing imposes order on ideas. Writing creates structure. It's important to notice, however, that the verbs we've used to describe the process of writing are active. They refer to that dynamic process we spoke of above. The written text, on the other hand, *is* ordered. It *reflects* the decisions that have been made. One of the difficulties novice writers experience derives from the fact that they sometimes imagine that the text emerged, fully formed and perfectly arranged. They believe that someone composed it in exactly the form it appears. That is not the case. Though the structure of the written text may appear inevitable, as if it could never have been otherwise, it is, in fact, the result of active decisions that were made during the composing process. The writer responsible for the text determined that ideas would proceed in a particular way and that one aspect of the text would govern the argument, while others would be subordinated to that principal idea. The order was fixed only when the essay emerged in its final form. Until that time, the writer was free to circle back repeatedly to ensure that the decisions that were made served to create the intended meaning.

1.7.2 Writing and Linearity

Novice writers often find one particular aspect of writing to be especially problematic. They have come to believe that writing is a linear process. As readers, they have learned to expect that the texts they encounter will be, more or less, linear, with the development of ideas following a logical path from the introduction to the conclusion. They imagine (as perhaps they ought to do) that the process that results in those finished texts will have been equally linear: write an introduction (check); write a body paragraph (check); write another body paragraph (check); write more body paragraphs (check, check, check...); tack on a conclusion (check). Things do not, however, usually work that way.

Novice writers typically think that they must write in a particular order. They are conditioned to the notion that writing an essay must start with the introduction and proceed through to the conclusion. Students sometimes confess, usually a little apologetically, that they write their introductions last (the word *confess* is appropriate here; the manner in which students speak suggests that they've broken some kind of rule). You're free to write the introduction last if that works for you, though you're probably better advised to write your thesis statement first (doing so provides you with a sense of direction). As we will see in the next section, experienced writers don't usually follow a linear path in their composing process but instead shift back and forth through the stages of planning, writing, and reviewing (revising and editing) their texts, adjusting the composition on an ongoing basis. They monitor the text production actively and, as they discover new information that challenges previous assumptions, they bring the text into alignment with the new assumptions. Though experienced writers commonly work from outlines, they are not married to them. The outlines are guides to the composing process, reflecting the general intentions of writers and providing a sense of direction. As new ideas emerge over the course of the writing process, however, experienced writers renegotiate their outlines, conceding that the essay will continue to the original conclusion but follow a different path, or abandoning the original conclusion altogether and restructuring the essay to satisfy a new purpose.

1.7.3 Writing and Recursivity

One of the curious things about writing is that, though the written text is generally characterized by order and linearity, the process of writing is not. It appears to be a paradox. It's not. Strangely, it is an essential feature in the cognitive process of translating ideas into written text. In order to create a text that is logical, coherent, and linear, the writer must go through a writing process that is recursive. The ideas that emerge during the writing process do not necessarily emerge in a logical, coherent, and linear fashion. In addition, at a certain point in the process, the text itself starts to exert an influence. Experienced writers recognize that they need to monitor the text and make adjustments on an ongoing basis in order to ensure that the written product corresponds with their intentions. Recursivity is the practice of circling back to correct the alignment of the text to maintain its internal logic and coherence. This allows you to concentrate on specific problems, exploring the ideas fully, without simultaneously attempting to attend to an idea's place in the larger essay structure. You don't have

Practising recursive writing means that you do not follow a linear path. Recursivity is the practice of circling back to correct the alignment of the text to maintain its internal logic and coherence.

to be certain during the composition process because you know you will have an opportunity to come back and refine the text at a later point.

Think of the way in which you make decisions in your personal life. You probably do not follow a linear path. For example, if you want to buy a new car, you might follow a process that goes something like this: (1) you decide on the features you want, (2) you carry out some initial research to see what kinds of cars are available with those features, (3) you narrow your search on the basis of the cars that match your criteria most closely, (4) you solicit information and advice from your friends and family, and (5) you make your decision. You select a particular make and model. On your way to the dealership, however, you notice a car of the same make and model parked on your street. It looks fairly new but appears worn and rusted. The owner comes out and you ask about the car. The owner suggests that you consider something else. The car has been a nightmare from the moment it was driven off the lot. The vehicle is unreliable. The dealership is untrustworthy. Buying the car was the worst decision the owner ever made. Despite your initial enthusiasm, you consider buying a different car on the basis of the new information. That is a simple example of a recursive practice. You monitored the decision you made and altered it on the basis of the new information.

The same thing happens when you are making writing decisions. Your initial decisions are not necessarily incorrect. They are the best decisions you can make with the information you have at the time. As you move forward, however, you have to be prepared to change those decisions based on new information. In Figure 1.1 we provide a simple illustration of the process.

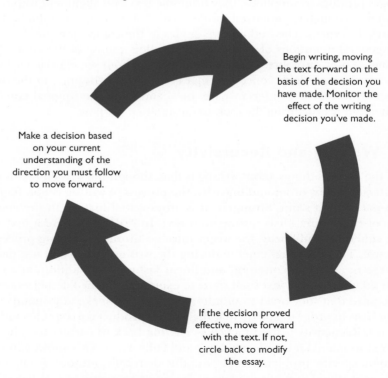

Begin writing, moving the text forward on the basis of the decision you have made. Monitor the effect of the writing decision you've made.

Make a decision based on your current understanding of the direction you must follow to move forward.

If the decision proved effective, move forward with the text. If not, circle back to modify the essay.

Figure 1.1   Recursive Model of the Writing Process

1.7.4 Linear Texts and Recursive Writing: Putting It Together

It all seems a bit abstract, doesn't it? Let's try to bring it down to earth again by returning to the concept of metacognition. If you remember, metacognition is a concept of learning that suggests individuals acquire understanding more easily when they understand the relationship between the goals they are trying to achieve and the procedures they must follow to meet the goals.

The Writing Process	The Written Text
The writing process works with a number of ideas with the intention of finding an organizing principle for them. One of the goals of a writer of essays is to impose order on a series of related ideas. Idea Idea Idea Idea Idea	**The written text is ordered.** Introduction Controlling idea or thesis Discussion of one idea or theme that serves the thesis Discussion of second idea or theme that serves the thesis Discussion of third idea or theme that serves the thesis Discussion of fourth idea or theme that serves the thesis Concluding discussion of controlling thesis
The process of writing is driven by decisions. *Examples:* What is my purpose? Who is my audience? What happens if I arrange the ideas in a different way?	**The written text is a reflection of the effects of decisions.** Effects of decisions are reflected in the essay.
The process of writing is recursive. As the writer works through the composing process, the effects of decisions made may demand that those decisions be revisited and revised.	**The written text is generally characterized by linearity.** The written text has a beginning and an end. If the essay is successful, the reader sees a logical path between the two. Beginning ⇩ End

In the case of writing, the goal is the essay. The procedure is the writing process. By understanding the relationship between the process of writing and the product it creates, you will better understand the decisions you must make to achieve the essay you intend to create.

1.8 DIFFERENCES BETWEEN THE SECONDARY AND POST-SECONDARY WRITING ENVIRONMENTS

LO 4

At the beginning of the chapter, we discussed the degree to which effective writing depends on its context. That was the whole point about audience and purpose. The same principle applies to the distinction between writing in high school and writing at university. One of the great differences that students experience, regardless of the age at which they begin their college or university studies, is in understanding that the strategies they acquired when they first learned to organize ideas into essays were appropriate for that environment and yet may not be appropriate for college or university writing. There is a body of research knee-deep that identifies the difference between the high school writing environment and the university writing environment. The difference between the two environments is more important than you may realize. If you believe that a single set of features characterizes good writing (as perhaps you had been led to believe), then the difficulty you will experience is in understanding why the work you're producing—work that subscribes to those important principles—is less successful in the new writing environment than it was in the old one.

In the next chart, we've identified some of the important differences between writing as it is usually taught in high school and the writing challenges students often experience in college or university. You'll notice that there are three general categories of difference: (1) students usually receive more explicit direction in high school than in university; (2) high school students are expected to display and report on learning in high school writing assignments, while university students are expected to analyze arguments or phenomena, and to synthesize the information coherently; and (3) high school students often work with a single writing template (e.g., the five-paragraph essay), while university students are expected to adapt to the distinct writing protocols of different disciplines or discourse communities.

Some might think that the distinction between the high school writing environment and the university writing environment is meant to serve as a tacit criticism of high school writing instructors. It's not. High school writing instructors are generally teaching students whose writing skills are still developing, and they therefore provide instruction appropriate to that stage of development. They are also teaching students in a writing environment in which different fields of study do not usually demand that students use different writing protocols and strategies. Finally, they are teaching a broad range of students, some of whom will enter the world with writing skills that will be appropriate to their needs and some who will later attend college or university, which will require that they gain more specialized writing training.

There are a number of good reasons, however, for identifying the differences between the two writing environments. Most people, whether they are traditional first-year students or not, acquired their understanding of essay writing when they were in high school. Many imagine the essay-writing strategies they learned then to be universally applicable. By learning to recognize the important differences between writing expectations in the two environments, you will be able to adapt to the new environment more easily.

1.8.1 Differences between Writing in High School and First-Year University

There are a number of noteworthy differences between writing in high school and writing in college or university. For instance, in your writing assignments in high school, you may have been asked to write from your own perspective on an issue. That doesn't usually happen in university classes. In most university essay

Writing in High School	Writing at University
■ Students generally receive some explicit instruction in writing.	■ Students are often assumed to have "mastered" the skill of essay writing.
■ Students generally receive explicit directions for writing assignments.	■ Students do not always receive explicit directions for writing assignments.
■ Generally, in high school, students follow a prescribed model for writing essays. In most cases, that model can be transferred from one class to another and from one year to the next. Good writing, it is assumed, is good writing. Students generally assume that the difference between one subject and another lies in the content.	■ In college and university, students move from a high school writing environment—in which writing situations were differentiated by audience or purpose but not by subject—to the university environment, where every discipline is its own discourse community* (i.e., the rules of writing change from one field of study to another).
■ Though essays are usually expected to subscribe to the rules of formal writing, students are often encouraged to experiment with other genres of writing.	■ Writing is usually formal in its diction (i.e., word choice), logical in its structure, objective in its tone, and governed by very specific rules of format, evidence, and organization.
■ The terminology used to describe various features of the essay is relatively standard.	■ Students find that identical, or very similar, terms for specific features of writing (e.g., thesis, documentation style, sources, organization, grammar, and mechanics) are used from one course to another, but they seem to refer to very different things.
■ Essays are typically first and final draft.	■ Students are encouraged (though not always taught) to concentrate on the process of writing.
■ Essays are usually brief (often one or two pages), which allows for the reporting of ideas but not for the development of them. Because of the relative brevity of the essays, there is less of a requirement for organization.	■ In general, writing at the university level requires that students develop ideas at length. Organization becomes increasingly important as the essay gets longer.
■ Topics for writing assignments are usually designed to test previous learning of information or skills. Hence, the students' task is to get the answer "right" rather than to convince, inform, or entertain their respective audience.	■ Written assignments at the university level generally demand that students explore and analyze topics or phenomena in depth. Students are expected to move beyond the reporting of surface details.
■ Writing in high school employs a greater degree of summarization than analysis.	■ Writing at the university level almost always requires that a writer analyze and synthesize the information that is being presented.
■ Writing in high school often involves the repeating of information that has already been organized by the teacher or the text.	■ Because the university writer is generally expected to bring together new ideas from a number of sources, the writer is required to organize the material in a novel way.

---

* A discourse community is a community (subject area) that has a common set of goals (e.g., language, rules).

assignments, you will be expected to argue from evidence of some kind. The nature of the evidence may vary from one course or discipline to another, but, in general, essay assignments in university make reference to supporting evidence.

Students wrestling with essays at university for the first time sometimes find this a difficult concept to grasp. You may well be one of those students. You may wonder why you cannot simply include information that you believe everyone knows to be true. We'll discuss this in greater detail in Chapter 5 but, at this point, we want to mention a couple of concerns with that practice:

1. In the first place, common knowledge is more uncommon than you might think, with many of the things we believe to be true emerging from culturally based assumptions that are particular to one social group or from commonly held beliefs that are, well, wrong.
2. Secondly, the strength of the evidence you offer is related to the authority of the source from which it comes. Without intending to offend you in any way, we have to tell you that you, quite simply, do not have the expertise on most subjects to convince your reader of the validity of your claims. If you are meaning to convince your reader on the basis of evidence, that evidence ought to be reliable, convincing, and authoritative.

1.8.2 How Do High School Writing Assignments Differ from Writing Assignments in University?

One of the ways in which high school writing differs from university writing is the variety of kinds of writing in which students are asked to engage. While university writing assignments may differ in a number of ways, you will, in most cases, be asked to submit reports or essays. In the following table, on the other hand, is a list of the various forms that writing assignments often took in high school. The purpose of the chart is to provide you with a greater understanding of the university writing environment by comparing it to the thing it is not.

High School Writing Assignments	First-Year-University Writing Assignments
1. Personal Narratives (a non-fiction essay with the writer as its subject)	
A personal narrative is a story about you, generally guided by a particular theme. Personal narratives are usually accounts written from the perspective of the writer that do not require a great deal of research. Instead, the writer tries to recreate an experience in such a way as to allow readers to feel as though they are living the experience.	There are not many courses that will require you to write a personal narrative in first-year university. If you are required to write a personal narrative, you will likely be asked to relate it to the course content in some way (e.g., you are taking an architectural course and the instructor asks you to write a personal essay on your preference for a certain type of design). Students often find personal narratives are easy to write because they are, well, personal. Nevertheless, for the most part, university instructors usually expect the narratives to be guided by a specified theme.

2. Creative Writing	
In high school, students are often asked to complete creative writing assignments in order to gain a better understanding of the writing form. For instance, students might be asked to write poetry (such as haikus, sonnets, limericks, or free verse), song lyrics, or short stories.	In first-year university, the likelihood that you might be asked to express yourself creatively is pretty slim. English courses you will be able to take are general courses. Though you may be asked to write an analysis of poems, stories, or novels, it's unlikely that you will be asked to produce them. The expression of your inner self will likely be restricted to work you do on your own time.

3. Analysis of a Poem, Story, Play, or Novel	
In high school, you might have had to read poems or stories, and analyze them for their meanings. The essay you wrote was one in which you related your analysis and defended it on the basis of textual evidence.	Finally, something you might have to do in first-year-university courses with which you've had some experience. Of course, the requirement to analyze literature will depend on the courses you have selected. If you don't enjoy analyzing poems, you can generally avoid it—don't register for a literature course. However, if you choose to take a literature course, or are required to do so, you may find that the analysis of literary work is not as painful as you remember (the variety of courses available in university catalogues may allow you to find one that is based on a theme that intrigues you). In addition, you may find that the process of writing your required essays is easier once you have mastered the form of the argumentative essay (i.e., the type of essay on which this text focuses).

4. Lab Report	
You may have had to write a lab report in high school. A lab report is a short paper that delivers the results of an experiment. A lab report usually presents data, discusses results, and gives a conclusion. You may also include a description of the experiment and the procedures that you followed when conducting the experiment.	If you're taking one of the sciences, there is a good chance that you will have to write a lab report. The form that your lab report takes will generally depend on the area of science you're studying. Biology lab reports will differ from chemistry lab reports, which, in turn, will differ from physics lab reports. There are certain commonalities, however. Once you have learned to structure an argumentative essay, you should be able to adapt the form to lab reports (see a further discussion of this in Chapter 14).

5. Research Essay	
You may have been introduced to the research essay at some point in high school. A research essay is usually an argumentative essay in which the writer argues for a particular view on the basis of evidence. However, you may also have been asked to write an expository essay, in which you provided information but did not argue for a particular interpretation of that information or take a position on an issue. (The distinction between the argumentative essay and expository essay is discussed in Chapter 2.)	You will probably be asked to write research essays over the course of your university career. The principal difference between research essays in high school and those in university lies in the quality of the evidence you're expected to provide. In high school, your research may have been limited to general-purpose sites or Google searches. While those resources may have been accurate and reliable, there is also a chance that they were not. It is almost certain that they were not scholarly. The kind of research essay you write in university will require resources that have been written by experts and published in academic journals. *Dr. Phil* may not cut it.

After reviewing the differences between the writing you did in high school and the writing you will do in university, you can be forgiven for thinking that the kinds of writing you did in high school are not going to help you now. Not necessarily. Many of the writing and reasoning skills you acquired in high school are still relevant. You just have to learn how to adapt them to your new writing environment. This book will help you navigate the new writing demands you face by giving you a structure that can be adapted to most new writing situations you find yourself in (i.e., the IDDL model, in Chapter 3).

1.8.3 Expectations of Instructors in High School and University

Many first-year students have just left the relatively safe writing environment in high school and are about to embark on a process of learning that includes learning to write in a completely different writing environment. You have, no doubt, already been warned that the expectations of writing instructors in university are going to be different from the expectations of writing instructors in high school. Unfortunately, that is usually true. What you may not realize, however, is that you can take some of the strategies you acquired in your high school classes and adapt them to the new writing environment of college or university.

What kinds of writing skills can be transferred from high school to first-year university? Well, first, you should understand that, in any class but a composition or writing class, most university instructors will mark for grammar, spelling, and punctuation but they generally will not teach it explicitly. While these skills are important, university instructors are usually looking to see whether you understand the material and can demonstrate that understanding in a coherent way. Of course, you need to know how to spell correctly (or, at least, know how to use a spell-checker) and it never hurts to conform to the rules of grammar. Frankly, your instructor, like any other reader, will look at your writing more favourably if you have taken the trouble to write a text that is easy to read. However, having said that, we should point out that clear writing is unlikely to seem remarkable to your instructors. That's kind of what they're expecting from you.

The chart on the following page lists some common differences between instructor expectations of writing in high school and instructor expectations of writing in university.

1.8.4 Understanding the Differences between Writing in High School and Writing in University

There is a reason to reflect on the differences between the writing you have produced in the past and the writing you will be expected to produce in university classes. Your knowledge of those differences will allow you to adjust more efficiently to the change. It's that metacognitive perspective we told you about. The capacity to recognize the differences between the writing you did in high school

High School Expectations	First-Year-University Expectations
In high school, it's not uncommon for students to write papers in which they simply repeat the information they've received from their teachers.	In university, most instructors don't expect you to tell them what they already know. They are, for the most part, experts in their field. They're usually familiar with the material already. They want to know whether you can analyze the content and come to some sort of an evaluation or synthesis of it.
In high school, you may have been led to believe that complicated, and often obscure, language works better than, well, language that is more common. This strategy is meant to impress the reader.	Your instructors generally want to hear your voice and your style (although the style is meant to be appropriate to the circumstance). They want you to write precisely and to use words that are suitable to the topic about which you are writing. It is most important that you to learn to write clearly and logically.
You may have gotten away with the use of familiar language or tone in high school. If you used slang or first person, you were often not penalized.	In university, informal language and familiar writing are generally frowned upon. Your instructor does not expect to read a paper that seems as if it were written for a friend or a Facebook posting. While your language is not meant to be artificially profound, it ought to be formal.
You may not have had to write to a page length or a word count in high school.	In university, the page length of an essay is usually specified, often with a minimum word count identified to discourage clever manipulations of margins and font sizes. These are generally not guidelines but expectations. If your instructor tells you that you need to deliver a paper of 3000 words, the instructor is expecting to receive a paper of 3000 words.
In high school, there is a good chance that you learned to write an essay following the five-paragraph model. Despite what you may have been told, your understanding of the model is useful. It can be used to organize your thoughts for essay assignments in university. It just needs to be adapted to the new writing environment.	In most university classes, you will not be given a model or template to follow. In addition, you will probably find that the five-paragraph model will not allow you to explore a topic in the detail and depth expected of university-level essays. Nevertheless, you can still use a model to develop your essays (we suggest the IDDL model, to which you will be introduced in Chapter 3). You must, however, understand that writing models are not meant to relieve you of your obligation to make decisions. They are only meant to assist the decision making.
You may have learned how to properly format an essay, using one of the most common formatting styles (APA, MLA, *Chicago*). On the other hand, you may be hearing about the practice of formatting for the first time now.	In university classes, essays are generally formatted in accordance with one of the common writing styles. Your instructors will advise you of the style they want you to follow (see Chapter 12 for a discussion on the importance of formatting).

and the writing you are doing in college or university is more useful than it may appear. It is, again, one of the great advantages of the metacognitive perspective. By understanding the change from the expectations in high school to the expectations in college or university, you are able to adjust to that change more efficiently.

| Making Writing Decisions | About Writing in College and University |

What is the purpose of this writing decision?

Adapting to the differing expectations for written work is one of the challenges students face in their transition to college or university.

What is the effect of this writing decision?

Your awareness of the characteristics of the writing environment in high school and the writing environment at college and university allows you to adjust to the new environment by systematically comparing the significant differences between the two.

What considerations inform this decision?

As was the case in the discussion of using the metacognitive approach to change your writing process to resemble that of the experienced writer, the change from writing practices associated with writing in high school to writing practices associated with writing in college or university requires that you be able to identify the *significant* similarities and differences between the two.

Suggested strategy for making this decision.

The suggested strategy for altering your writing practices to correspond with the expectations of written assignments in college or university is very much like the suggested strategy for altering your writing practices to correspond with those of experienced writers. Identify the five most important differences between the writing practices in high school and the writing practices in college or university. To help make that decision, ask yourself which five of the differences you've identified are the most important and why.

Questions to guide decision making in your own essay.

1. Look back to the chart in section 1.8.1 to identify the differences between writing in high school and writing in college or university. To what extent do the characteristics ascribed to writing in high school correspond with your experience? To what extent do the characteristics ascribed to writing in college or university correspond with your experience?
2. What changes do you need to make to your own writing process to bring it closer to the expectations of writing assignments in college or university?
3. What changes should you make in the planning stage? What effect do you think the proposed changes will have on your planning process?
4. What changes should you make in the composing stage? What effect do you think the proposed changes will have on your composing process?
5. What changes should you make during the revising stage? What effect do you think the proposed changes will have on your revising process?

1.9   CONCLUSION

In this chapter, we have identified some of the problems you face as a writer. Fortunately we've also suggested that some of those difficulties are less of a problem than you might think. It's true that, as you begin to write in an unfamiliar writing environment, you may be overwhelmed by the sense that you don't entirely understand how to do the thing that you are being asked to do. You may look at a successful essay, compare it with your own, and wonder how others appear to create a coherent and sophisticated piece of work while you struggle to understand how to wrestle the information you are using into shape.

One of the greatest difficulties novice writers face is the challenge of trying to manage the wild meandering of the emerging text at the same time as they focus on the rules they're meant to follow. Successful writers generally have an idea of the elements that characterize a successful essay. They understand that the ultimate purpose of writing—the goal of writing assignments—is not the avoidance of mechanical errors but the representation of meaning. The choices they make are governed by the understanding that writing is a process of decision making. Based on their understanding of the purpose of the essay, they also usually have an idea of the form their own essays will take.

The point we have tried to make, however, is that your awareness of the difference between your own writing process and the writing process of those who appear to be more successful than you is a good thing. By reflecting on those differences, and by using your metacognitive abilities to recognize the effect that different decisions might have on your writing, you will begin to start working within the text, driving its development intentionally.

MyCompLab®

How Do I Get a Better Grade?

Go to MyCompLab for additional help with your grammar, writing, and research skills. You will have access to a variety of exercises, instruction, and videos that will help you improve your basic skills and help you get a better grade.

CHAPTER 2

Academic Writing and the Argumentative Essay

Learning Objectives

At the completion of this chapter, you will be able to:

1. Illustrate the differences between the ways in which novice and experienced writers compose academic essays.

2. Identify the characteristics of an academic essay.

3. Explain the importance of reflecting on audience and purpose while planning, writing, and revising your essay.

4. Distinguish between the written product (i.e., the essay) and the process of writing.

5. Compare the unique features of the argumentative essay to other forms of writing.

2.1 INTRODUCTION

In this chapter, we discuss some of the general features of academic writing, identifying the value of attending to the importance of audience and purpose, and the effect that those considerations have on your writing. Our main focus, however, is on the argumentative essay, and on paying particular attention to thesis statements and arguable claims. We identify the way in which the essay itself emerges from the claims you make in the thesis, and the way in which the reader's expectations derive from those claims. There are a number of reasons for the focus on the argumentative essay, reasons that we will discuss at greater length in the chapter itself. The most important of the reasons are these:

1. The argumentative essay is the most common genre in college and university writing.

2. It's easier to transfer the organizational patterns of the argumentative essay to other genres than it is to transfer the organizational patterns of other genres to argumentative essays (or, in fact, to one another).

2.2 DIFFERENCES BETWEEN NOVICE WRITERS AND EXPERIENCED WRITERS

LO 1

The differences between novice and experienced writers are particularly significant in the writing of academic essays. Formal academic writing is, to a certain extent, a deceptively foreign language for many college and university students. On one hand, you're familiar with the language, and, generally, familiar with the practice of writing essays. On the other hand, there may be significant differences between the writing practices that have worked for you in the past and the expectations of your instructors at college or university.

There are two purposes for foregrounding the differences between the practices of novice and experienced writers in the preparation of academic essays:

1. We wanted you to know that *you* are not the problem.
2. In general, using the metacognitive perspective (see Chapter 1) allows you to change your writing practice as you reflect on the differences between practices that work and those that don't, so your awareness of the differences will help you to become a more successful writer.

Novice Writers	Experienced Writers
■ Require thought for procedural, or "mechanical," writing functions.	■ Have, to a significant degree, automated procedural functions.
■ Focus on error avoidance rather than meaning.	■ Focus on developing or refining meaning.
■ Begin writing without planning, and edit, if at all, for grammatical errors.	■ Invest time and energy in planning and reviewing.
■ Focus on "knowledge telling" (i.e., relating all the information they have and can find on a topic, rather than exercising critical judgment to determine relevance).	■ Organize, and reorganize, essay structure to allow individual ideas to serve the overall purpose of the essay.

Because novice writers are often unaware of the writing conventions of academic writing, they tend to *begin writing without planning; edit, if at all, for grammatical errors*; and *focus on "knowledge telling" (i.e., relating all the information they have and can find on a topic, rather than exercising critical judgment to determine relevance)*. In addition, because novice writers *require thought for procedural, or "mechanical," writing functions*, part of the difficulty they experience comes from an overload of the working memory. They have to monitor more information than do the experienced writers. The writing model we introduce in this chapter (and discuss further in Chapter 3) is designed, in part, to off-load some of that information to the page. The final characteristic that the first chart in this chapter notes about novice writers is the degree to which they tend to *focus on error avoidance rather than meaning.* They do so, it seems, because error avoidance is an easier task to understand (though it is, in fact, a much harder thing to do).

Experienced writers, by contrast, *have automated procedural functions to a significant degree* and, thus, are able to *focus on developing or refining meaning.* They *invest time and energy in planning and reviewing,* and they *organize, and reorganize, essay structure to allow individual ideas to serve the overall purpose of the essay.*

Novice-ness, you have to understand, is not meant to be a pejorative term. There is no shame in being a novice writer. And being a novice writer is going to happen again. In fact, it's going to happen every time you enter a new field of study. In each field, you will find that there are subtle differences between the rules that apply to writing assignments. To a certain extent, then, each move to a new writing situation is like a bold leap into the unknown. It's like bungee jumping that way (well, it's like bungee jumping for those of us who are too clever to have done it). If you've never jumped off the side of a bridge that is half a mile high, suspended only by the utterly unreasonable faith that a tiny elastic band will hold you, you're a novice.

LO 2, 3   2.3   WHAT IS ACADEMIC WRITING?

Writing is a form of communication, and all forms of communication depend, to some degree, on the shared expectations of the person who creates the communication (in this case, the writer) and the person who receives the communication (in this case, the reader). The simplest way to explain the essential characteristics of academic writing is to refer to the expectations the reader has of it and the ways that the writer goes about meeting those expectations. The difficulty students often experience when they begin to work within the genre of academic writing is that it is not immediately clear why a writer has to follow particular rules when the message could be as clearly delivered in another form. The reason is this: the reader of academic writing expects the text to conform to certain rules and, if the writer fails to observe those rules, the reader may either experience some sense of dislocation or reject the text as being unauthoritative.

2.3.1 Writing for an Audience

In Chapter 1, we discussed the importance of adopting a metacognitive perspective on your writing process (i.e., learning to think critically about the decisions you make and to monitor the effect those decisions have on the text). To monitor that effect, however, you need to have a way of measuring it. Your understanding of audience (and your understanding of purpose, which we go on to discuss) allows you to do that. The effect of your writing decisions is, in the end, determined by the degree to which your audience is able to engage with your ideas. Writing is a communicative act and the reader's understanding of your essay testifies, to some degree, to your success as a writer. Many of the decisions you make will be influenced by your understanding of the target audience.

It's important, then, to identify your audience. If your goal in writing is to address a specific essay to a specific audience, that goal is better served by your recognition of the nature of that audience. In academic writing, writers address their arguments to the reason, or intellect, of readers. However, the question of who your audience is for a writing assignment depends on the point at which you're asking the question. At this stage, while you are planning your essay—while you are making decisions about genre, scope, length, and format—your target audience is your instructor. Your interest in a grade will guide many of the decisions that you are making about the writing assignment at this point. In the long run, however, there seems to be little evidence to suggest that selecting your instructor as the audience helps you to learn to write a better essay. Therefore, we are going to define your audience for you. Your audience is made up of intelligent individuals who are familiar with the practice of reasoning and are willing to be persuaded by evidence.

Your understanding of that audience is important. It determines the way in which you are going to deliver your message. You probably dress differently for a job interview than you do to visit with your grandmother, understanding that your presentation is dictated by social circumstance. Similarly, you write differently for different audiences, understanding that different audiences have different expectations. By reflecting on the nature of your audience, and by recognizing the different expectations that each audience holds, you can tailor your text to meet those expectations.

The better you are able to visualize the audience, the easier you will find it to recognize the kind of information they need to follow your argument. Novice writers often make the mistake of believing there is only one way to write for an audience in an academic setting. They use scholarly language in an attempt to impress the audience with their erudition (using *erudition* is an example of the phenomenon: it means learning or knowledge, so you could use *learning* or *knowledge*). Remember that the words you choose ought to be selected on the basis of their meaning; you're aiming for clarity rather than an impressive number of syllables. Though you want to avoid slang, you also want to avoid using language that serves no purpose but to show off your remarkable vocabulary (or, worse still, your computer's woefully unreliable thesaurus). The belief that instructors will be impressed by the use of overwrought language is mistaken for several reasons, not the least of which is this: they've already heard the word. In fact, they may have heard it more than once. An instructor will be more impressed by your adept use of a humble, but correct, word than by the clumsy stumbling about with a word that's too big to handle.

What are the sorts of things you need to consider when thinking about your audience? That's an excellent question. You might want to consider the reader's background knowledge about the topic. It's certainly easier to write for a reader who is already armed with some knowledge about the topic (this allows you to assume that the reader already knows fundamental principles of the topic). But it's not significantly more difficult to write to an audience that has no knowledge about the topic. You simply need to recognize that you have to approach the topic differently. Let's say, for the purposes of this discussion, that your reader has no knowledge about the topic. If that is the case, you could start by providing the reader with necessary background information about the topic, explained in terms that are relatively easy to understand so that novices in the field are able to develop a foundational knowledge of the concepts. It would also be important to clearly identify the main ideas of your essay, so that readers can anticipate the chain of reasoning you will follow. It's important to read your essay critically, looking for gaps in your reasoning and checking for aspects of the essay that might prove problematic for a reader. This requires you to practise metacognition (we did warn you that the method this book follows was going to require you to monitor your thinking while writing).

You may also want to consider how your audience's point of view could affect their reception of your essay. How do they feel about the topic on which you are writing? If you are writing to persuade a reader to accept a position that they might be skeptical of, then you may have to proceed differently than if you are writing to an audience that is already sympathetic to your view. If you define your target audience as your instructor, for instance, then you can make certain assumptions as to his or her attitude to the topic. In all likelihood, the instructor's position will be relatively easy to determine. The essay usually addresses a topic to which the instructor has already spoken. If you are writing about a subject that the instructor has already covered in class, and if you are writing to demonstrate your understanding of course material, you might reasonably assume that your instructor will be sympathetic to the view you are expressing. If, on the other hand, you are speaking to an issue from a perspective that is different from the perspective of your instructor, you will probably need to provide greater evidence for your position and argue more persuasively.

2.3.2 Identifying the Purpose of Your Essay

Just as it was important for you to identify the audience for your essay, so is it important for you to identify your purpose in writing. In planning your essay, you need to reflect on the purpose of your essay (metacognition again) and allow that purpose to dictate the nature of the essay you're preparing to write. Are you writing to inform and entertain (writing a letter to your grandmother, perhaps, or an article for a magazine), writing to convince your reader on the basis of reason (writing an argumentative essay), or simply writing for your own enjoyment or reflection (maintaining a journal)? The purpose determines the tone you will take, the degree of formality you will use, and the writing conventions you will follow.

Your understanding of the purpose of academic writing ought to come from an understanding of the audience for whom you write. If the audience of academic writing has been identified as being logical, relatively objective, and willing to be convinced by evidence rather than emotion, then the purpose of academic writing is to provide an argument that both reveals a logical train of thought and rests upon evidence. In short, in academic writing, your purpose is to appeal to the reader's intellect by providing evidence that your arguable proposition (i.e., thesis) is reasonable.

Let's be honest, however. Your goal may simply be to get the best grade that you can possibly get. Unfortunately, as long as you allow the grade to be your goal, you will be focusing on error avoidance rather than the development of your ideas. We're going to make a compromise: we're going to suggest that you begin by being motivated by desire for a particular grade and, in accordance with that goal, that you will be guided both by your instructor's purpose for the assignment and by your instructor's rubric or marking policy. As soon as you've established those parameters, however, your goal will become that of developing a particular idea through writing. At that point, you're driving. You need to assume responsibility for the decisions you will make.

Read the examples below to see whether you can recognize each writer's purpose for writing.

Example 1

One of the most popular movies in the theatres now is a film called *The Hunger Games*. The movie is based on a young adult fiction book by Suzanne Collins that is set in a future. In brief, the film is a dystopian view of an amoral culture in which children are forced to fight one other to the death in a form of entertainment called the Hunger Games. The inhabitants of the fictional world of Panem wager on the games, betting on the child they believe will be the ultimate survivor.

What is the purpose of this text?
In this case, it appears as if the writer's purpose is to inform.

How did you identify the purpose?
The fact that the passage provides information with no obvious bias or attempt to persuade suggests that the writer's purpose is to inform.

What clues did you find that hinted at the purpose?
Though the language of the passage suggests a certain judgment (e.g., "dystopian view," "amoral culture"), the overall tone of the piece is relatively neutral.

Example 2

Increasingly, children are becoming addicted to computer games, either online or on game systems. It is far too easy to spend time playing games these days because the games provide a source of inexpensive entertainment that is available twenty-four hours a day. Many games are now available over the internet, which allows children to play computer games with others without ever having to leave their respective homes. While there may be some benefits to playing computer games, for the most part, studies have shown that playing computer games is not good for people. This is particularly true for children. Playing computer games is harmful to a child's development because the games can cause children to become aggressive, they can affect children's overall health, and they can lead to addiction.

What is the purpose of this text?
The purpose of this text is to convince you on the basis of an argument. If you check the thesis statement at the end of the paragraph you will be able to see that the author is trying to convince you that playing video games is harmful to a child's development.

How did you identify the purpose?
In addition to the thesis statement noted above, the pattern of the paragraph, with a series of statements that lead to a logical conclusion, suggests that the writer is making an argument.

> *What clues did you find that hinted at the purpose?*
> Just as the thesis statement provided the clue that this is an argumentative essay, so does the tone. Statements like "It is far too easy to spend time playing games these days" and "studies have shown that playing computer games is not good for people" also suggest that the writer is writing from a particular perspective. Though the writer concedes that "there may be some benefits to playing computer games," it seems clear that the essay is arguing against the practice in general.

How did you do? Were you able to identify the purpose in each of the samples? You can see from the two samples that writing purpose has a profound effect on the way in which a writer proceeds. It is the basis for making other decisions.

LO 1, 2, 3

2.4 HOW ACADEMIC WRITING DIFFERS FROM OTHER FORMS OF WRITING

It's often easier to explain what a thing is by comparing it to similar things that it isn't. For example, if you know how to throw a football and want to learn to throw a baseball, you might want to have someone identify the similarities and differences between the two motions. By learning to recognize the ways in which the new skill is similar to the skill you've already mastered, and also the ways in which it differs, you can build on your existing knowledge to acquire the new skill. You can do the same thing when you're trying to adapt to a new form of writing. Though academic writing shares a number of features with other forms of writing, it can also be distinguished, generally, by reference to its audience and purpose. The nature of the audience and purpose of the academic essay leads to the difference in some of its representative characteristics.

Writing Form	Audience	Purpose	Representative Characteristics
Familiar Writing	You write for those you know in a very different way than you write for strangers. You take advantage of common experience (which allows you to make reference to shared experiences without providing much detail), and your tone and language reflect the intimacy of your relationship.	The purpose of familiar writing may be to share information, but it also may simply be a textual form of visiting.	An informal tone and a casual manner usually characterize familiar writing. Because your audience knows you, you are able to describe events and experiences by using a kind of shorthand that's based on shared experience. It is not necessary for you to explain things as carefully as you would with an audience with whom you share no history.

Journalism	The audience for journalism is generally an individual, or individuals, seeking information about phenomena or events.	The purpose for journalism is the delivery of information.	Lean, spare prose that delivers information without drawing attention to its language generally characterizes journalism.
Literature	The audience for literature is an individual, or group of individuals, reading for pleasure, diversion, intellectual engagement, and/or aesthetic delight.	The purpose of literature is complex. It ranges from narrating an event to the evocation of deep emotion.	Though the characterization of literary writing is difficult because of the range of genres and styles, it is often true of literature that it contains a density of meaning. The annoying ambiguity of literary text is usually purposeful: the ambiguity of literature is the feature that permits a range of interpretation. Unlike the other forms of writing discussed in this table, ambiguity and complexity are often desirable features in literature.
Oration	The audience of an orator is generally one that is willing to be persuaded by both reason and passion.	The purpose of oration usually, is to inspire emotional responses and, in many cases, action.	Historically, orators have used appeals to emotion to effect a call to action.
Academic Writing	The audience for academic writing is generally one that is prepared to be persuaded by reference to evidence and reason.	The purpose is to represent information fairly and accurately.	In academic writing, the writer makes a case on the basis of evidence. Academic writing is generally characterized by precise language, logical structure, and the use of some form of publicly available evidence. Academic writing refers to a general category of writing: academic writing is usually formal in its diction (i.e., word choice), logical in its structure, and objective in its tone. On the other hand, however, academic writing is also characterized by the very specific rules of format, evidence, and organization that belong to individual disciplines.

2.4.1 A Brief Discussion about Genre

Genres are specific types of writing, each governed by different principles and different rules. As much as questions of grammar and format need to be considered, an understanding of genre and of the various writing rules that each genre demands creates particular difficulties for the novice writer. That's not surprising. For years, you have imagined that good writing is good writing, and that the artful expression of an idea is more important than any other consideration. You are, then, understandably confused when your instructor observes that you have written the wrong *kind* of essay. You might find, for instance, that you have written a descriptive essay (i.e., describing a person, place, or event) when you were meant to write a narrative essay (i.e., telling a story from a personal perspective), or written an expository essay (i.e., explaining a concept or theory, or simply relating information without interpreting it) when you were expected to write an argumentative essay (i.e., presenting an argument through reasoning and the use of evidence). Under those circumstances, unfortunately, the essay—however well it might be written—fails to satisfy the requirements for the assignment because it is the wrong *type* of essay.

In many ways, an understanding of essay genre makes it easier to plan the essay you are about to write. Every genre dictates, to some extent at least, the range of voices that are permitted (i.e., first, second, or third person), the degree of subjectivity that is allowed, the nature of the evidence that is expected, and the patterns of organization that are likely to succeed.

2.4.2 Making Decisions about Genre

In many cases, the decision about genre will be made for you. Your instructor will tell you that your assignment requires that you write an essay of a particular kind. There will be times, however, when you will be obliged to determine the kind of essay that you need to write on the basis of the form that best serves the purpose of your essay. On those occasions, it is important to remember that genre serves the purpose of an essay. That is, you select the genre that allows you to develop a particular idea in a particular way. If your purpose is to describe an event, emphasizing its sensual character, you would select the genre of descriptive essay writing. If your purpose is to relate information from a personal perspective, emphasizing the impact of the information on the narrator or the degree to which the narrator's personal character affects a situation, then you might choose narrative. If your purpose is to report on an event or a phenomenon, you might choose an expository essay. If your purpose is to use reason and evidence to convince your reader of the validity of a particular proposition, you might select the argumentative essay.

In this text we focus almost exclusively on the writing of argumentative essays. In no way do we mean to diminish the importance of other genres of essay. Each has its purpose, and each, without question, is very dear to the essay mother that bore it. We focus on the argumentative essay because the argumentative essay is the single most versatile genre available to students. Though the argumentative essay may differ in format from one academic discipline to another, it operates much the same way in each discipline. The argumentative essay permits you to investigate a question on the basis of evidence, to reflect on alternative explanations, and to arrive at a reasonable conclusion (i.e., a conclusion whose strength is directly related to the evidence on which it rests).

2.4.3 Thinking about Genre

Given the number of things you already have to worry about, you may be wondering why you would be further burdened with concerns about obscure subjects like genre. It's a fair question. You concern yourself with questions of genre because genre makes your writing process more efficient. It also affects the degree of success your essay might enjoy. More importantly, perhaps, genre provides a road map to your reader. In recognizing the genre in which an essay is written, readers can use their background knowledge of that genre to anticipate the structure the essay will use and the information they can expect to find. In some cases, genre also tells readers the point of view to expect in the essay. Building on their prior knowledge of a genre, readers are better able to navigate the text. The selection of a particular genre creates a kind of a contract between you and your audience in which you agree to write in accordance with the genre's rules.

The following chart will guide you when you need to select the appropriate genre.

Making Writing Decisions | About Genre

What is the purpose of this writing decision?

Because each genre carries with it distinct expectations on the part of the reader, your awareness of audience demands that you write with an understanding of genre.

What is the effect of this writing decision?

By recognizing the distinct features that characterize any particular genre, you are better able to anticipate the expectations of your reader. Writing a brilliant essay in an inappropriate genre is like serving a nice steak to a vegetarian. It doesn't matter how good it is, it has failed its audience.

What considerations inform this decision?

In many cases, the choice of genre will be made for you. Your instructor may prescribe the expected genre. In the absence of that explicit direction, your understanding of the audience for whom you are writing may lead you to make a particular choice.

Suggested strategy for making this decision.

If you are obliged to select the appropriate genre yourself, think about your audience and refer to other essays that address the same audience. What tone do those essays adopt? What voice do they use (i.e., first, second, or third person)? Are the essays written in the present tense or the past tense? What is the nature of the evidence they use?

2.5   WRITING AN ACADEMIC ESSAY

The great challenge for students is often not the writing of an academic essay but rather the conceiving of the academic essay. In Chapter 1, we talked about linearity as one of the significant characteristics of writing: that is, every text has a beginning and an end. The first suggestion we make to you (and this is a suggestion that, in and of itself, is worth the price of the textbook) is based on that observation: if you want to know where you're going, start at the end and work your way back. Articulate a clear (though provisional) thesis statement, one that specifically identifies the ultimate purpose of your essay. Think of that purpose as your destination. Given that destination (however provisional), and given your understanding that an academic essay must move systematically toward its final purpose, presenting a coherent argument on the basis of evidence, you will now be able to see the various steps you need. The task becomes pragmatic rather than creative. In Chapter 3, we will introduce a writing model that is designed to assist you in drafting a coherent essay.

For now, the next chart might serve as a guide to the kinds of strategies that work when you write an academic essay, and the kinds of strategies that do not. You will notice, as you read through the chart, that many of the differences between the two have to do with planning and organization. We will discuss these in greater detail later. For now, we want you to start thinking about the ways in which successful writers undertake the writing of an essay and thinking about the decisions you must make to write more successfully yourself.

A Short List of Things That Do Not Work as Well as You Think They Will	A Short List of Strategies That Might Prove More Useful
Start with no idea of where you are going, thinking that it will become more clear as you go along.	Develop a provisional thesis statement to identify the relationship between key ideas in the essay. This thesis statement should include an arguable proposition (an arguable proposition is a statement that includes the reasons for the claim you're making; we will talk more about this later). If you can't express your thesis in a single sentence, you haven't yet figured out how the key ideas fit together.
	You can use your provisional thesis statement to develop a provisional outline (in essence, the thesis statement contains the DNA of the essay; every idea and every relationship between ideas ought to have been anticipated in the thesis statement).
Brainstorm to discover more ideas.	Contrary to what you may have heard, brainstorming is not nearly as effective a technique as people imagine it to be. It is more useful to use your provisional thesis statement to limit the scope of your essay and operate within that scope.

Take out every book in the library that is even remotely related to the topic. Augment that information with everything you can find on the internet.	One of the great advantages that experienced writers have is they know when to say when. Remember that the purpose of the information you gather is to serve the essay. There are few ways of avoiding writing that are more effective than excessive research (some of the other things you might want to do to avoid writing are cleaning your room and reorganizing the phone numbers in your cell phone; to a certain extent, each of these is as useful as gathering information you do not need).
Dump the information on the page indiscriminately. Your instructor will figure out how it ought to be connected.	Writing is a process of making meaning. A good essay is one that connects information and ideas to serve a purpose. If you do nothing else, ensure that your essay has a structure that permits the reader to derive its meaning.
Work toward the required word count. You're finished when you reach the minimum number of words.	Essays are not haikus. Though your assignment might prescribe an expected number of words, the essay itself might argue that you need more. You ought not to write to a minimum word count, you ought not to imagine that every essay has a limit of five paragraphs, and you ought not to be guided by the number of pages you think you might get away with. You are only finished when the essay says you are finished.

2.5.1 Common Characteristics of Effective Academic Writing

In the table that follows, you'll find a short list of the common features of effective academic essays. Despite the variations you may discover in the expectations of instructors across the disciplines, effective essays will usually be characterized by these features: (1) awareness of audience, (2) attention to purpose, (3) a commitment to the creation of meaning, (4) a sense of coherence, and (5) awareness of the rules of specific genres.

Effective Academic Writing
1. **Acknowledges its audience.** In academic writing, you assume that your reader is willing to be persuaded by reason rather than passion. That is, you expect that, by providing evidence that is ordered logically, and by providing a complete and fair exploration of competing explanations, you will be able to establish that the proposition you forward is, at the very least, feasible.
2. **Is guided by an observable sense of purpose.** The purpose of academic writing comes from an understanding of the audience. If the audience of academic writing has been identified as one that is willing to be persuaded by reason rather than passion, then your purpose is to provide an argument that both reveals a logical train of thought and rests upon evidence.

(*continued*)

(*continued*)

3. Works toward the creation of meaning.   This is a theme that we are going to return to repeatedly. Having identified your audience and purpose, your goal is to work toward meaning. Every sentence you write, every paragraph you craft, serves to develop the overall meaning of the essay.
4. Is coherent.   Coherence is the sort of thing that is easier to maintain in a text that is guided by purpose and moving toward the creation of meaning. Coherence ensures that each element of the essay is coordinated with each other element of the essay and moving toward the final purpose of the essay.
5. Observes the protocols of specific writing genres or rhetorical modes.   If writing, like other forms of communication, depends on the satisfaction of expectations in its audience, then one of the ways in which those expectations are met is by behaving oneself properly. Protocols of specific writing genres and rhetorical modes are rules of behaviour.

2.5.2 Understanding the Context for Making Writing Decisions about Effective Academic Writing

We've already discussed the importance of making writing decisions as you write. The process of constantly monitoring the emerging text of the essay is a skill that experienced writers possess. They understand the importance of writing for meaning, in part, because they have trained themselves to read for meaning. That is, they monitor the essay they are writing, thinking about the way in which readers might understand it. Because novice writers tend to focus on discrete elements of their essays in isolation, rather than looking at the effect that the individual elements have on the larger essay, they have a tendency to lose track of their purpose in writing.

Use the next chart to guide your thinking about general characteristics of academic writing.

Making Writing Decisions   About Effective Academic Writing

What is the purpose of this writing decision?

As we noted in the chart discussing the purpose of understanding genre, an understanding of the nature of academic writing is necessary if you are to address questions of writing purpose and audience effectively.

What is the effect of this writing decision?

Knowing that the audience of academic writing expects to be convinced of the validity of your argument on the basis of reason and evidence allows you to tailor your essay to that expectation.

What considerations inform this decision?

It's important to remember that your writing is guided by a specific purpose. In academic writing, the essay is characterized by a logical progression from the claims you make (or the questions you implicitly pose) in the introduction, through an explora-tion of the validity of those claims, to a conclusion. As you monitor your emerging text, pay attention to the degree to which the individual parts are serving the larger argument.

Suggested strategy for making this decision.

In Chapter 3, we will demonstrate the way in which the IDDL model can be used to guide you through the process of academic writing. Using a visual representation of the relation-ship between the component parts of an academic essay, the model leads you through the writing process using a series of embedded questions.

2.6 ARGUMENTATIVE ESSAYS

LO 5

Given its name, you may be inclined to believe that the argumentative essay is, well, a little quarrelsome. You may imagine it to be the kind of essay that doesn't get along well with others, initiates conflicts, and stubbornly refuses to back down in the face of competing ideas.

Not exactly. An effective argumentative essay is one that (1) appeals to the intellect of its audience, (2) fairly represents multiple perspectives on an issue, and (3) explores those perspectives carefully and respectfully. The purpose of the essay is not to win at all costs but rather to arrive at a reasonable conclusion that is supported by evidence. Though you are arguing for a particular position, you are doing so with an understanding that reasonable, well-meaning individuals might disagree, and that you are arguing, therefore, with a certain degree of humility. Your purpose is to represent the validity of your position, with authori-tative evidence arranged in such a way as to demonstrate the logical connection between the ideas and the conclusion that follows from the argument, but also to reveal that you have considered alternative positions. Your purpose, therefore, is not to prove your point beyond any shadow of a doubt but, rather, to convince the reader that your argument has merit.

On the other hand, the development of an effective argument demands more than a mere statement of opinion on a topic. Sadly, it's not that simple. An argument is a structure in which reasons lead logically to a conclusion. The argu-mentative essay emerges from that structure. It's a form of writing that involves forming reasons, checking for evidence, drawing conclusions, and then applying them in a discussion of your arguable proposition. An effective argumentative essay clearly reveals the process of reasoning from the introduction, through the body of the essay, to the conclusion.

The commitment to rationality that characterizes the effective argumenta-tive essay serves two purposes: (1) it allows you, as the writer, to examine an issue dispassionately, seeking the most reasonable position rather than your preferred position, and (2) it provides your writing with authority. If you have demonstrated that you are willing to explore opposing views, your reader is more inclined to trust you.

LO 2 , 3 , 4 , 5

2.7 DEVELOPING A PROVISIONAL THESIS STATEMENT

If, as we have said, experienced writers organize, and reorganize, essay structure to allow individual ideas to serve the overall purpose of the essay, the thesis statement provides the governing principle of that organization. A thesis statement articulates and limits the scope of an essay and usually includes an arguable claim that can be judged on the basis of evidence. The thesis statement forecasts, for the reader, the way in which you will approach the subject matter under discussion. It provides a road map for the essay. It usually makes a claim that might be disputed by others (let's face it, writing to prove an indisputable fact can get tedious very quickly) and it's generally an exploration of a particular aspect of a subject, rather than an encyclopedic account of the entire subject.

In contrast, a topic is a general category. Because a topic lacks limits, and usually fails to make a specific claim, it is very difficult to organize an essay around a topic. Figure 2.1 is an image of the way your thesis statement and your topic relate to one another.

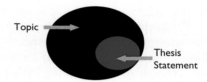

Topic

Thesis
Statement

Figure 2.1   The Thesis Statement in Relationship to the Topic

2.7.1 Drafting a Provisional Thesis Statement

As we've noted, the thesis statement is a sentence that articulates your purpose in writing. It carves out a particular aspect of the topic you've selected, imposing both form and limits on the essay you will write, and identifies the specific proposition you will explore or argue. It is necessary, therefore, that the drafting of a thesis statement be an exercise that you undertake with care. You are no better served by a thesis statement that only vaguely hints at a general intention than you are by a roadmap that suggests that Winnipeg is "over there somewhere."

You may argue that precision is difficult to achieve at the outset. You may suggest that you don't know what you mean to say until you begin to write the essay. In your writing experience, you've found that things emerge in the writing processes that lead you in directions you hadn't anticipated. After all, you note sagely, when you were ten, you thought you wanted to be a lion tamer, and, now, well, you don't. Those are just and apt objections. It's true that the process of writing is dynamic (an idea to which we return frequently in this text), and one that requires ongoing monitoring and revision, but it's also true that you can't begin any journey without postulating, however provisionally, the direction in which you intend to travel. Deciding on the parameters of the essay during the planning stage permits you to identify what aspects of the topic will be relevant to your discussion. Failure to do so leads you into an abyss of confusion, with no guiding principle by which to sort information into groups that might prove useful and those that won't.

Consider, for a moment, the following example of a vague thesis statement:

> **Example:** *Students often find the process of studying difficult.*

While the statement does offers a general sense of a topic, it does little to limit the scope of the essay you intend to write. The range of possibilities is too great to provide you with much direction. It is, generally, more effective to make a claim that is specific and verifiable. Notice the difference in the limits imposed by the example below:

> **Example:** *Students who locate themselves in noisy rooms often find the process of studying to be difficult.*

By identifying the parameters of the essay in the thesis statement, you are able to focus more clearly on a particular aspect of the larger topic. We discuss the process of refining your thesis statement at greater length in section 2.8 (i.e., "The Arguable Proposition").

2.7.2 Thinking about Your Thesis Statement

A thesis statement is usually a brief (one-or two-sentence) statement of the argument or chain of reasoning you will follow in your essay. It's an expression of your purpose, an answer to the question that you're exploring. When drafting a thesis statement, you generally take the following principles into consideration: a thesis statement (1) usually identifies the position you will take in an essay (i.e., the position you are going to be arguing), (2) provides the significance of the argument (i.e., explains why a reader should care about the topic), (3) expresses the principal theme(s) the essay will explore, and (4) is specific and clear (if the readers have no greater understanding of your argument after reading the thesis statement than they had before, you've written a bad thesis statement). Use the following chart to guide you when you're drafting your thesis statement.

Making Writing Decisions	About a Provisional Thesis Statement

What is the purpose of this writing decision?

In drafting a provisional thesis statement, you provide yourself with a clear sense of purpose and direction for your essay.

What is the effect of this writing decision?

A well-articulated thesis statement, however provisional it may be, allows you to explore your theme systematically. As we will discuss in Chapter 3, the thesis statement can be used to create an outline in which all elements of your essay are purposeful and integrated.

What considerations inform this decision?

In most cases, your writing process is best served by a thesis statement that is precise in its conception and its articulation. The more clearly you define your purpose in the thesis statement, the easier it is to monitor the emerging essay for adherence to that purpose.

Suggested strategy for making this decision.

One of the difficulties that novice writers report when attempting to begin the writing process is that they don't yet know what they mean to say. In the first place, that's probably not entirely true. Take, for instance, one example we've used—*Students often find the process of studying difficult.* While it may be the case that we haven't fully articulated our thesis, we do know that we won't be talking about elves dropping by the study hall to tutor. If you know what you're not going to discuss, then you must have some idea of the things you are considering. Accept that you may need to draft, and redraft, the thesis statement until you've refined it to your purpose.

Questions to guide you in the drafting of a provisional thesis statement.

1. What is the topic?
2. Is the topic worthy of investigation? Is it broad enough to permit discussion?
3. What is the specific thesis statement? Does it permit discussion or is it a statement of belief?
4. Is the thesis statement specific?
5. How does it limit the scope of the essay?
6. How does the thesis statement articulate and limit the focus of an essay?

LO 1, 2, 3, 4, 5

2.8   THE ARGUABLE PROPOSITION

In an argumentative essay, the thesis statement usually includes an arguable proposition of some kind. In order to move beyond simple assertions of opinion, it is necessary to base your argument on an arguable proposition. An arguable proposition is a statement that (1) clearly articulates the proposition being argued, and (2) provides the reasons for the claim being made.

The arguable proposition identifies the relationship between the claim that is being made and the reasons for that claim. It allows a reader to determine whether the writer has provided sufficient evidence for an argument. It also provides the basis for the essay's structure (a point that will be discussed further below and in Chapter 3) and it helps you maintain coherence in your essay.

2.8.1 The *Because* Clause

An arguable proposition usually includes a *because* clause. The purpose of the *because* clause is to identify the relationship between the reasons for a claim and the claim itself (we're not married to the word *because;* any word or phrase that identifies a causal relationship between the claim and the reasons will work just as well).

Example: *Listening to music while studying is often ineffective* because *music introduces a competing stimulus that distracts the student.*

- The claim being made is that *listening to music while studying is often ineffective.*
- The supporting reason for the claim is that *music introduces a competing stimulus that distracts the student.*
- The causal connector is *because.*

The relationship between the claim that is being made and the reasons for that claim is, in effect, the substance and soul of your essay. It gives shape to the essay and direction to the writer. A more scientific metaphor might be that the arguable proposition in an argumentative essay operates pretty much the way that

DNA operates: despite the seemingly miraculous complexity of each higher animal, the general shape and form was guided by the DNA code.

2.8.2 Drafting an Arguable Proposition

Arguable propositions are not questions. They may derive from questions but they are not, in themselves, questions. Questions cannot be affirmed or rejected. You are better advised to articulate an arguable proposition as a statement that can be argued for or against.

In the following chart, you'll find a concise discussion of the characteristics of, and purpose for, the arguable proposition.

Making Writing Decisions About an Arguable Proposition

What is the purpose of this writing decision?

In drafting an arguable proposition, you're attempting to develop the pattern of organization that will govern your essay, establishing a clear relationship between the main theme of the essay and subordinate ideas.

What is the effect of this writing decision?

A well-articulated arguable proposition gives shape to your essay, articulating the principal claim you are making, and identifying the reasons for that claim. It allows you to establish a benchmark against which to measure the emerging essay (i.e., as you are writing, the individual elements of the emerging essay can be measured against your intended purpose, which you articulated in the arguable proposition).

What considerations inform this decision?

Effective essay writing is precise and clear. The arguable proposition must reflect, and drive, that precision and clarity.

Suggested strategy for making this decision.

In the initial stages of planning your essay, write the thesis statement as a single sentence, including an arguable proposition that uses a *because* statement to link your claim and the reasons for that claim. You may choose to rewrite the thesis statement in the final draft, but the use of a single sentence will ensure that the connection between the claim and the reasons is clear.

Questions to guide you in the drafting of a provisional thesis statement.

1. What is the arguable claim the thesis statement makes?
2. What are the reasons for that claim?
3. Are the reasons causally related? Are they thematically related?
4. How have you identified the connections between the claim and the reasons for that claim?
5. Do the connections between the claim and the reasons make sense? Do they reflect your intentions?
6. Using only the arguable proposition, would a reader be able to anticipate the general thrust of the argument you intend to make?
7. Does the arguable proposition permit you to conceive of an outline for the essay in which there is a clear relationship between the individual paragraphs (or series of related paragraphs) and the controlling thesis of the essay?

Practice Exercise 1

Working toward a Clear, Concise Thesis Statement

(1)   The first step is to *identify your topic*. A topic is the broad general overview of what you want to discuss.
In this example, the larger topic is sex education.

(2)   The second step requires that you decide upon a *stance* for the topic. A stance is the position you are going to argue.
For example, you might argue that teaching students sex education in public schools is either a good idea or a bad policy.

(3)   The thesis is still rather general. You should now consider the reasons why you have taken the stance you have. These reasons allow you to refine your thesis. If you have chosen to write in favour of sex education, you might argue on the basis of reasons like:

    a. *Providing students with information about sex may reduce teen pregnancy.*

    b. *Providing students with information about sex may lead to fewer sexually transmitted diseases.*

    c. *Providing students with information about sex may take the mystery out of sex.*

    d. *Providing students with information about sex may promote safer sex practices.*

(4)   Let's recap. If this were your essay, you would now have identified your topic, your stance, and the reasons for your position. What comes next? At this point, you would develop a provisional thesis statement. Here are examples of two provisional thesis statements, each reflecting a different stance on the issue. The first one argues that safe sex education is a reasonable practice, and the second argues that safe sex education is not a reasonable policy. You'll notice that the stance you take informs the thesis statement.

Safe sex education is a reasonable social policy because it helps young people understand that unprotected sex can lead to unwanted pregnancy, to infection with sexually transmitted diseases, and to other negative consequences.

> *OR*

Safe sex education encourages promiscuity because it teaches children that they can prevent sexually transmitted diseases, avoid pregnancy, and enjoy casual sex without consequence.

Examine the first of the two examples. Is it an effective thesis statement? Is there a clear relationship between the arguable claim and the reasons?

Safe sex education is a reasonable social policy because it helps young people understand that unprotected sex can lead to unwanted pregnancy.

Safe sex education is a reasonable social policy because it helps young people understand that unprotected sex can lead to infection with sexually transmitted diseases.

Safe sex education is a reasonable social policy because it helps young people understand that unprotected sex can lead to other negative consequences.

By framing the argument around the *because* clause it is much easier to see which of the elements in the argument work and which ones don't.

The first of three is relatively clear. It argues that:

Safe sex education is a reasonable social policy because it helps young people understand that unprotected sex can lead to unwanted pregnancy.

In this case, the relationship between the claim and the reason for that claim is obvious. You understand immediately what it is you need to prove: that there is an identifiable link between sex education and the rate of teen pregnancy.

The second element of the thesis also appears to be phrased effectively. It argues that:

Safe sex education is a reasonable social policy because it helps young people understand that unprotected sex can lead to infection with sexually transmitted diseases.

In this case, you would need evidence that supported the connection between safe sex education and teen awareness of sexually transmitted diseases.

The third element of the thesis is more problematic. It does not appear to make a claim that could be proven or disproven:

Safe sex education is a reasonable social policy because it helps young people understand that unprotected sex can lead to other negative consequences.

Because the claim isn't specific, it's hard to see how you might proceed to find evidence to support it. You can frame the individual statement of claim in a number of different ways, but it must provide an observable connection between the claim and the specific reason. Look again at the third aspect of the argument to see whether you can rephrase it into something that clearly articulates a particular, testable argument.

The argument here is that *"safe sex education is a reasonable social policy because it helps young people understand that unprotected sex can lead to other negative consequences."*

Safe sex education is a reasonable social policy because:

1. *it can empower students.*
   OR
2. *it can assist students in making the right choices for their emotional health.*
   OR
3. *it can assist students in understanding that the choices they make can affect their emotional health.*

Any one of the options above will work because each makes a claim. There's no guarantee that any of the choices are supportable (i.e., that you will find evidence to bear out one of the claims), but each, potentially, could be argued.

(5) Now, finally, we have a workable thesis statement with an arguable proposition:

Safe sex education is a reasonable social policy because it helps young people understand that unprotected sex can lead to unwanted pregnancy, allows them to recognize the relationship between unprotected sex and sexually transmitted diseases, and guides them to an understanding that the choices they make can affect their emotional health.

Do you see how you can take a broad topic and narrow it through the considerations of the stance you will take (the position for which you are arguing), the scope of your argument, and the reasons on which you will base your claim?

✓•─Practice

Practice Exercise 2

Work through the second thesis statement yourself or with a partner, taking into account the points that have been raised in the example above.

> *Safe sex education encourages promiscuity because it teaches children that they can prevent sexually transmitted diseases, avoid pregnancy, and enjoy casual sex without consequence.*

2.8.3 Using the Arguable Proposition to Draft a Provisional Outline

Earlier in this chapter, we observed that novice writers tend to focus on knowledge telling (i.e., relating all knowledge on a topic as the ideas occur to the writer). Knowledge telling often results in an essay that lacks coherence, leaving the reader to provide a pattern of organization to the writer's ideas. By contrast, writing that is *coherent* displays a pattern of organization in which similar ideas are grouped together and arranged in such a way as to serve the overall purpose of the writing assignment. Problems with coherence can affect either the overall structure of your essay, or the structure of the individual paragraphs, or both.

Most writers—even good writers—write better with an outline. An outline allows you to plan, and planning allows you to identify key elements of the essay at the outset, to explore alternatives in the preliminary stages of the writing process, and to revise the organization of your ideas in a preliminary outline, as you move through the writing process. If ideas have been introduced that do not serve the purpose of your writing assignment, they are more easily seen when you use an outline.

Unfortunately, effective outlines require more than a simple listing of ideas that may be tangentially related to your topic. Effective outlines require that you think carefully about the essay you intend to write, identify your controlling thesis, and organize supporting ideas in a logical order. The arguable proposition provides you with that information. An outline that is drafted using an arguable proposition establishes a pattern by which to organize your ideas. It highlights the relationships between important ideas, organizes those ideas into related groups, and ensures that the ideas are presented in a logical order. It also provides a mechanism you can use to monitor the relationship between the various ideas that, collectively, comprise your essay.

✓•─Practice

Practice Exercise 3

A good thesis statement provides the basis for the outline of your essay. That principle is reflected in the example below. This example uses the sample thesis statement that was developed in the previous section.

> *Safe sex education is a reasonable social policy because it helps young people understand that unprotected sex can lead to unwanted pregnancy, allows them to recognize the relationship between unprotected sex and sexually transmitted diseases, and guides them to the understanding that the choices they make can affect their emotional health.*

If you take each of the individual arguments from the thesis statement, organizing them logically, ensuring that one flows to the next, you will have a manageable outline. (See Chapter 3 for a more complete model of the process of translating a thesis statement into an outline.)

2.8.4 Making Writing Decisions about Outlines

The process of drafting an outline for an argumentative essay reflects the nature of the essay itself. The essay is bound together by the relationship between the claim you make (i.e., the arguable proposition) and the evidence you offer in support of that claim. The outline ought to reflect that relationship. The following chart contains a brief discussion of the principles involved in using the arguable proposition to draft an outline.

Making Decisions About Using the Arguable Proposition to Draft an Outline

What is the purpose of this writing decision?

One of the most important developments in the movement of a writer from the stage of novice writer to the stage of experienced writer is the recognition of the need for planning. The use of the arguable proposition to draft an outline ensures that you are thinking about a meaningful pattern of organization for your essay.

What is the effect of this writing decision?

The use of the arguable proposition to draft an outline for your essay leads to an essay that is coherent, with all ideas integrated to serve a single purpose.

What considerations inform this decision?

An outline ought to reflect the pattern of reasoning that will govern your essay. Outlines that derive from lists of random ideas that occurred to you while you were watching a movie are usually not outlines at all. Challenge your outline to demonstrate the reasoning that is implicit in your thesis statement.

Suggested strategy for making this decision.

There is an implicit logic in your arguable proposition that runs horizontally (i.e., claim *A* is the case because of reason *B,* reason *C,* and reason *D*). If you tilt that proposition to the vertical (shown below), you have an outline in which the individual elements of the essay are connected by the same logic.

> *Introduction: Claim* A *is the case because of reason* B, *reason* C, *and reason* D.
> *Paragraph One: Prove or explore reason* B.
> *Paragraph Two: Prove or explore reason* C.
> *Paragraph Three: Prove or explore reason* D.

That, in brief, is your outline (it's not as complicated as it appears; we will work through the process at greater length in Chapter 3).

Questions to guide you in using your arguable proposition to draft an outline.

1. Look at the arguable proposition in your thesis statement. What claim are you making? What are the reasons you've identified in support of that claim?
2. Use the first reason to create the following question: What evidence is needed to substantiate or explore the first reason? This will be your first paragraph (or series of related paragraphs).

3. Use the second reason to create the following question: What evidence is needed to substantiate or explore the second reason? This will be your second paragraph (or series of related paragraphs).

4. Use the third reason to create the following question: What evidence is needed to substantiate or explore the third reason? This will be your third paragraph (or series of related paragraphs).

5. Use the same process for each of the reasons you identified in the arguable proposition.

2.8.5 The Arguable Proposition and Evidence

The arguable proposition also allows you to select the supporting resources you will need more effectively. When you've identified both your arguable claim and the reasons for that claim, you've also identified the scope of your research. If, for instance, you are arguing that *Listening to music while studying is often ineffective __because__ music introduces a competing stimulus that distracts the student*, you have already determined the nature of the research you will undertake:

1. What evidence is needed to show that *listening to music while studying is ineffective?*
2. What evidence is needed to show that *music introduces a competing stimulus that distracts the student?*
3. What evidence is needed to show that there is some connection between the two phenomena?

In short, because the arguable proposition contains the essential argument that you are making to your reader, it serves as a constant reminder of the burden of proof you assumed in your thesis statement.

2.8.6 Using the Arguable Proposition to Manage Evidence in Your Essay

The objective of an argumentative essay is to demonstrate the validity of your argument. One of the ways in which you can do that is by ensuring that the reader is able to recognize the connection between the claim you are making and the evidence you have put forth to support that claim. Use the following chart to guide your decision making about selecting and managing evidence, or other supporting documentation, in your essay.

Making Writing Decisions	About the Relationship between the Arguable Proposition and Evidence

What is the purpose of this writing decision?

The use of evidence and other supporting documentation in your essay should be purposeful and intentional.

What is the effect of this writing decision?

By connecting your documentation to the specific needs that you identified in the arguable proposition, you are able to avoid the characteristic information dump of novice writers.

What considerations inform this decision?

It's important to remember that individual facts, authoritative quotations, and other pieces of information do not write an essay. You do. Resource materials must be subordinate to your purpose as a writer.

Suggested strategy for making this decision.

The best strategy for undertaking research for an essay is to use the arguable proposition, and the questions that derive from that proposition, to identify the specific information you need (this is discussed further in Chapters 4 and 6).

Questions to guide you in the management of evidence in your essay.

1. Return to the questions you developed while drafting an outline for your essay. What evidence is needed to substantiate or explore the first reason? How does that information strengthen your argument or lead to a deeper understanding of that particular aspect of the essay?
2. What evidence is needed to substantiate or explore the second reason? How does that information strengthen your argument or lead to a deeper understanding of that particular aspect of the essay?
3. What evidence is needed to substantiate or explore the third reason? How does that information strengthen your argument or lead to a deeper understanding of that particular aspect of the essay?
4. Use the same process for each of the reasons you identified in the arguable proposition.

2.8.7 Arguable Propositions and the Reader

A well-articulated arguable proposition serves your reader in two principal ways:

1. It establishes a pattern of organization that permits the reader to follow, and even anticipate, the pattern of reasoning the essay will follow.
2. It allows the reader to see whether you've met your burden of proof.

The first advantage is a particularly significant one. Reading is a more efficient, and more pleasant, experience when the reader is comfortable in the text, and the reader's comfort derives, in large part, from an understanding of the pattern of organization. The second advantage, however, has its own merits. It reminds both you and the reader that your essay has a purpose, a purpose that is only satisfied when you have demonstrated, on the basis of some form of evidence, that your thesis is a reasonable one.

Establishing a pattern of reasoning for the reader is more than simple courtesy. Most research into the process of reading shows that readers use context to decipher meaning. That is, readers will reason inductively from a well-articulated thesis statement to interpret some aspect of the text that is harder to understand. The thesis statement allows your reader to guess what you *mean* to say. Similarly, the topic sentence of each paragraph establishes a pattern of reasoning for the respective paragraph. We're not suggesting that you take the day off when you're working on other sentences, or that you casually string words together, relying on thesis and topic sentences to carry the load for you. We are suggesting, however, that you will do a great service, to both your reader and yourself, if you embed the arguable proposition in your thesis statement.

In identifying the relationship between the claim you're making and the reasons for that claim, the arguable proposition also allows your reader to determine whether you have provided sufficient evidence for your argument. While that might seem to impose a bit of an obligation on you (and it does), it also offers a compensatory benefit. Just as the arguable proposition foregrounds your writing purpose for your reader, reminding the reader of the promises you made in your introduction, it also reminds you of your writing purpose, allowing you to monitor the degree to which the essay is satisfying your intentions.

2.8.8 Thinking about Arguable Propositions and the Reader

The goal of an argumentative essay is to provide your reader with the evidence necessary to establish that your arguable proposition is reasonable. The following chart offers a brief discussion of the advantage to your reader of a well-crafted arguable proposition.

Making Writing Decisions   About Arguable Propositions and the Reader

What is the purpose of this writing decision?

At the beginning of this chapter, we identified your reader as belonging to an audience of intelligent individuals who are familiar with the practice of reasoning, and willing to be persuaded by evidence. The purpose of this writing decision is to help facilitate the satisfaction of that reader's expectations by using the arguable proposition to ensure the logic and coherence of your essay.

What is the effect of this writing decision?

By using the arguable proposition to establish an organizational pattern for the essay, you create an effective transition into the essay. You also establish expectations that allow the reader to understand your writing purpose and to determine whether you've satisfied that purpose.

What considerations inform this decision?

Writing is a communicative act in which you, as a writer, assume some degree of responsibility for ensuring that your reader has enough information to interpret your text. Your arguable proposition ought to provide the basis for your reader's interpretative strategy.

Suggested strategy for making this decision.

Read your thesis statement (and the arguable proposition it contains), imagining that you are going to convey the essence of your essay in that single statement. Would that statement allow a reader to anticipate both the structure and substance (or content) of the essay you are going to present? If not, it needs to be reworked.

LO 2, 3, 4, 5

2.9   EXPLORING OPPOSING VIEWS (COUNTER-ARGUMENT)

Some people believe that organic farming is the best thing since, well, organic farming (i.e., organic farming is not an entirely new development; it's an updated version of older practices). Others argue that organic farming is not efficient enough to feed the world's population. Which side is correct? Probably, a little bit of column A and a little bit of column B. Organic farming is, in many ways, kinder to the environment but it does not usually provide the yields necessary to feed billions of people. How, then, are you meant to write an argumentative essay on the issue? You do so by drafting a thesis statement that allows you to argue for the advisability of organic farming in some circumstances, while acknowledging the competing merits of large-scale farming operations.

An argumentative essay is, by its nature, designed to favour a particular point of view on an issue. The thesis statement you draft, the evidence you provide, and the structure of reasoning that guides your essay all reflect the position you've taken on an issue. Nevertheless, effective reasoning requires that you look at an issue from multiple perspectives, examining each to determine the most reasonable position on the basis of the available evidence. The practice of systematically examining alternative views ensures that you will do this. It also signals to the reader that you are a reliable source of information.

One of the defining characteristics of academic writing is a demonstrated commitment to the thorough and balanced exploration of competing perspectives. Unfortunately, many students have been taught to strengthen their own arguments by anticipating alternative views, misrepresenting those views as ridiculous and untenable, and moving on to demonstrate the obvious superiority of their positions. It is, of course, much easier to make one's own case if the alternative view has been established as unworthy of consideration.

There are a couple of problems with that strategy. The first is that it short-circuits your reasoning process. Before you try to convince your reader of the validity of your position, you need to ensure that your position is, in fact, defensible. One of the difficulties that students encounter when writing academic essays is the practice of reverse reasoning (i.e., prematurely committing to a conclusion and then, selectively, searching out the evidence that supports it). You are not meant to make the lesser argument seem the stronger (this was the much-maligned custom of the Sophists in Greece in the sixth-century B.C.E.; they had a good run with it, but Plato, exposing many of the practices we're discouraging here, ensured that history would judge those Sophists harshly). Your obligation as an academic writer is to assess the evidence carefully, asking yourself why a reasonable person might disagree with the position you hold, and report your conclusions fairly, acknowledging the points at which intelligent and well-informed individuals oppose your views.

The second problem with an unfair representation of opposing views is that it is usually transparently dishonest. You defined your audience as intelligent and well versed in logic, remember? That audience is not likely to be fooled by any attempt to unfairly vilify those who might disagree with you. It is more likely, in fact, that you will diminish your own authority with the reader. In contrast, acknowledging the validity of alternative views strengthens your argument by demonstrating that you've carefully considered the evidence—reflecting dispassionately on the merits of competing positions—before arriving at a conclusion that seems reasonable. This commitment to reason will make you a better writer (it will also, by the way, make you a more pleasant guest at cocktail parties; that's not entirely relevant here, of course, but it is, nevertheless, a thing to remember).

What is the best place to place a counter-argument? Unfortunately, there is no clear answer to that question. It will depend on both the context and the purpose for introducing it. You should always refer to it in your introduction as a means of limiting the scope of your thesis statement. After you've introduced the counter-argument, you might choose to place a larger discussion of it in either (1) the paragraph immediately following the introduction, using it to establish the view against which you are arguing, or (2) a paragraph immediately preceding the conclusion, using it to identify competing positions to the one you hold. As a general rule, you should avoid playing Ping-Pong between your thesis and its counter-argument in a single paragraph. The effect tends to be a little confusing and often works against the unity of the paragraph.

How do you signal to your reader that you're going to be presenting a counter-argument? The table below provides examples of words and phrases that indicate that you might be presenting an alternative view to the thesis you're arguing.

Words That Can Signal the Counter-argument:	Words That Signal That You're Turning the Argument Back to Your Reader:
In contrast; some might object, however; it might seem that; in the contrary view.	Yet; however; nevertheless; still; nonetheless; notwithstanding the above.

You may notice the similarity between the phrases in each category. That similarity isn't surprising. In both cases, you're signalling that you're changing direction.

2.9.1 Thinking about Counter-argument in Your Writing

A thoughtful and carefully reasoned discussion of opposing views makes your argument stronger and enhances your credibility with the reader. It is important, however, to ensure that you've presented the counter-argument fairly and objectively. Do not resort to misrepresentations of opposing views that suggest your apparent even-handedness is nothing more than a transparently deceptive rhetorical device. It just doesn't fool anybody. Instead, look for arguments that you, and your reader, might consider to be reasonable.

The following chart identifies some of the key ideas to consider when making decisions about counter-arguments in your essay.

Making Writing Decisions | About Counter-arguments

What is the purpose of this writing decision?

Academic writing derives from a process of reasoning, and the process of reasoning demands that the question under consideration be examined from multiple perspectives.

What is the effect of this writing decision?

The analysis of competing views or alternative explanations ensures that you have explored your topic thoroughly. It also enhances your authority with the reader, demonstrating that you've investigated the respective issue comprehensively and represented all views fairly.

What considerations inform this decision?

There are very few interpretations of text, responses to philosophical paradoxes, or explanations for natural phenomena that are so compelling that they exclude any alternative.

Intelligent and decent human beings may disagree with you. The representation of the counter-argument acknowledges the possibility that others may understand an issue differently.

Suggested strategy for making this decision.

The simplest strategy for investigating counter-arguments is one of the most useful tools in all of reasoning: set aside your initial explanation or hypothesis, and ask yourself what other explanation there might be. Be guided by a sense of humility.

Example of a counter-argument   Suppose you argued in your thesis statement that video games were not harmful to a child's development. What process might you follow to develop your counter-argument? First, you might consider whether there are any limits to the claim you are making. You might ask, for instance, whether it is always true that video games are not harmful. Does the degree of harm depend upon the nature of the game? Are violent games more harmful? Is it possible that some children are more likely to experience harm? Does the degree of harm depend on the degree of exposure to the games? The answers to each of these questions might serve both to refine the claim you're making and to indicate counter-arguments that you should be addressing in your essay.

Thesis Statement:
Video games are beneficial to children's development.
Reasons:
1. Video games can improve children's problem-solving skills,
2. They can give children self-confidence.
3. The skills children learn can be useful in real-world situations.

Counter-argument:
However, there are circumstances under which video games do appear to have some negative effects on children.

Example: *Children who play violent video games have a tendency to become violent themselves.*

Resolving the apparent conflict between the thesis and the counter-argument effectively:
Although video games can cause some children to become more violent, most studies show that only a limited number of children who play video games subsequently display violent tendencies. Thus, it may be the case that there are other factors that contribute to the behaviour of those children who do become violent after playing violent video games.

Though the process of examining competing views identifies some circumstances in which the original argument does not hold, those circumstances do not invalidate the argument. They do, however, require an explanation. The counter-argument allows you to provide that.

2.10 CONCLUSION

In this chapter, we have reviewed the general features that characterize academic writing in general, distinguishing it from other forms of writing in order to foreground the features that typify it. We noted that one of the difficulties that novice writers face is the variety of writing forms they might encounter in their college or university career. We also acknowledged that, in this textbook, we concentrate on developing general strategies for academic writing by focusing on a generic essay that doesn't exist. We believe that, by mastering a general process of essay writing, you will develop a model of essay writing that will be useful in most circumstances (at the end of the textbook, we have provided templates that will allow you to adapt those general writing principles into the specific formats required for individual disciplines). To that end, we reviewed some of the processes of argumentative writing in particular. In the next chapter, we will show the way in which you might be able to acquire a working understanding of argumentative essay writing using the IDDL model.

MyCompLab®

How Do I Get a Better Grade?

Go to MyCompLab for additional help with your
grammar, writing, and research skills. You will have access to a variety of
exercises, instruction, and videos that will help you improve your basic
skills and help you get a better grade.

Sample Essay

The following is an example of an essay that offers a clear, concise thesis statement, and how that thesis statement informs the outline of the essay.

A Final Look at the Considerations that Guide Decision-Making in Writing a Thesis Statement in a Student Essay

Video Games Are Not Harmful to a Child's Development

1 The introductory paragraph provides the reader with a road map to the essay. The thesis statement at the end of the introduction clearly articulates the organizational pattern the writer will follow.

[1]The reliance on technology is pervasive in today's society. Almost everyone owns some piece of technology such as cell phones, tablet computers, or video game consoles. People have become so reliant on these devices that they would find it difficult to function without them. The same could be said for video games. Video games have become so ingrained in children's daily lives that they would find it difficult to go without playing a game even for a day. Video games provide a source of entertainment much the way television does. There have been many articles written about the negative effects of playing video games on a child's development (Brown, 2010; Green, 2011; Morgan, 2009). However, there are just as many articles written about the positive aspects attributed to playing video games (Hall, 2010; Plank, 2008; Shepherd, 2012). It is difficult to know what to think with so many competing articles pointing out not only the negatives but

the positives associated with playing video games. [2]Video games are not harmful to a child's development because they improve reflexes and problem-solving skills; they give children something to be successful at; and they help develop skills that will prove useful in the future.

[3]Playing video games can improve reflexes and problem-solving skills (Hall, 2010). In a series of studies conducted with children ages 10–15, Hall (2010) reported that children who play video games had higher scores on a variety of visual attention tasks than children who did not play video games. His research found that video game players are less easily distracted, better able to make quick decisions, and better able to focus on tasks for long periods of time. In addition, video game players have greater peripheral vision than non-video game players.

[4]There are many different types of video games on the market. Some require little skill, such as the games that are limited to aiming and shooting at a target, but others require complex thinking and problem-solving skills (Shepherd, 2012). Shepherd (2012) found that children who play games that require greater concentration can actually improve their overall thinking skills. Some games require players to solve problems that will allow them to gain access to the next level (Henderson, 2008). Henderson (2008) discovered that if children are not good problem-solvers, they will not be able to advance in the game. The ability to concentrate is a trait that not only helps children stay on task when playing video games but also helps them in school-related tasks (Plank, 2008).

[5]The ability to make quick decisions is also a trait of video game players (Hall, 2010). In each game, there is a limited amount of time for each player to make a decision before they are killed and sent back to the start of the game. Players cannot afford to be indecisive (Hall, 2010) or they risk losing everything they have acquired up to that point. Hall (2010) theorized that the ability to make quick decisions is a life skill that should be encouraged in children. Playing video games is one way that this skill can be developed.

[6]In addition, children who play video games develop the ability to stay focused on the task (Jenkins, 2009). Jenkins (2009) discovered that children who play video games can shut out distractions that take their attention away from the game. The ability to concentrate for long periods of time can also help children with school work (Jenkins, 2009). In a study of 15-year-olds, Jenkins (2009) found that children who play video games were better able to concentrate on the task of finishing their homework in a timely fashion than students who did not play video games.

---

2 This is the thesis statement. Notice that it details for the reader the writer's stance on an issue and the reasons for that stance. The author establishes the argument for the reader in a clear, concise manner. An essay that starts with a clear thesis statement practically organizes itself.

3 The first line of the paragraph is the topic sentence. Notice that the topic is the same as the first point of the thesis statement. It is important in terms of organization that you follow the same order established in your original statement of argument (thesis statement).

4 The second paragraph of the first point continues with the theme established in the first paragraph. Generally, a paragraph is organized around a single organizing idea. When you are exploring a complex concept, you may want to break it into a series of related themes, with each being discussed individually in its own paragraph.

5 Again, the writer has moved on to a new paragraph to explore a different aspect of the theme discussed above.

6 Notice that the writer is starting the paragraph with a clear topic sentence. This signals to the reader the principal theme for the paragraph.

7 This paragraph introduces the second argument from the thesis statement. The topic sentence relates directly to the point being argued.

[7]Children who play video games can become very successful in a game in a short period of time (Welsh, 2011). Welsh (2011) pointed out that it is important for children to achieve early success in whatever they do. He further hypothesized that if children are not successful they become discouraged and may not want to continue with the task. Welsh (2011) discovered that children who are easily discouraged have not had much success and therefore give up on tasks too easily. However, he discovered that children who were persistent in improving their skills in a video game had greater success in school-related tasks. Welsh concluded that it is beneficial for children to develop self-confidence and being successful at playing video games is one way for them to develop self-confidence.

8 In a new paragraph, working from a clear topic sentence, the writer provides support for the second point of the thesis statement.

[8]Welsh (2011) further found that children who play video games develop positive feelings about themselves which can lead to increased enthusiasm for other tasks, and self-motivation and interest for tasks that might be more difficult. When children are successful they gain confidence in their abilities and feel better about themselves. Playing video games can be beneficial to young people because it increases their self-esteem.

9 This topic sentence introduces the discussion of the third argument from the thesis statement. Again, the writer has signalled the theme of the paragraph with a clear topic sentence.

[9]Playing video games can also help develop skills that children can use in the future such as perseverance and communication. Grove and Waters (2010) discovered that children who play video games exhibit behaviour that is purposeful and goal-directed. Many computer games have more than one level, and each level must be conquered before the player can move on. Players who are more goal-directed will continue to play the game until they can move on to the next level (Grove & Waters, 2010). In addition, the authors reported that games become more complex as the players progress through the levels thus requiring even more perseverance in overcoming obstacles. This skill can be transferred to life situations. If children learn the importance of continuing on with a task until they are successful rather than giving up at the first sign of trouble, they will be better able to cope with disappointment and failure later on in their life (Welsh, 2010).

10 The writer begins with a clear topic sentence, indicating that the essay has moved to a discussion of a different aspect of the third argument.

[10]Some video games can be played online, thus encouraging cooperation among players. Players who play games online wear headsets and can communicate verbally with other players. Since children play video games a lot they can develop friendships with the people they play with (Bond, 2008). The ability to form friendships and teams can help build positive communication skills. When children play video games as a member of a team, they have to learn to work together with the other team members if they want to progress through the game and be successful

(Bond, 2008). Learning important communication skills will help children become successful in their dealings with others such as family members, friends, classmates, and teachers (Bond, 2008).

Video games can also be used in the work place as training tools. For example video games such as flight simulators are used by the Air Force and NASA to train pilots how to fly (Gorky, 2011). The practical application of video games has also been adapted by some schools that use video games to teach skills such as algebra and computer programming (Gorky, 2011). Video games are not just for entertainment purposes and children who develop skills learned from playing video games early in life will have a greater success rate with computer simulations when they join the work force (Gorky, 2011).

[11]Despite the benefits of playing video games, there are some side-effects that have been attributed to playing video games. The most common one is that exposure to violent video games can cause children to become more violent (Gray, 2009). [12]Gray (2009) studied children who were 12–16 years of age over three months, and found that some children did exhibit feelings of anger or hostility after playing video games but he concluded that not all children displayed these behaviours. He found that, though video games could increase violent feelings in the player, it depended on the character of the child.

[13]Another problem with players who spend a lot of time playing video games is that they get desensitized to violence and lack empathy towards others (Gray, 2009). Gray (2009), in his study, discovered that for some children exposure to violent video games did lead to a decrease in emotional reactions to violence and other people's pain. It has been hypothesized (Hum, 2010) that children who play violent video games could become more violent themselves and could harm others. This desensitization factor could lead to children hurting others because they might think it really doesn't hurt the other person because they are so used to the violence they see on the games they play. [14]This does not pertain to all children so it cannot be argued that violent video games necessarily lead to desensitization of all players.

[15]When discussing the role of video games in the development of a child, it is important to remember that moderation is the key. It is up to parents to monitor the types of games their children play, and the amount of time they spend playing games. [16]Video games have been shown to contribute to a child's overall development in terms of helping them develop skills that have proven to be beneficial such as improving reflexes and

11 This statement introduces an opposing view to one articulated in the thesis statement. It is important to include a counter-argument that demonstrates why a reasonable person might disagree with your point of view.

12 The writer argues that, despite some evidence to the contrary, the writer is not convinced by the thesis statement; the overall findings are not conclusive.

13 This paragraph continues the discussion of the counter-argument, offering yet another perspective on the issue.

14 Once again, notice that the writer examines the evidence for the argument but argues the original thesis is still viable.

15 The start of the conclusion does not just restate the thesis statement. It is important to remember that conclusions should not merely repeat the thesis statement. A conclusion synthesizes the evidence and demonstrates the conclusions that can be drawn from it.

16 This is the evidence that the writer used to prove that video games are not harmful to a child's development.

problem-solving skills; improving self-esteem; and improving skills that can be used in the future. There are some negative effects associated with playing video games but these seem to be related to the individual. Not all children who play violent video games develop violent tendencies so perhaps there are other factors that contribute to some children becoming violent. Video games cannot take the blame for children who may have other issues unrelated to playing games. In addition, not every video game has violence in it, and so parents have to make sure that the video games they buy are not all one kind. [17]There are many educational games on the market (Hum, 2010) so drawing the conclusion that all video games are harmful to a child's development is not a valid reason to avoid their use. Some video games can be beneficial to a child's development.

17 The writer leaves the reader with a brief statement of the conclusion.

✓•⎡Practice   **Thesis Statement Peer-Review Worksheet**

Writer's Name: _____

Reviewer's Name: _____

What is the thesis statement?

_____

_____

1. **In two or three sentences, identify the argument being suggested in the thesis statement. What is the claim that is being made? What is the basis of that claim?**

2. **In two or three sentences, explain how the scope of the argument has been limited to a specific and manageable claim.**

3. **Reflect upon the thesis statement. What evidence might be needed to support its argument?**

Arguable Proposition Peer-Review Worksheet ✓• Practice

Writer's Name: _____

Reviewer's Name: _____

What is the arguable proposition?

_____

_____

1. In two or three sentences, identify the argument being suggested in the arguable proposition. What is the claim being made? What is the basis of that claim?

2. In two or three sentences, explain how the arguable proposition has been limited to a specific and manageable claim.

3. Reflect upon the arguable proposition. What other evidence might be needed to provide support to its argument?

Counter-argument Peer-Review Worksheet ✓• Practice

Writer's Name: _____

Reviewer's Name: _____

What are the most important counter-arguments that are being made?

_____

_____

1. In two or three sentences, summarize the counter-arguments being suggested in the essay. What effect do they have on the writer's argument?

(continued)

(*continued*)

2. In two or three sentences, explain the way in which the counter-arguments limit the writer's thesis. In your opinion, are the counter-arguments strong enough that the writer needs to consider the validity of the thesis? Why?

CHAPTER 3

Getting Started Using the IDDL Writing Model

Learning Objectives

At the completion of this chapter, you will be able to:

1. Explain the differences between the organizing structures that novice and experienced writers use to compose essays.

2. Explain how the IDDL model reflects the writing process of the experienced writer.

3. Explain the purpose of the embedded questions in the IDDL model.

4. Demonstrate the ability to use the IDDL model to organize your own essay.

3.1   INTRODUCTION

First-year students in writing classes often complain that they don't know what is expected of them. They're handed assignments in one or more classes and asked to provide a paper of some length on a subject of some kind. For the most successful students, this means going home and immediately scribbling the due date onto a calendar, before trotting off to the library to check out every book that is even tangentially related to the subject (the advantage of this, of course, is that no one else will get the books). The next step? Settling down to read everything there is to read on a general topic before drafting an impossibly broad outline.

Students who are less successful? They notice that the essay is due the evening before they have to submit it, scramble to find the resource materials that the other students have left behind, and race through a similar process in a shorter period of time (in effect, they attempt to complete in one night what the success-ful students spent a month doing).

Despite the obvious differences, both groups of students are often undone by the same error in judgment. At no point, you will notice, did either group of students stop to ask the kind of questions that would permit them to explore a focused and coherent idea in writing. Instead, they all began with the assump-tion that most of us had when we were novice writers: that the purpose of writing was to relate as much knowledge as one could possibly manage to an instructor.

And then there were those students who drive us all mad. Those are the ones who don't begin early—may even begin late—but begin with a well-articulated understanding of purpose. They analyze their respective assignments, focus their ideas through the ongoing refinement of their thesis statements and outlines, organize material to correspond to the patterns of organization suggested in the outlines, and produce better essays than the rest of us—apparently with less effort. It seems wrong, doesn't it? It seems like it violates the principles of natural justice, which dictate that people's rewards will be proportionate to the sweat and toil they have invested.

Sadly, in this fallen world, life is not always fair. The papers these students submit are papers that are guided by purpose, informed with careful reason-ing, and demonstrably committed to the development of ideas rather than the simple transmission of unrelated facts. In this chapter, we'll use the IDDL model to demonstrate the steps you can follow to ensure that your essay will exhibit a similar commitment to meaning, purpose, and structure.

In Chapter 1, we discussed the nature of writing in general, the problems that novice writers sometimes experience in orienting themselves to the textual world, the differences between novice and experienced writers, and the differ-ences between writing in high school (which is, for many, the last stage at which they received formal instruction in writing) and writing in college or university settings. We also introduced you to the concept of metacognitive learning, a pro-cess that allows you to acquire writing skills (1) by attending to the decisions you make while writing, and (2) by comparing the differences between the nature of the work you're producing and the nature of the work you would like to pro-duce. In Chapter 2, we identified some of the specific characteristics of academic writing, focusing for the most part on the argumentative essay, and discussed the importance of identifying the relationships between key ideas during the planning stage. And, all the while, we acknowledge that the process of writing is complex and, sometimes, difficult.

In this chapter, we introduce you to a model that will assist you in making the types of writing decisions we have discussed in the previous chapters. It is called the IDDL decision-making model. It's a little different from writing models to which you may have already been introduced (e.g., the five-paragraph model). The five-paragraph model is that very structured, formulaic pattern of writing that you may have been taught in high school. We want to be clear here. There is nothing wrong with the five-paragraph model. In fact, we like it. It's a useful structure for students who are learning to organize their thoughts for the writing of essays. It allows you to plan the larger structure of your essay before you begin to work on its individual components or sections. However, in many instances, writers permit the model to become formulaic. They assume that the steps the model follows (e.g., write an introduction, write three body paragraphs, write a conclusion) will inevitably result in a successful essay. That process sometimes fails to transfer to university writing assignments because most university writing assignments are more complex than those in high school and, therefore, require greater depth than the five-paragraph model allows.

The IDDL model (pronounced *ideal*) is an acronym for a linked series of strategies designed to aid invention and organization during the planning stage of the writing process. (An acronym is an abbreviation formed using the first letters of a word or phrase.) IDDL stands for:

1. **I**nscribe the writing space (i.e., create the structure of the essay using the thesis statement to identify the individual components or sections the essay will explore). You use the outline that emerges from the argument you identified in your thesis statement to map the direction your essay will follow from the beginning. The map may be altered as you progress through the writing (sadly, sometimes things don't work out as well as you had intended and you're obliged to circle back to correct your course; we discuss this process in greater detail in Chapter 11). It is, nevertheless, a lot easier to move forward when you have some sense of the direction you intend to follow. This is one of the great advantages of writing models: they change the writing process, from one in which you scramble to fill empty pages to one in which you work through the steps you must follow in order to advance from the beginning to the end. It helps you get started. Getting started is often the hardest part.

2. **D**efine the rhetorical problems locally. After mapping out the general shape of your essay, you will find that you have a series of themes, or subtopics, that need to be explored, discussed, or substantiated (i.e., supported by evidence). These themes will become either paragraphs or groups of related paragraphs. The advantage of looking at each individually is that you can concentrate on one idea at a time, exploring it fully, without simultaneously having to concentrate on the rest of the essay. You know that each section is connected to the controlling thesis because you got the idea from the thesis in the first place (this will become clearer when you work through the example later in the chapter). You also know that you will be able to make adjustments to ensure that the individual pieces fit together properly. The fourth stage in the model asks you to examine the individual sections of the essay and link them together logically.

3. **D**iscover the information necessary to solve the local rhetorical problems. In the second stage of the process, you defined themes for each of the individual sections of the essay. In Stage 3, working with one theme or subtopic at a time, you will undertake the research necessary to fully explore the themes or substantiate the claims you have just identified. You'll find it's much easier to conduct research when you're focusing on a single aspect of a larger question (we discuss this in greater detail in Chapter 4).

4. Link the individual units of the essay logically. In the final stage of the IDDL model, you will be asked to review the order of the individual sections and to consider the connections you have made between the individual sections of the essay. Using the thesis statement as a guide to your original purpose, you'll reflect on the order of the paragraphs, or groups of paragraphs, to ensure that you're guiding your reader through the essay in a way that makes sense. You'll also think about the connections you've made between sentences and paragraphs, asking yourself whether those connections link the ideas together in the way you intended.

The IDDL model has a number of advantages:

- It uses a pattern of organization with which you are already familiar (i.e., the five-paragraph essay) and builds on it.
- It offers a visual representation of the essay's organizational structure, highlighting the relationships between ideas and helping you become aware of those relationships.
- It's flexible (e.g., though the model requires that you organize your thoughts into units of related ideas, it doesn't tell you how many paragraphs you must have in your essay).
- It allows you to manage the complex series of decisions that writing demands by presenting those decisions one at a time.
- It includes embedded questions that encourage you to make decisions the way experienced writers make decisions (the questions are addressed to you; the essay you write depends on the answers you give; the questions are only meant to focus your attention on the decisions you have to make).

The IDDL model does not diminish the complexity of the writing process, but it may make it a little more manageable.

LO 1, 2 ## 3.2 DIFFERENCES BETWEEN NOVICE WRITERS AND EXPERIENCED WRITERS

The following chart, which you will recognize from previous chapters, is meant to highlight some of the important differences between the writing practices of novice writers and experienced writers. In this chapter, we want you to focus on the two last sections of the chart, which pertain to planning, reviewing, and organizing. The IDDL model is designed to help developing writers acquire some of the planning and organizational strategies used by experienced writers.

As we noted in Chapter 2, the differences between novice and experienced writers are particularly significant in the writing of academic essays, which, in addition to the usual writing challenge of developing coherent meaning in text, have a number of distracting formal requirements. Because novice writers *require thought for procedural, or "mechanical," writing functions,* they have less memory capacity for attending to the development of meaning. Because they are unfamiliar with the conventions of academic writing, they also tend to *focus on error avoidance rather than meaning.* Most importantly, perhaps, novice writers *focus on "knowledge*

Novice Writers	Experienced Writers
■ Require thought for procedural, or "mechanical," writing functions.	■ Have, to a significant degree, automated procedural functions.
■ Focus on error avoidance rather than meaning.	■ Focus on developing or refining meaning.
■ Begin writing without planning and edit, if at all, for grammatical errors.	■ Invest time and energy in planning and reviewing.
■ Focus on "knowledge telling" (i.e., relating all the information they have and can find on a topic, rather than exercising critical judgment to determine relevance).	■ Organize, and reorganize, essay structure to allow individual ideas to serve the overall purpose of the essay.

telling" (i.e., relating all they know and can find on a topic, rather than exercising critical judgment to determine relevance) and, as a consequence, tend to insert information into their essays without tailoring it to their respective purposes. Experienced writers, in contrast, *have, to a significant degree, automated procedural functions*, and, thus, are better able to *focus on developing or refining meaning*. In addition, because experienced writers are generally purpose driven in their writing, they are more likely to *organize, and reorganize, essay structure to allow individual ideas to serve the overall purpose of the essay.*

During the planning stage, there is another significant difference between novice and experienced writers that is particularly noteworthy. Novice writers often *begin writing without planning, and edit, if at all, for grammatical errors*, while experienced writers *invest time and energy in planning and reviewing*. The IDDL model is designed to encourage you to follow the same practices that experienced writers follow, developing a unifying thesis, and using that thesis to govern decision making.

The process that is used by both the successful student writers mentioned in the introduction to this chapter and the experienced writers is one that privileges logical essay structure and purposeful patterns of organization over word count and long strings of unrelated thoughts. It's an important difference. The coherence of an essay derives from its organization, and organization derives from a clear sense of purpose and careful planning. Readers will forgive many smaller failings if you are able to produce a piece of work that is logical and well ordered. In fact, because readers generally interpret text inductively, relying upon key sentences to contextualize other information, the crafting of a clear thesis statement and outline is the greatest gift you have to offer them.

3.3 USING THE FOUR-STAGE IDDL MODEL TO PLAN YOUR ESSAY

LO 2, 3, 4

In the face of the blank page, some students wander aimlessly. Most writers, even good writers, write better with an outline. Planning allows you to explore alternatives in the movement toward the final articulation of an idea. The characteristic information dump of inexperienced writers (i.e., relating all the knowledge one has on a topic, rather than exercising critical judgment to determine its relevance or organizing the information to serve a point) generally results from a lack of planning.

Planning is an integral part of the process of writing. It does, of course, take more time and effort during the early stages of writing than, say, not planning. On the other hand, planning pays off in a number of ways. Not planning doesn't. That is, planning generally saves you time in the long run and renders the writing process much easier. It permits you to frame your argument carefully, reflecting on your purpose and audience, and thinking about the ways in which you will craft an essay that will meet your reader's expectations. It gives you time to think about the kinds of information you will need while writing and time to reflect on potential flaws or weaknesses in your argument. It allows you to make a number of the larger writing decisions in advance, relieving you of the obligation to manage multiple decisions while you are concentrating on refining individual sentences or paragraphs for meaning. Not planning often leads to essays that break down midpoint, leaving you to struggle with a thesis that cannot be proven or to manage an idea that is too ill-defined to be resolved.

The IDDL model is designed to guide the planning and the composition of an academic essay. The model employs a system that allows you to plan your essay and helps you to maintain a pattern of organization that provides the essay with coherence by (1) developing a thesis statement that clearly articulates both an arguable proposition and the reasons on which that proposition is based, and (2) using those reasons to chart a clear path from the introduction to the conclusion. Unlike the five-paragraph model, however, the IDDL model is both active, with embedded questions that prompt you to develop content in accordance with your own writing purpose, and dynamic, allowing you to monitor the effect of the writing decisions you are making.

The following chart provides an abbreviated description of the steps you will follow using the IDDL model. In the examples afterwards, you will work through the individual steps.

The IDDL Model for Essay Writing
Inscribe the writing space.   ■ Use the arguable proposition of your thesis statement to create a working outline for your essay.
Define the rhetorical problems locally.   ■ Use the individual claims of the arguable proposition to define the subtopics that you will explore as individual components in the essay.
Discover the information necessary to solve the local rhetorical problems.   ■ For each of the subtopics, undertake a research process that allows you to explore the theme or prove a claim. Because you have already defined the subtopic in the second stage, you are able to carry out a research process that is guided by a specific need.
Link the individual units of the essay logically.   ■ Using your thesis statement as a guide, organize the individual units to provide your reader with a logical path from the beginning of the essay to its conclusion.

3.3.1 Stage 1: Inscribing the Writing Space

The difficulty that many students have with writing assignments is that they don't know what they're meant to do. They often don't have that problem with other courses. They understand, for instance, that a physics assignment requires them to work through a problem and arrive at an answer. They understand that a reading assignment in psychology requires them to read and remember the assigned content. The writing assignment, however, is challenging because it seems to lack both boundaries and step-by-step rules. They struggle to find a road map to guide them.

The next box represents the blank page that torments the novice writer. Unlike experienced writers, most of whom have already developed writing strategies that—implicitly at least—divide the act of writing into a series of individual steps, novice writers often see the process as a single act of creation. In the absence of the models that experienced writers carry around in their heads, novice writers have to develop the structures for their essays and then find the information to put into those structures. It seems a little unfair, doesn't it?

(Uninscribed Writing Space)
There's nothing here.

It may be a little easier to get started if you're able to think of the essay as a practical problem, one in which there are a series of steps that will move you from the introduction to the conclusion, allowing you to stop occasionally to develop a particular idea, moving logically from one idea to the next, addressing individual challenges as each comes up, confident that the planning you did at the outset will ensure that the ideas will ultimately serve the general purpose of the essay (i.e., proving the thesis). That's really all you have to do:

1. Figure out where you're going.
2. Identify the necessary steps to get there.
3. Get started.

The IDDL model uses a series of boxes to represent a writing space that has been broken down into individual steps (i.e., inscribed). You'll notice that each of the steps relates to the essay's general purpose (i.e., the arguable proposition of the thesis statement). In the second stage of the process, we'll fill in the remaining boxes with the subtopics that need to be explored as you work your way through the essay.

Compare the previous box (i.e., the uninscribed writing space) with the one on the following page (i.e., the inscribed writing space). The first offered no direction, relying on you instead to invent an essay out of thin air. That's not an easy thing to do. The box that follows identifies what you must do in the course of writing your essay.

While the following example may appear a little formulaic, creating a simple link between the introduction and the conclusion, it's only meant to get you

(Inscribed Writing Space)
Introduction: Thesis statement with *because* connector between the claim and the reasons for that claim.   **Example:** It is reasonable to believe that global warming is the result of human activity <u>because</u> **(1) global warming seems to correspond with the greenhouse effect, (2) increased carbon emissions contribute to the greenhouse effect,** and **(3) carbon emissions have increased as a result of human activity.**
Subtopic 1:
Subtopic 2:
Subtopic 3:
Consideration of counter-argument:
Conclusion: Thesis statement proven.   **Example:** As the evidence has shown, it is reasonable to believe that global warming is the result of human activity <u>because</u> **(1) global warming seems to correspond with the greenhouse effect, (2) increased carbon emissions contribute to the greenhouse effect,** and **(3) carbon emissions have increased as a result of human activity.**

started. The IDDL model is not intended to reduce the writing process to a fill-in-the-blanks exercise and it does not excuse you from the obligation to make difficult decisions about the development of the argument. It does, however, permit you to inscribe the writing space with a general road map you can follow.

In other words, as promised, it allows you to begin writing without facing the dreaded blank page. Think about the thesis statement in the box above: *It is reasonable to believe that global warming is the result of human activity* <u>because</u> *(1) **global warming seems to correspond with the greenhouse effect, (2) increased carbon emissions contribute to the greenhouse effect,** and (3) **carbon emissions have increased as a result of human activity.*** Reflect on the way in which it identifies the individual elements of the essay.

The simple act of writing a thesis statement is, in fact, the act of creating structure for your essay. It provides you with the information you need to draft your outline. It also defines the relationship of the main ideas in your essay. You may find that, in your final draft, you want to express the thesis more artfully. Express it, perhaps, in a number of sentences rather than one or identify the relationship using phrases other than the *because* clause. At this point, however, the way in which the thesis statement is structured allows you to map a logical path through the essay.

3.3.1.1 Writing Exercise

Draft a thesis statement that includes an arguable proposition. Use that thesis statement to fill in the first and last box of the following chart.

Topic
Thesis Statement: ■ **Is it clear?** ■ **Is it focused?** ■ **Is it measurable?**
Subtopic 1: What is the relationship to the main thesis? What information is needed to explore or substantiate the claim of subtopic 1? ■ Evidence ■ Evidence ■ Evidence
Subtopic 2: What is the relationship to the main thesis? What information is needed to explore or substantiate the claim of subtopic 2? ■ Evidence ■ Evidence ■ Evidence ■ Evidence
Subtopic 3: What is the relationship to main thesis? What information is needed to explore or substantiate the claim of subtopic 3? ■ Relationship to Main Thesis ■ Evidence ■ Evidence ■ Evidence
Counter-argument: Why would a reasonable person disagree? ■ Evidence ■ Evidence
Conclusion:

Use the next chart while you're writing to evaluate the degree to which you've effectively mapped a path to follow. Often the hardest aspect of writing is getting started. Having a path defined before you begin writing allows you to recognize the individual steps you must follow. While the course of the essay may change slightly as you work through your ideas, the outline you've developed will provide you with a sense of direction.

Making Writing Decisions | About Inscribing the Writing Space

What is the purpose of this writing decision?

The naked page poses a number of challenges, requiring that you simultaneously manage the organizational structure and engage in the exploration of the essay's ideas. Inscribing the writing space allows you to concentrate, first, on the organizational structure, and, later, on the development of your ideas.

What is the effect of this writing decision?

By explicitly identifying the organizational structure your argument will follow, and by using the IDDL model to embed that structure in your outline, you are able to overcome the initial challenge of generating your ideas systematically. Later, as you move through the writing process, you will also find it easier to revise the essay.

What considerations inform this decision?

Though the writing process is dynamic, and usually characterized by a series of tentative steps forward and hopeful forays into promising tangents, your goal as a writer is to produce a finished essay that is essentially linear, with all individual themes serving to move the reader toward a conclusion.

Suggested strategies for making this decision.

The IDDL model allows you to use the logic of the arguable proposition—which is expressed, horizontally, in the thesis statement: *It is reasonable to believe that global warming is the result of human activity <u>because</u> (1) global warming seems to correspond with the greenhouse effect, (2) increased carbon emissions contribute to the greenhouse effect, and (3) carbon emissions have increased as a result of human activity*—to create a coherent outline, which is expressed vertically:

> *It is reasonable to believe that global warming is the result of human activity <u>because:</u>*
>
> *(1) global warming seems to correspond with the greenhouse effect,*
> *(2) increased carbon emissions contribute to the greenhouse effect, and*
> *(3) carbon emissions have increased as a result of human activity.*

Questions to guide decision making in your own essay.

1. Reflect on the topic you've chosen or been assigned. How can you refine that topic to a specific claim that's supported by specific reasons?
2. Is the claim arguable (i.e., can it be proven in one way or another)?
3. Is it manageable within the word limit you've been assigned?
4. Do the reasons support the claim you're making? Do they lead to a particular conclusion?
5. Does the order of the reasons make sense? Is there one reason that provides a foundation for the others? Have you structured your outline so that the foundational reason comes first?

3.3.2 Stage 2: Defining the Rhetorical Problems Locally

The second strategy of the IDDL model asks you to use the arguable proposition to define the rhetorical problems locally (i.e., the local rhetorical problems emerge in the essay as paragraphs, or a series of related paragraphs). The local rhetorical problems are the individual themes or claims that emerged in the arguable proposition of the thesis statement. The arguable proposition, which includes both the claim that the essay is exploring and the reasons for that claim, guides your writing process by specifically identifying the subtopics that need to be investigated and/or substantiated. By defining those problems, you're able to break the larger essay into component parts and work on each one individually. At this point, you don't need to think about other aspects of the essay. The individual subtopic becomes the focus of your attention.

In the following example, the individual subtopics have been inserted into the individual boxes in the IDDL model.

Introduction:

Thesis statement with *because* connector between the claim and the reasons for that claim.

> **Example:** It is reasonable to believe that global warming is the result of human activity **because (1) global warming seems to correspond with the greenhouse effect, (2) increased carbon emissions contribute to the greenhouse effect, and (3) carbon emissions have increased as a result of human activity.**

1. It is reasonable to believe that global warming is the result of human activity **because global warming seems to correspond with the greenhouse effect.**

2. It is reasonable to believe that global warming is the result of human activity **because increased carbon emissions contribute to the greenhouse effect.**

3. It is reasonable to believe that global warming is the result of human activity **because carbon emissions have increased as a result of human activity.**

Conclusion:

Thesis statement proven.

It is reasonable to believe that global warming is the result of human activity because **(a) global warming seems to correspond with the greenhouse effect, (b) increased carbon emissions contribute to the greenhouse effect, and (c) carbon emissions have increased as a result of human activity.**

In the wilderness of the blank page, it's easy to go astray. The IDDL model guards against undisciplined wandering by ensuring that the paragraphs, or series of paragraphs, in which the writer explores supporting themes or provides supporting evidence are logically connected to each other and to the controlling thesis. Because each of the individual themes of the essay were derived from the thesis statement, there is less danger that you will drift off course, chasing after intriguing ideas that have no relevance to the essay that is being written. There is a second advantage to this strategy. One of the differences between the writing challenges faced by novice and experienced writers (as discussed in Chapter 1) is the degree to which experienced writers are able to devote their working memory to the development of their respective arguments. Novice writers, in comparison, are obliged to concentrate on both maintaining the essay's overall structure and writing the content for each individual part of the essay.

By using the IDDL model, you're able to level the playing field. The model becomes a memory aid, off-loading questions of structure to the page, and allowing you to concentrate on the specific task of developing and refining meaning either in individual paragraphs or in a series of related paragraphs.

3.3.2.1 Writing Exercise

Use the individual reasons or themes that you identified in the arguable proposition of your thesis statement to populate the following body paragraph boxes.

Topic
Thesis Statement: ■ Is it clear? ■ Is it focused? ■ Is it measurable?
Subtopic 1: What is the relationship to the main thesis? What information is needed to explore or substantiate the claim of subtopic 1? ■ Evidence ■ Evidence ■ Evidence
Subtopic 2: What is the relationship to the main thesis? What information is needed to explore or substantiate the claim of subtopic 2? ■ Evidence ■ Evidence ■ Evidence ■ Evidence
Subtopic 3: What is the relationship to the main thesis? What information is needed to explore or substantiate the claim of subtopic 3? ■ Relationship to main thesis ■ Evidence ■ Evidence ■ Evidence
Counter-argument: Why would a reasonable person disagree? ■ Evidence ■ Evidence
Conclusion:

Using the next chart, reflect on the degree to which you have effectively defined your rhetorical problems locally.

Making Writing Decisions | About Defining Rhetorical Problems Locally

What is the purpose of this writing decision?

The purpose of this writing decision is to isolate the individual themes, or subtopics, of the essay, relying upon the IDDL model to ensure that you maintain a logical connection to the controlling thesis of the essay.

What is the effect of this writing decision?

By using the IDDL model to maintain a connection between the various themes of the essay and the larger essay structure, you are able to concentrate on one specific aspect of the essay at a time.

What considerations inform this decision?

In order to use the IDDL model effectively, you must ensure that your thesis statement clearly reflects the relationship between the claim you're making and the evidence you're offering in support of that claim. The model does not, independently, create or generate coherence. It can't do that. The model reflects the logical relationship between themes that you have articulated in your thesis statement.

Suggested strategies for making this decision.

This process is embedded in the IDDL. If you're using the model, you're already using a strategy. If you don't use the model, you can use a similar strategy: identify the individual points you need to explore during the planning stage by critically examining your thesis statement and use each of these points to create an outline. Your outline must derive from your thesis. Writing from an outline that was generated by brainstorming often results in an essay that explores a number of ideas that, however interesting, have no relationship to your specific writing purpose.

Questions to guide decision making in your own essay.

1. Looking at the essay you're currently writing, ask yourself whether you have articulated a clear thesis statement. Have you identified the controlling thesis of the essay?
2. Have you identified the individual points, or subtopics, that you will discuss in the course of your exploration of the controlling thesis?
3. Reflect on each of the individual points or subtopics. In what way is each related to the controlling thesis? In what way does each contribute to your exploration of the thesis?
4. Has each subtopic been articulated clearly enough that you are able to identify the information you need to either substantiate the claim or explore the subtopic thoroughly?

3.3.3 Stage 3: Discovering the Information Necessary to Resolve the Local Rhetorical Problems

This is where the practice of careful planning pays its dividend. Because you've already defined the rhetorical problems of your essay locally, you are able to focus your attention on those problems. The decisions you make at this stage of the writing process concern a search for the kinds of evidence or background information that you need to explore or substantiate your subtopic. You need to do some research. While you might imagine that you can measure the effectiveness of your research process by the volume of information you find, that, sadly, this is not always the case. You are looking for *relevant* information, and the more information you're able to find on your topic the better your paper will be. The advantage of using a model like the IDDL model is that it allows you to assess the value of the information you find relative to the needs you identified in the second stage of the process. (Refer to Chapter 4 for a more thorough discussion of strategies for conducting research using the IDDL model.)

In the example below, we have suggested some questions to guide you in your search for, and development of, the information that will be used to write the individual paragraphs. You should notice that, though the questions are general, your answers will be specific to the subtopic.

Introduction:
Thesis statement with a *because* connector between the claim and the reasons for that claim.

> **Example:** It is reasonable to believe that global warming is the result of human activity <u>because</u> global warming seems to correspond with the greenhouse effect, increased carbon emissions contribute to the greenhouse effect, and carbon emissions have increased as a result of human activity.

(continued)

(*continued*)

It is reasonable to believe that global warming is the result of human activity <u>because</u> global warming seems to correspond with the greenhouse effect.

What needs to be proven?
What evidence is required?
Are there exceptions or limits to the claim?

It is reasonable to believe that global warming is the result of human activity <u>because</u> increased carbon emissions contribute to the greenhouse effect.

What needs to be proven?
What evidence is required?
Are there exceptions or limits to the claim?

It is reasonable to believe that global warming is the result of human activity <u>because</u> carbon emissions have increased as a result of human activity.

What needs to be proven?
What evidence is required?
Are there exceptions or limits to the claim?

Conclusion:
Thesis statement proven.

It is reasonable to believe that global warming is the result of human activity <u>because</u> **(a) global warming seems to correspond with the greenhouse effect, (b) increased carbon emissions contribute to the greenhouse effect, and (c) carbon emissions have increased as a result of human activity.**

In the examples above, we used the IDDL model to organize the major themes of an essay. We also looked at some of the questions you need to consider when looking for the information you need to explore those themes fully. At this point, it's probably useful to remind you that the IDDL model is different in a number of important ways from the five-paragraph essay that many students used in high school. One of the criticisms of the five-paragraph essay is that it sometimes leads students to plug information into a template and assume that they have satisfied their obligations. You can't do that. Facts and quotations don't testify on their own; they require your deft touch to shape them to their intended purpose. As a writer, you need to remember that the individual bits and pieces of information you employ when writing are very much like the ingredients you use when baking. Unless they're brought in at the appropriate time, and introduced in the appropriate measure and manner, well, unfortunately, you end up with a well-intentioned but largely inedible cake.

3.3.3.1 Writing Exercise

Using the individual subtopics you identified in Stage 2, conduct a focused search for the information you need to thoroughly explore the theme or substantiate the claim you made in each individual subtopic. You must be sure to include bibliographic data for each piece of reference material you use. The use of the IDDL model is not preparation for the process of writing your essay. It *is* the process of writing your essay. Each of the paragraph boxes will become the paragraphs, or series of related paragraphs, in your essay, and each of the paragraphs will derive, to some extent, from your critical examination of the resource material you've included in this stage. It would be a shame to have to give it up because you forgot to include a citation.

You'll also notice that the model includes a box for recording any counter-arguments that need to be addressed. As you write, you might want to maintain a record of the counter-arguments as they occur to you. If those counter-arguments come from external sources, you need to make a record of the source for your citations. Remember that the counter-argument is a thoughtful and carefully reasoned discussion of opposing views. It strengthens your argument and enhances your credibility with the reader. (See Chapter 2 for a more thorough examination of counter-argument.)

Thesis Statement:
Paragraph 1:
Subtopic:
Relationship to Main Thesis
- Evidence with citation
- Evidence with citation
- Evidence with citation
- Evidence with citation

Paragraph 2:
Subtopic:
Relationship to Main Thesis
- Evidence with citation
- Evidence with citation
- Evidence with citation
- Evidence with citation

Paragraph 3:
Subtopic:
Relationship to Main Thesis
- Evidence with citation
- Evidence with citation
- Evidence with citation

Counter-argument:
Why would anyone disagree?
- Evidence with citation
- Evidence with citation

Conclusion:

It's important to remember that your goal is not to find just any evidence. You must find relevant evidence. Use the following chart to evaluate the degree to which you successfully explored the themes or substantiated the claims identified in the individual paragraphs above.

| Making Writing Decisions | About Discovering the Information Needed to Solve Local Rhetorical Problems |

What is the purpose of this writing decision?

The development of content for an essay ought to be driven by purpose. It is difficult, however, to concentrate on a number of different themes simultaneously and do any one of them justice. This strategy is intended to help you manage the various threads of thought that constitute your essay.

What is the effect of this writing decision?

Research that is guided by reference to the specific subtopics of an essay tends to be more efficient (i.e., your searches are better focused) and more fruitful (i.e., if you're researching a particular subtopic, you're more likely to discover information that addresses that subtopic directly).

What considerations inform this decision?

It's much easier for you to undertake research of any kind when your search is guided by a clearly defined thesis or subtopic. It's not enough, however, to content yourself with articles or reference materials that speak to the general thesis but don't address the specific points you are making in your essay. If you're arguing a particular position on the basis of a number of subtopics, you ought to explore each of those subtopics individually.

Suggested strategies for making this decision.

As was the case in our discussion of Stage 2 of the IDDL model, the use of the model is the suggested strategy for making this decision. However, if you choose not to use the model you are able to use a similar process: isolate each of the individual subtopics of your thesis and undertake a search for the information necessary either to demonstrate the validity of the subtopic or to investigate it thoroughly.

Questions to guide decision making in your own essay.

1. Reflect on the essay you're currently writing and isolate each of the principal themes or subtopics. Have you articulated each one specifically enough that you are able to state, clearly, what it is you mean to say?
2. Select the first of the subtopics and ask yourself how you can substantiate, or thoroughly explore, that theme. What question lies at its heart? It's much easier both to research and to write in response to a question.
3. How can you most effectively justify the claim you're making? Do you require evidence from science or social science? Do you require scholarly opinion?
4. Does your investigation of the subtopic demand that you recognize some limits to the claim you're making? What are those limits? Academic writing embraces, rather than retreats from, nuanced discussions of complex ideas. That kind of subtlety requires that you acknowledge the counter-argument (i.e., the opposing view) of your position. How can you integrate opposing ideas without appearing to argue against yourself?

3.3.4 Stage 4: Linking the Individual Units of the Essay Logically

In the fourth stage of the IDDL model, you return again to the thesis of the essay to ensure that, in the wild enthusiasm of the writing process, you haven't strayed from your intended organizational pattern. As you may recall from Chapter 1, there is an interactive relationship between the *process* of writing (which is active and inclined to circle back on itself) and the *product* of writing (which is static and linear). The vitality of the process allows you to explore possibilities while you're writing. That's good. It keeps you from surrendering to stale formulae that limit your ability to innovate. On the other hand, the logic and linearity of the written product have their charms too. They permit your reader to recognize the connections between the guiding thesis of the essay and the individual ideas that support the thesis.

At this stage in the process, you will critically review the essay you're writing, reflecting on the organizational pattern. It is important to remember that, though the model is designed, in part, to allow you to work on each of the supporting themes independently, they are meant to serve a larger purpose. They're meant to work together to reflect a logical train of thought. You now have to coax the various themes into line, linking them to ensure that your reader is led from the thesis, through the individual sections of the essay, to the conclusion. Though the model seems to suggest that revision only happens at the end of the writing process, the monitoring of the text for coherence should occur on an ongoing basis (see Chapter 13 for more on revision).

Example   Earlier in the chapter, we looked at the way in which the thesis could be used to develop a structural outline for your essay. In the boxed example that now follows, we've returned to that sample thesis statement again to demonstrate the way in which the IDDL model allows you to recognize the connections you must make to ensure your essay will proceed coherently. The bulleted sentences in the following example suggest some of the questions you might ask yourself as you monitor the organizational structure of your own essay and work to link the units logically.

Introduction:
Thesis statement with a *because* connector between the claim and the reasons for that claim.

> **Example:** It is reasonable to believe that global warming is the result of human activity <u>because</u> global warming seems to correspond with the greenhouse effect, increased carbon emissions contribute to the greenhouse effect, and carbon emissions have increased as a result of human activity.

Subtopic 1:
> It is reasonable to believe that global warming is the result of human activity <u>because</u> global warming seems to correspond with the greenhouse effect.
> - What is the relationship of this paragraph, or series of related paragraphs, to the introduction?
> - Does the pattern of organization reflect that relationship?

Subtopic 2:
> It is reasonable to believe that global warming is the result of human activity <u>because</u> increased carbon emissions contribute to the greenhouse effect.
> - What is the relationship of this paragraph, or series of related paragraphs, to the introduction?
> - Does the pattern of organization reflect that relationship?

(continued)

(*continued*)

Subtopic 3:
It is reasonable to believe that global warming is the result of human activity <u>because</u> carbon emissions have increased as a result of human activity.
■ What is the relationship of this paragraph, or series of related paragraphs, to the introduction?
■ Does the pattern of organization reflect that relationship?

Conclusion:
Thesis statement proven.
It is reasonable to believe that global warming is the result of human activity <u>because</u> (a) global warming seems to correspond with the greenhouse effect, (b) increased carbon emissions contribute to the greenhouse effect, and (c) carbon emissions have increased as a result of human activity.

If everything has gone according to plan, you will have inscribed the writing space, using your thesis statement to represent, provisionally, the point of departure (the introduction), the major subthemes (the individual subtopics), and the intended destination for your essay (the conclusion). You will have used the themes you identified in your thesis statement to identify the individual units that will comprise your essay, thereby ensuring that each of the body paragraphs is relevant to the thesis, and you will have used specific themes to provide each of the individual units with its unifying purpose. You will also have organized the individual subtopics in the same order in which they appeared in the thesis statement, following the pattern you established previously. Stage 4 of the IDDL model encourages you to return to the thesis statement again, using it as a benchmark against which to judge the degree to which the emerging essay continues to reflect a logical progression.

3.3.4.1 Writing Exercise

Take a thesis statement you've developed yourself and develop a short essay draft using the IDDL model. On this one occasion only, feel free to invent your own evidence. The purpose of the exercise is not to draft an essay for submission, but to practise monitoring your writing to ensure that there's a clear path from the introduction to the conclusion, that each paragraph has a clear relationship to the controlling thesis, and that the individual paragraphs, or series of related paragraphs, are logically connected to one another.

Thesis Statement
Subtopic 1:
What is the relationship to the main thesis?
■ Evidence with citation
■ Evidence with citation
■ Evidence with citation
■ Evidence with citation

Subtopic 2: What is the relationship to the main thesis? ■ Evidence with citation ■ Evidence with citation ■ Evidence with citation ■ Evidence with citation
Subtopic 3: What is the relationship to the main thesis? ■ Evidence with citation ■ Evidence with citation ■ Evidence with citation
Counter-argument: Why would anyone disagree? ■ Evidence with citation ■ Evidence with citation
Conclusion:

Use the next chart to guide you as you evaluate the coherence of the essay draft you prepared in the writing exercise.

Making Writing Decisions | About Linking the Individual Units of the Essay Logically

What is the purpose of this writing decision?

In Stage 4 of the IDDL model, you're monitoring the emerging essay to ensure that there are logical connections between (a) the thesis and the body paragraphs, and (b) the individual paragraphs themselves.

What is the effect of this writing decision?

By foregrounding both the relationship of the paragraphs to the controlling thesis and the relationship of the paragraphs to one another, you're able to determine whether the individual components of your essay are connected together logically.

What considerations inform this decision?

The argument of your thesis statement ought to be reflected in the logic of the essay. If the thesis statement clearly articulates the nature and the scope of the essay you are writing, it will provide a benchmark against which to measure the coherence of the emerging essay.

Suggested strategies for making this decision.

By using the IDDL model to organize a draft for your essay, you'll find that the structure of the essay will correspond with the structure of the thesis statement.

Questions to guide decision making in your own essay.

1. Look at the thesis statement you've drafted for the essay you're writing. Does it include an arguable proposition? Does the arguable proposition clearly identify the claim being made and the reasons for that claim?
2. Are you able to identify the pattern of reasoning that derives from the arguable thesis? Does your essay correspond to that pattern?

3. Are the paragraphs, or series of related paragraphs, arranged logically? Are you leading your reader from one point to another in a way that's consistent with the argument you're making?
4. Have you indicated the relationship of one paragraph to another using transitions? (See Chapter 9 for more information on transitions.)

3.4   CONCLUSION

In this chapter, we discussed the ways in which the IDDL decision-making writing model might be used to organize and write an essay draft that reflects a focus on the development of ideas and the maintenance of coherence. Unlike the models to which you may have been introduced in high school or other educational settings, this model is designed to guide you through the composition process with a series of questions that require you to actively engage with the emerging text, making decisions on the basis of your understanding of the effect those decisions might have. The types of decisions you make as you write will determine the nature of the essay you produce. The IDDL model doesn't guarantee that you will produce an essay that is governed by logic and is seamlessly coherent. It can't do that. Your writing purpose is not embedded in this or any other writing model. Unfortunately, you will always have to struggle with a difficult planning process to find a way of exploring your topic in a way that's both intriguing and comprehensible. What the model does is provide you with a mechanism that you can use to work through the challenges of exploring your topic systematically. It allows you to construct a pattern of organization that derives from your thesis statement and to draft an essay that corresponds to that pattern. It also allows you to break the process of writing into manageable sections, attending to the various writing decisions you need to make one at a time and reflecting on the effect of those decisions. In short, the model allows you to write the way experienced writers write: intentionally and purposefully.

MyCompLab®

How Do I Get a Better Grade?

Go to MyCompLab for additional help with your grammar, writing, and research skills. You will have access to a variety of exercises, instruction, and videos that will help you improve your basic skills and help you get a better grade.

Thesis Statement Peer-Review Worksheet

 Practice

Writer's Name: _____

Reviewer's Name: _____

What is the thesis statement?

_____

_____

1. In two or three sentences, identify the argument being suggested in the thesis statement. What is the claim that is being made? What is the basis of that claim?

2. In two or three sentences, explain how the scope of the argument has been limited to a specific and manageable claim.

3. Reflect upon the thesis statement. What evidence might be needed to provide support for its argument?

Essay Outline Peer-Review Worksheet

 Practice

Essay Written By: _____

Peer Reviewer: _____

Topic

What is the thesis statement:

- Is it clear?
- Is it focused?
- Is it measurable?

Paragraph 1:

What is the subtopic (i.e., the theme of this paragraph, or series of related paragraphs)?
How is the subtopic related to the thesis?
What is the key argument of paragraph 1?
What evidence is needed to support the subtopic?
What evidence does the writer offer?
How does the evidence support the argument?

(*continued*)

(*continued*)

Paragraph 2:

What is the subtopic (i.e., the theme of this paragraph, or series of related paragraphs)?
How is the subtopic related to the thesis?
What is the key argument of paragraph 2?
What evidence is needed to support the subtopic?
What evidence does the writer offer?
How does the evidence support the argument?

Paragraph 3:

What is the subtopic (i.e., the theme of this paragraph, or series of related paragraphs)?
How is the subtopic related to the thesis?
What is the key argument of paragraph 3?
What evidence is needed to support the subtopic?
What evidence does the writer offer?
How does the evidence support the argument?

Counter-argument:

Why would a reasonable person disagree with the argument?
How has the writer identified and explored the counter-argument to the argument?

Conclusion:

Does the conclusion follow logically from the argument? Has the thesis statement been proven?

✓•⊣Practice   **Practice Example: Stage 1**

1. Use your word processor to create a table like the one below.
2. Develop a thesis statement that includes an arguable proposition.
3. Insert your thesis statement in the first box. Use the example as a guide.
4. Use your thesis statement to identify the individual claims that need to be substantiated or explored (there are examples in boxes titled "Section 1," "Section 2," and "Section 3").

Thesis Statement:

■ Is it clear?
■ Is it focused?
■ Is it measurable?

Metacognition allows students to learn more effectively because it identifies goals and procedures for meeting those goals, it encourages students to reflect on their progress and adjust as necessary, and it encourages students to learn from previous performance in similar tasks.

Section 1:

Subtopic:

Metacognition allows students to learn more effectively because it identifies goals and procedures for meeting those goals.

What needs to be proven?
- Evidence
- Evidence
- Evidence
- Evidence

Section 2:

Subtopic:

> *Metacognition allows students to learn more effectively because it encourages students to reflect on their progress and adjust as necessary.*

What needs to be proven?
- Evidence
- Evidence
- Evidence
- Evidence

Section 3:

Subtopic:

> *Metacognition allows students to learn more effectively because it encourages students to learn from previous performance in similar tasks.*

What needs to proven?
- Evidence
- Evidence
- Evidence

Counter-argument:

Why would anyone disagree?
- Evidence
- Evidence

Conclusion:

Practice Example: Stage 2

1. Using the example questions below as a guide, devise your own questions to guide your research process.
2. You will use those questions to guide your research process in the next stage.

(continued)

(*continued*)

Thesis Statement:

- Is it clear?
- Is it focused?
- Is it measurable?

Metacognition allows students to learn more effectively because it identifies goals and procedures for meeting those goals, it encourages students to reflect on their progress and adjust as necessary, and it encourages students to learn from previous performance in similar tasks.

Section 1:

Subtopic:

How can you prove that "Metacognition allows students to learn more effectively because it identifies goals and procedures for meeting those goals"?

- Evidence
- Evidence
- Evidence
- Evidence

Section 2:

Subtopic:

How can you prove that "Metacognition allows students to learn more effectively because it encourages students to reflect on their progress and adjust as necessary"?

- Evidence
- Evidence
- Evidence
- Evidence

Section 3:

Subtopic:

How can you prove that "Metacognition allows students to learn more effectively because it encourages students to learn from previous performance in similar tasks"?

- Evidence
- Evidence
- Evidence

Counter-argument:

Why would anyone disagree?

- Evidence
- Evidence

Conclusion:

Practice Example: Stage 3

1. Using the questions you developed in Stage 2, begin your research process, guided by the specific questions you need answered.

2. As you're reading the sources you discover, keep notes on the relevant information you find. Record that information as quotations, paraphrases, or summaries. Take care to attach the name of the author of each piece of source material, the year of publication, and the page number.

3. Using the material you discover, insert relevant quotations, paraphrases, and summaries, including the bibliographic information (i.e., name of author, year of publication, page number) in the evidence boxes of the claims to which they refer.

4. You should note that, in many cases, a single reference document may be relevant to a number of the claims you've made.

5. In the "Counter-argument" section, include any information that limits the scope of your claim.

Thesis Statement:

■ Is it clear?

■ Is it focused?

■ Is it measurable?

Metacognition allows students to learn more effectively because it identifies goals and procedures for meeting those goals, it encourages students to reflect on their progress and adjust as necessary, and it encourages students to learn from previous performance in similar tasks.

Section 1:

Subtopic:

Metacognition allows students to learn more effectively because it identifies goals and procedures for meeting those goals.

■ Evidence

■ Evidence

■ Evidence

■ Evidence

Section 2:

Subtopic:

Metacognition allows students to learn more effectively because it encourages students to reflect on their progress and adjust as necessary.

What needs to be proven?

■ Evidence

■ Evidence

■ Evidence

■ Evidence

(continued)

(*continued*)

Section 3:

Subtopic:

> *Metacognition allows students to learn more effectively because it encourages students to learn from previous performance in similar tasks.*

- Evidence
- Evidence
- Evidence

Counter-argument:

Why would anyone disagree?
- Evidence
- Evidence

Conclusion:

✓• Practice   **Practice Example: Stage 4**

1. In the section of the model titled "Section 1," organize the source material you've gathered to support the specific subtopic. At this stage, you should note that Section1 is, in fact, a series of related paragraphs, linked by a common theme.
2. Interpret the information, explaining its relevance to your thesis.
3. In each paragraph, organize the material to support the paragraph's unifying theme (i.e., ensure that the material is organized around one controlling idea).
4. Using the thesis statement to guide you, ensure the paragraphs have been linked together in such a way as to create a logical path through the essay for the reader.

Thesis Statement:

- Is it clear?
- Is it focused?
- Is it measurable?

> *Metacognition allows students to learn more effectively because it identifies goals and procedures for meeting those goals, it encourages students to reflect on their progress and adjust as necessary, and it encourages students to learn from previous performance in similar tasks.*

Section 1:

Subtopic:

> *Metacognition allows students to learn more effectively because it identifies goals and procedures for meeting those goals.*

- Evidence
- Evidence

- Evidence
- Evidence

What Is the Relationship to the Main Thesis?

Section 2:

Subtopic:

> *Metacognition allows students to learn more effectively because it encourages students to reflect on their progress and adjust as necessary.*

What needs to be proven?

- Evidence
- Evidence
- Evidence
- Evidence

What Is the Relationship to the Main Thesis?

Section 3:

Subtopic:

> *Metacognition allows students to learn more effectively because it encourages students to learn from previous performance in similar tasks.*

- Evidence
- Evidence
- Evidence

What Is the Relationship to the Main Thesis?

Counter-argument:

> *Why would anyone disagree?*

- Evidence
- Evidence

Conclusion:

CHAPTER 4

Research

Learning Objectives

At the completion of this chapter, you will be able to:

1. Identify the differences in the ways that novice and experienced writers conduct research.
2. Describe the process of research.
3. Justify the practice of isolating research questions using the IDDL model.
4. Demonstrate the ability to use the IDDL model to organize your own essay.

4.1 INTRODUCTION

Do you know whether organic farming produces safer foods than large-scale farming operations do? Neither did we. We looked it up. Though we may have believed one thing or another with regard to the subject, we had no real evidence to support those beliefs. We turned to those who have the expertise to answer the question. That's research. Research provides the information you need to explore the thesis that lies at the heart of your essay. However gifted a writer you may be, however skilfully you may weave a sentence together, you can't write about nothing. You need access to content. This is true of writing in general. In the case of academic essays, however, it is particularly true. When you're writing an academic essay, you're expected to know what you're talking about.

Good research provides you with a number of other advantages as well:

1. It gives you access to the information that you need to develop a broader understanding of your topic. It also allows you to examine an issue from

multiple perspectives, which is important in both critical thinking and academic writing.

2. It lends credibility to your essay. It allows you to speak with the authority of your careful reasoning and the authority of the experts you discover in the course of the research process.

3. It also allows you to suggest relevant resources to your reader. That is, in addition to your own analysis of the topic you're exploring, you provide a list of the resources that guided your thinking. Those references permit the reader to investigate your topic independently.

In this chapter, we explore the process of research, identifying some of the general principles of the process along the way and suggesting some strategies that you might use to make your own practice more efficient.

4.2 DIFFERENCES BETWEEN THE WAY IN WHICH NOVICE WRITERS AND EXPERIENCED WRITERS CONDUCT RESEARCH   LO I

Experienced writers were not born with an innate understanding of effective ways to gather information. Over time, they learned to develop precise and specific thesis statements, to look for information in the sort of places information hides, and to evaluate the relative authority and reliability of individual sources of information. The most significant advantage that experienced writers enjoy, however, derives from the practice of researching intentionally. Because they've taken the time to plan their writing projects carefully, they have a much clearer understanding of the information they need to find. In the following chart, you'll notice that the most relevant difference between novice and experienced writers at this point in the writing process concerns the degree to which experienced writers have invested time in planning before beginning to write.

Novice Writers	Experienced Writers
■ Require thought for procedural, or "mechanical," writing functions.	■ Have, to a certain degree, automated procedural functions.
■ Focus on error avoidance rather than meaning.	■ Focus on developing or refining meaning.
■ *Begin writing without planning*, and edit, if at all, for grammatical errors.	■ *Invest time and energy in planning and reviewing.*
■ Focus on "knowledge telling" (i.e., relating all the information they have and can find on a topic, rather than exercising critical judgment to determine relevance).	■ Organize, and reorganize, essay structure to allow individual ideas to serve the overall purpose of the essay.

Unlike the experienced writer, novice writers frequently fail to take the time necessary to develop a focused arguable proposition before dashing off madly to gather as much information as possible on a general, and often ill-defined, topic. This haphazard process works about as well as you would expect it to do. It results in large piles of documents that serve no real purpose but to artificially flesh out a bibliography. In addition, because novice writers sometimes begin to write their essays the night before the due date, they're pretty much stuck using whatever information is available. Under the circumstances, relevance may not be a consideration.

LO 2 ## 4.3   RESEARCHING INTENTIONALLY

You may have been taught that the best way to both generate and identify ideas in the research process is to brainstorm. That doesn't seem to be as effective a strategy as you might think. Imagine, for a moment, that you're writing an essay on the effect of human development and urbanization on elephant populations in Africa. In order to generate ideas, you brainstorm. If you brainstorm using only the word *elephant* to generate ideas, you might end up with intriguing but irrelevant branches for your research. For instance, you might think of differences between African and Asian elephants, the gestation period of elephants, diet, mating practices, and Walt Disney's representations of elephants (in particular, Dumbo, who is extraordinarily cute, despite his big ears). You ought to recognize that some of the branches of the brainstorming session will prove unfruitful. Even if you were to add in the other key idea—the effect of human development—you would find that you were generating large numbers of ideas for which you have no use. The IDDL model for invention and decision making, to which you were introduced in Chapter 1, encourages you to be far more intentional in your research process by identifying the specific information you need to solve your research problems locally. That is, by identifying the specific aspects of the argument that require support, you are able to begin the research process with a much clearer sense of the evidence you need to find.

LO 1, 2 ## 4.4   THINGS TO KEEP IN MIND WHEN CONDUCTING RESEARCH

The process of research doesn't have to hurt. In fact, if it's undertaken purposefully and systematically, it is, for some, the most enjoyable part of the process of writing an academic essay. The "systematic" part is important, however. Writers at all stages of their academic careers, from undergraduates to Ph.D. candidates, occasionally lose themselves in the process of research, choosing to gather twenty or thirty more books and articles rather than begin the process of writing. It's a tantalizing trap. Others hunt endlessly for pertinent information because they fail to focus their search at the outset. To research efficiently, you need to know what you're looking for and when you have found it. The following suggestions can help you to research more strategically.

1. Work with a clear sense of purpose. By reflecting on your purpose before you begin, you're able to sift through information more quickly. This is not meant to suggest that you should be so single-minded in the search that you ignore articles that offer a competing perspective on the topic you're investigating. It does mean, however, that you will be able to skip past books or articles that are clearly irrelevant. Remember that one of the differences between novice and experienced writers in their respective processes of research is that the novice writer often fails to plan adequately beforehand. The time novice writers save at the outset is usually lost many times over as they dig blindly through reams of documents they won't use. It's a bad bargain.

2. Take your time. Again, think of the novice writer's approach to research. By working slowly through lists of articles or books, you're more likely to find the information you need. Remember also that search engines suggest results on the basis of the keywords you have entered. It's always possible that the article you want is on the fifth page of the 1,987,011 hits. It didn't register first because the search engine didn't recognize its relevance on the basis of the search terms you used. That does not mean that you should work through all 1,987,011 hits; below, in point 4, we'll suggest a strategy for determining when your search can be safely concluded.

3. What information do you really need? Once you've identified the type of evidence you need (the IDDL decision-making process, which will be discussed next, may help you make those kinds of decisions), it's much easier to search out information that is appropriate to your argument. Remember that the purpose of research is to find answers to the questions that need to be answered. In short, you should not look at the process of research as being simply an instructor's requirement. It is meant to serve the needs of your specific essay.

4. How much information do you need? In some ways, this is a difficult question to answer. There are no specific guidelines as to the number of articles that are needed. Instead, we'll offer this principle: when, in the course of your research process, you discover that you are no longer finding new ideas (either in favour of or in opposition to your thesis), you're probably done.

5. Types of references. There are two basic kinds of sources that you might use: (a) primary, and (b) secondary.

Primary Sources	Secondary Sources
These represent the original authors' understanding of the events as they occurred. Primary sources may include those written by individuals who experienced an event or those written by an individual who conducted research and prepared a discussion of the research and conclusions drawn from it.	These reflect authors' interpretations of other individuals' original material. The sources may have been included in a research article where they were used to lend support to the author's own argument. Secondary sources are usually an interpretation or analysis of events that another individual experienced and/or recorded. Secondary sources are usually one or more steps removed from the original document.

(*continued*)

(*continued*)

Primary sources include original documents like diaries, speeches, manuscripts, letters, interviews, autobiographies, and official documents.	Secondary sources include textbooks, magazine articles, histories, encyclopedias, and commentaries.
Primary sources are sometimes subjective and may reflect a personal bias. It is important that you read critically and reflect on the authority of the author(s).	When using a secondary source, you are relying on the second author's judgment and interpretation of information.

Making Writing Decisions   About Your Own Research

What is the purpose of this writing decision?

The purpose of this writing decision is to make your research process more effective and more efficient.

What is the effect of this writing decision?

Effective research is informed with a clear sense of purpose. By explicitly identifying the kinds of evidence you need, you're more likely to find that your research process will result in relevant information.

What considerations inform this decision?

Searches of any kind are better executed when you have a clear sense of what you're seeking and a general sense of where you might find it. In academic research, you will generally find that you have greater success with less time and effort if you identify the information for which you are looking before you begin. That initial idea may be only provisional (i.e., it may change as you read through the articles you find), but it is better to alter the nature of the search as needed than to begin a search with no real sense of the thing you're looking for.

Suggested strategies for making this decision.

By isolating the arguable claim of your thesis and the individual themes or subtheses of that claim, you're better able to undertake a search that is specific to the needs of your essay. The IDDL model helps you to make decisions that effective research requires by asking you to think about the specific purpose of reference material at each stage in the writing process.

Questions to guide decision making in your own essay.

1. Turn to the essay you're working on now and look at your own arguable proposition. What is the claim being made in the arguable proposition? What evidence is needed to substantiate that claim?

2. Are there subtheses with their own claims? How can you clearly identify the individual claims? Are each of the individual claims provable (i.e., is each claim the kind of claim for which you might find supporting evidence)?

3. Look at the first claim. What evidence is necessary to support that claim? What is the best source for that evidence?

4. Look at the second claim. What evidence is necessary to support that claim? What is the best source for that evidence?

5. Look at the third claim. What evidence is necessary to support that claim? What is the best source for that evidence?

6. Look at each subsequent claim and ask yourself the same questions. What evidence is necessary to support the claim? What is the best source for that evidence?

Practice Exercise

Read the following thesis statement and determine the kinds of evidence that you will need to support each of the subtheses.

✓•─Practice

Example:

Organic farming is preferable to industrial farming because *it uses no harmful pesticides, it employs an effective process of crop rotation,* and *it does not use growth hormones to enhance the development of livestock.*

The first step in the process is to identify the three subtheses of the argument. You may remember that we talked about this in Chapter 2. We'll do the first one for you.

Subthesis 1:

Organic farming is preferable to industrial farming because it uses no harmful pesticides.

What evidence do you need to establish that this claim is reasonable?
1. You need evidence that organic farm operations do not usually use pesticides and that factory farm operations do.
2. You need to find evidence that the pest control agents used by organic farmers are a better alternative than pesticides.
3. You need to find evidence that the use of pesticides is harmful to crops, the environment, or the consumer.

Follow the same process for the second and third subtheses. At the end of the exercise, we provide a key to possible answers.

Subthesis 2:

_____

_____

What evidence do you need to establish that this claim is reasonable?

_____

_____

Subthesis 3:

_____

_____

What evidence do you need to establish that this claim is reasonable?

_____

_____

Answer Key

Example:

Thesis:

Organic farming is preferable to industrial farming because *it uses no harmful pesticides, it employs an effective process of crop rotation,* and *it does not use growth hormones to enhance the development of livestock.*

Subthesis 2:

Organic farming is preferable to industrial farming because it employs an effective process of crop rotation.

What evidence do you need to establish that this claim is reasonable?

1. You need evidence that organic farmers practise crop rotation and factory farmers do not.
2. You need evidence that crop rotation is a useful and sustainable practice for farmers.
3. You need evidence of the advantages of crop rotation over the use of artificial applied soil nutrients.

Subthesis 3:

Organic farming is preferable to industrial farming because it does not use growth hormones to enhance the development of livestock.

What evidence do you need to establish that this claim is reasonable?

1. You need evidence that speaks to the practice of factory farmers feeding their animals growth hormones to stimulate unnatural growth.
2. You need evidence that speaks to the natural process of effecting growth that is used by organic farmers.
3. You need evidence that speaks to the benefits of using a more natural approach to raising livestock.
4. You may also want to find evidence that testifies to the harmful effects of using growth hormones on animals and the possible danger for consumers.

In the example, you may have noticed that your search for information was governed by a specific need in the essay. In the following discussion of the IDDL model as a guide to research, we will walk through an example of how you can use the model to identify the kinds of information you will need.

4.4.1 Using the IDDL Model to Guide Research

You will remember that we were encouraging you to use the IDDL model because of the degree to which it allows you to become far more practical in your essay writing. Instead of trying to invent your way from the beginning of an essay to the end, the IDDL model allows you to develop your essay by posing specific questions and answering them. Your content is generated by your response to the questions that need to be answered in order to support the argument you're making. Your first step was to identify an arguable proposition in which your claim was linked causally to the reasons for that claim. In the case of our elephant example above, your arguable proposition might be: *Human development is having an adverse effect on the African elephant population because elephant populations are inherently fragile due to their long gestation period, human development proceeds more quickly than elephants can adapt, and human development deprives elephant herds of the large expanse of area needed to sustain the herds.* The arguable proposition allows you to inscribe your writing space. The next boxed example demonstrates this.

I. Inscribe the writing space:

The first step in the IDDL model allows you to frame your essay using the ideas that you identified in the arguable proposition. Because the arguable proposition identifies both your claim and the basis for your claim, it also identifies the end point for your essay (i.e., the conclusion) and the individual steps that will lead to that conclusion. It allows you to:

   a. Inscribe, or invent, your writing space.
   b. Define the essay's purpose holistically.
   c. Identify the steps necessary to get from the beginning of the essay to the end.

In the example below, there is a thesis statement that includes an arguable proposition. You will notice that we've used the arguable proposition to identify both the beginning of the essay and the conclusion.

> *Inscribing or defining the writing space is the act of creating an explicit plan for moving from the beginning of an essay to the end. In order to be effective, this should include an understanding of the individual steps that you will follow.*

Introduction:

What is the arguable proposition?

| **Example:** *Human development is having an adverse effect on the African elephant population because (a) elephant populations are inherently fragile due to their long gestation period, (b) human development proceeds more quickly than elephants can adapt, and (c) human development deprives elephant herds of the large expanse of area needed to sustain the herds.*

What is the claim?
- *Human development is having an adverse effect on the African elephant population*

What is the causal connector?
- *because*

What are the reasons in support of the claim?
- *elephant populations are inherently fragile due to their long gestation period*
- *human development proceeds more quickly than elephants can adapt*
- *human development deprives elephant herds of the large expanse of area needed to sustain the herds*

Conclusion:

What must be proved?

You must prove that *Human development is having an adverse effect on the African elephant population because:*
- *elephant populations are inherently fragile due to their long gestation period*
- *human development proceeds more quickly than elephants can adapt*
- *human development deprives elephant herds of the large expanse of area needed to sustain the herds*

In the second stage of the IDDL model, you will see how to use the information implicit in the arguable proposition to break the essay down into a series of local problems with local solutions. As we suggested previously, this makes essay writing more manageable by identifying the individual questions that you need to answer in order to prove your argument. By identifying the overall purpose of the essay in the arguable proposition, the model allows you to see the way that the individual steps of the essay-writing process are linked to provide a path from beginning to end. This allows you to focus specifically on the individual steps.

4.4.2 Making Writing Decisions about Inscribing the Writing Space

For many students, the greatest challenge in writing is getting started. In Chapter 3, we discussed the advantage of using the IDDL model to create an outline that reflects both the general purpose of your essay and the steps you must follow to achieve that purpose. The following chart provides a summary of the process you should follow to organize your writing space using the IDDL model.

Making Writing Decisions	About Using Your Arguable Claim to Inscribe Your Writing Space

What is the purpose of this writing decision?

The arguable claim identifies both the beginning and the end of the essay. That is, it allows you to create boundaries for the essay, isolating the ideas that will be relevant to the essay.

What is the effect of this writing decision?

It's easier for you to compose an essay when you've marked out the boundaries and limited the number of questions you need to address.

What considerations inform this decision?

In order to use the arguable claim to inscribe the writing space, you need to be sure that you have clearly articulated both the claim you are making and the reasons on which you are basing that claim.

Suggested strategies for making this decision.

In order to use your arguable claim as a means by which to map out your writing space, you must ensure that it's clear and specific. When you're looking at your own arguable proposition, ask yourself whether the claim you're making is well defined. Look at each of the reasons in support of that claim. Is each reason well defined? Finally, look at the causal connector (e.g., *because, as a result of*): Does the causal connector reflect the relationship you intend between the claim and the reasons for that claim?

Questions to guide decision making in your own essay.

- Turn to the essay you're working on now and look at your own arguable proposition. Is it clear enough to suggest to you the things you need to prove before you get to the conclusion? Remember that the purpose of the IDDL model, in part, is to transform a blank page into a series of questions that will lead to the conclusion. Does your arguable proposition tell you where you are going? If it doesn't, it needs to be refined. Clarity is more important at this point than ornamentation. However tempting it may be to make a grand and impassioned claim in your thesis, overblown rhetoric doesn't provide you or your reader with a sense of direction.
- If the arguable proposition clearly identified the reasons for your arguable claim, then it also identified each of the specific themes for your essay. Do you know, specifically, what themes you need to explore and what questions you need to answer if the reader is to follow the logic of your argument from the beginning of your essay to the end?

II. **D**efine the problems locally (i.e., at the level of the paragraph or series of related paragraphs).

    The second stage of the IDDL model asks you to use the arguable proposition to define the specific questions that you need to answer in order to demonstrate that your argument is reasonable. In the following chart, we offer examples of how you can break the arguable proposition into individual questions.

Introduction:
What is the arguable proposition?

> **Example:** *Human development is having an adverse effect on the African elephant popula-tion because elephant populations are inherently fragile due to their long gestation period, human development proceeds more quickly than elephants can adapt, and human development deprives elephant herds of the large expanse of area needed to sustain the herds.*

What is the claim?
- *Human development is having an adverse effect on the African elephant population*

What is the causal connector?
- *because*

What are the reasons in support of the claim?
- *elephant populations are inherently fragile due to their long gestation period*
- *human development proceeds more quickly than elephants can adapt*
- *human development deprives elephant herds of the large expanse of area needed to sustain the herds*

Identify the first local problem
- How will you prove that *elephant populations are inherently fragile due to their long gestation period?*

Identify the second local problem
- How will you prove that *human development proceeds more quickly than elephants can adapt?*

Identify the third local problem
- How will you prove that *human development deprives elephant herds of the large expanse of area needed to sustain the herds?*

Why would a reasonable person disagree?
- Are there any exceptions to the points you have made above?

Conclusion:
What must be proved?
You must prove that *Human development is having an adverse effect on the African elephant population because:*
- *elephant populations are inherently fragile due to their long gestation period*
- *human development proceeds more quickly than elephants can adapt*
- *human development deprives elephant herds of the large expanse of area needed to sustain the herds*

The individual questions are specific and well defined. This allows you to seek out the particular information you need.

4.4.3 Making Writing Decisions about Defining Rhetorical Problems Locally

As we discussed in Chapter 3, there is an advantage to narrowing your focus when you are writing. In terms of the research process, this allows you to clearly iden-tify the specific themes that need to be explored. The following chart provides

Rhetorical problems are the key issues that must be resolved in order to move an essay forward.

a summary of the process you should follow to define those themes of your essay using the IDDL model.

| Making Writing Decisions | About Defining Rhetorical Problems Locally |

What is the purpose of this writing decision?

In the IDDL model, the purpose of the arguable proposition is to clearly identify the beginning and end of the essay and to break the essay into a related series of individual units.

What is the effect of this writing decision?

The effect of this writing decision is to allow you to concentrate on the composition of the individual units (i.e., either a paragraph or a series of related paragraphs), so that you can explore a single theme of the essay without having to simultaneously manage its connection to the overall thesis. Sounds complicated. It isn't. Because you have already determined the purpose of each of the individual units, it's not necessary for you to think about the larger essay while you are composing the component parts.

What considerations inform this decision?

Again, it's important that the arguable proposition clearly reflects the relationship of the individual reasons to the claim you're making. If the arguable proposition was sufficiently precise, it ought to be clear what it is you have to prove over the course of the essay.

Suggested strategies for making this decision.

Look at your own arguable proposition and separate each of the reasons that you've supplied for the claim you're making. Ask yourself whether each of those reasons can be proven and, if so, how?

Questions to guide decision making in your own essay.

1. Reread your arguable proposition, identifying each of the reasons you've supplied in support of your claim. Move each of the reasons into its own box, as we demonstrated in the example above.
2. Examine the first reason. Is it specific? Is its purpose clear (i.e., is the way in which it provides support obvious)? How will you support that reason? Is it, in fact, a thing that can be proven or supported by evidence? (If not, it's probably not the sort of reason you ought to use.)
3. For each of the other reasons, follow the same process. In each case, ask yourself whether it's possible to support the reasons that you've given. If so, how?

III. **D**iscover the evidence necessary to resolve each of the local problems.

The third stage of the IDDL model asks you to focus your research using the questions that you defined in the second stage. Your research becomes more purposeful when you're guided by specific and identifiable needs, rather than haphazardly gathering resources that vaguely refer to the general topic of the essay.

> Introduction:
> What is the arguable proposition?
>
> > **Example:** *Human development is having an adverse effect on the African elephant population because elephant populations are inherently fragile due to their long gestation period, human development proceeds more quickly than elephants can adapt, and human development deprives elephant herds of the large expanse of area needed to sustain the herds.*

What is the claim? ■ *Human development is having an adverse effect on the African elephant population*
What is the causal connector? ■ *because*
What are the reasons in support of the claim? ■ *elephant populations are inherently fragile due to their long gestation period* ■ *human development proceeds more quickly than elephants can adapt* ■ *human development deprives elephant herds of the large expanse of area needed to sustain the herds*
What evidence is needed to prove that *elephant populations are inherently fragile due to their long gestation period*? ■ Quotation, paraphrase, or summary of evidence, including citation ■ Quotation, paraphrase, or summary of evidence, including citation ■ Quotation, paraphrase, or summary of evidence, including citation
What evidence is needed to prove that *human development proceeds more quickly than elephants can adapt*? ■ Quotation, paraphrase, or summary of evidence, including citation ■ Quotation, paraphrase, or summary of evidence, including citation ■ Quotation, paraphrase, or summary of evidence, including citation
What evidence is needed to prove that *human development deprives elephant herds of the large expanse of area needed to sustain the herds*? ■ Quotation, paraphrase, or summary of evidence, including citation ■ Quotation, paraphrase, or summary of evidence, including citation ■ Quotation, paraphrase, or summary of evidence, including citation
Why would a reasonable person disagree? ■ Are there any exceptions to the points you have made above?
Conclusion: **What must be proved?** You must prove that *Human development is having an adverse effect on the African elephant population because* ■ *elephant populations are inherently fragile due to their long gestation period* ■ *human development proceeds more quickly than elephants can adapt* ■ *human development deprives elephant herds of the large expanse of area needed to sustain the herds*

4.4.4 Making Writing Decisions about Discovering Evidence

Having identified the rhetorical problems in the second stage of the IDDL process, you are now in a position to search out the information you need to resolve those problems. Remember that you're looking for the information you need to explore a theme or substantiate a claim. Your search should be purposeful. That is, research is meant to answer the questions you posed.

The next chart summarizes the process you should follow when looking for information that clarifies your reasoning, substantiates your claims, or offers an alternative view.

Making Writing Decisions	About Discovering the Evidence Necessary to Resolve Local Rhetorical Problems

What is the purpose of this writing decision?

The purpose of this writing decision is to seek out the particular evidence that is necessary to underpin each of the reasons you supplied in support of your arguable claim.

What is the effect of this writing decision?

By focusing specifically on each reason at one time, you may find that you are able to conduct your research more efficiently and effectively. Rather than wading through reams of documents to find the ones that are relevant to your argument, you are able to identify keywords that limit your search.

What considerations inform this decision?

It's easier to undertake research when you're seeking support for one particular point. Again, this allows you to focus your search for information.

Suggested strategies for making this decision

The best advice that we can give at this point is to ensure that you clearly identified the rhetorical problem in the second stage of the IDDL model. The more precisely you identified the reason, the more efficiently you can seek out evidence in support of that reason.

Questions to guide decision making in your own essay

1. Look at the first of the rhetorical problems you defined in the second stage of the IDDL model. What evidence do you need to resolve the rhetorical problem (i.e., what evidence is necessary to convince the reader that the reason you've offered is reasonable)? What is the best source for that evidence (e.g., will you seek evidence from a text, as is often the case in many of the humanities, or will you seek evidence from research studies, as is generally the case in the social sciences and the sciences)? In Chapter 7, we identify strategies for selecting authoritative evidence.
2. When you look at the sources that emerge from your research, record quotations, paraphrases, or summaries of the ideas that you find. These will allow you to construct the individual units of the essay on the basis of supporting evidence. To select your evidence, ask yourself what quotations, paraphrases, or summaries provide the greatest support for this particular reason.
3. When you record your supporting evidence, it's important to ensure that you also scribble down the source of your information. You need to cite your evidence, and there are few things more frustrating than having to give up a particular idea or quotation because you can't remember its source. Have you recorded the bibliographic information necessary to properly cite the source (your instructor will have told you what format to use for citations, e.g., APA, MLA, *Chicago*)?
4. Think about the evidence that's needed to substantiate each claim. What source of information provides the greatest authority?
5. Seek out that authoritative evidence for each reason. If you're unable to find reliable and authoritative evidence in support of a particular reason, you may want to consider whether or not the reason is a good one.

LO 2 ## 4.5 A QUICK REVIEW OF THE RESEARCH PROCESS

When conducting research, your job is not only to gather evidence but also to evaluate it and determine its worth to your argument. In most cases, you will be working with articles written by individuals who are experts in their fields and there will be an understandable temptation to scribble down everything that each has to say. This is one of the great challenges of the twenty-first century. It used to be the case that the search for information was a bit of a chore. These days, with the seemingly endless stream of information coming from the internet, the greater difficulty is the need to sift through sources to find those that are appropriate to your purpose. Before you begin to do research on your topic, then, it is important to develop a research strategy.

Here are some things that you ought to think about before you begin.

Select a Topic

In many cases, your topic will have been selected for you by your instructor. Believe it or not, that makes your life much easier. You can assume that your instructor will have provided you with a list of topics that lend themselves to argument. In the event that you can or must select your own topic, you need to ensure that the topic you select will allow you to develop an argument that is practical and arguable. It has to be specific and it has to be, in some way, measurable. Once you've selected a topic, think of questions within the topic that interest you. What do you want to know?

Develop an Arguable Proposition

Phrase your thesis in a way that allows you to develop your arguable proposition (we discussed the arguable proposition in Chapter 3). Remember that it will be easier to undertake your research if you know specifically the questions you're investigating and the evidence you need.

Develop Research Questions Based on Your Arguable Proposition

As we discussed at the beginning of the chapter, the arguable proposition comprises a claim and the reasons for that claim. Your research questions are embedded within the arguable proposition. In the example at the beginning of the chapter, we included this thesis statement: *Human development is having an adverse effect on the African elephant population because elephant populations are inherently fragile due to their long gestation period, human development proceeds more quickly than elephants can adapt, and human development deprives elephant herds of the large expanse of area needed to sustain the herds.* In this case, your research questions would be: (1) *Are elephant populations inherently fragile due to their long gestation period?* (2) *Does human development proceed more quickly than elephants can adapt? and* (3) *Does human development deprive elephant herds of the large expanse of area needed to sustain the herds?*

Think of Keywords

The research questions provide you with keywords. One of the great advantages of conducting research in the twenty-first century is that computers now do much of the legwork. Before you send the computer scurrying off to find something, however, you want to ensure that it has the information necessary to select documents that are relevant and exclude the ones that are not. Keywords let you do that. Keywords are words that guide your queries (queries are computer searches) by providing the computer with the information it needs to limit a search. When you begin to do your research, you need to select the most important words from your arguable proposition and input them into your search engine. For example, in the first research question above, you might choose the words *elephants, gestation period,* and *population stability.* By using keywords in your searches, you won't end up retrieving information that has no relevance to your thesis. On the other hand, you're less likely to discover some incredibly intriguing tidbit of information accidently (e.g., elephant mothers breastfeed their young up to the age of five; didn't know that, did you?).

Choose Resources Carefully

Think about the nature of the resources you need. Does your instructor require specific resources (e.g., academic journals, specific online journals)? Regardless of the medium you choose, you can save yourself a lot of time by selecting the resources that are most likely to be authoritative (we discuss this in Chapter 7). If you begin with Google Scholar rather than Google, you are more likely to find authoritative sources. Similarly, if you conduct your research using either academic journals in your library or academic journals online, you can be relatively certain that the information you find will be reliable.

(continued)

(*continued*)

Use Online Resources with Caution

The internet is often a good place to begin your research because it frequently provides you with a general overview of your topic. The internet will identify points to consider about the topic and may suggest ideas you hadn't yet thought of. In fact, the use of Wikipedia as a starting point is not entirely a bad idea. Wikipedia often presents a useful, though sometimes surface, summary of a particular topic. You do have to remember, however, that you need to verify much of the information you find on the internet.

Read Intentionally

Once you have selected a resource, skim it quickly to ensure that it is, in fact, relevant to your thesis. In most cases, academic articles will begin with an abstract that summarizes the article. You can generally tell by reading the abstract whether the article is likely to be useful. Discard any resources that don't appear to offer the information you need and put aside those that hold promise so that you can read them more carefully at a later time.

Monitor Your Research Process

As you're conducting your research, you ought to be monitoring your progress. Are you finding that there's enough information? Are you relying exclusively on a single document? Are you finding reliable resources? If you discover that you can't find any information, there are two things you may want to consider: (1) Perhaps there is no information on the topic (though that seems unlikely), or (2) perhaps you aren't doing it right (e.g., you've chosen the wrong keywords or you're looking in the wrong place). If you're convinced that you've done everything right, and still can't find any information, it may be time to come up with a new topic. You'll have plenty of time in grad school to investigate obscure ideas. On the other hand, if the search was initially successful but is now yielding the same results over and over again, you're done.

Modify Your Search if Necessary

There are a number of ways to modify your search. You may have found that your thesis was too broad (this happens a lot, even when the writers are experienced). If you find that the volume of information is unworkable, you may want to narrow your focus by selecting a specific aspect of a larger topic. It's easier to write about something specific and it's easier to research something specific. If, on the other hand, you discover that you can't find any information, you may need to broaden your thesis.

Take Notes

It's important to remember that, when you're conducting research, you are not merely identifying information but also interpreting it. In other words, you have to make decisions about what to include and what to leave out. Taking notes during the research process allows you to do this more effectively. If, as you go along, you write brief summaries of the resources you plan to use, you'll find that it's much easier to integrate the information into your essay during the writing process. Summaries ought to include the following features: (1) a general summary, in your own words, of no more than three sentences (in order to write the summary in three sentences, you need to have a general sense of what the article has discussed), (2) a summary of specific details that are relevant to your argument (one of the great difficulties students experience in citing external sources is identifying the degree of detail that is required; however interesting they may be, some details in an article may not be relevant), (3) specific details that you intend to use as direct evidence (these can be recorded as quotations or paraphrases), (4) bibliographic information (this will make citing sources easier), and (5) a brief statement indicating the way in which the information will be used in your essay.

Cite Sources

It's very important to keep track of any references you may use as you're going along. This is an essential part of research. There are few things more frustrating than arriving at the end of your writing process and not being able to find a source that you wanted to use in your paper. In Chapter 12, we discuss methods of citation in greater detail. At this point, all you need to know is that, regardless of the format you're using, you ought to have the name of the author, the title of the article, the name of the journal, and the page number if you have quoted an author directly.

4.5.1 Citing Sources during the Research Process

Whenever you quote, paraphrase, or summarize information in a resource, you're obliged to cite your source using parenthetical documentation, endnotes, or footnotes. Similarly, if you want to make reference to an idea, word, or phrase that is closely associated with a particular author or group of authors, you may want to identify the source in a citation. Refer to Chapter 12 for a more comprehensive discussion of citation procedures.

4.6   CONCLUSION

In this chapter, we have discussed the purpose and practice of academic research, focusing, in particular, on the advantage of working from questions that emerge from the specific needs of your particular essay. We've tried to base our discussions on two principles that ought to guide your research practices.

1. The search for reference material is not merely an instructor's requirement. It's dictated by the needs of the writer and the audience. The resources you consult permit you to develop a better understanding of the subject. Those resources also reassure the reader that your exploration of the subject is informed with the authority of experts.
2. The search for reference material should be purposeful. If you work from the specific questions that emerge from the arguable proposition of your thesis statement, you will find the keywords you need to conduct your research efficiently. That is, you will find that you are better prepared to search for information that is relevant to the particular argument you're making.

The effort you invest in understanding the purpose of your research process will be rewarded by the efficiency with which you are able to conduct the research process.

MyCompLab®

How Do I Get a Better Grade?

Go to MyCompLab for additional help with your grammar, writing, and research skills. You will have access to a variety of exercises, instruction, and videos that will help you improve your basic skills and help you get a better grade.

✓•─[Practice]

Practice Exercise

Using the IDDL Model to Prepare a Research Strategy

Using the IDDL model makes your decision making easier at discrete points in your essay by providing you with a way of recognizing the specific needs that emerge in the writing process. Read the thesis statement in the example below and isolate the individual claims that emerge from the thesis statement. In the following exercise, develop a strategy for discovering the evidence you would need to explore and substantiate the claims.

Topic: Video Games

What is the thesis?
- *Video games are harmful to a child's development because they can cause addiction, they can lead to aggression, and they can lead to social isolation.*

What is the claim?
- *Video games are harmful to a child's development*

What is the causal connector?
- *because*

What are the reasons in support of the claim?
- *they can cause addiction*
- *they can lead to aggression*
- *they can lead to social isolation*

Identify the first local problem
- *Video games are harmful to a child's development because they can cause addiction.*

What evidence is needed to prove that video games cause addiction?
- *You need to find articles that talk about video games and addiction.*

Identify the second local problem
- *Video games are harmful to a child's development because they can lead to aggression.*

What evidence is needed to prove *that playing video games causes aggression?*
- *You need to find evidence that proves playing video games causes aggression in children.*

Identify the third local problem
- *Video games are harmful to a child's development because they can lead to social isolation.*

What evidence is needed to prove tha*t playing video games leads to social isolation?*
- *You need to find evidence that proves that playing video games leads to social isolation.*

Why would a reasonable person disagree?

Are there any exceptions to the points you've made above?
- *Some people might argue that playing video games also has benefits for children because they provide recreational activities that can be educational and developmental. Video games can increase motor skills, enhance problem-solving skills, and boost self-confidence.*

Conclusion:

What has been proven?
Video games are harmful to a child's development because:
- *they can cause addiction*
- *they can lead to aggression*
- *they can lead to social isolation*

Research Strategy Exercise

1. The guiding thesis is that *video games are harmful to a child's development because they can cause addiction, they can lead to aggression, and they can lead to social isolation.* Where would you look for information that might allow you to explore that thesis? What specific steps would you follow?

   _____

   _____

   _____

2. The first local rhetorical problem is proving that *video games are harmful to a child's development because they can cause addiction.* Where would you look for information that might allow you to explore that thesis? What specific steps would you follow?

   _____

   _____

   _____

3. The second local rhetorical problem is proving that *video games are harmful to a child's development because they can lead to aggression.* Where would you look for information that might allow you to explore that thesis? What specific steps would you follow?

   _____

   _____

   _____

4. The third local rhetorical problem is proving that *video games are harmful to a child's development because they can lead to social isolation.* Where would you look for information that might allow you to explore that thesis? What specific steps would you follow?

   _____

   _____

5. The counter-argument is that *some people argue that playing video games may have the following benefits for children: the games provide recreational activities that can be both educational and developmental, provide activities that can increase motor skills, provide activities that enhance problem-solving skills, and provide activities that might boost self-confidence.* Where would you look for information that might allow you to explore that thesis? What specific steps would you follow?

   _____

   _____

   _____

✓•—Practice   **Self-Evaluation Worksheet for the Research Process**

The evaluation worksheet below includes a series of questions to reflect on your own research. The worksheet is designed to make your research process more efficient by encouraging you to focus on the specific themes and claims that require investigation.

1. Review your essay. Does it have a clear and specific thesis statement? What is the specific claim the thesis statement makes? What reasons have you offered in support of that claim? What keywords will you use to guide your research process?

_____

_____

2. Look at the first reason. What evidence is needed to show that the reason you have provided is consistent with your arguable proposition? What is the best source of that evidence? Which specific statements in the resource you have chosen make your point most effectively? Should you use a direct quotation (which provides the authority of the author's own words), a paraphrase (which allows you to integrate the ideas into your essay more easily), or a summary (which allows you to convey a larger volume of information in more general terms)? Have you noted those statements, including the bibliographic information you will require for your citations and references?

_____

_____

3. Look at the second reason. What evidence is needed to show that the reason you have provided is consistent with your arguable proposition? What is the best source of that evidence? Which specific statements in the resource you have chosen make your point most effectively? Should you use a direct quotation (which provides the authority of the author's own words), a paraphrase (which allows you to integrate the ideas into your essay more easily), or a summary (which allows you to convey a larger volume of information in more general terms)? Have you noted those statements, including the bibliographic information you will require for your citations and references?

_____

_____

4. Look at the third reason. What evidence is needed to show that the reason you have provided is consistent with your arguable proposition? What is the best source of that evidence? Which specific statements in the resource you have chosen make your point most effectively? Should you use a direct quotation (which provides the authority of the author's own words), a paraphrase (which allows you to integrate the ideas into your essay more easily), or a summary (which allows you to convey a larger volume of information in more general terms)? Have you noted those statements, including the bibliographic information you will require for your citations and references?

_____

_____

Use the same line of questioning to evaluate the research you have undertaken for any subsequent points.

_____

_____

_____

5. Have you identified any competing views that you discovered in the research process? Do you have the bibliographic information necessary to cite those sources?

_____

_____

_____

Peer-Evaluation Worksheet for References ✓• Practice

Title of the Essay _____

List of References Submitted By: _____

Peer Evaluator: _____

Based on your understanding of the essay's thesis, what evidence is needed to support the argument?

_____

_____

_____

Source #_____ Title of Source Material:	
How does this source strengthen the argument being put forth?	
What specific aspect(s) of the argument does this resource address?	

(continued)

(*continued*)

What evidence can you find to suggest that the source is authoritative, reliable, objective, and current?	
What information has the writer provided that would permit you to locate the source?	

Source #_____
Title of Source Material:

How does this source strengthen the argument being put forth?	
What specific aspect(s) of the argument does this resource address?	
What evidence can you find to suggest that the source is authoritative, reliable, objective, and current?	
What information has the writer provided that would permit you to locate the source?	

Source #_____
Title of Source Material:

How does this source strengthen the argument being put forth?	
What specific aspect(s) of the argument does this resource address?	
What evidence can you find to suggest that the source is authoritative, reliable, objective, and current?	

What information has the writer provided that would permit you to locate the source?	
Source #_____ **Title of Source Material:**	
How does this source strengthen the argument being put forth?	
What specific aspect(s) of the argument does this resource address?	
What evidence can you find to suggest that the source is authoritative, reliable, objective, and current?	
What information has the writer provided that would permit you to locate the source?	

CHAPTER 5

Using an Annotated Bibliography as a Research Tool

Learning Objectives

At the completion of this chapter, you will be able to:

1. Identify the differences between the ways in which novice and experienced writers use annotated bibliographies.

2. Distinguish between lists of references (e.g., references pages, bibliographies) and annotated bibliographies.

3. Demonstrate the ability to create and format an annotated bibliography.

4. Explain the way in which the annotated bibliography can be used to guide the composition of an essay draft.

5.1   INTRODUCTION

In this chapter, we discuss the value of using an annotated bibliography as a research tool. The annotated bibliography allows you to keep a record of the books and articles you've read, the major themes in each of them, and the degree to which they might be relevant to your essay. An annotated bibliography demands that you interpret the book or article you're reading, rather than having you merely scribble down ideas to be shoe-horned into your essay kicking and screaming, independent of the degree to which the article is sympathetic to your argument. It also obliges you to keep track of the source of your ideas (that is no small advantage; it often happens that writers have to set aside wonderfully useful ideas because they are unable to remember the books or articles from which those ideas came). Most importantly, the annotated bibliography can serve as an interface between you and the research documents you're using.

Because it forces you to interpret and summarize the research material, the annotated bibliography allows you to recontextualize the information (without betraying its original meaning) and record it in a form that you can integrate into your essay. In this way, the annotated bibliography helps with the efficient transfer of ideas from their original sources (i.e., books or articles) to the place you want them (i.e., your essay).

5.2 DIFFERENCES BETWEEN NOVICE WRITERS AND EXPERIENCED WRITERS

LO 1

In the chart below you will notice that novice writers often focus on relating all the information they can find on a topic without making the critical decisions necessary to separate important information from interesting but irrelevant information. Experienced writers take the time to organize their thinking so that the material they choose is relevant to their thesis.

Novice Writers	Experienced Writers
■ Require thought for procedural, or "mechanical," writing functions.	■ Have, to a significant degree, automated procedural functions.
■ Focus on error avoidance rather than meaning.	■ Focus on developing or refining meaning.
■ Begin writing without planning, and edit, if at all, for grammatical errors.	■ Invest time and energy in planning and reviewing.
■ *Focus on "knowledge telling" (i.e., relating all the information they have and can find on a topic, rather than exercising critical judgment to determine relevance).*	■ *Organize, and reorganize, essay structure to allow individual ideas to serve the overall purpose of the essay.*

As noted in the chart above, novice writers often do not exercise *critical judgment to determine relevance* of information to their specific purpose. Experienced writers, on the other hand, monitor their writing to ensure that *individual ideas serve the purpose of the essay.* In previous chapters, we stressed the importance of making critical decisions about the information you use. An annotated bibliography can help you do that. When preparing an annotated bibliography, you have to analyze the documents with which you're working, reading to discover their essential meaning. If you're using the documents as evidence in a paper, you need to think about the degree to which they support your argument or challenge it. Are they relevant? Do they provide evidence that directly supports your argument or are they offering support of a more general nature? How can you integrate them into your essay? If the material challenges your position, you need to determine whether the challenge is serious enough to cause you to modify your position to some degree or to include the challenges in a discussion of counter-arguments. It is not always an easy process. It does, however, allow you to create a document that helps you integrate resource material into your essay.

LO 2   ## 5.3   UNDERSTANDING THE DIFFERENCE BETWEEN LISTS OF REFERENCES (E.G., REFERENCES PAGES, BIBLIOGRAPHIES) AND ANNOTATED BIBLIOGRAPHIES

The annotated bibliography is often a source of confusion for students on account of its apparent similarity to its better-known cousin, the bibliography. There are similarities, of course, but there are also important differences. A bibliography (which is also known as a *reference*, or *works cited*, page, depending on the style format that your instructor has asked you to use), is an integral part of any academic essay. It requires you to cite your sources in alphabetical order, including the bibliographic information needed to locate those sources (i.e., name of author, date of publication, title of article or book, name of city where published, and the name of the publisher). The purpose of a bibliography is threefold: (1) to acknowledge the original source of the ideas and to guard against the charge of plagiarism, (2) to provide enough information that your reader will be able to seek further information from the original source, and (3) to provide your essay with the authority that derives from the expertise of the original author of the material.

By contrast, an annotated bibliography is a summary, or an evaluation, of the material. Though it's not an essential feature of the essay itself, it's an invaluable aid to the writing of the essay. It provides a specific record of each of the sources you've consulted, including bibliographic information (which is useful in and of itself, since it allows you to keep track of the source of the information you're using, and thus allows you to cite each idea easily during the writing process). The annotated bibliography also allows you to synthesize and summarize the texts, rendering them suitable to their new purpose as evidence in your argument. Often, writers will stack the works they've consulted on a desk, with Post-it® Notes identifying the pages that might prove useful. Those stacks of books and articles are reassuring. It seems as if something is being done. Unfortunately, having the material piled in great heaps beside the computer (however well organized those piles might be) doesn't get the information into the essay as easily as we might all hope. In fact, it can be a little frustrating. The information is so close, and yet it stubbornly refuses to take that final step and integrate itself into the essay. By maintaining an annotated bibliography during the research process, you will find that you (a) have a record of the ideas that are relevant to your essay, and (b) have already begun to translate them into a form that allows you to integrate them into the essay easily.

An annotated bibliography allows you to summarize your sources early in the research process and helps you to narrow your search. It allows you to move from the research process to the writing process with relatively little effort. This is especially useful when you're dealing with a large number of sources. One of the advantages of a decision-making model like the IDDL model is that you can link it to the writing of an annotated bibliography to simplify the research process.

The IDDL model identifies the specific questions that need to be answered, narrowing your search to a more manageable process of inquiry and rescuing you from an endless investigation for information that has little relevance.

5.4 PURPOSE OF AN ANNOTATED BIBLIOGRAPHY

LO 2, 3, 4

The purpose of an annotated bibliography is to provide you with an accurate summary and analysis of your sources. In order to be effective as a research tool, an annotated bibliography should encourage you to think critically about each article and consider the way in which the article relates to your own argument. On the other hand, if the annotated bibliography is intended to stand alone as a review of literature in a particular field, it should give readers an understanding of current thinking in the field and provide background information for other researchers who might be interested in pursuing the questions in that field.

Classes that require you to conduct research will also sometimes require you to prepare an annotated bibliography. Believe it or not, there is some benefit to that. An annotated bibliography helps you to organize your research and to assess the relevance of the articles or books you read. In writing an annotation for each source, you acquire a better understanding of the information it includes and a better understanding of the way in which each source relates to the other sources. The annotations also allow you to refresh your memory on both the essence and the details of individual articles or books as you write your essay. Working with an annotated bibliography beside you, you'll have access to the supporting material you need to construct your essay.

In the introduction to this chapter, we suggested that the preparation of an annotated bibliography provides an opportunity to summarize and interpret the information you find in the articles or books you read. Sadly, the titles of documents sometimes lead you to believe that certain articles may be more relevant to your topic than they are. An annotated bibliography can prove useful in helping you make critical judgments about the value of the material (again, it's a metacognitive practice). The process of writing an annotated bibliography also allows you to entertain multiple perspectives on the same topic. This will be useful when you construct your argument and write your counter-argument (see Chapter 2 for a discussion of counter-arguments).

A good annotated bibliography has multiple features that will prove useful in organizing and analyzing the sources you're going to use in your essay. The following chart summarizes the main features of an annotated bibliography.

An Annotated Bibliography Enables You to:
Maintain a record of references during the research process.
Survey the field of perspectives on the topic, identifying the views that are generally accepted and those that are more controversial. This allows you to acquire a general understanding of the range of accepted scholarship on a particular subject. A well-crafted annotated bibliography also demonstrates to your reader that you are a fair-minded and careful researcher who has looked at multiple perspectives on your topic.

(continued)

(*continued*)

Provide examples of the type of resources available on a given topic.
Describe and evaluate those references. Again, a good annotated bibliography allows you to make critical decisions about the value of the material you're using.
Actively reflect on the references, assessing their relevance to the essay and considering ways in which the information will be used. An annotated bibliography can provide your reader with an understanding of the way in which you came to the conclusions you did. It can also provide your readers with a summary of your sources so they can determine for themselves the way in which each source contributed to your overall argument.
Develop your own understanding of the topic through the process of critically analyzing and articulating a response to other treatments of the subject.
Illustrate the range and quality of your own research.
Demonstrate the relevance of the references to your argument. An annotated bibliography can help your readers make their own decisions about the sources you've used.

Exercise 1

In the following writing exercise, your goal is to assess the annotated bibliography entry to determine whether the document to which it refers might be relevant to the thesis identified in the thesis statement. Remember that your purpose is to find information that will help you explore that thesis. Resist the temptation to be led astray by interesting but irrelevant facts or comments.

Notice that only the last name and the first initial of the first name are used in the citation.

The name of the journal is italicized.

The volume number is part of the required bibliographic information.

Page numbers are listed without the use of the word *page*, the designation *p* or the designation *pp*.

The statistics will be used to prove that pollution affects the water supply.

Sample Exercise 1

Thesis Statement

Governments ought to regulate pollution because pollution poisons the air, poisons the water supply, and endangers the food supply.

Annotated Bibliography

Gordon, H., Haiku, L., & Frost, B. (2010). How pollution poisons the environment. *Journal of Environmental Studies, 3,* 46–58.

In this article, the authors offer information about the effects that pollution has on the water supply. They provide statistics that prove how manufacturers and large-scale farms dump waste into waterways without thought of how the waste affects the water supply. The authors graphically represent the path followed by waste products from the time waste is dumped into the water until it reaches the water supply of cities and towns. This information will be used in my essay to provide evidence that pollution should be regulated by the government because it poisons the water supply.

Did the annotated bibliography entry provide enough information to allow you to determine whether the document is useful? Did it appear worth pursuing?

Exercise 2

Here's another example. Again, your goal is to assess the annotated bibliography entry to determine whether the document to which it refers might be relevant to the thesis identified in the thesis statement.

Sample Exercise 2

Thesis Statement

Governments ought to regulate pollution because pollution poisons the air, poisons the water supply, and endangers the food supply.

Annotated Bibliography

Forest, A., & Tree, K. (2011). Pollution and the chain of food preparation. *Journal of Food Services, 6,* 25-40.

In this article, the authors described a study in which two cows were observed from the time of their birth to the time they were sent to market to be slaughtered for food. The authors charted the growth of the cows, the waste produced by the cows, and the types of food that each cow consumed over a three-year period. The cows weighed approximately the same at birth. The first cow was raised on a more traditional farm where cattle were raised outdoors and were allowed to graze for their food. The second cow was raised on a factory farm where cattle were fed nutrient-enriched food, given growth-hormone injections, and were not allowed outdoors. At the end of the three years, the cattle were weighed before they were sent to market. The factory cow was twenty-five pounds heavier than the traditional farm cow even after taking into consideration the slight difference in their birth weight. After the cows were slaughtered, the authors inspected the meat and found that the factory farm cow had less fat than the traditional farm cow. The authors reported that factory farm cows are bred to have less fat because most consumers want less fat in their meat. The authors also followed the disposal of the manure generated by the two cows. They noted a number of differences. The traditional farm cow "produced less manure and, because it was raised outdoors, that manure decomposed naturally" (Forest & Tree, 2011, p. 35). By contrast, the factory farm cow's manure was mixed with that of the other 300 cows in the barn, and was processed artificially before being dumped into a lagoon. The processing of the manure in the case of the cow from the factory farm led to the pollution of the groundwater on the factory farm, which impacted other farms that were dependent on the groundwater for their water supply. The authors tested some of the crops grown on the other farms and "found that the level of toxicity of some of the food crops was more than five times higher than the food that was grown on farms near the traditional farm" (Forest & Tree, 2011, p. 37). This article could be used to show the way in which pollution affects the water supply and endangers the general food supply.

Did the entry in this annotated bibliography provide you with enough information to assess its relevance to the thesis statement? Were you able to get a sense of the article it summarizes? Did you feel it required more information? More analysis of the information?

5.5 HOW TO PREPARE AN ANNOTATED BIBLIOGRAPHY

LO 3, 4

Writing an annotated bibliography requires you to think critically, to summarize data succinctly, and to analyze and evaluate material. You can, however, work only from the information you have at hand. The first step in the preparation of an annotated bibliography is to go through a rigorous research process (see Chapter 4). Using the same critical skills that you will employ in the analysis and summarizing of books and articles, you must seek out the best sources available on a particular subject. As you're leafing through the vast resources available to you in the world of electronic document delivery, you begin the process of cutting away those that are dated, lacking in authority, or irrelevant. Only then can you begin the process of preparing your annotations.

Each annotation has two parts. The first part is the recording of the bibliographic information (i.e., the information you will later require for citations and references). You will format the bibliographic information in accordance with the formatting style you're using.

In APA style, for instance, the information is formatted in the following way:

> Brown, J. (2009). Water quality at risk. *Journal of Farming Practices, 4,* 16–30.

If there is more than one author, you would cite like this:

> Brown, J., & Blue, B. (2009). Water quality at risk. *Journal of Farming Practices, 4,* 16–30.

If there are three or more authors, the format stays the same:

> Brown, J., Blue, B., & Gifford, R. (2009). Water quality at risk. *Journal of Farming Practices, 4,* 16–30.

Notice that, in APA, you start with the last name of the author, then the name of the article, then the name of the journal in italics, then the volume number also in italics, followed by the page numbers with no page header.

Second and subsequent lines are indented.

The annotated bibliography is organized alphabetically using the author's last name as the key to the index.

The second part of an annotated bibliography is the annotation itself. In an annotation, you prepare a concise summary of the principal ideas of the book or article. In some cases, you might include a sentence or two that describes the background of the author, the purpose of the article, and the intended audience of the article. You would also include both the observations and conclusions that the author(s) reached, and your assessment of those observations and conclusions. If you're undertaking the annotated bibliography as an assignment, your instructor will, of course, dictate the list of elements to be included (you always include the information that the assignment identifies as required). If the annotated bibliography is being prepared as a tool for essay writing, you may also want to add a sentence or two to remind yourself of the way in which you might use it in your essay. It's also useful to include quotations, paraphrases, and summaries of information that you might want to use in your essay.

LO 3, 4   5.6   FORMATTING AN ANNOTATED BIBLIOGRAPHY

Learning to properly format an annotated bibliography is just as important as learning to properly format a references page (see Chapter 12). The format of an annotated bibliography can vary in accordance to its specific purpose.

Annotations may be longer and more in-depth for longer research papers or they may emphasize particular aspects of the reference material. If you're undertaking an annotated bibliography as part of a class assignment, it's important to ask for specific guidelines.

5.6.1 Sample Annotated Bibliographies for a Journal Article

The following example uses the APA format for the journal citation (note that APA requires single spacing within citations).

> Moulder, J., Erdreich, L., Malyapa, R., Merritt, J., Pickard, W., & Vijayalaxmi, L. (1999). Cell phones and cancer: What is the evidence for a connection? *Radiation Research, 151*, 513–531.
>
> This article gives a brief overview of existing RF radiation cancer studies. The article is divided into three sections: the first section provides a brief review of the physics and technology of cell phones; the second section reviews the existing epidemiological studies of RF radiation, identifying gaps in general knowledge; and the third section discusses the cytogenetics literature on RF radiation and the whole-animal RF radiation carcinogenesis studies. In their analysis of the existing studies on RF radiation and the connection to cell phone use, the authors found that any evidence provided was weak and inconsistent. They reported that the studies do not provide any conclusive evidence that cell phone RF radiation has any connection to cancer, and suggested that, in their opinion, a connection between the two was implausible. This article will be used to prove that cell phone use does not cause cancer.

The example above demonstrates the way in which you should structure an entry in an annotated bibliography. The entry is written in paragraph form, and includes the name(s) of the author(s), year of publication, title of article, journal title, volume, and the page numbers of the article. Remember that authors are listed by their last name first, followed by the first initial of their given name.

Let's take a closer look at three other examples of an annotated bibliography. One is written in APA format, one in MLA format, and one in *Chicago* style. At first glance, they may appear to be the same. They're not. The most effective way to acquire a working knowledge of the formats is to pay attention to the first five features of one style (don't try to memorize more than five) and then examine the other two styles for similarities and differences. After all, you will usually have access to a guidebook or online resource. It's important, however, to develop a general sense of principal features that characterize each of the formats. This will allow you to develop an operational knowledge of the format and save you the trouble of trying to write with a style manual on your lap.

There are more styles of annotated bibliographies than the three mentioned here. We've chosen to focus on these three as they are the most common formats you will encounter in university.

5.6.2 APA Formatting

Sample APA Formatted Annotated Bibliography

When writing an annotated bibliography in APA, keep in mind that all annotations are single-spaced. In APA documents everything is typically double-spaced, including the references page, so this is something you have to pay attention to.

Hugger, J. (2012). Water pollution and the dangers to human food consumption. *Journal of Environmental Science, 4,* 20–39.

The citation begins with the author's last name first, followed by a comma, then the first initial only, followed by a period. Then the date in parentheses, ending with a period. Next comes the name of the article, followed by a period. The name of the journal is italicized. Then there is a comma, followed by the volume number, then a comma, then the page numbers. Notice that we don't use any designation for page.

Hugger provides a well-reasoned argument that environmental pollution, especially water pollution, has risen in the last ten years to such an extent that food sources for both humans and animals are being compromised. He further argues that this should be a concern to everyone who depends on a supply of fresh water. He supplies statistical data to prove his point that the number of freshwater lakes has dramatically decreased in the last ten years; he discusses the dangers to human and animal food from farm runoff and the overuse of pesticides; and he provides information on how much human waste cities are still pumping into lakes despite more strident laws governing the practice. This article will be useful in providing evidence to prove my point that water pollution is on the rise due to factory farming practices.

General APA Format

Author(s). (year). Title of article. *Title of Journal. Volume,* pages. doi:00.0000000.

Begin the annotation with a statement that gives the main point of the article. This is the author's topic sentence.

In this section you provide a summary of all of the pertinent information from the article, documenting the evidence that is provided by the author.

Then you conclude with a statement that indicates how you will be able to use the evidence provided in the article to prove your thesis statement.

A DOI is known as a Digital Object Identifier. It is used because online materials may change over time. DOI's provide information that is stable for a longer period of time.

All annotated bibliographies in APA are formatted alphabetically, using the author's last name.

5.6.3 MLA Formatting

As you're reading the following section on the MLA format for annotated bibliographies, think about the similarities to, and differences from, the principal features of APA format. It's often easier to acquire an understanding of the formats by comparing the significant features of one to the other.

If that doesn't work for you, focus on the style you need in your course at this time. The information on the other styles will still be here when you come back. It's not going anywhere.

Sample MLA-Formatted Annotated Bibliography

In MLA style the annotation is single-spaced.

Hugger, Jim. "Water Pollution and The Dangers to Human Food Consumption." *Journal of Environmental Science.* 4.4 (2012): 20-39.

> Hugger provides a well-reasoned argument that environmental pollution, especially water pollution, has risen in the last ten years to such an extent that food sources for both humans and animals are being compromised. He further argues that this should be a concern to everyone who depends on a supply of fresh water. He supplies statistical data to demonstrate that the number of freshwater lakes has dramatically decreased in the last ten years; he discusses the dangers to human and animal food from farm runoffs and the over-use of pesticides; and he provides information on how much human waste cities are still pumping into lakes despite more strident laws governing the practice. This article will be useful in providing evidence to prove my point that water pollution is on the rise due to factory farming practices.

General MLA Format

Author(s). "Title of Article." *Title of Journal.* Volume. Issue (year): pages. Date of Access <electronic address>.

As with the APA annotation, you need to give a brief summary of the article. It's acceptable in both formats to give a brief introduction of the author if you think that the information is relevant to your summary.

5.6.4 *Chicago*-style Formatting

Sample *Chicago*-style Formatted Annotated Bibliography

Single-space annotated bibliography in Chicago *author-date style.*

Hugger, Jim. 2012. "Water Pollution and The Dangers to Human Food Consumption." *Journal of Environmental Science 4 (4):* 20–39.

> *Author's last name first, followed by full first name, period, then year, period. The name of the article, period. Name of the journal, period. Volume number, period. Issue number, colon, page numbers.*

> Hugger provides a well-reasoned argument that environmental pollution, especially water pollution, has risen in the last ten years to such an extent that food sources for both humans and animals are being compromised. He further argues that this should be a concern to everyone who depends on a supply of fresh water. He supplies statistical data to illustrate that the number of freshwater lakes has dramatically decreased in the last ten years; he discusses the dangers to human and animal food from farm runoffs and the over-use of pesticides; and he provides information on how much human waste cities are still pumping into lakes despite more strident laws governing the practice. This article will be useful in providing evidence to prove my point that water pollution is on the rise due to factory farming practices.

Margin notes (MLA):

When citing sources in MLA, you include the full name of the author.

The name of the article is enclosed in quotation marks.

The name of the journal article is next, followed by the volume and issue number of the journal, a colon, and then the page numbers.

Introduce the author and his overall purpose for writing the article.

Provide a concise summary of the information in the article.

Include a statement that will indicate how you are going to use the information from the article to make your argument stronger.

All annotated bibliographies in MLA are formatted alphabetically using the author's last name.

Margin notes (Chicago):

Introduce the author and his overall purpose for writing the article.

Provide a concise summary of the information in the article.

Include a statement that will indicate how you are going to use the information from the article to make your argument stronger.

General *Chicago*-style Format

Author(s). Year. "Title of Article." *Title of Periodical* volume (issue): pages, URL.

You may notice if you have looked closely at the three different formatting styles that the difference between the three styles lies in the citations, not in the annotations. Each style requires a brief summary of the article and some degree of analysis. If you're using an annotated bibliography as an aid to the writing of an argumentative essay, you might also include a line or two identifying the specific evidence you will be using from the article.

5.7   VARIETIES OF ANNOTATED BIBLIOGRAPHIES

LO 3, 4

Though you may dress annotated bibliographies in different ways, altering their outward appearance to suit a specific formatting convention (e.g., APA, MLA, etc.), they generally serve a common purpose. There are, however, two forms of the annotated bibliography that are distinguished by a significant difference in purpose: (1) the annotated bibliography that focuses on summary, and (2) the annotated bibliography that focuses on analysis.

Summary
An annotated bibliography that emphasizes summary will provide a concise review of the essential content of the document being cited. In this type of annotation, you present a synopsis of the general thesis or main points of the article. You do not, however, evaluate the sources. When writing a summary, ask yourself: ■ What is the theme of the book or article? ■ What topics are covered? ■ How would I explain the article or book in a text message? (The use of text-message protocols is a useful exercise for developing summarizing skills; the limit in the number of characters obliges you to get to the point quickly.) The length of each annotation will depend on the details you include in your summary, but it should be consistent and should be as concise as possible.
Critical Analysis
Annotated bibliographies that emphasize analysis generally provide both summary *and* analysis of content. When writing a critical analysis, you will first present a brief synopsis of the principal themes of the work in question. You will then analyze the work critically, asking yourself questions like: ■ What is the source of the document? ■ What expertise does the author have? ■ Is the information consistent with, or in opposition to, other experts in the field? ■ Does the author have an identifiable bias? ■ What is the purpose of the document (i.e., what does the author seek to accomplish in writing the document)? ■ How old is the document? Is the information still current?

While some instructors might ask that you adopt one format or another for an annotated bibliography, those differences might be less significant than the differences between the annotated bibliography that focuses on summary and the annotated bibliography that focuses on analysis. It's important to pay attention to the instructor's directions. For the purposes of composing an argumentative essay, the annotated bibliography that focuses on analysis is generally more valuable.

5.8 SELECTING SOURCES TO INCLUDE IN YOUR ANNOTATED BIBLIOGRAPHY

LO 3, 4

The usefulness of your annotated bibliography will depend on the strength of the sources you choose to include. Before you begin searching for sources, you need to define the scope of your research. The IDDL model, which requires you to clearly articulate your arguable proposition and specifically identify the individual subtheses of the argument, can help you to do this. Though you want your search to be as thorough as possible, it's also important to limit the scope of your research to resources that are relevant. The questions in the following chart should help to refine your search parameters and make your search more systematic.

- What is my thesis?
- What is the problem I am investigating?
- Has my argument been defined precisely enough to facilitate focused and systematic research?
- What kinds of materials am I looking for?
- What degree of authority do I need?
- Do I want to only look at peer-reviewed books and academic journals?
- Will I check magazines and newspaper articles?
- Can I access the information online or will I need to find information that is only available in hard copy?
- When I am looking at journal articles, do the names of the same authors keep appearing? (If so, it's probably a good idea to check those names for further information.)
- Am I paying attention to the references lists of the articles I'm reading? Often the best source of prospective texts and journals is the references list at the end of the article.
- Am I finding that new searches are not yielding any new information? (This may be a sign that this particular search is unlikely to provide new ideas and that the search terms or keywords should be changed.)

5.9 READING CRITICALLY WHEN PREPARING AN ANNOTATED BIBLIOGRAPHY

LO 3, 4

The value of the annotated bibliography as a research and writing tool depends on the information it provides. It's important, therefore, that you read the abstract and the article or the text carefully (the abstract is a great aid in reviewing large numbers of documents quickly, but it isn't a substitute for reading the article itself).

It's also important to represent the cited material fairly. While it may be tempting to cite from a reference document selectively, using discrete fragments of information that support your position while ignoring the fact that those fragments clearly do not represent the author's intention, it's a little dishonest to do so (actually, it's very dishonest to do so; it just seemed a bit impolite to state it as strongly as that).

In the following chart, you'll find some questions to guide your analysis of a reference document.

What is the author's thesis or research question? ■ Look at the introduction and the conclusion, the points at which many authors state their respective purposes.
How does the author define the key terms that are used? ■ These key terms in the thesis or research question can help you identify the main point of the article.
How is the text organized? ■ Text organization may help you set up your own bibliography; it is important, however, to avoid the temptation to limit your annotation to a mere list of the contents of the article; even in a summary-style annotation, you need to identify the meaning and the relevance of the information.
What method does the author use to present the argument and the evidence? ■ By identifying the structure of the argument, you may find it easier to contextualize information.
What is the point that the author is making in the respective topic sentence of each paragraph? ■ This is often an index to the purpose of the information in the paragraph.
Are there any sections of the article that provide a summary of the argument (e.g., the abstract, the introduction)?

Remember that you are reading to discover the meaning of the document in its entirety. Though you want to record supporting details, your principal purpose is to summarize the essence of the article, capturing the author's purpose in two or three sentences. It's important, therefore, that you not get lost in the minutiae.

LO 3, 4 5.10 WRITING AN ANNOTATED BIBLIOGRAPHY

The writing of an annotated bibliography should be guided by an awareness of its function. For our purposes, the annotated bibliography is meant to serve as an interface between the reference document and the essay you're writing. That is, it's intended to help with the transfer of information from the source document and the essay, while maintaining a running record of the bibliographical information necessary to document the source properly.

For Each Entry, the Writer Will:
Actively <u>assess</u> the reference, evaluating the information critically. ■ In what way is it relevant to the argument? ■ How does this document compare with other sources of information in the bibliography? ■ Is the information reliable? ■ Does the document demonstrate a bias? Does it have a stated or implicit agenda of its own?

Critically <u>reflect</u> on the reference.
- Does it raise questions about the validity of the thesis?
- Does it lend support to the thesis?
- Where does it fit within your intended argument?
- In what way does it enrich your understanding of the topic?
- Does it agree with, or depart from, the general understanding of the issue in the other articles you've read?

Carefully <u>summarize</u> the reference.
- What is the main thesis of the book or article? How can I summarize the essence of the book or article in fewer than 150 words?
- What are the main arguments?
- What is the scope of the book or article? What topics are covered?
- Does the text address some controversy? Does the author argue for or against a proposition?
- How does the argument of this text compare with others you've reviewed for the annotated bibliography?

Often the easiest way to write a summary is to read the document you're reviewing without taking notes, and then put it away while you compose the first few sentences of the annotation. This allows you to concentrate on the overall meaning of the document without getting lost in the details. In writing an annotation, you're attempting to capture the essence of the article or book. You are not trying to reproduce it in its entirety.

5.11 CONCLUSION

Annotated bibliographies can serve a number of purposes. Sometimes, as is often the case with summary-style annotated bibliographies, you're writing an annotated bibliography to assist you when reviewing the current research in a particular field. On other occasions, you're preparing a systematic analysis of the relationship of individual articles to the general consensus of opinion in the research or scholarly literature. In that case, you would generally prepare an annotated bibliography that foregrounds analysis. And, sometimes, you might be undertaking the exercise because an instructor has asked you to do so (in which case, of course, you defer to the wishes of the instructor and follow the specific directions of the assignment).

When used as a writing tool, annotated bibliographies can help to focus and manage your research process. An annotated bibliography is a list of reference resources that includes three key elements: (1) a summary of the document's content, (2) a brief contextualization of that content, including, in most cases, an evaluation of the significance of the document's contribution to the subject area, and (3) a bibliographic reference for the document. It's usually characterized by brevity (i.e., generally fewer than 150 words). Annotated bibliographies allow you to maintain an organized summary of the references that you've consulted during the research process and to actively reflect on reference material during the research process.

In this chapter, we've suggested that the annotated bibliography might serve yet another purpose. By using the IDDL model to identify the individual aspects of an argument for which you will require support from external authorities, and by using an analytical style of annotated bibliography to identify sources that meet that need, you will be able to create a dialogue between your essay and the reference material. It will create a bridge between the reference source and your essay, allowing you to transfer the supporting documentation more effectively.

MyCompLab®

How Do I Get a Better Grade?

Go to MyCompLab for additional help with your grammar, writing, and research skills. You will have access to a variety of exercises, instruction, and videos that will help you improve your basic skills and help you get a better grade.

 Practice   **An Evaluation Worksheet for Writing Annotated Bibliographies**

Use the questions in the following worksheet when you're preparing an annotated bibliography.

Annotated Bibliography Worksheet

Review and evaluate your own annotated bibliography.

1. Have you identified the format you are expected to use (e.g., APA, MLA, *Chicago* style)?
2. Have you identified the purpose of the annotated bibliography? Is it meant to be a summary or analysis of the document you're annotating? In most cases, if you have not been asked to restrict yourself to a summary, it's a good idea to default to analysis.
3. Have you identified the general thesis of the document? Have you reported on that general thesis or are you trying to use details in a different way than they were used in their original context (i.e., have you used details to support an argument to which the author of the document is demonstrably opposed)?
4. Have you captured the essence of the document in its entirety? Though you might be interested in only one aspect of the author's argument, you're generally obliged to report on the context of the information you're using.
5. Have you written each entry in the annotated bibliography as concisely as possible? Try, at first, to capture the document's meaning in two or three sentences. By imposing a limit on yourself, you are more likely to focus on the author's general purpose and less likely to lose yourself in details.
6. Have you provided enough detail to make the entry useful? Though your primary task is to capture the author's general purpose, it's useful to include some specific details to demonstrate the validity of your interpretation of the document.

7. Have you assessed the authority of the document (i.e., have you determined whether the information is reliable)? Have you reported on your assessment of that authority?

8. Have you provided a complete citation, including all bibliographic information for the document? The annotation will only be useful, both to you and to others, if you've provided enough information that will ensure you or your reader can find the document again.

Practice Exercises for Annotated Bibliographies

In the section below, you will find three fictitious articles. Read each one and prepare an annotated bibliography. In these exercises, you are creating a document that will be useful when you write your essay. The thesis statement provided will help you to identify your writing purpose for the exercise.

Annotated Bibliography Sample Exercise 1 (APA style)

Read the article once and take a moment to reflect on its relevance to the argument being put forth in the thesis statement. Identify the article's principal thesis and then go back and underline the main points of the article.

Thesis Statement: *Governments ought to regulate pollution because pollution poisons the air, poisons the water supply, and endangers the food supply.*

Small-scale Pollution: A Hidden Danger
George Orgood (2009)
Journal of Bio-Systems, volume 6, issue 5, 34–54
        Though environmentalists have historically concerned themselves with large-scale sources of pollution like manufacturing industries, emissions from automobiles with internal combustion engines, and the immoderate use of toxic chemicals, it has become increasingly clear that there is also a significant danger in the daily practices of individuals at a micro level. This article will explore the hidden sources of pollutants that accompany the ordinary citizen's daily practices.
        Environmental pollution refers to a level of contamination of the biospheric and atmospheric systems on Earth to the extent that normal environmental development is adversely affected. Human beings have been contaminating their environment for so many years that the environment can no longer absorb and adapt to changes brought about by human activity. Unfortunately, the effects of long-term polluting only become obvious when the environment cannot process and neutralize the

(*continued*)

(continued)

toxins that are being released. Contrary to the sentiments expressed in the prevailing public discourse, pollution is not a new problem. It predated even the Industrial Revolution, the time when technological progress facilitated the rapid development of manufacturing plants. However, beginning with the Industrial Revolution, there was a rapid growth of industrial production. At the same time, a revolution in efficient business practices led to cheaper production costs, which further fed industrial expansion. That is, as costs went down, businesses were encouraged to increase the levels of production. The level of carbon emissions increased and greater amounts of waste products were pumped into the water systems without any significant regulatory control. Large-scale farming operations have also contributed to air pollution through the ammonia emissions of livestock. The congestion of automobiles in large cities has long been identified as a major source of air pollution.

Pollution can come from a single source like a factory, an oil spill, or farming, but it can also come from individuals changing their car oil and pouring the oil down a drain. A great deal of water pollution does not come from a single source but actually comes from different sources. Sometimes water pollution affects the immediate area of the contamination, like an oil spill, but sometimes the pollution affects the environment kilometres away. There are some people who argue that water pollution is an inevitable part of life on Earth. They point to the conveniences that are enjoyed by people in industrialized countries: flush toilets, washing machines, dishwashers, cars, and airplanes all contribute to the modern lifestyle, but they also contribute to the pollution of water either directly or indirectly. Most people would not be willing to give up their household conveniences even if it meant reducing the amount of pollutants that enter our water systems. It can be argued that Earth's environment is capable of cleaning up some water pollution so there is no need to worry about dumping things down drainage systems. It is true that the Earth can clean up small spills, but that is not the case with large spills.

Water becomes polluted when substances build up to such an extent that they cause problems for humans and animals. A small amount of any substance poured into a water system will not cause major problems because the substance can be harmlessly absorbed into the water. The problem arises when large quantities of a polluting substance are released into an ocean, lake, or stream. The severity of the damage to the water system is determined by the size of the body of water compared to the size of the spill. Water pollutants include insecticides and herbicides, food-processing waste, pollutants from farm operations, organic compounds, heavy metals, and chemical waste.

One of the major pollutants of water is human and animal sewage. As the population increases so does the problem of disposing of sewage waste. According to the Environment for Safe Water, 20 million hectolitres

(440 million gallons) of sewage are dumped each year into the water system in Canada. Some of this waste is treated, but after it leaves the sewage treatment plants there is still waste to be disposed of. Some countries do not have access to sewage treatment plants and their sewage is pumped untreated into their water supplies. Improper sewage disposal affects people's immediate environment and can lead to water-related illnesses such as hepatitis, typhoid, and cholera. These illnesses can kill millions of individuals a year.

When people think of water sources they think of oceans, lakes, rivers, and streams. These are called surface waters, but much of the Earth's water is underground and waters such as these are known as groundwater. Water stored underground feeds the rivers and supplies much of the drinking water. It can become polluted when pesticides and herbicides are used as weed killers in crops and gardens. When it rains or individuals water their gardens, the groundwater can become polluted. A study conducted in Canada in 1999 found that more than half of the groundwater wells were contaminated.

Worksheet for Annotated Bibliography Exercise 1   Practice

Record the necessary bibliographic information for the article.

Identify the writer's principal thesis for the article. Record it below.

Summarize the article in five or six sentences.

Identify any quotations or paraphrases of information that might be useful to you when you write an essay on this subject. Record them below, including the bibliographic information necessary for citations and the references.

✓•─Practice   **Annotated Bibliography Sample Exercise 2 (APA style)**

Write an annotated bibliography entry for the article below. As you did before, you can use the thesis statement provided to identify your writing purpose for this exercise.

Thesis Statement: *Governments ought to regulate pollution because pollution poisons the air, poisons the water supply, and endangers the food supply.*

Environmental Pollution: The Air We Breathe
Brent Walnut and Gregory Oak (2011)
Journal of Safe Air, volume 2, issue 2, 60–75

Dangerous levels of air pollution are appearing in urban settings in the emerging nations due to the dramatic increase in the number of vehicles on the road and the corresponding exhaust emissions. In addition, due to an increased reliance worldwide on a number of time-saving machines like gas water heaters, fireplaces, wood stoves, gas stoves, and gas dryers, the levels of dangerous emissions being released to the atmosphere is growing at a rate not seen since the 1970s. These pollutants are having a profound effect on the health of the population. Humans can be exposed to different air pollutants through inhalation of the harmful chemicals. In studies of air quality, researchers (Barns & Fields, 2008; Grass & Crop, 2010) found that air pollutants contribute to increased mortality and hospital admissions. There are many different compositions of air pollutants and the amount and time of exposure can lead to diverse impacts on human health. Some of the effects can range from nausea and difficulty breathing to skin irritation and cancer. Other effects include birth defects, developmental delays in children, and can also lead to a compromised immune system. Air pollution can have acute and chronic effects on human health and can affect a number of different systems and organs. These can range from minor upper-respiratory irritation to chronic respiratory diseases. There is also a danger that air pollution can cause heart disease, lung cancer, and can lead to acute respiratory infections in children and chronic bronchitis in adults. Air pollution is also a problem for people who suffer from asthma and other respiratory ailments. The short- and long-term exposures to air pollution have been linked with premature mortality and reduced life expectancy.

Sulphur dioxide is one of the many pollutants that can cause air pollution. In people, breathing in sulphur dioxide is generally a moderate to strong irritant that does not penetrate much beyond the nose and throat. There might be minimal amounts that reach the lungs, unless a person is doing physical exercise and breathing heavily through the mouth. However, sensitivity to sulphur dioxide varies among people, and Brown (2008) found that even short exposures (1–5 hours) can cause a decrease in lung function and constriction of the bronchial tubes. In a study with fifty adults, Brown discovered that people who were exposed to low levels of sulphur dioxide (8 ppm) experienced reddening of the throat and mild nose and throat irritation. As Brown increased the level of sulphur dioxide, the participants reported an increase in discomfort. When Brown raised the concentration to over 400 ppm, the participants found that they could no longer take a deep breath. High levels of sulphur dioxide in industrial sites, especially closed areas, can cause severe airway obstruction, a decrease in the oxygen levels of the blood, buildup of fluid in the lungs, and eventually death. The effects of sulphur dioxide poisoning can include coughing and shortness of breath, which can be delayed for hours or even days after the exposure. These symptoms can be increased by physical activity. Prolonged exposure can cause permanent lung damage.

Sulphur dioxide can also cause problems when it comes in contact with skin. The sulphur dioxide reacts with the moisture on the skin and may cause irritation. Symptoms of sulphur dioxide poisoning can include numbness, prickling, and itching. The skin may become white or yellow, and blistering, dead skin, and gangrene may develop in severe cases. Sulphur dioxide can also irritate the eyes. Brown (2008) discovered that the participants in his study experienced mild eye irritation at levels of 8 ppm. As the levels of sulphur dioxide increased, so did the degree of eye irritation. Brown found that increasing sulphur dioxide levels to above 8 ppm caused participants to experience moderate eye discomfort resulting in burning, itching, and running eyes. Prolonged exposure to sulphur dioxide can cause permanent damage to the nerves in the eye, which can lead to blindness caused by corneal burns.

Sulphur dioxide can also cause respiratory problems. In the study carried out by Brown (2008), it was discovered that repeated exposure to low levels (under 8 ppm) of sulphur dioxide caused some pulmonary discomfort. The effects were not permanent on his participants because the participants were not exposed to the sulphur dioxide levels for an extended period of time. However, George (2009) reported that people who work in industries that have low levels of sulphur dioxide emissions (e.g., smelters) had decreased lung function when exposed to sulphur dioxide for over a year. They also experienced a higher incidence of chronic bronchitis.

Another source of concern is carbon monoxide. Carbon monoxide is a colourless, odourless gas that is emitted when fossil fuels are burned. It forms when the carbon in fuels such as gasoline, heating oil, natural gas, wood, and charcoal does not burn completely. Carbon monoxide cannot be seen or smelled but is, nonetheless, dangerous to people's health. Carbon monoxide can reduce oxygen delivery to organs like the heart and

(*continued*)

(*continued*)

brain. At high levels, carbon monoxide can cause illness such as fatigue and stomach problems. Exposure to low levels over a long period of time can cause heart disease and damage to the nervous system. At very high levels, however, carbon monoxide can be life-threatening.

Carbon monoxide enters the bloodstream through the lungs and attaches itself to the blood that carries oxygen to the cells. This works to reduce the amount of oxygen that reaches the body's tissues and organs, especially the heart and brain. Gold (2008) studied the effects of low-level exposure to carbon monoxide on mice. When mice were exposed to low levels of carbon monoxide over a long period, the results indicated that their blood vessels were more constricted than in mice that were not exposed to carbon monoxide. The mice that had been exposed to carbon monoxide also had more problems breathing and had less energy to move around (Gold, 2008). They also, on average, did not live as long as the mice that were not exposed to the carbon monoxide. Howard (2011) conducted a study with twenty participants who lived in a large city and spent a minimum of two hours in traffic each day. Howard observed that daily exposure to carbon monoxide impaired their judgment and reduced their ability to respond rapidly to changes in traffic. The health threat from exposure to carbon monoxide is greatest for those who already suffer from some form of cardiovascular disease. They may experience chest pain and other cardiovascular symptoms if they are exposed to carbon dioxide, particularly while exercising. Exposure to carbon monoxide even for individuals who are in good health can lead to headaches and can affect manual dexterity, mental alertness, ability to work, and vision.

There are viable alternatives to the use of fossil fuels that will not affect air quality or cause health problems. Alternative fuel sources include wind energy, water energy, solar energy, and the use of vegetable oils to create fuel for transportation. The American petroleum industry predicts that by the year 2020, one-third of the world's energy is going to have to come from solar, wind, and other renewable resources. The increasing amount of the dwindling supplies of fossil fuels that are being depleted each year means that renewable resources will become more important as energy sources. Alternative energy sources provide two advantages: they are more sustainable and they have lower carbon emissions than fossil fuels.

The use of solar energy can cut greenhouse gas emissions by 25 percent over the next ten years (Bland, 2012). Solar energy means that there is no acid rain, no urban smog, and no pollution of any kind. This will lead to cleaner air, and cleaner air will lead to fewer health problems for people. Wind power is also an alternative energy source to fossil fuels and it does not cause air pollution. Bland (2012) reported that the cost of wind power has dropped by 20 percent in the last ten years. He predicted that wind power could become one of the main sources of electricity in the near future. Not only is wind power more affordable, it is also pollution-free.

As people begin to realize the effect that fossil fuels have on natural development, and on their health, more alternatives to the dependence on fossil fuels will be developed. Unfortunately, developing alternative energy sources is an expensive proposition right now. Solar energy is a possible alternative but not every country has sustained solar energy that can be harvested on a daily basis. Likewise, not every place can sustain a wind farm. The threat of air pollution and the depletion of fossil fuels are going to necessitate a change in lifestyle if people hope to protect themselves from the harmful effects to their health caused by air pollution.

The negative health effects of air pollutants are a concern for everyone. This is, however, particularly true for those who already have chronic symptoms such as asthma, bronchitis, and heart disease. Even limited exposure to these gases over time can have a negative effect on the health of the public. Control of these emissions ought to be a priority for regulators.

Worksheet for Annotated Bibliography Exercise 2   Practice

Record the necessary bibliographic information for the article.

Identify the writer's principal thesis for the article. Record it below.

Summarize the article in five or six sentences.

Identify any quotations or paraphrases of information that might be useful to you when you're writing an essay on this subject. Record them below, including the bibliographic information necessary for citations and the references.

Annotated Bibliography Sample Exercise 3 (APA style)

Write an annotated bibliography entry for the article below. As you did before, you can use the thesis statement provided to identify your writing purpose for this exercise.

Thesis Statement: *Governments ought to regulate pollution because pollution poisons the air, poisons the water supply, and endangers the food supply.*

Water Pollution: Pollution as an Infection of the Ecosystem
Jessica French and Gertrude Stask (2011)
Journal of Water Safety, volume 4, issue 3, 34–45

Water pollution affects food chains throughout the world. Water sources such as lakes, rivers, streams, creeks, and oceans can become poisoned in a number of different ways, most of which have been well documented in discussions of industrial waste and effluents over the past decades. There was, for instance, the much-publicized disaster in 2010 following an explosion on a deep-sea oil well in the Gulf of Mexico. The resulting oil spill killed more than 6000 animals (Brown, 2011), with the affected species including birds, turtles, and dolphins. In a very short time, the disaster began to adversely affect the local food chain. The death of so many predatory birds led to a spike in fish populations, while the death of so many dolphins resulted in a corresponding decrease in the shark population. Overlooked in the frenzy over large-scale disasters, however, is the incremental increase in the number of pollutants being introduced to the water systems through the deceptively dangerous practices of individuals and small-scale agricultural operations.

In the extreme example cited in the introduction, great slicks of leaking oil mesmerized the international community. Less dramatic, but just as significant, are daily trickles of oil entering the water systems due to the casual disposal of household waste. When pollutants enter water-supply systems like oceans, lakes, rivers, or creeks, those systems become, in a manner of speaking, infected. However, because of the nature of water systems, the infection is not contained. It also affects the surrounding environment, beginning a chain of events that ultimately can result in damage to areas that are geographically connected or to species that are connected through the food chain.

In the first instance, the nature of the contagion effect is initially a result of geographical proximity. As waste is dumped into rivers or streams, it can begin to clog creeks, rivers, and streams. When creeks and streams get clogged, fish are contained and can no longer swim upstream or downstream to spawn. This will generally weaken the local population. Household garbage, particularly plastics, creates its own hazard to the local population. Plastics, which take an enormous amount of time to break down, remain in the environment long after disposal. Animals frequently fail to discriminate about the things they swallow, generally eating first and regurgitating what cannot be digested later. When eaten, plastics can cause a blockage in the digestive system of fish. In addition, fish and other animals that live in water systems can become trapped by plastics. Items, such as the rings used to hold cans together, can get stuck around animals' mouths, making them unable to eat and thus causing them to starve to death. Plastic items can also get stuck around the neck of the animals in the water and cause them to choke to death or to starve because they cannot hunt. Metal, rope, nets, and Styrofoam are similarly harmful to aquatic wildlife. Finally, depending on the amount of garbage dumped into the water, waste can also lead to the blockage of sunlight and the death of plant life that lives in the water. As plants die, the animals that depend on plants for food also begin to die, leading to a series of events that will impact the entire food chain.

The second line of infection is one that runs through the food chain. Plants such as vegetables, crops, and trees become contaminated with the pollutants from the environment through their roots. When the ground-water is polluted, the crops that get nutrients from the polluted water also become polluted. When fish or other prey animals become infected, the population of predators that depend on those prey animals also suffers. There are also a number of pollutants that introduce toxins that can cause problems for animals at the top of the food chain. Apex marine animals are exposed to higher levels of toxins because they get toxins both from the water and from eating fish exposed to the toxins in the water. Marine mammals that rely on their blubber to regulate their body temperatures suffer when the blubber gets contaminated from toxins and the animals have a harder time regulating their body temperature. Bird populations may also be affected by the absence of prey and the transmission of toxins through the food chain.

This is the nature of water-borne pollution. It will not be contained. It moves beyond the immediate site to which the pollutants are introduced, drifting through the ecosystem, following a course through the connecting streams, rivers, lakes, and seas of a water system and through the hierarchy of a food chain.

✓● Practice   **Worksheet for Annotated Bibliography Exercise 3**

Record the necessary bibliographic information for the article.

Identify the writer's principal thesis for the article. Record it below.

Summarize the article in five or six sentences.

Identify any quotations or paraphrases of information that might be useful to you when you're writing an essay on this subject. Record them below, including the bibliographic information necessary for citations and the references.

Use the following worksheet to assess annotations of a classmate. Think about the purpose of the annotations as you're reviewing. They are meant to provide enough information to allow you to determine the value and relevance of the article to which they refer.

✓● Practice   **Peer-Evaluation Worksheet for Annotated Bibliographies**

Title of the Essay _____

Annotated Bibliography Submitted By: _____

Peer Evaluator: _____

Thesis Statement: _____

_____

_____

Based on your understanding of the essay's arguable proposition, what evidence is needed to support the argument?

_____

_____

_____

Annotated Entry # _____ Title of Source Material:	
How does this source strengthen the argument being put forth? In what way is it relevant to the issue?	
How well has the writer of the annotation summarized the article? Are you able to understand the general theme of the article?	
In what way has the writer identified the article's main ideas?	
What analysis of the original article has the writer provided?	
Annotated Entry # _____ Title of Source Material:	
How does this source strengthen the argument being put forth? In what way is it relevant to the issue?	
How well has the writer of the annotation summarized the article? Are you able to understand the general theme of the article?	

(_continued_)

(continued)

In what way has the writer identified the article's main ideas?	
What analysis of the original article has the writer provided?	
Annotated Entry # _____ **Title of Source Material:**	
How does this source strengthen the argument being put forth? In what way is it relevant to the issue?	
How well has the writer of the annotation summarized the article? Are you able to understand the general theme of the article?	
In what way has the writer identified the article's main ideas?	
What analysis of the original article has the writer provided?	

CHAPTER 6

The Importance of Authoritative Sources

Learning Objectives

At the completion of this chapter, you will be able to:

1. Identify the differences between the ways in which novice and experienced writers select sources.
2. Demonstrate the ability to select authoritative sources.
3. Demonstrate the ability to introduce sources to your essay effectively.
4. Demonstrate the ability to cite sources.

6.1 EVIDENCE AND THE ARGUMENTATIVE ESSAY

In Chapter 2, we discussed some of the important differences between writing in high school and writing in college or university. One of those differences was the importance of learning to write an argumentative essay (if you are unsure of what is meant by argumentative essay, go back to Chapter 3 for a more detailed explanation than we will give here). In Chapter 3, we defined the argumentative essay as one in which the conclusion is logically linked to the evidence. In writing an argumentative essay, you're expected to do more than simply summarize the information or discuss an issue from your own perspective (unless, of course, you happen to be an authority on the topic). When marking argumentative essays, instructors are generally going to assign significant weight to your demonstrated ability to reason from good evidence to a conclusion.

Of course, you're also expected to introduce evidence in such a way as to indicate its relevance to the argument you're making. In this chapter, we discuss the importance of incorporating evidence into your essay. We will also review different ways in which the evidence can be introduced into the essay, and we will identify the relative advantages of quotations, paraphrases, and summaries.

LO 1 6.2 DIFFERENCES BETWEEN NOVICE AND EXPERIENCED WRITERS IN THE SELECTION OF EVIDENCE

The following chart identifies the specific difference between novice and experienced writers in the selection of supporting evidence. Where novice writers often gather information that is only tangentially connected to a general topic, experienced writers work more purposefully, using the arguable proposition to identify the specific information they need and, by extension, the most useful source of that information.

Novice Writers	**Experienced Writers**
■ Require thought for procedural, or "mechanical," writing functions.	■ Have, to a significant degree, automated procedural functions.
■ Focus on error avoidance rather than meaning.	■ Focus on developing or refining meaning.
■ Begin writing without planning, and edit, if at all, for grammatical errors.	■ Invest time and energy in planning and reviewing.
■ *Focus on "knowledge telling" (i.e., relating all the information they have and can find on a topic, rather than exercising critical judgment to determine relevance).*	■ *Organize, and reorganize, essay structure to allow individual ideas to serve the overall purpose of the essay.*

As we've noted elsewhere, the greatest advantage that experienced writers have over novice writers is that experienced writers have learned to make decisions at particular points in their writing process through years of practice. Their abilities to make provisional judgments about the relevance and authority of particular kinds of evidence derive from their ability to recognize certain cues. The bad news is that many novice writers don't recognize those cues. The good news is that the recognition of the cues can be taught. In this chapter, we identify some of the ways in which you can learn to select authoritative evidence on the basis of your essay's purpose. One of those ways is to use the arguable proposition to identify the specific information you need.

6.3 USING THE ARGUABLE PROPOSITION TO GUIDE RESEARCH

LO 1, 2

In Chapter 3, we discussed the importance of making a clear and specific arguable claim (an arguable claim is a statement that clearly articulates the claim being made and provides the reasons for that claim). When you're thinking about the sort of evidence you need, you should be guided by the claim you've made.

- What do you have to prove?
- How are you going to prove it?

Your claim has to be supported by evidence. However, you can't simply collect materials filled with facts. If you don't undertake your research carefully and critically, your paper becomes a dumping ground for information that may, or may not, be relevant to the argument you're making. In addition (and this might be the best selling point for reading this chapter carefully), research is easier to do when you have a clear understanding of what it is you're looking for. Experienced writers will usually spend more time developing their arguments than novice writers do, but, in return, experienced writers will find their research to be more rewarding. It's easier to find something when you know what you're looking for.

The following chart will help guide you in making decisions about the kinds of information you need to explore your thesis.

Making Writing Decisions	About Using Your Arguable Claim to Guide Your Search for Authoritative Evidence

What is the purpose of this writing decision?

The more specific you are in identifying your arguable claim, the easier it will be to identify the kind of authority you need.

What is the effect of this writing decision?

If the arguable claim tells you the kind of authority you need to support a claim, it also narrows your focus during the research process. It allows you to seek out supporting resources more effectively.

What considerations inform this decision?

In order to use your arguable claim to guide your research, you must first ensure that the claim is specific and, in some way, measurable.

Suggested strategies for making this decision.

Identify the claims that you're making in your argument. Are they claims that can be proven? What evidence is needed to prove them? What is the best source of evidence? Who has the greatest authority in this area?

Questions to guide decision making in your own essay.

1. Reread your arguable proposition. Is the claim specific? Is the claim measurable? If not, refine the claim until you know exactly what you mean to prove and how you mean to prove it.

2. Identify the specific reasons you've offered in support of the claim. For each reason, determine what evidence is needed to substantiate the claim.
3. Think about the evidence that's needed to substantiate each claim. What source of information provides the greatest authority?
4. Seek out that authoritative evidence for each reason. If you're unable to find reliable and authoritative evidence in support of a particular reason, you may want to consider whether or not the reason is a good one.

LO 1, 2

6.4 WHY WRITERS NEED AUTHORITATIVE SOURCES

In the introduction to this chapter, we observed that most instructors evaluate argumentative essays by assessing the degree to which a student has demonstrated the ability to reason from good evidence to a logical conclusion. The "good" evidence part is important. If you're going to take the time to search for evidence in the first place, why not look for good evidence? Weak evidence may satisfy the word count, but it doesn't improve the argument. If you remember (1) that your purpose in seeking evidence is to strengthen your position, and (2) that readers aren't going to simply take you at your word (however much you think they ought to do so), you'll recognize the importance of taking a moment or two to assess the quality of the evidence you've selected. Think about it this way. Let's say that during your visit to the playground, the neighbourhood bully pushed you to the ground and stole your hat. In order to persuade the bully to return the hat, you go home looking for something, or someone, to strengthen your position. Are you going to bring a younger, smaller sibling back to the playground or are you going to bring your older, bigger sibling? In most cases, the larger sibling will be more convincing. Similarly, since your purpose in looking for evidence is to increase the likelihood that your reader will accept your argument, you want the best evidence you can find.

LO 1, 2

6.5 CRITICAL READING

When you're looking for evidence, you need to be aware that all texts are written with their own specific purpose in mind. That is, every text is written from a particular perspective. In much the same way that you're writing to convince your reader of the validity of a particular point of view, so the writer of the text you've chosen as evidence has argued from his or her own perspective. Here's the treacherous thing: good writers can make bad ideas seem reasonable, independent of the merit of their argument. You're too clever to fall for that. When you're examining resource materials, you need to train yourself to separate the power of a writer's rhetoric from the validity of the writer's argument.

In the following chart, we've provided some suggestions to guide your critical reading process. Each of the questions derives from a larger, more general question: On what basis has the author arrived at his or her conclusion?

Questions to Consider When Reading Source Material
1. What is the author's purpose in writing this article (i.e., what is he or she attempting to prove)?
2. Has the author provided reasons in support of the position she or he has chosen?
3. Does the author identify competing views?
4. Is the author's argument based on factual evidence, professional experience, personal opinion, or personal experience?
5. Is the argument logical? Can you follow the author's train of thought?
6. What are the author's credentials and how are they relevant to the topic? Sadly, many intelligent and well-educated individuals comment on issues in which they have no expertise, believing that their intelligence and education applies equally to all subjects. It doesn't. When an individual is writing within the field of his or her expertise, that individual is generally speaking authoritatively. When an individual is writing about matters beyond the field of his or her expertise, that individual is often expressing an opinion.
7. What evidence can I use from this article to support my argument? Have I taken the evidence out of context? Have I interpreted the evidence fairly or have I misrepresented the author's intent?
8. Which of the author's points do I agree with? Why? Do I agree with the author because the author agrees with me or have I been convinced on the basis of the author's evidence and reasoning? Is there some information missing that would have been useful to know?

6.6   WHAT CONSTITUTES GOOD EVIDENCE?

LO 1, 2

The purpose of an argumentative essay is to convince the reader of your point of view on the basis of evidence. It, therefore, follows that the writer should seek out the best, or most authoritative, evidence. Sometimes, however, it's hard to tell whether a source is authoritative or not. Writers learn that through experience. The world you occupy provides you with cues that aid you in your decision making. Your experience tells you that it's probably a bad idea to stick your hand in a fire or to pet a mountain lion. You've made a general rule based on your general experience in life. Now, it might happen that the mountain lion has been domesticated or is naturally gentle, but the rule is still a good one (by the way, there are fewer exceptions to the rule about sticking your hand in the fire; *that* is almost always a mistake). Unfortunately, when novice writers are looking for evidence, they may not have had enough experience in conducting research to develop the cues that will guide them effectively. As a result, they turn to information sites that are the intellectual equivalent of a guy selling knock-off wristwatches from a briefcase in an alley. In this section, we've provided some rough guidelines to assist you in identifying the best sources of information.

6.6.1 Weak Evidence and Strong Evidence

Not all evidence is created equal. If, as we've suggested, evidence is meant to carry the weight of your argument, you might say that some types of evidence are better suited to the task than others. Some sources of evidence that you may want to be a little nervous about are intuition, personal experience, and anecdotes, testimonials, or hearsay.

Types of Evidence	Degree of Reliability and Authority
Intuition	Intuition is a "gut feeling." It's surprisingly effective in guiding you away from danger (the explanation for that phenomenon is fascinating but, sadly, too complicated for a parenthetical aside), but it's difficult to quantify. It also tends to be more convincing to those to whom the insight belongs than it does to the rest of us.
Personal Experience	Like intuition, the advantage of personal experience as evidence is that it's very convincing to those who've had the experience. Like intuition again, however, it's less convincing to those who are only hearing about the experience. Sadly, your reader is not likely to take your word as evidence.
Anecdotes/ Testimonials/ Hearsay	Evidence that derives from anecdotes, testimonials, or hearsay is, more or less, personal experience once removed. If your readers are reluctant to take your word as evidence, they're even less likely to be swayed by the recollections of some guy you met on your trip to Montana.

There are still other ways in which evidence might disappoint you. Many unfocused searches for supporting evidence result in the discovery of information that is both scholarly and reliable but, sadly, not relevant. It's like finding a shirt that looks good on the hanger and taking it home, only to discover that it makes you look as pale as the underbelly of a dead fish. There's nothing wrong with the shirt and, heaven knows, there's nothing wrong with you. It's just that the two of you together, well, the two of you don't work.

Example of Evidence That Is Authoritative but Irrelevant

Subthesis: *Talking on a hand-held cell phone while operating a vehicle is not a safe practice because it can result in driver inattention.*

The evidence is authoritative but not relevant to the claim being made.

The use of hand-held cell phones is not a safe practice because of the emission of high-frequency electrical waves and the proximity of the device to the user's brain. Though the degree of danger has not yet been determined definitively, there is no question that the use of cell phones may pose an unnecessary risk. A study on the use of cell phones indicates that people are at higher risk of developing brain cancer when they use a hand-held cell phone (Holmes, 2012). While some might argue that it is premature to recommend that individuals respond to a risk that has not been verified, the potential for profound health problems among a great number of cell phone users is too great a danger for policy makers to ignore.

Consider the relevance of the evidence in this example to the argument it is meant to support. While the example offers authoritative evidence of the dangers of cell phone usage, it does not support the particular claim that is being made in the subthesis. The risk it identifies is an illness that may occur in the future to cell phone users regardless of the degree to which they engage in the practice of speaking on cell phones while driving. The question you're asking yourself is the same one that readers might ask: What does the possible connection between cell phone use and brain cancer have to do with driver inattention?

In contrast, the evidence offered in the following example is both authoritative and relevant.

> ## Example of Evidence That Is Authoritative and Relevant
>
> **Subthesis:** *Talking on a hand-held cell phone while operating a vehicle is not a safe practice because it can result in driver inattention.*
>
> The use of hand-held cell phones while operating a vehicle is inherently unsafe because of the effect it has on the driver's capacity to pay attention to the road. In addition to more obvious problems (e.g., drivers attempting to manipulate the phone while driving), the simple fact that drivers are talking while driving generally results in a lack of focus. That is, the driver's attention is divided between the traffic ahead and the conversation that is being conducted. This has the effect of impairing a driver's judgment, often leading to situations in which the driver fails to recognize that traffic has slowed or stopped until it is too late for the driver to avoid an accident. A recent study found that drivers who use hand-held cell phones are three times more likely to get into a traffic accident than people who do not use cell phones while driving (Constable, 2012). Operating a motor vehicle demands strict attention to the emerging traffic circumstances. That attention is impossible to maintain when drivers attempt to focus on both the use of their cell phones and the road conditions.

Supports the argument that the use of cell phones while driving can lead to accidents.

Where the first example offered evidence that the use of cell phones may be hazardous to individuals who may or may not be operating a motor vehicle, the second example provides evidence that speaks directly to the claim being made. It is both authoritative and relevant.

6.6.2 Authoritative Sources of Evidence

For the purposes of academic writing, authoritative sources are those individuals or groups who, by virtue of their respective expertise, are best qualified to comment on the phenomenon in question. Admittedly, that seems a little vague. It's difficult to say whether a particular resource is appropriate as a reference without looking at the context of the specific writing situation, In part, the suitability of the resource will depend on the writer's purpose. However, based on our understanding of the purpose of the academic essay (i.e., to convince the reader on the basis of evidence), we can formulate a general guideline: it is usually the case that the most authoritative resources will come from those relatively objective commentators who have the greatest expertise in the subject.

6.6.3 Evaluating the Authority of Sources

Developing the ability to judge the authority of the sources is one of the many challenges novices face in their development as academic writers. This task is further complicated by the sheer volume of information that's available in journal articles, books, and electronic formats. If, for example, you were to enter the keywords *cell phones* and *driving* in the Google search engine, you would, within seconds, receive links to more than 52 million sites. Of course, some of the information isn't applicable, useful, or accurate. It's not enough, therefore, to glance through the first journal you find or click on the first three random sites that appeared in a Google search. You have to be able to evaluate the information you find.

In the following chart, we've identified some of the things you might want to consider when assessing a resource's authority, relevance, and objectivity.

1. Things to Consider about the Author

Credentials
- What are the author's credentials?
- What is the author's institutional affiliation, educational background, publishing history (i.e., a list of other publications), or experience?
- Are details of the author's qualifications or the organizations they are associated with provided with the article?

Expertise
- Is the book or article written on a topic in the author's area of expertise? When authors write in an area in which they have no expertise, the opinions expressed may be less authoritative.

Audience
- What type of audience is the author addressing?
- Is the publication aimed at a specialized or general audience? In most cases, books and journals that are intended for specialized audiences provide information that is more specific and more authoritative.

Point of view
- Recognize the point of view of the author and assess it accordingly.
- Is the information based on fact, opinion, or propaganda?
- Does the information appear to be valid and well researched, or is it questionable and unsupported by evidence?
- Are the ideas and arguments advanced in line with other works on the same topic?
- What point of view does the author represent? Is the article an editorial that is trying to argue a position?
- Is the text or article associated with a company or organization that advocates a certain philosophy?
- Is the article published in a magazine that has a particular editorial position?
- Though a specific viewpoint does not, necessarily, render a resource invalid or unreliable, it's important to consider that perceived bias when judging the work.
- The perceived bias of a particular reference should always be acknowledged in one's evaluation of the reference (i.e., the bias should be noted in the paper).

2. Date of Publication

- When was the source published? The date is often located on the face of the title page, below the name of the publisher, or on the reverse of the title page. Recent publications, even those that are dealing with historic events, tend to reflect contemporary scholarly views.
- In general, more recent information is considered to be more authoritative.
- However, if the thesis requires an investigation of the views or ideas that were prevalent at a particular time, one might choose to use historical documents.
- If you're looking at a website, when was it last updated?

3. Publisher

- Consider the publisher. If the source is published by a university press, it's likely to be scholarly.
- An academic press adds its authority to the authority of the writer.

4. Title of Journal

- The title of a journal may indicate if the publication is a scholarly journal or a popular journal. This distinction is important because it indicates different levels of complexity in conveying ideas.
- Scholarly journals are generally preferred for academic writing.

5. Scope of the Content

What is the breadth of the article or book?
- Is it a general work that provides an overview of the topic or is it specifically focused on only one aspect of the topic?
- Does the resource cover the right time period?

6.7 MAKING WRITING DECISIONS ABOUT SELECTING EVIDENCE

LO 1, 2

Remember that your research purpose is to discover information that is *reliable* and *relevant*. The ability to sift through the pile and find that information is, therefore, an important one. The following chart provides a series of questions that you can use to evaluate the authority of evidence for your own essay.

Making Writing Decisions | About Selecting Evidence for Your Own Essay

---

What is the purpose of this writing decision?

The purpose of systematically challenging the authority of your own evidence is to ensure that it will stand up to the scrutiny of the reader.

What is the effect of this writing decision?

Challenging your own evidence for its relevance and authority leads to a more purposeful selection of supporting resources. Let's face it. If you're not entirely certain you can trust your sources, it's not really fair to expect your reader to do so.

What considerations inform this decision?

Remember that the purpose of supporting evidence is not simply to satisfy an instructor's expectation or a formal requirement. You've sought out supporting evidence to persuade the reader that your argument is reasonable. If you think about your purpose, you're more likely to challenge yourself to find the most authoritative evidence available.

Suggested strategies for making this decision.

Use the questions in the previous chart to interrogate your own sources of evidence. Ask yourself, for example, whether you accept the authority of the author of the research you're using. Ask yourself whether the work is sufficiently current to be reliable and persuasive. Ask yourself whether the document demonstrates a bias.

Questions to guide decision making in your own essay.

1. Think about the essay you're working on now. You've made specific claims and your reader, reasonably enough, expects you to substantiate those claims. Read over your arguable proposition, looking at the claim you've made and the reasons for that claim.

2. What evidence have you provided in support of the first reason? Is the source relevant? Is the source authoritative? In what way does the source demonstrate its authority?

3. Follow the same process for each of the reasons you provide in support of your claim.

4. We shouldn't really have to say this, but we will: we've never met a writer who didn't allow himself or herself to be persuaded of the authority of evidence simply because that evidence supported a particular point of view. Wrestle against the inclination to accept evidence that is not authoritative just because it agrees with you.

6.7.1 Scholarly Resources

In the section above, you may have noticed that scholarly resources are usually preferred for academic writing. There are a number of reasons for that preference. Scholarly resources (journals, periodicals, scholarly texts) are those that:

- Are written by experts in a field.
- Have undergone peer review (i.e., the articles or books have been evaluated by other experts in the field).
- Have been judged to have followed the accepted research protocols of the field.
- Have been judged either to reflect the current understanding of experts in the field or to represent a dissenting opinion that is recognized, nonetheless, as being reasonable.

The advantage of using peer-reviewed resources is a significant one. Before a scholar's work is published, it undergoes examination by other experts to determine whether it demonstrates the required rigour for the field. That is, other scholars assess the work to ensure that it meets the standard for scholarship in the discipline. In effect, a resource that has survived the scrutiny of the peer-review process has both the authority of the scholar who produced it and the authority of those who judged it to be worthy of publication.

In addition to the authority provided by peer review, scholarly resources also provide writers with access to other relevant articles on a particular subject. Because scholarly articles generally include a concise summary of the current research on the question that's being examined, they eliminate the need for the writer to begin his or her own investigation at the most preliminary stage.

Advantages of Scholarly Resources
1. Scholarly resources are assumed to represent the findings of objective, or unbiased, investigators.
2. Scholars follow accepted practices of investigation.
3. Scholarly articles have usually undergone peer review by other scholars.
4. Scholars are expected to report findings in precise terms, limit their conclusions to that which has been proven, and identify areas in which the research has been inconclusive.
5. Scholarly articles generally locate the author's work within the larger context of scholarship on the particular subject.

6.7.2 How Do Scholarly Sources Differ from Newspapers or Magazines?

Historically, the majority of mainstream news-gathering organizations have prided themselves on their accuracy and reliability. For the most part, that pride is well deserved. Reporters and editors have worked hard to uncover and package news stories as those stories have emerged from the rapidly changing events of day-to-day history. By their very nature, however, those stories reflected incomplete pictures of phenomena that were not yet completely understood. Newspapers and news magazines tend to report events as they occur, provisionally offering interpretations that make sense based on the information available at the time (i.e., newspapers and news magazines often do not have the luxury of considering a particular event in the larger context of historical patterns). News reporters provide current information on events as they are occurring. Because the event is still unfolding, we don't yet recognize the significance of the information. Because they might be called upon to cover any number of different events, reporters must possess general knowledge on a broad range of topics. They are usually not meant to be experts in any particular field but, rather, well versed in a number of fields.

If you watch twenty-four-hour news channels, you may have noticed that they report stories in which cats are stuck in trees with the same degree of gravity and concern that they do a national catastrophe. They can't help themselves. There are days, apparently, when nothing of note happens. Scholars, on the other hand, have often been investigating one particular phenomenon for their entire careers and are, therefore, better able to comment on subjects within their respective fields in greater depth and with a greater appreciation of the aspects that are noteworthy.

In the following chart, we've outlined some of the differences between scholarly sources, magazines, and newspapers. This brief overview of the three different types of sources is designed to provide you with an understanding of some of the defining characteristics of each.

	Scholarly Sources	Magazines	Newspapers
Format	Articles are written using an established format and usually published quarterly, semi-annually, or annually. They sometimes include charts and graphs but less frequently include pictures (the exceptions would be those publications in which visual representations are necessary). The typeface is usually standardized and the type is usually black on white paper. There are usually no advertisements in articles.	Articles are often short (one or two pages), with slick, glossy layouts and full-colour photos. Magazines are usually published monthly. Magazines have advertisements.	Articles tend to be relatively short. Newspapers are usually published daily. They are generally produced on cheap paper. They include some use of colour for emphasis, but the majority of the paper is in black and white. Newspapers have advertisements.
Sources	Scholarly articles are generally expected to make use of scholarly sources, which are cited both within the article and on a references page at the end of the paper.	Though they may include references to other sources, magazine articles rarely include the citation of sources as evidence. When they do so, the sources are not usually scholarly.	Newspapers articles may include some references to sources, but those sources are usually not scholarly. Because the articles generally refer to events as they occur, they may not provide a context for the information they report.

(*continued*)

(continued)

Authors	The authors are experts in a field. Articles are usually written for other scholars in the same area.	Articles are written by staff writers or freelance writers. The articles are targeted to a wide audience.	Articles are written by reporters, staff writers, or freelance writers, and are intended for a wide audience.
Language	The language tends to be formal and specific to a particular academic discipline. The language may be complex, as it is directed to scholars in the same field of study.	The language is generally meant to be engaging and entertaining, using diction that is accessible to a diverse set of readers.	The language tends to be direct. It's meant to be simple, easy to read, and easy to understand.
Purpose	The purpose of a scholarly article is to inform and/or report on original research. It contributes to the scholarly community.	The purpose of a magazine article is to entertain, enlighten, or persuade.	The purpose is to provide timely information to an interested audience.
Publishers	Scholarly periodicals are generally published by professional non-profit organizations.	Magazines are generally published for profit.	Newspapers are generally published for profit.

The chart identifies a number of important differences between the various sources of information. The first is a difference in audience, with a corresponding difference in purpose and tone. Because scholarly publications are intended for an academic audience, they tend to use language that is formal and specific to a particular discipline. They also tend to be more concerned with adherence to a particular format and less concerned with the aesthetic appeal of the page. Finally, scholarly publications usually consist of articles that explore a particular subject in depth. Magazines, on the other hand, are generally intended to inform and entertain a general audience, a fact that is reflected in a greater concern both with the aesthetic appeal of the page and with language that is accessible to the general public. Newspapers are also intended for consumption by a general readership and, thus, must use language that is accessible. In addition, because newspapers generally report on events as they happen, the analysis they offer is conditional. As new information becomes available, the analysis may change. Finally, magazines and newspapers are, directly or indirectly, dependent on readership for their economic survival. The way in which they present information reflects their need to appeal to a broad audience.

LO 1, 2

6.8   ASSESSING THE AUTHORITY OF INFORMATION ON THE INTERNET

The internet provides access to a volume of information that would have been unthinkable even ten years ago. Unfortunately, much of it is incomplete or simply wrong. It's important, therefore, to remember that much of the information on the internet is neither scholarly nor authoritative. Because the internet doesn't require an evaluation of either the contributing author or the information that's being posted, it's more difficult for readers to assess the validity of the information they find.

In addition, the information on the internet is fluid (i.e., the information is easily altered, and, in many cases, there's no guarantee that the evidence on which one could build an argument will exist in the same form when one returns to the site). Wikipedia, for example, permits users to alter entries on an ongoing basis. While the use of Wikipedia to gain an overall understanding of a particular topic is often a good strategy, you should probably resist the temptation to use it as your only source.

6.8.1 Guidelines for Assessing Authority on the Internet

There are some general rules to follow when assessing the authority of internet websites. Sites that are attached to government agencies or universities and colleges are generally examined carefully and, thus, tend to be reliable. In addition, scholarly articles that have been published electronically have undergone the scrutiny of peer evaluation. They have the same authority as those that have been printed in print journals.

What follows are general principles to consider when doing research on the internet. Before you use the information you find on the internet, use the questions in this table to assess its reliability.

1. Who is the author and is the author an authority in the field?
Author's Credentials   When looking at articles on the internet, check for the author's credentials. Ask yourself the following questions: ■ Is the author identified?   ■ What is the author's expertise and/or credentials (i.e., education, experience, position, etc.)?   ■ Is the author qualified to write this information?   ■ With what institution or organization is the author connected?   **Accuracy of Information**   ■ Can the information be verified by other sources?   ■ Does the author cite the sources of information used?   ■ Does the article seem to be well researched?
2. Who is the intended audience?
■ Is the article addressed to those who are already convinced of its conclusion, or does it appear to be intended to speak to a wider audience?
3. Is the site relatively objective?
■ What is the bias of the site?   ■ Are multiple viewpoints presented?   ■ Is the information presented as fact or opinion?   ■ What organization sponsors or hosts the web page?   ■ Does the host or sponsor hold a particular view or opinion?   ■ What is their purpose in sponsoring the web page?

(continued)

(continued)

4. How current is the site?
■ When was the information on the page produced? ■ When was the web page itself produced? ■ When was it updated? ■ Are any links on the page kept up-to-date?
5. How comprehensive is the site in its coverage of the topic?
■ What is included and what is not included? ■ Does it provide information in all areas it claims to cover? ■ Is the information uniformly complete for all areas or is it uneven? ■ If there are links, what are the criteria for including them in the site? ■ Are the links evaluated?

6.8.2 Making Writing Decisions about Assessing Evidence on the Internet

In the following chart, you'll find a brief discussion of the factors to consider when you're assessing the authority of information that you find on the internet. Use the questions at the bottom of the chart to ensure that you're comfortable with the authority of the evidence you're using.

Making Writing Decisions	About Selecting Evidence from the Internet for Your Own Essay

What is the purpose of this writing decision?

The internet is a treacherous ally. It provides access to a volume of information that would have been unimaginable even a decade ago. Unfortunately, some of that information has been posted by individuals who, in the most generous analysis, are not reliable. When you're using information from the internet, you must be particularly careful to ensure that it's accurate and authoritative.

What is the effect of this writing decision?

The first concern that you ought to have when using material that you've found on the internet is one that derives from the internet's role in modern urban legends. It's easy to be misled by exciting ideas that emerge on the internet, and, unfortunately, easy to appear gullible because you've done so. The careless acceptance of unsubstantiated claims from the internet diminishes your authority.

What considerations inform this decision?

Think about all of the factors that undermine the authority of the information on the internet (e.g., questions about the reliability of the author, the accuracy of the information, and the objectivity of the site). How can you ensure that the information on which you're basing your argument is reliable and authoritative, and how can you convince your reader that the information is reliable and authoritative?

Suggested strategies for making this decision.

Use the questions in the chart in section 6.6.3 to interrogate your own sources of evidence. How do you determine the author's credentials on the internet? Is the site attached to a reliable institution or entity? Is the information on the site relatively stable or does it change frequently (e.g., Wikipedia)?

Questions to guide decision making in your own essay.

1. Return to the essay you're working on and look at the claims you've made. Do any of those claims rest entirely on information that's come from a single internet site? If so, you need to scrutinize that site most carefully.

2. Look at the other claims that have been supported by information on the internet and think again about the factors that affect the reliability of information on the internet. If the information comes from an online academic journal, you can assume that it will have the same authority as information that would come from any other academic journal. If the information comes from a university or government site but has no author attached to it, it's probably reliable but it's often less authoritative.

3. Think carefully about using any information that cannot be verified elsewhere.

4. Be particularly critical of any information that you derive from an advocacy site, a commercial site, or a political action site. The information is not necessarily incorrect but, by their very nature, these sites operate with a bias.

5. Do not mistake rhetorical brilliance for a guarantee of accuracy. Just because an idea, or series of ideas, has been well expressed, you cannot assume that it's accurate. Similarly, you cannot assume that the author is an authority simply because he or she writes well.

6.9 WHERE TO PLACE EVIDENCE IN YOUR PAPER

LO 3, 4

You have to remember that the purpose of evidence is to enhance the quality of the argument you're making. As we've mentioned before, you don't conduct research merely to satisfy a formal requirement of an instructor or a particular writing format. You include evidence to prove a particular point, and it's important, therefore, that you connect the evidence to the point to which it refers. One of the characteristics of novice writers is the tendency some have to dump information on the page. That strategy is not as helpful as you may think. Including information for the sake of including information doesn't make your argument stronger. However, demonstrating the way in which your evidence leads to a particular conclusion does.

6.9.1 Introducing External Sources to Your Essay

There are several ways in which you can introduce external ideas to your work:

6.9.1.1 Direct Quotations Direct quotations are exact, word-for-word, copies of the content and the phrasing of the original source. A direct quotation uses the source's spelling, capitalization, and punctuation, and is generally identified by the presence of quotation marks at the beginning and end of the quotation.

There are a number of advantages to using a direct quotation. A direct quotation speaks with the authority of the original and it sometimes includes the expression of an idea that is too brilliant to be passed over. You should, however, use direct quotations with caution. They should not be used to replace your own ideas or analysis and should only be used when they connect directly to a point you are making. The reader should not have to guess about the relevance of the quotation.

Direct quotations should be introduced to the text carefully. They usually require a phrase that signals their arrival to the reader.

Words you can use to signal to your reader that you're using a direct quotation (the tense will depend on the formatting convention you're using).	Smith _____: notes(d), argues(d), observes(d), writes/wrote, emphasizes(d), says/said, reports(ed), suggests(ed), claims(ed), remarks(ed), declares(d), states(d), affirms(ed), asserts(ed), maintains(ed), testifies(d), contends(ed), reasons(ed), concludes(d), believes(d), understands/understood, finds/found, describes(d), discovers(ed), determines(d), realizes(d), notices(d), articulates(d)

In the boxes that follow, we've included two examples in which the writer has used direct quotations. One is more effective than the other.

Example of an Ineffective Way to Introduce a Direct Quotation

Driving while talking on a cell phone is a dangerous habit for any driver. "When teenagers talk on their cell-phones while driving, their ability to pay attention to the road is compromised" (Minnie, 2012, p. 45). Accidents can cause harm to the driver, the passenger, a pedestrian, an animal, or another driver.

In the example above, the writer has introduced a direct quotation without taking the time to integrate it. The writer has simply dropped the quotation into the paragraph without making any connection between it and the surrounding text.

Example of an Effective Way to Introduce a Direct Quotation

Driving while talking on a cell phone is a dangerous habit for any driver. This is, however, particularly true for young drivers. Minnie (2012) observed that "when a teenager attempts to drive while talking on a cell-phone his or her ability to pay attention to the road is severely compromised" (p. 45). Inexperienced drivers, like teens, often have greater trouble driving while distracted because they have to pay much closer attention to the operation of the car. Their driving skills have not yet become automatized.

This example demonstrates a more effective way to introduce a direct quotation to the essay. The writer has established the quotation using the author's name, with the date in parentheses, and the words *observed that*. More importantly, the writer has integrated the quotation into the essay, demonstrating its relevance to the text around it.

6.9.1.2 Block Quotations   Block quotations are direct quotations that are longer than forty words (APA format), or longer than four sentences (MLA format). In APA format, when a quotation is longer than forty words, it's indented and double-spaced. You don't use quotation marks, and you place a period at the end of the quotation. The page number comes after the period and should be placed in brackets—e.g., (p. 40)—with no period after the page number.

Keep in mind that block quotations should not be used as a way to make your essay longer. You should use block quotations sparingly. Attempting to artificially inflate the size of an essay with unnecessarily lengthy quotations is not going to fool anybody.

Example of a block quotation

Brown (2008) found that

> cell phone use among teenagers (aged 14–18) has increased 100 percent in the last ten years. Before that time, teens did not have access to cell phones. The rise in cell phone use can be attributed to several factors: (1) the relative cost of cell phones has decreased in the last ten years; (2) more parents are purchasing cell phones for their children as a way to stay in contact with them; and (3) more teens are working and can afford their own cell phones. (p. 50)

The ease with which teens can obtain a cell phone has led to an increase in their use. This has created problems in schools, where teachers and administrators are scrambling to put rules into place to limit the use of cell phones in classrooms.

In the example above, you'll notice that the writer signalled the use of a block quotation in a number of ways. The first and most obvious of these was the indentation of the quotation. The second way in which the direct quotation was identified was by the introduction of the original author. The writer of the example used the phrase *Brown (2008) found that* to indicate that the words following belonged to Brown. You should also notice that the writer did not leave the block quotation to make the argument, but instead wove the information into the text that surrounded it by explaining the quotation's significance: *The ease with which teens can obtain a cell phone has led to an increase in their use. This has created problems in schools where teachers and administrators are scrambling to put rules into place to limit the use of cell phones in classrooms.* Quotations should not be expected to speak on your behalf. They are meant to support your argument. They are not meant to replace it. This is particularly true with block quotations.

6.9.1.3 Summary and Paraphrase   Incorporating evidence into your paper requires you to make decisions about the best way to introduce the external information you find. In the section above, you learned to place direct quotations in your essay. There are times, however, when you may want to use another individual's ideas but express those ideas in your own words. In those instances, you can use a paraphrase or summary. Each has its own particular advantage:

   a. The advantage of a paraphrase is that it permits you to weave the idea into the text seamlessly.
   b. The advantage of the summary is that it permits you to capture the main themes of a book or article in relatively few words.

Paraphrase and summary employ similar methods. Both permit you to take the original author's ideas and restate them in your own words. There are rules, of course. In the case of the paraphrase, for example, you're expected to go beyond a mere tinkering with one or two words (if that's your intention, you might as well quote it directly). In addition, whether you're writing a paraphrase or a summary, you're obliged to remain true to the original author's intent. You cannot alter the author's meaning to suit your own purposes. You may analyze the information, but you cannot change its meaning. Finally, though the material is not being presented in its original form, it still represents another individual's ideas. You are, therefore, still required to cite the source.

Paraphrasing   You may choose to paraphrase rather than quote directly when you think you can state an idea more clearly and concisely using your own words or when you find that it's difficult to integrate the quotation smoothly. As we've already noted, your paraphrase needs to be faithful to the intention of the original writer (i.e., you cannot change the meaning of the article to suit your own purposes). You cannot, however, be so faithful that you simply change a word or two, or replace key words with synonyms. If you're going to paraphrase, you must rework and rephrase the material in your own words. One of the ways in which you can ensure that you're paraphrasing properly is to put some distance between yourself and the original text. For example, you might find it useful to read the article first and then put it away while you try to express the ideas in your own words.

When paraphrasing, it's important that you clearly signal where your paraphrase begins and ends. You do this by referencing the author and the year of publication at either the beginning or the end of the paraphrase. The original source of the ideas deserves credit even when you're paraphrasing. If the author uses words or phrases that are distinctive, you may even choose to put those words in either italics or quotation marks.

Example of a Paraphrase

This is a paraphrase of Kehler's findings. Note the way in which the paraphrase is introduced. The idea has been attributed to Kehler.

Kehler (2011) has argued that university students should be free to make their own decisions about attending class. He reported that the students he surveyed gave a variety of reasons in support of the position that they should be the ones to make the decision of whether to attend or not attend class. In the survey, 60 percent of the students agreed or strongly agreed that, because they were adults and capable of making their own decisions without interference from other adults such as parents and instructors, the decision should be theirs. A study conducted by Hopkins (2012) found comparable results. Hopkins surveyed students at a large Canadian university and reported that upper-year students (those who were in their third or fourth year) were more likely to attend class than were first-year students. Fifty-five percent of first-year students admitted to missing three or more lectures in a thirteen-week class, while only 10 percent of fourth-year students admitted to missing three or more classes. Hopkins concluded that upper-year students do not miss as many classes as first-year students.

Summarizing   The difference between a summary and a paraphrase is that a summary is meant to capture the essence of a large section of text while a paraphrase is intended to represent an author's expression of one or two smaller ideas. Summarizing follows a similar process to paraphrasing, with the principal difference being the greater degree of compression. When summarizing information to use in your essay, it may be helpful to follow these steps: (1) read the article or section of the article, (2) read it again, underlining or highlighting the main points, and then (3) put the article away and try to capture a general sense of the section you're summarizing in one, two, or three sentences. A summary should be a thorough, balanced, and objective encapsulation of the main themes of the original text.

Example of a Summary

Kehler (2011) argues in this article that university students should not have to attend classes if they choose not to do so. He gives several reasons to support his position: (1) university students are considered to be adults and, thus, should be permitted to decide for themselves the importance of class attendance; (2) students are, essentially, consumers of education and are entitled to decide how they will employ the product they purchased; (3) students do not perceive attendance to be a requirement if instructors do not take attendance; (4) some students will not perceive a need to attend classes if lecture notes are posted online; and (5) students may not feel that they have to attend the lectures if the material requires little more than rote learning.

Kehler also provides evidence for the benefits of attending class, suggesting that: (1) lectures are more detailed discussions of the themes being addressed in a course and, thus, some material will not be available in the online notes; (2) opportunities for participation in class discussion and interaction with other students and the instructor are only available in the classroom; (3) assignments are often explained and elaborated upon in class; (4) questions that emerge from the lecture can be addressed immediately; and (5) films, guest speakers, and other presentations are usually only available to students who attend class.

Kehler concludes that, despite the benefits of classroom attendance, students must be permitted to make the decision to attend class or not. In the computer age, mandatory attendance policies do not have the relevance they once did.

6.10 THE EFFECTIVENESS OF USING CHARTS, TABLES, PHOTOGRAPHS, AND ILLUSTRATIONS AS EVIDENCE

LO 2, 3, 4

There are some advantages to using charts, tables, photographs, and illustrations as evidence. Charts and tables have an authority that derives from their apparent objectivity. Photographs testify to the fact that a recorded event did, in fact, occur. Illustrations often help the reader to visualize a particular point. It's important to remember, however, that information only becomes evidence when the writer explains its significance. Dumping raw information on the page without explaining its significance doesn't help as much as you think (and though a picture may be worth a thousand words, those words usually don't help with the required word count in an essay).

A visual aid can often be used to clarify the points you're making. In some cases, particularly in instances in which you're presenting statistics or other data, you can use tables, graphs, and charts to represent the relationship between numerical findings more easily and more clearly than you might do with language. It's important, however, that all tables, graphs, and charts include explanations in the text of the essay. These visuals should be labelled very clearly, allowing the reader to recognize the section of text to which they refer.

6.10.1 The Difference between Tables and Charts

While tables and charts both serve to provide a visual representation of ideas and/or data, they do so in slightly different ways. The differences reflect a difference in purpose. Tables are often sets of data that are arranged in rows or columns to allow the reader to see the relationship between the individual parts. Though they are rarely used in the humanities, they are effective tools for writing in the sciences and social sciences. As you will have noticed, we also use tables in this textbook to organize categories or facilitate our discussions of the differences between one thing and another. Charts are often used to represent processes, sequences of events, and the relationship between individual parts and the whole. Again, the use of charts is less common in the humanities than it is the sciences and social sciences.

6.10.2 Making Decisions about Using Tables

A table is used to show large amounts of data in a small space. It's a way to organize your data so that the reader can see the information quickly and efficiently. Tables can display numbers or text.

Example of a Table

Table 6.1: Cell Phones and Driving

Questions	Distribution of Answers	
Do you think that talking on cell phones while driving should be banned?	Strongly Agree	50%
	Agree	25%
	Disagree	20%
	Strongly Disagree	5%
Do you think that talking on cell phones while driving can cause an accident?	Strongly Agree	60%
	Agree	20%
	Disagree	10%
	Strongly Disagree	10%
Do you think that talking on cell phones while driving can lead to an increase in accidents?	Strongly Agree	45%
	Agree	20%
	Disagree	25%
	Strongly Disagree	10%

6.10.3 Making Decisions about Using Charts

Charts are often used in an essay when the writer needs to display data and the connection between the different parts of the data. It's often easier for a reader to understand data when it's displayed in a chart. Pie charts (see Figure 6.1) are an effective way to display percentages, bar charts and graphs (see Figure 6.2) are useful for displaying trends, and flow charts (see Figure 6.3) assist the reader in understanding the relationship between individual events and the larger process to which those events belong.

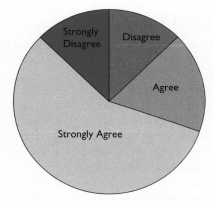

Figure 6.1   **Example of a Pie Chart**

The number of people who think that talking on a cell phone while driving can cause an accident.

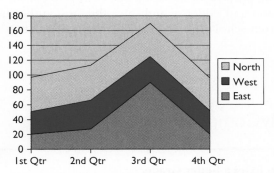

Figure 6.2   **Example of a Graph Showing a Trend**

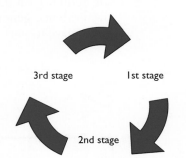

Figure 6.3   **Example of a Flow Chart**

6.11 CITATIONS AND AUTHORITY: HOW CITATIONS INCREASE THE AUTHORITY OF YOUR ESSAY

LO 1, 3, 4

There are a number of reasons to cite one's sources: good karma, good manners, and a fear of the consequences of academic dishonesty. Most of those are discussed in Chapters 4, 5, and 11. Most of those reasons have to do with avoiding unpleasant consequences. However, there are also benefits to the use of citations that go beyond protection from the charge of plagiarism. Citations increase the authority of your work by pointing to the source and saying "See, the important and well-regarded individual who wrote that article agrees with my position." However highly you may esteem your grandmother, it's unlikely that the reader will be convinced on the basis of her authority alone (don't get us wrong—we love your grandmother, but we're just not sure that your readers will feel the same way).

6.12 CONCLUSION

In this chapter, we discussed the importance of authoritative sources and identified some of the ways in which you can use those sources to strengthen an argumentative essay. We also discussed the importance of citing experts to enhance your credibility with the reader and of the need to provide facts, statistics, or other evidence to support your position. Academic essays are addressed to an audience that expects to be convinced by solid reasoning and reliable evidence. To that end, we also discussed the need to acquire the skills necessary to evaluate reference material for its objectivity, relevance, and authority. We noted that, for the purposes of academic writing, scholarly resources tend to be the most reliable source of information. Scholarly resources generally provide the most authoritative evidence because the author is expected to be an expert in the particular field and the articles or texts have been peer-reviewed (i.e., reviewed by a panel of other experts in the field). Scholars are expected to report their findings in precise language. Since the purpose of the academic essay is to convince the audience on the basis of reason and evidence and since the most authoritative evidence generally comes from scholarly references, it seems like that is a good place to start.

MyCompLab®

How Do I Get a Better Grade?

Go to MyCompLab for additional help with your grammar, writing, and research skills. You will have access to a variety of exercises, instruction, and videos that will help you improve your basic skills and help you get a better grade.

Evaluation Worksheet for Identifying Authoritative Sources   Practice

The following worksheet provides a series of general questions for use in evaluating the evidence in your essay. Use it to ensure that the resources you've used are authoritative.

1. Review the evidence you've provided for your essay. Does your essay rely on a single source? If so, you should return to your essay and ask yourself whether one source is enough. It's rarely the case that a single source will provide you with the multiple perspectives on an issue that critical thinking demands. Your instructor is probably looking for evidence that you have explored the issue in greater depth than a single resource offers.

   _____

   _____

   _____

   _____

   Next, look at the resources you've chosen. Are they reliable? How do you know?

   a. Are they from authoritative sites?
   b. Is the author credible?
   c. Is the information free of bias?

   _____

   _____

   _____

   _____

2. Though we discuss the importance of ensuring that your evidence is relevant to your argument elsewhere, it's worth noting again. Regardless of how well the source is written, or how learned it sounds, it will not improve your argument if it is not relevant. Challenge every source that you have included in the same way: What is the connection between the claim you have made and the evidence you have included to support it? Have you made the identification clear between your argument and the evidence you are using? What is it meant to prove? How is it meant to prove it?

   _____

   _____

   _____

   _____

✔•─[Practice]   **Peer-Evaluation Worksheet for Assessing the Authority of Reference Materials**

Title of the Essay: _____

Written By: _____

Peer Evaluator: _____

Thesis Statement: _____

_____

_____

Source #_____ Title of Source Material:	
What evidence can be found to suggest that the source is authoritative, reliable, and objective?	
How do you know that the author cited is qualified to comment on the topic?	
Is the source unbiased? On what basis can you judge the objectivity of the source?	
Is the source current? On what basis is that judgment being made?	
How many sources have been used? Can the evidence be verified by reference to other sources?	
Source #_____ Title of Source Material:	
What evidence can be found to suggest that the source is authoritative, reliable, and objective?	
Is the source current? On what basis is that judgment being made?	
Is the source unbiased? On what basis can you judge the objectivity of the source?	

How many sources have been used? Can the evidence be verified by reference to other sources?	
Source #_____ **Title of Source Material:**	
What evidence can be found to suggest that the source is authoritative, reliable, and objective?	
Is the source current? On what basis is that judgment being made?	
Is the source unbiased? On what basis can you judge the objectivity of the source?	
How many sources have been used? Can the evidence be verified by reference to other sources?	

Practice Exercise 1 (APA Style)

Sample Article
An Exploration of the Harmful Effects of Video Games
By Christopher Zuuk
Journal of Parenting, 2012, volume 3, 45–47

The video game industry is one of the fastest-growing sectors in entertainment. The industry has grown quickly from its early days, back in the 1970s, when people had to own a desktop computer to be able to play games, to the present time, when video games can be accessed from almost anywhere at any time. Video games are available online, through games systems such as Nintendo, PlayStation, and Dreamcast, and, now, through cell phones and computer tablets. It is not unusual to find some homes with more than one game system and it is also not unusual to find that some children and teens play up to six hours of video games on a daily basis (Snow, 2010). Parents do not appear concerned about their children playing video games because they see video games as a form of cheap entertainment and they are comforted to have the children at home (Snow, 2010).

(continued)

(continued)

Parents do not understand all of the problems that video games can cause their children and teenagers. A study was conducted with a hundred young adults (males and females) aged 18–21 in a small Midwestern city in the United States. The study was designed to measure the incidence of violent behaviour in young adults that could be related to the playing of violent video games. The study sought to determine if young adults' levels of aggression increased in accordance with the duration and frequency with which they played video games. The study recruited young adults from the community through the use of printed invitations that were dropped off at 500 homes in one suburban neighbourhood. The participants were invited to come to a monitored centre and play video games for a total of eight hours one Saturday in July. The participants were divided into two groups (50 in each group): one group played games that were identified as violent and the other group played non-violent video games. Each group was housed in a separate room and, in each room, there were 50 televisions, 50 video game consoles, 50 comfortable chairs, 50 sets of headphones, and 150 games. In addition, each room contained tables with supplies of food and a fridge with soft drinks, juice, and water.

Upon entering the room, each group member was given a chance to choose one game from the three options available. The games classified as violent were rated *M* for mature and included a violence warning. The games that were classified as non-violent had a rating of *E* for everyone. In this study, participants each had their own game consoles and were separated by dividers from the other participants. Participants were also issued headsets so that they did not hear other players.

A snack table was set up in each of the rooms and participants were told that they could access the snacks at any time. As the day went on, and the snack pile dwindled, children who were playing the violent video games became increasingly aggressive and more adamant that they should get their share of the snacks. There were arguments over the snacks, with participants calling each other names if they felt someone was eating more than he or she should. This progressed to pushing and shoving. In contrast, the participants who played the non-violent video games did not resort to any physical violence in response to the decreasing supply of snacks. In fact, as the snack pile went down, participants were observed to offer to share, saying things like "There is only one chocolate bar left: does anyone want it?" and, "Does anyone want to share this with me?" The rate of violence among the participants who had been playing violent video games escalated the longer they played and no cooperation was observed among the participants.

It was noted that the level of violence and aggression depicted in the video games caused some of the participants to lose sensitivity to the feelings of the other participants. It appeared that excessive video playing may have reduced their empathy or willingness to cooperate with their fellow game players. There was no indication that the participants in the violent video game shared the snacks as the group who were playing the non-violent video games had done. It was also observed that the participants in the non-violent group began to play the games together after a few hours. They became friendly to each other, were seen talking and laughing together, and began to play the games in a cooperative manner.

Also, as the time drew near for the players to stop playing for the day, there was an increase in the level of play for those teens that were playing the violent video games. Participants became more agitated and their play became more frantic as they rushed to finish off a level before they had to leave. It was almost as if they had become addicted to the games and the high that they received every time they managed to gain the next level, or they managed to kill off one of their adversaries. The games from which the participants could choose offered a high degree of instant gratification, players were constantly being rewarded, and, if the players made a mistake and lost, they could easily start over again. The players in the group who played non-violent games did not express a desire to stay longer to finish off a level. Their level of play did not escalate the closer they got to quitting for the day.

The participants who were playing violent video games were also observed becoming more violent as they got closer to winning the game. This was especially noticeable in the games in which players took on characters and experienced the game through the eyes of their characters. Children who play video games become active participants in the game, which may be one of the reasons why they become more aggressive when they play violent video games. Unlike television, in which participation is more passive, video games encourage players to become part of the game. The participants who were observed playing non-violent video games did not appear to make a strong connection with their respective characters and did not become as engaged in the games as the participants playing violent video games had done.

Bell (2009) reported that playing video games excessively in isolation may contribute to social disorders. Social interaction teaches children how to deal with other people and allows them to gain an understanding of behaviours that are appropriate and those that are not. Children who spend a great deal of time playing video games may have trouble learning to relate to other people. The participants who were playing violent video games in this study appeared to get more isolated as the day progressed, whereas the participants who were playing the non-violent games abandoned their own game consoles and went in search of others with whom to converse.

In 1993, video game manufacturers were required by law to put the following ratings on video games: *E* (for everyone), *T* (for teen), and *M* (for mature) (Gustaf, 2000). However, Gustaf (2000) discovered that it was still relatively easy for teens to buy games labelled "Mature" since the stores selling video games do not monitor the ages of those who purchase

> This statement could be used to prove the first problem, which was that video games are harmful because they lead to addiction.

(*continued*)

(*continued*)

video games. He also found that the number of games that depict violence has increased in the last five years and that the number of advertisements showing violent video games has also increased over the same period.

The results from these studies indicate that playing violent video games does have a harmful effect on children's behaviour. The participants in the study who played violent video games were seen to become more aggressive the longer they played, to become more socially isolated from the other participants, and to show signs of apparent dependence on the stimulation. With these findings in mind, parents are well advised to monitor the amount of time their children play video games, to pay particular attention to the kinds of video games children play, and to engage their children in activities that take them away from video games on a daily basis.

Summarize the article here.

Paraphrase a number of important points here.

Record two or three direct quotations that reflect the general themes of the article here.

Practice Exercise 2 (APA style)

 Practice

Sample Essay 2

Read the sample essay below and write a brief summary of the main points. It's easier to do this if you first read the article once to get an overall impression, then reread, underlining or highlighting the main points. The second reading also provides the opportunity for you to identify direct quotations, paraphrases, or summaries that might be useful in an essay that emerges from the thesis statement.

After you have read the article the second time, complete the exercises that follow the article.

Topic: Cell Phones

Thesis Statement: *The practice of operating a cell phone while driving is hazardous because it demands that drivers attend to multiple tasks at a single time, it leads to delayed reaction times, and it overtaxes drivers' respective capacity to process visual stimuli.*

Teenagers, Cell Phones, and Motor Vehicle Operation—A Dangerous Mix
By Frederick Fontblanc (2012)
Journal of Car Accidents, volume 3, issue 5, 57–70

The use of cell phones has become such an accepted part of society that it is rare to hear of someone today who does not own a cell phone. Ten short years ago, there were only a handful of people who owned cell phones and those phones were not used as a replacement for landlines as they are now. The old cell phones were large, heavy, and expensive to own. Due to their size, they were not convenient to carry around and, therefore, most people usually left them in their cars to use only for roadside emergencies. Another problem with the old phones was that the signal was often erratic and unreliable. This has all changed in the past ten years. Cell phones are now inexpensive, small, and user-friendly. Cell phone users no longer have to worry about getting a signal unless they are indoors, since signal towers are plentiful and phones are rarely out of range.

Cell phones have proven to be popular with people of all ages, but users under the age of thirty have adopted them in the greatest numbers and with the greatest enthusiasm. This generation has grown up using cell phones and sees them as a great convenience. Cell phones are not mere telephones as the early models had been. The new phones serve as mini-computers, allowing users to check email, send text messages, and access the internet. It is no wonder that cell phone use has quadrupled in the last five years.

(continued)

(continued)

As with many revolutionary changes in social practice, however, there are some risks associated with cell phone use. These risks are especially applicable to teenage drivers. Statistics Canada (2012) reported that 50 percent of all accidents involving teenage drivers could be attributed to cell phone use. Teenagers are novice drivers and, as such, have not developed the automated skills associated with driving that older, more experienced drivers have. They still have problems attending to more than one stimulus at a time and the use of a cell phone when driving introduces competing stimuli that novice drivers may not be prepared to manage.

A great deal of attention is required when driving a vehicle. Drivers must concentrate on the operation of the vehicle, making decisions about simple mechanical functions like the correct time to apply the brake and the correct time to apply the accelerator. They have to attend to their surroundings at all times to avoid collisions with vehicles, pedestrians, cyclists, or animals. They also have to know the rules of the road to ensure they can make judgments about stopping distance and speed based on the road conditions. In other words, their level of concentration must remain high if they are to operate the vehicle safely.

Cell phone use, both hand-held and hands-free, has proven to be dangerous for all drivers when they are operating a motor vehicle. This is especially true for teenage drivers between the ages of sixteen and twenty-five. Johnson (2009) found that teenage drivers lose concentration when they talk on their cell phones while driving. He conducted a study with one hundred teenage drivers who had been involved in a car accident while they were talking on a cell phone. He interviewed each participant in an attempt to discover what it was about talking and driving that contributed to the accident. Johnson (2009) discovered that the reported difficulties that led to the traffic accidents primarily had to do with driver inattention. Forty of the one hundred teens admitted that they were busy talking on their cell phones and did not notice that a vehicle in front of them had slowed down. A further thirty teens confessed that they were not aware that the traffic lights had changed to red and proceeded through the intersection on the red. Ten teens reported that they drove through stop signs without noticing them, which resulted in eight accidents involving other cars and two accidents involving pedestrians. In addition, twenty teens stated that they were going too fast for the road conditions, which led to a variety of accidents, including collisions with road repair vehicles, collisions with road signs, collisions with parked cars, and collisions with trees and fences.

In a different study, Long (2010) examined police reports for the past ten years and noticed that there was a marked increase in the number of accidents involving teens and cell phone use over the past five years. Ten years ago there were no accidents involving teenage drivers and the use of cell phones. Last year, there were over a hundred accidents involving teen drivers and cell phone use. Long attributed the results to delayed reaction time on the part of the teen drivers. When Long read the police reports, he discovered that the teens reported that they were not paying attention to the road because they were talking on their cell phones. An analysis of the police reports indicated that teen drivers who were talking on their cell phones were five times more likely to be involved in an accident that caused some sort of bodily harm. The teens who spoke to Long said that they were distracted by their individual cell phone conversations and realized too late that they needed to apply their brakes to avoid a collision.

Another problem identified by Jones (2009) is visual distraction. Drivers do not need to take their eyes off the road for more than a few seconds to miss changing road conditions that lead to accidents. It is relatively easy for drivers to take their eyes off the road when they are trying to answer a ringing phone. Teenage drivers are also guilty of attempting to drive and text at the same time. This has proven to be a particularly dangerous thing as even glancing down for a few seconds can cause the driver to collide with another car or a pedestrian. Jones found that, in two hundred accidents caused by the cell phone use of teenagers, one hundred had been caused by drivers who were texting and driving. Strangely, these teens reported that, though they were aware of the dangers of driving while speaking on a cell phone, they were not aware of the dangers of texting and driving.

In 2009, a test was conducted by a university in the United States to determine the differences between the reflexes of drivers who were using hand-held cell phones, hands-free cell phones, or no cell phones at all. Sixty first-year students took part in the study using driver simulators. Twenty of the teens were tested using hand-held cell phones, twenty were tested using hands-free cell phones, and twenty students were tested while operating the simulator without a cell phone. The test was conducted with participants attempting to operate a simulator with a steering wheel, a brake, and an accelerator. The accelerator was set at 30 mph regardless of the pressure put on it by the participants. The simulation was preprogrammed to represent a city street, complete with houses on both sides of the road and appropriate traffic signs such as stop signs, yield signs, and school zones. In the simulation, a number of obstacles were randomly introduced, including other vehicles, fences, potholes, animals, pedestrians, bicyclists, road repair crews, and two small children who run into the road chasing a ball. The simulator was designed to measure the time it took for the driver to react, starting at the moment at which the obstacle was introduced and ending when the driver applied the brake. Another device kept track of the number of obstacles that were hit during the fifteen-minute simulation.

(*continued*)

(*continued*)

Two second-year university students were also hired as research assistants. Their job was to make phone calls to the drivers who had the hand-held cell phones and the hands-free phones. They were instructed to carry on a normal conversation with the drivers for a total of two minutes per call. They made ten phone calls during the fifteen-minute simulation. Researchers provided scripts to the research assistants to ensure that the conversation would last for two minutes. The research assistants were also instructed to leave time for the driver to respond.

The results from the study indicated that both groups who were talking on cell phones and driving at the same time had slower reaction times when compared to the drivers who were not talking on a cell phone. The drivers who used hand-held devices hit the obstacles ten times in the fifteen-minute period, the drivers who used the hands-free devices hit the obstacles nine times in the fifteen minutes, and the drivers who did not use cell phones only hit an obstacle on average one time in the fifteen minutes. The researchers further discovered that drivers who were talking on hand-held phones had a reaction time of twenty seconds between the time the obstacle was introduced and the brake was applied, the drivers who used a hands-free device also had a reaction time of twenty seconds, while the drivers who did not have a cell phone had a reaction time of five seconds. The researchers determined that the use of cell phones led to drivers displaying slower reflexes and slower reaction times when introduced to the obstacles. There were no noticeable differences between the drivers who used the hand-held devices and those who used the hands-free devices. Contrary to popular opinion, hands-free cell phones did not appear to be safer than hand-held cell phones.

In general, research indicates that there is a high incidence of traffic accidents involving teen drivers and the use of cell phones. The use of hands-free cell phones has not proven to be any safer than the use of hand-held cell phones. Teenage drivers are especially susceptible to periods of driver inattention when talking on cell phones or texting when driving. The laws for talking on cell phones and driving have to be strictly enforced if the number of accidents caused by cell phone use is to be reduced. This seems to be more important for teenage drivers. Cell phones are convenient and have many positive benefits, but teens have to realize that there is a time and a place for using a cell phone, and a car is not one of those places.

Summarize the article here.

Paraphrase a number of important points here.

Record two or three direct quotations that reflect the general themes of the article here.

REFLECTING ON THE TEXT I: THE PLANNING STAGE

The Planning Stage

During the planning stage of the writing process, you've been focused on the conception of your essay. You've thought about the nature of the writing process itself, about the importance of understanding writing as a series of decisions, about the process of acquiring writing skills by considering the effect of the decisions you make, and about the need to identify an effective organizational pattern for your essay. The most significant thing you've done, however, is to recognize that, in writing, you're attempting to say something specific (i.e., you have a well-articulated purpose) to someone in particular (i.e., you have a well-defined audience). You're monitoring your emerging text to ensure that your writing decisions derive from that recognition.

Having identified your audience and purpose, you've begun to develop a provisional outline for the essay. You've drafted that outline in response both to your purpose and to the expectations that you attribute to the audience you've identified. Using a thesis statement that includes an arguable proposition, you've narrowed your focus, making a specific claim about the idea, phenomenon, or interpretation that was your topic. You've thought about the logical connections between the major ideas of your essay, and have reflected on the outline you drafted to ensure that those connections are represented in the outline. Finally, you've begun to research the individual elements of your thesis statement purposefully, exploring reference material to find whether the argument you're making can be sustained by reference to evidence or authoritative sources, selecting supporting documents when it seems reasonable to do so, and modifying your thesis when the evidence suggests you should.

In the following sections, we've provided brief synopses of Chapters 1 through 6, with a series of questions to guide your reflections on the effect of the principles and concepts discussed in each chapter.

CHAPTER 1: MAKING THE TRANSITION TO WRITING AT COLLEGE OR UNIVERSITY

In Chapter 1, we introduced a different way to acquire writing skills, suggesting that the practice of thinking about your writing process—during which you reflect on the differences between *the work you are doing* and *the work you would like to do*—allows you to intentionally alter the process you're following to one that might prove more effective. The metacognitive approach to writing encourages you to think about the decisions you're making and to recognize the effects of those decisions. There were two particular examples of the different stages of writing that we discussed in Chapter 1: (1) differences between the writing processes of novice writers and experienced writers, and (2) differences between writing in high school and writing in college or university. Use the questions below to guide your reflections on the kinds of decisions you need to make to produce the writing you intend to produce.

Understanding the Nature of Writing
1. What is the effect of understanding writing as a decision-making process?
2. What is the importance of understanding the difference between the *process* of writing and the *product* of writing?
3. How do the two differ?
4. What effect does that difference have on your understanding of writing?
Differences between Novice Writers and Experienced Writers
1. What are the important differences between the writing processes of novice and experienced writers?
2. Which of the two writing processes do you follow most closely?
3. How can you alter your writing process to move closer to the writing process of experienced writers?
4. What specific decisions do you have to approach differently?
5. How are you going to change your decision-making process to effect that change?
Differences between Writers in High School and Writers in College/University
1. What are the important differences between the writing processes of writers in high school and writers in college or university?
2. Which of the two writing processes do you follow most closely?
3. How can you alter your writing process to move closer to the writing process of writers in college or university?
4. What specific decisions do you have to approach differently?
5. How are you going to change your decision-making process to effect that change?

CHAPTER 2: ACADEMIC WRITING AND THE ARGUMENTATIVE ESSAY

As we moved from Chapter 1 to Chapter 2, we began to reflect on the specific characteristics of academic writing. Though we acknowledged that you might encounter writing assignments that ask you to work in any one of a number of distinct genres, we focused on the argumentative essay. We did so for a number of reasons. The first reason for the focus on the argumentative essay was the breadth of its applicability. It is, in one form or another, the kind of essay that's assigned most often in college and university. The second reason for the focus on the argumentative essay is similar to the first. Because the argumentative essay reflects the kind of reasoning that underpins thinking in most disciplines in the academic realm (i.e., a reasoning process through which one advances to a conclusion on the basis of a logical presentation of evidence), it provides an organizational pattern that's easily adapted to other writing assignments.

Academic Writing
1. Have you identified an audience for your essay?
2. What is your understanding of that audience?
3. What are the expectations of the audience you've identified?
4. How do you intend to address those expectations?
5. Have you identified a purpose for your essay?
6. Is that purpose specific and well defined?
7. How would you express your specific writing purpose in a single sentence (i.e., a sentence that contains both the claim you're making and the reason, or rationale, for that claim)?

Argumentative Essays
1. How have you identified the arguable proposition of your essay?
2. What is the claim you're making?
3. What are the reasons for that claim?
4. What is the specific relationship between the claim you're making and the reasons for that claim?
5. Are you able to draft a provisional outline for your essay in which the reader is introduced to your argument through your thesis statement?

CHAPTER 3: GETTING STARTED USING THE IDDL WRITING MODEL

In Chapters 1 and 2, we identified some of the difficulties you might experience when you're adapting to the writing circumstances of college or university. We noted that novice writers sometimes experience excessive memory demands because they have not yet internalized strategies for writing, because they attempt to manage too many writing decisions simultaneously, and because they are not able to effectively off-load memory-intensive procedures to the page. In addition, novice writers often fail to recognize that an academic essay requires that they interpret, analyze, and explain ideas, rather than simply list them.

In Chapter 3, we introduced the IDDL model as a strategy to address some of those challenges. The model is designed to make the writing process more manageable by providing a dynamic structure that allows you to impose order on your ideas, without robbing you of the opportunity to explore those ideas in your own way. In fact, because the model includes a series of questions that guide your informed analysis of the essay's theme, each step forward is predicated on your answer to previous questions. In short, the model demands that you inform the essay with your specific purpose.

Inscribing the Writing Space and Defining Rhetorical Problems Locally
1. Does your thesis statement identify a specific claim (the controlling thesis) and the reasons for that claim (the subtheses or subthemes)?
2. How can you group the subtheses to create individual paragraphs or individual groups of paragraphs?
3. How will you identify the relationship of each of the subtheses to the controlling thesis?

Discovering the Information Necessary to Resolve the Local Rhetorical Problems

1. Looking at the first of the subtheses, what kind of evidence do you need to establish it as reasonable or credible? (It's important to remember the nature of your audience; what kind of evidence does that audience expect?)
2. Looking at the second of the subtheses, what kind of evidence do you need to establish it as reasonable or credible?
3. Looking at the third subthesis (and all subsequent subtheses), what kind of evidence do you need to establish it (or them) as reasonable or credible?

Linking the Units Logically

1. In academic writing, your purpose is generally to convince a reasonable audience on the basis of evidence. Your thesis statement, though it's situated in the introduction to the essay, also identifies the essay's ultimate destination: a conclusion in which the challenges raised in the thesis statement are resolved. Look at the organization of the individual subtheses as they are presently arranged in your outline.
2. Are there paragraphs, or groups of related paragraphs, that logically ought to precede other paragraphs? Does the order in your outline reflect that logic?
3. Does the order lead the reader through the essay in a way that makes sense?
4. Can you change the order of the individual paragraphs to render your argument easier to understand?

CHAPTER 4: RESEARCH

One of the effects of using the IDDL model to foreground the thesis of your essay is that it allows you to clarify the individual claims that need to be substantiated or themes that need to be explored. In isolating the specific reasons on which your argument is based, you clearly identify themes and keywords to guide your research process. Rather than charging off to gather all information that is even remotely related to your topic, you select resources on the basis of their respective capacity to answer the needs you identified in the second stage of the IDDL process (*defining rhetorical problems locally*).

Thinking about Preliminary Research

1. Looking at the first of the subtheses you identified in the second stage of the IDDL process, identify the claim you're making.
2. Looking at the first claim or reason, what do you need to do to establish it as reasonable or credible?
3. What is the best source for information on that particular question? An online university database? Your university's library? Why have you chosen that source?
4. Looking at the second claim or reason, what do you need to do to establish it as reasonable or credible?
5. What is the best source for information on that particular question? An online university database? Your university's library? Why have you chosen that source?
6. Looking at the third claim or reason (and all subsequent claims), what do you need to do to establish it (or them) as reasonable or credible?
7. What are the best sources for information on those particular questions? An online university database? Your university's library? Why have you chosen those sources?

1. For the first claim or reason, draft a specific question that will guide your research, remembering that the time you spend refining the question will reduce the time you spend researching. Use keywords to guide your research. What were the questions you generated in the third stage of the IDDL process for the first of the reasons you offered in support of your thesis?
2. What were the questions you generated in the third stage of the IDDL process for the second of the reasons you offered in support of your thesis?
3. What were the questions you generated in the third stage of the IDDL process for the third of the reasons you offered in support of your thesis?
4. Use the same process for each of the reasons you offered in support of your thesis.

CHAPTER 5: USING AN ANNOTATED BIBLIOGRAPHY AS A RESEARCH TOOL

In Chapter 5, we looked at the advantages of using an annotated bibliography to create an interface between the resources you've selected and the essay you're writing. As we noted, novice writers often dump information onto the page, usually in accordance with an obvious organization, but often without pausing to interpret that information, to challenge it for relevance, or to tailor it to its new purpose. That practice is hardly surprising. The process of summarizing an entire article or book in a few sentences, or of selecting those key statements that capture the essence of an article or book, is more difficult than it appears. It's particularly difficult when you're attempting to make a direct transfer from the resource document to your essay. You are able to refine the process of integrating external documents to your essay by using an annotated bibliography to (1) record your interpretation of the resource document, noting important quotations or paraphrases, then (2) identify the way in which it can be used, and finally (3) record the essential bibliographic information required for proper citations.

CHAPTER 6: THE IMPORTANCE OF AUTHORITATIVE SOURCES

In this chapter, we discuss the importance of authoritative evidence. We also review some of the different ways in which evidence can be introduced into an essay, identifying the relative advantages of quotations, paraphrases, and summaries. In keeping with the practices that we've discussed elsewhere in the text, we also identified some of the ways in which you can learn to seek evidence strategically by tailoring your search to the specific purpose of your essay. We noted, in particular, the value of using the arguable proposition to identify the specific information you need. As we had noted in Chapter 2, it's important to have a clear and specific arguable claim (an arguable claim is a statement that clearly articulates the claim being made and provides the reasons for that claim). When you're thinking about the sort of evidence you need, you should be guided by the claim you've made.

Thinking about the Relevance of Secondary Sources

1. Look at the first resource document you've selected. What specific purpose will it serve in your essay?
2. Does the document address any of the specific questions you're exploring? In what way does it do so?
3. How will you use the information from this document to enhance your essay?
4. In what specific way does the document strengthen your argument or enrich your understanding of the essay's topic?
5. How would the essay be different without this particular resource document?
6. Follow the same process to challenge the relevance of each of the documents you have selected.

Thinking Critically about Secondary Sources

1. Look at the first resource document you've selected. Why would you accept its authority?
2. Is the author an expert in the field? How do you know?
3. Is the source of the article scholarly? What evidence can you offer to substantiate the authority of the source?
4. Is the information current? How can you tell?
5. Follow the same process to challenge the authority of each of the documents you have selected.

SECTION II: WRITING AND REVISION

CHAPTER 7

Thinking in Meaningful Units

Learning Objectives

At the completion of this chapter, you will be able to:

1. Discuss the differences between the ways in which novice and experienced writers construct sentences and paragraphs.

2. Demonstrate the ability to choose specific sentence structures to achieve specific effects.

3. Explain the importance of monitoring paragraphs for internal unity and purpose.

4. Explain how the IDDL model can be used to guide decisions about paragraph construction.

7.1 TRANSLATING YOUR THOUGHTS INTO LANGUAGE

There is some debate about the best way to teach writing. Some believe that students learn best by focusing on sentences first, and then learning to link those together to create a larger unit. Others argue that students are better advised to concentrate on the larger rhetorical structure (e.g., the essay) first, and polish the sentences later. Who's right? It's probably a little bit of column A and a little bit of column B. It's hard to see how you might write an essay without first knowing how to write a sentence. On the other hand, it's also difficult to understand how you would write one of the sentences that will become a component part of an essay without knowing how that sentence fits into the larger structure.

In Chapter 3, we introduced you to the IDDL writing model. One of the aims of that model is to encourage you to think, first, about the purpose of the writing assignment, and then, about the way the individual parts of your text serve that purpose. By understanding the way in which decisions about sentences and paragraphs affect the larger structure, you will be able to make those decisions more effectively.

7.2 UNDERSTANDING THE DIFFERENCE BETWEEN THE PRACTICE OF THE NOVICE WRITER AND THE PRACTICE OF THE EXPERIENCED WRITER IN THE USE OF SENTENCES

LO 1

In the following chart, you'll notice that there are a number of differences between the ways in which novice writers and experienced writers make decisions about sentences. Novice writers tend to *focus on error avoidance rather than meaning, begin writing without planning,* and *focus on "knowledge telling,"* while experienced writers *focus on developing or refining meaning; invest time and energy in planning and reviewing;* and *organize, and reorganize, essay structure to allow individual ideas to serve the overall purpose of the essay.*

Novice Writers	Experienced Writers
■ Require thought for procedural, or "mechanical," writing functions.	■ Have, to a significant degree, automated procedural functions.
■ *Focus on error avoidance rather than meaning.*	■ *Focus on developing or refining meaning.*
■ *Begin writing without planning, and edit, if at all, for grammatical errors.*	■ *Invest time and energy in planning and reviewing.*
■ *Focus on "knowledge telling" (i.e., relating all the information they have and can find on a topic, rather than exercising critical judgment to determine relevance).*	■ *Organize, and reorganize, essay structure to allow individual ideas to serve the overall purpose of the essay.*

In effect, the essential difference between the novice and the experienced writer is that the experienced writer is making decisions, thinking about purpose, and using sentence variety to serve that purpose.

LO 1   ## 7.3   UNDERSTANDING THE DIFFERENCE BETWEEN THE PRACTICE OF THE NOVICE WRITER AND THE PRACTICE OF THE EXPERIENCED WRITER IN THE USE OF PARAGRAPHS

In the next chart, you'll notice that we have identified the most important difference between the way in which novice writers and experienced writers make decisions about paragraphs. Because novice writers tend to *focus on "knowledge telling,"* their work is often characterized by the information dump. That is, they insert information without organizing it for meaning. In contrast, experienced writers focus on *organizing, and reorganizing, essay structure to allow individual ideas to serve the overall purpose of the essay.* They make decisions about paragraphs intentionally, organizing information into units that serve the larger purpose of the essay.

Novice Writers	Experienced Writers
■ Require thought for procedural, or "mechanical," writing functions.	■ Have, to a significant degree, automated procedural functions.
■ Focus on error avoidance rather than meaning.	■ Focus on developing or refining meaning.
■ Begin writing without planning, and edit, if at all, for grammatical errors.	■ Invest time and energy in planning and reviewing.
■ *Focus on "knowledge telling" (i.e., relating all the information they have and can find on a topic, rather than exercising critical judgment to determine relevance).*	■ *Organize, and reorganize, essay structure to allow individual ideas to serve the overall purpose of the essay.*

LO 1, 2   ## 7.4   A BRIEF DISCUSSION ABOUT SENTENCES

To be clear, we have not underestimated your ability to compose sentences. We assume that you're familiar with the process, that you know how to write a sentence, that you've been writing sentences from the time you were in primary school, and that you were speaking in sentences before you started writing them. Why, then, are we wasting your valuable time with this discussion of sentences? It's a fair question. There is a marked difference between possessing the understanding necessary to compose a sentence in isolation and having the skill to exploit the different sentence structures to communicate your ideas effectively. In order to write successfully, you first have to understand the way in which different types of sentences can be used to organize and communicate your ideas.

7.4.1 Three Basic Types of Sentences

> **1. Simple Sentences:**
> A simple sentence, also called an independent clause, contains a subject and a verb, and it expresses a complete thought.
> **Some examples of simple sentences:**
> - Jack goes to the zoo every Sunday. (*Jack* is the subject and *goes* is the verb.)
> - Jack and Jill went up the hill. (*Jack, Jill* are the subjects; *went* is the verb.)
>
> **2. Compound Sentences:**
> A compound sentence contains two independent clauses joined by a conjunction. The conjunctions are as follows: *for, and, nor, but, or, yet, so.* Except in very short sentences, a conjunction is always preceded by a comma. Sentences are made up of clauses. To distinguish between a simple and a compound sentence you have to remember that a simple sentence has just one independent clause, and a compound sentence has more than one independent clause.
> **Some examples of compound sentences:**
> - George was watching baseball, so Meghan went to the movies. (*George was watching baseball* is an independent clause; *Meghan went to the movies* is an independent clause; *so* is the conjunction that joins the two clauses together to make a compound sentence.)
> - Bob liked to play soccer, but Paul preferred to play football. (*Bob liked to play soccer* is an independent clause; *Paul preferred to play football* is an independent clause; *but* is the conjunction that joins the two clauses together to make a compound sentence.)
>
> **3. Complex Sentences:**
> A complex sentence has an independent clause that is modified or qualified by one or more dependent clauses. A complex sentence always has a subordinator, such as *because, since, after, although,* or *when,* or a relative pronoun such as *that, who,* or *which.*
> **Some examples of complex sentences:**
> - When Paul bought his textbook, he forgot to buy some paper to write on. (*When Paul bought his textbook* is a dependent clause modifying the independent clause *he forgot to buy some paper.*)
> - Doris and Jim went shopping after they finished watching the soccer game. (*Doris and Jim went shopping* is an independent clause; *after they finished watching the soccer game* is the dependent clause.)

7.4.2 Another Variation

Sometimes a writer may choose to depart from the "natural" structure of the sentence, inverting it to achieve variety or greater clarity. The box below offers a brief explanation of the inverted sentence.

> In an inverted sentence, the subject is moved from its customary place at the beginning of the sentence.
> **An example of an inverted sentence:**
> - Tired of using simple sentences repeatedly, the author inverted the order.
> In the sentence above, the subject (*the author*) follows a dependent clause (*Tired of using simple sentences repeatedly*).

7.4.3 Why It's Important to Understand the Various Forms a Sentence Can Take

The different forms of sentences are much like synonyms. That is, though it is possible to express an idea in a number of different ways, there are usually shades of difference that emerge from the choices you make as a writer. By thinking about the different sentence structures, you are better able to find the structure that suits your purpose. For instance, the simple sentence is both easier to write clearly and easier for the reader to process. Compound sentences allow you to combine two independent clauses, identifying the relationship between them. The complex sentence links two or more ideas but does so by using dependent clauses to expand upon, limit, or justify the independent clause.

There are a number of reasons why you might want to use a variety of sentence structures in your essay. We're going to focus on two: (1) rhythmic variation keeps the text from becoming stale and repetitive, and (2) different sentence structures allow you to accent or emphasize the various ideas in a sentence in different ways. Too many sentences with the same structure and length can grow tiresome for the reader. More importantly perhaps, by varying sentence style and structure you can add emphasis to points that are important to your overall essay. You can use long sentences to explore complex relationships between a number of ideas, and short sentences to make important points.

Read the sample essays that follow, noting the different sentence structures the different writers are using. In particular, pay attention to the effect that the sentence structures have on you as a reader.

Sample Essay 1: Simple Sentences

There is a problem with cell phones. The problem is talking while driving. When you drive, you need to focus. When you talk on a cell phone you need to focus. When you try to talk on a cell phone you cannot focus. It is difficult to do two things at one time. Driving can be distracting. Talking on cell phones can be distracting. Taken together you have doubled the distraction. It does not work.

Talking on a cell phone while driving can cause an accident. Driver inattention is one of the problems. Drivers cannot pay attention to the road when talking on cell phones. They can hit a lot of things. They can hit other cars. They can hit pedestrians. They can hit bicyclists. They can hit animals. They can hit fences. Hitting things can be dangerous. They can injure themselves. They can injure other drivers. They can injure their passengers. They can injure pedestrians. They can injure bicyclists. They can injure animals. It is dangerous to talk on cell phones.

Talking on a cell phone can also impact drivers' reflexes. When talking on their cell phones, drivers do not have time to react. They can run into cars stopped at stoplights. They might not be aware the other car stopped. They can run into small children. Children might run in front of the car. The driver might not see them. They might hit the child. This can be dangerous. Children can be injured. They can be killed. Drivers can also hit road repair crews. The drivers might not realize they have to slow down. They keep going at the same speed. They are not able to react in time to stop. Again, injuries can occur. Talking on cell phones affects drivers' reflexes.

Reaching for a cell phone can be a problem. Taking hands off the wheel can cause an accident. Drivers should not be talking on a cell phone. They should not take their hands off the wheel. They should not take their eyes off the road. Even if they only look away for a couple of seconds, they can run off the road. They can also hit something. They can hit a cow if they are out in the country. They can miss a stop sign. They can hit a crossing guard. They can hit a child walking to school.

Talking on a cell phone is dangerous. People should not talk on the phone while driving. Driving requires concentration. Talking requires concentration. Drivers cannot do both. Either they should talk or they should drive. It is dangerous to do both.

That was painful, wasn't it?

Admittedly we exaggerated to make a point, but you now know the mind-numbing effect of an unrelenting list of assertions in simple sentence form. A simple sentence is easy to understand because it has only one idea in it. However, the pace that it imposes on the reader has the same effect as standing at the automated checker behind a shopper who doesn't understand how to scan a bar code. The reader becomes impatient, wanting to hurry the process along by combining a series of simple sentences into a single compound or complex sentence.

Compare the effect of the sentence choices above to the effect of the following sentence choices.

Sample Essay 2: Compound and Complex Sentences

Drivers who use cell phones while operating vehicles can become distracted from the emerging conditions on the road. When operating a vehicle, drivers need to focus on those emerging conditions, and focus is difficult while one is also operating a cell phone. It is always challenging for individuals to divide attention between two competing activities. The use of a cell phone while operating a car introduces an unnecessary distraction.

Using a cell phone while driving can lead a driver to unnecessary collisions due to driver inattention. Drivers cannot pay attention to the road because their attention is divided between the cell phone conversation and conditions on the road. This can result in drivers colliding with other cars, pedestrians, bicyclists, animals, and fences. The result of such collisions can be that drivers injure themselves, their passengers, other drivers, pedestrians, cyclists, or animals.

The use of cell phones while driving can also cause drivers' reaction times to be compromised. When talking on a cell phone, drivers shift their attention between the conversation and the traffic around them and, thus, often do not have time to react to emerging conditions. They often rear-end cars that are stopped at stoplights because they are not aware that other vehicles have stopped. They can also overlook small children who might dash out into the street, sometimes causing injury or even death. Drivers using cell phones have been known to hit individuals in road repair crews because they did not notice the signs that signalled road work ahead, did not notice signs calling for reduced speed, and did not notice flag persons who were attempting to slow the traffic. Even answering a ringing cell phone can cause problems. When drivers reach for the cell phone, they usually take their eyes off the road briefly. Even if they only look away for a couple of seconds, however, they can run off the road or collide with the traffic around them.

It is clear that the practice of using cell phones while driving is dangerous. It requires that drivers attend to too many tasks at one time, robbing each of the attention it requires. Because a driver is unable to manage multiple tasks at once, the driver should choose to do one or the other. That is, drivers should either drive their cars or stop to talk on the phone. It is dangerous to attempt to do both at once.

The second essay included much of the same information that was in the first one. The strategic use of various sentence constructions, however, improved the pleasure and coherence of the text. In the parlance of the writers, it read better. The simple direct sentence is not without its place and purpose, of course, and sometimes it speaks more effectively because it speaks directly. There are other times when you are better advised to weave a number of related thoughts into a single complex or compound sentence.

7.4.4 Principles to Consider When Thinking about Sentences and Sentence Variety

Though this chapter includes a number of discussions about the respective merits of sentence variety and complexity, sentences should not simply be modified to satisfy some arbitrary principle. Decisions about sentence structure should always be made on the basis of their effect. The chart below offers some strategies for making those decisions.

Think about the Purpose of the Sentence
A sentence that conveys a key or foundational idea is too important to be lost in ambiguity. Because it's easier to maintain clarity in a simple sentence, you may choose to use the simple declarative sentence to express thesis statements or topic sentences. Similarly, if you're having difficulty expressing a particular idea, you may want to articulate it first as either a simple sentence or a series of simple sentences. You can combine the sentences later if you choose to do so.
Think about the Idea You Want to Emphasize
In selecting the particular type of sentence you want to use at a particular point, you might want to think about the idea you mean to emphasize. If an important idea seems to be lost in a sentence, you should experiment with the sentence structure to see if you can find a way to add greater emphasis to it.
Think about the Unifying Idea of the Paragraph
Organizing a paragraph around a single controlling idea is a useful strategy for maintaining coherence in the paragraph. When drafting sentences within the paragraph, you ought to consider which idea needs to be emphasized in order to serve the overall purpose of the paragraph.
Think about the Way in Which a Particular Sentence Is Linked to the Previous One
To ensure that the reader is able to recognize the connecting ideas, link a series of sentences together using different sentence structures.
Alternate between Short and Long Sentences
Though the simple, declarative sentence is generally easier for your reader to process, it can also grow a little tedious. Varying the length and structure of sentences renders the text more interesting.
Vary Your Sentence Openings
Just as an endless series of sentences with the same structure can get tiresome, so too does the practice of beginning every sentence with the same word (e.g., *the, it, this*). You probably want to avoid that. Whenever possible, use a variety of sentence openings. However, if you need to choose between expressing your meaning clearly and introducing variety, chose clarity.

Examples of variations in sentence structure   You can achieve sentence variety in a number of ways. You don't have to rely exclusively on managing the length of the sentence to change the emphasis of the sentence or to introduce variety. In the following exercise, we'll demonstrate other simple strategies for controlling the emphasis of your sentences.

Front-Loaded Sentences

In front-loaded sentences, you present the subject and the verb first, followed by a variety of modifying phrases.

Example: It was typical of this government's legislation—short-sighted, self-interested, and indifferent to the needs of citizens.

Effect:
In this sentence, you should notice that the emphasis is on the first element of the sentence.

End-Loaded Sentences

In end-loaded sentences, you place the main idea at the end of the sentence.

Example: After having invested heavily in upgrading the plant, the company simply walked away.

Effect:
The emphasis of an end-loaded sentence is on the last element of the sentence. It often introduces a subtle change to the sense of the sentence.

Balanced Sentences

In balanced sentences, you generally use a conjunction (e.g., *and, or*) to join two ideas of equal importance in a single sentence.

Example: Texting while driving is dangerous and illegal.

Effect:
The use of balanced sentences uses a parallel structure to distribute the emphasis between two ideas of relatively equal importance.

Sentences That Begin with Verbal Phrases

To write a sentence that begins with a verbal phrase, identify the verb form that modifies the main idea in the sentence and move it to the front of the sentence.

Example: Alarmed by her midterm grade, the student began to attend tutorials.

Effect:
In this sentence type, the verbal phrase that modifies the main idea is emphasized.

Sentences That Begin with an Adverb

To write a sentence that begins with an adverb, you identify the principal action of the sentence and move its modifier to the front of the sentence.

Example: Reluctantly, he walked away from the table.

Effect:
By beginning your sentence with an adverb, you generally emphasize the way in which an action occurs in a sentence. It usually has the effect of establishing the tone of the sentence.

Sentences That Begin with Adjectives

To write a sentence that begins with an adjective, you identify the subject of the sentence and move its modifier to the front of the sentence.

Example: Elated and exhausted, the student handed in the overdue assignment.

Effect:
The effect of the sentence that begins with an adjective is to emphasize particular features or conditions of the subject.

Sentence Variety Exercises

1. Write your own examples of a simple sentence:

   _____

   _____

2. Write your own examples of a complex or compound sentence:

   _____

   _____

   _____

3. Write your own example of a front-loaded sentence. As you're doing so, think about the way in which the emphasis shifts.

   _____

   _____

4. Write your own example of an end-loaded sentence. As you're doing so, think about the way in which the emphasis shifts.

   _____

   _____

5. Write an example of a sentence that begins with a verbal phrase. What is the effect of this sentence structure?

   _____

   _____

   _____

6. Write an example of a sentence that begins with an adverb. What is the effect of this sentence structure?

   _____

   _____

   _____

7. Write an example of a sentence that begins with an adjective. What is the effect of this sentence structure?

   _____

   _____

   _____

LO 1, 2   ## 7.5   WRITING SAMPLE SHOWING DECISIONS ABOUT SENTENCE VARIETY

1 In this example, the writer has chosen to invert the sentence. The inversion has the effect of foregrounding, or emphasizing, *a study that focused on college students and the way in which college norms and religion affected alcohol consumption.*

2 Again, the sentence has been inverted. In this case, the effect of the inversion is to strengthen the connection between this sentence and the previous one.

3 The simple declarative sentence allows the writer to express a key idea clearly.

4 Despite the use of the colon to assist in the organization of a list, this key organizing idea has, again, been expressed using the simple sentence structure.

5 The use of the compound sentence structure with the conjunction *but* joining the two independent clauses lets the writer create a contrast between the two situations observed over time.

6 The writer has introduced a rhythmic variation to the text by inserting this short declarative sentence between two longer sentences.

7 The use of a complex sentence structure allows the writer to add greater detail to the independent clause (i.e., *The Christians from the American South ... were generally least likely to consume alcohol*) by inserting a dependent clause (i.e., *whose belief in the human body as God's temple generally encouraged them to restrain from alcohol*).

Example of a Paragraph Using a Variety of Sentence Structures

[1]In a study that focused on college students and the way in which college norms and religion affected alcohol consumption (Perkins, 1985), the researcher found that peer pressure was the most important factor in determining drinking behaviours. [2]Even more than was the case with adolescents, college students reported that the values held by significant peers, rather than the values held by parents, were the primary influence on their decisions about drinking. Perkins (1985) also noted that religious background had an effect on decision making. [3]Three main religions were considered in this study: Judaism, Catholicism, and Christianity from the American South. [4]The Jews in this study tended to consume less alcohol at the beginning of college, but eventually their drinking habits increased to fit the immediate campus norms.[5] [6]Nonetheless, it was found that Jews generally drank less than Catholics. [7]The Christians from the American South, whose belief in the human body as God's temple generally encouraged them to restrain from alcohol, were generally least likely to consume alcohol.

7.6   MAKING WRITING DECISIONS ABOUT SENTENCES

LO 1, 2

The following chart includes a list of principles and suggestions to consider when you're making decisions about writing and combining sentences. Use the questions at the bottom of the chart to guide you in your decision making.

Making Writing Decisions	About Sentences While Writing Your Own Essays

What is the purpose of this writing decision?

The obvious purpose in thinking about the different structures of sentences that are available to you is to introduce variety to your text. More importantly, however, understanding different sentence structures can provide you with a way to both express your ideas more clearly and link them more effectively.

What is the effect of this writing decision?

Writers who exploit the range of sentence structures available to them are able to link sentences more coherently, emphasize particular ideas intentionally, and introduce rhythmic variety to their work.

What considerations inform this decision?

As always, decisions about writing ought to be guided by the effect those decisions have on meaning. The ultimate test for every sentence you write is this: Does the sentence convey its intended meaning as precisely as it possibly can? Only after the sentence has passed this first test should you entertain secondary considerations. For example, is it possible to structure the sentence in a way that allows you to link it to surrounding sentences more effectively? Is it possible to express the idea in a more interesting way?

Suggested strategy for making this decision.

Any time that you find you're having difficulty expressing an idea in a sentence, return to the simplest sentence structure. Articulate the idea in a simple, declarative sentence and then modify it if you choose to do so. Think about the ideas you mean to emphasize in the sentence. Do those ideas stand out? If not, experiment with different sentence structures to see if you can foreground them more clearly.

Questions to guide decision making in your own essay.

1. Though sentences are meant to express a complete thought, they often depend on surrounding sentences to provide context, qualification (i.e., limits or exceptions to the expressed idea), or elaboration (i.e., greater detail to the expressed idea). It is useful, therefore, to examine your sentences in the context of surrounding sentences.

2. Looking at a group of connected sentences, ask whether each sentence expresses the idea you had intended clearly and precisely. Could you modify any of the sentences to express the idea more clearly? Should you break a complex sentence or compound sentence into smaller sentences for greater clarity?

3. Are there any individual sentences that you should structure differently to provide emphasis to a particular idea?

4. Are there any individual sentences that you should structure differently to make the connection to surrounding ideas clearer?
5. Have you used a variety of sentence structures to enliven your text? Have you used a variety of sentence openings?

LO 1, 3

7.7   A BRIEF DISCUSSION ABOUT PARAGRAPHS

In this chapter you have been introduced to sentences and the importance of varying your sentence structure when writing your essay. Now, we turn your attention to how those sentences come together in a paragraph.

7.7.1 When Is a Paragraph Not a Paragraph?

A paragraph is a larger unit of meaning. Pay attention to the *unit* part. The difference between a paragraph and an unrelated series of sentences is that the paragraph is unified by a single controlling idea. Often, novice writers begin to write by organizing a loose outline (or, worse still, without using an outline at all, apparently believing that they will arrive at their point serendipitously), and listing a series of ideas that are linked together, at best, by some obscure, unseen theme. There are a couple of problems with that strategy: (1) it provides the writer with no guidance during the composition process, and (2) it provides the reader with no way of understanding how the ideas are related. As you will see below, one of the most significant differences between the way in which novice and experienced writers compose paragraphs is that that first group frequently dumps information on the page while the latter group organizes, and reorganizes, for meaning. Think about it this way. You have a friend (we all have this friend) who begins stories by relaying an endless series of unrelated details, develops stories by relaying a second series of unrelated details, and concludes stories by relaying a third series of unrelated details. Whatever redeeming charms the friend might have as a human being, his or her failing as a storyteller lies in the inability to recognize that personal anecdotes, like essays and the paragraphs that comprise them, ought to have a point. Unity of purpose is the principle that guides the linking of ideas.

In order to maintain that unity of purpose, you need to identify the single controlling idea that will govern the paragraph. All supporting ideas will be subordinated to that main idea (i.e., supporting ideas will relate back to the paragraph's controlling idea). If you find yourself introducing an idea that cannot be related to the controlling idea, you may need to redraft the sentence to make the connection clearer, to move the idea to a different paragraph, or to cut the idea altogether (which is walking away, one of the most difficult things a writer will ever have to do).

Sometimes, a paragraph's controlling idea is stated explicitly in a topic sentence. The topic sentence will clearly articulate the controlling idea and explain the way in which supporting ideas are related to it. There's a great deal to recommend this practice. A good topic sentence provides a road map for the writer to follow during composition and for the reader to follow during the reading process. You need to know, however, that some disciplines (particularly those in the humanities) regard the use of the topic sentence as both formulaic and stylistically clumsy. In these disciplines, the controlling idea is suggested implicitly, and woven artfully into the text, operating without announcing itself. It has a lovely effect, if it's done well. However, because the theme of the paragraph isn't stated explicitly, there is a greater risk that the writer will lose focus. When writing the first draft of the essay, you may find it easier to work with a clear statement of the essay's purpose.

7.7.1.1 Making Decisions about Paragraph Breaks   We identified a paragraph as a unit of meaning in which all ideas are governed by a single controlling idea. The decision to begin a new paragraph should be based on that principle.

- You should start a new paragraph when you need to introduce an idea that you cannot accommodate within the scope of the current paragraph.
- You should start a new paragraph when the organization of ideas is better served by two paragraphs (e.g., when writing a compare and contrast essay, where separate paragraphs can be used to contrast sides in an argument; or when the paragraph is getting so long that it becomes difficult for the reader to manage the volume of information).
- You should start a new paragraph when you're writing introductory and concluding paragraphs.

If, on the other hand, you began a paragraph with great enthusiasm, only to discover that you weren't able to develop the controlling idea beyond two or three sentences, you may want to consider whether (1) it's an idea that could be incorporated into an existing paragraph, or (2) it's an idea that has no place in the essay.

7.7.2 Internal Coherence

Like many before you, you may believe that coherence is not a feature of the text but a matter of opinion for the reader. We admire your healthy skepticism. As it turns out, however, the principle of textual coherence is relatively easy to defend. A coherent paragraph is one in which all the component parts are governed by a single unifying theme and linked together by an observable organizing strategy. Understanding that coherence isn't merely an aesthetic consideration but also a reflection of the internal logic of a paragraph may help you to make decisions about structure in your own paragraphs. The chart below provides some strategies to use for maintaining coherence in your writing.

Strategies for Improving Coherence in a Paragraph
Ensure that each paragraph is governed by a topic sentence or main idea.
Ensure that all sentences within the paragraph serve to develop the main idea, to provide evidence for the main idea, or to provide examples related to the main idea.
Use repetition of a key term or phrase to focus ideas and to keep the reader on track.

(continued)

(*continued*)

> Use pronouns to refer back to the main idea.
> - *This, that, these, those, he, she, it, they,* and *we* are useful pronouns for referring back to something previously mentioned.
> - It's critical, however, that you clearly identify the relationship between the pronoun and the noun to which it refers. If the relationship isn't obvious, reorganize your sentence or restate the noun.
>
> Use transition words to indicate to the readers the relationships between sentences.
> - Effective transitions provide coherence to the essay and advance the process of the argument.
> - See Chapter 9 for examples of transition words.

✓•─ Practice

Writing Exercise 1

The paragraph below is not a good paragraph. It flits from one idea to another and displays little evidence of an organizing structure. Rewrite the paragraph to ensure that the pattern of organization serves the central theme. You may need to rephrase the topic sentence or to modify or delete some of the sentences. When you've completed your rewrite, compare it to the example of an organized paragraph at the end of this writing exercise.

Some parents appear comfortable with the time their children spend on game consoles (Snow, 2010). Video games are available online, through game systems such as Nintendo, PlayStation, and Dreamcast, and now through cell phones and computer tablets. Video games are one of the fastest-growing segments of the entertainment industries. Some parents favour the presence of video games because the games provide cheap entertainment and keep children safely at home (Snow, 2010). Some parents appear comfortable with the time their children spend on game consoles (Snow, 2010). The industry has grown quickly from the early days, back in the 1970s, when people had to own a computer to be able to play games. Parents do not appear particularly concerned about the amount of time their children spend playing video games (Snow, 2010). Video games can be accessed from almost anywhere at any time. It is not unusual to find some homes with more than one game system, and it is also not unusual to find that some children and teens play up to six hours of video games on a daily basis (Snow, 2010). Parents do not appear particularly concerned about the amount of time their children spend playing video games (Snow, 2010).

> Think of the following questions when you're rewriting the paragraph:
> 1. What is the central theme of the paragraph?
> 2. What is the relationship of each sentence to that theme?
> 3. What information ought to come first?
> 4. What information ought to be grouped together?

Compare your rewrite to the following example. You are not judging your work against the example, as there are a number of ways in which the paragraph could be organized. It may, in fact, be the case that your rewrite is superior to this one. You are only reflecting on the decisions you made and comparing your decisions to those that were made in this example.

> *Video games are one of the fastest-growing segments of the entertainment industry. The popularity of playing video games has grown quickly from the early days in the 1970s, when people had to own a computer to be able to play games, to the present circumstance in which video games can be accessed anywhere at any time. Video games are available online, through game systems such as Nintendo, PlayStation, and Dreamcast, and now through cell phones and computer tablets. It is not unusual to find some homes with more than one game system and it is also not unusual to find that some children and teens play up to six hours of video games on a daily basis (Snow, 2010). It does not appear, however, that parents are particularly concerned about their children playing video games since the video games are seen as a form of cheap entertainment that keeps children home and out of danger (Snow, 2010).*

Writing Exercise 2

 Practice

Organize the material in each of the following boxes to support the specific subthesis. You may have to modify sentences, move them to a different paragraph, or delete them altogether.

Paragraph 1
Subthesis: *Learning is a memory process.* All learning begins with memory. <ul><li>There are three stages of memory, each of which is necessary to achieve a single recollection.</li><li>In order to acquire understanding, one has first to remember the information.</li><li>Though it is possible to remember without understanding, it is not possible to understand without remembering.</li><li>The second stage of memory is storage, a process through which sensory stimuli move through short-term memory to long-term memory.</li><li>The first stage of the memory process is encoding, which is the process of translating sensory stimuli into meaningful ideas.</li><li>The third stage of memory is retrieval.</li><li>If a student does not pay attention during the encoding stage, the information he or she sees or hears is quickly forgotten.</li><li>Active learning requires individuals to think critically about new information and to consider the purpose behind the information one learns.</li></ul>

Practice Exercise for Paragraph 1
Organize the material above around the subthesis *learning is a memory process.*

Paragraph 2

Subthesis: *Memory works best when individuals can attend to a single stimulus.*
It is difficult to pay attention in a noisy environment.

- During the encoding stage, information from the external world must be selectively identified, understood, and stored.
- Some individuals attempt to watch television or listen to music when they are studying.
- In the initial stage of the memory process, attempts to pay attention to multiple sources of information may lead to information being missed or misunderstood.
- People remember better when they are able to focus their attention on a single stimulus.
- To avoid losing information in the initial stage of memory, individuals must actively pay attention to the information they want to remember.
- It is important to avoid competing stimuli when trying to concentrate on unfamiliar material.

Paragraph 2

Organize the material above around the subthesis *memory works best when individuals can attend to a single stimulus.*

Paragraph 3

Subthesis: *Music introduces a competing stimulus to the material the student is studying.*

- Some individuals believe that music improves their ability to concentrate on other things.
- Some music interferes with concentration.
- Music that does not have lyrics, a noticeable pattern, or heavy accents or strong beats is less likely to interfere with concentration.
- To test whether music is interfering with concentration, individuals should break from their studies for twenty minutes and ask themselves whether they can remember the music that was playing while they were studying.
- Music sometimes interferes with the encoding process.
- It is easier to encode information when one is learning actively.
- In a noisy room, students are less likely to remember the things they read.

Paragraph 3

Organize the material above around the subthesis *music introduces a competing stimulus to the material the student is studying.*

Once again, it may be useful for you to reflect on the decisions you made while you were rewriting and think about the effect that those decisions had on the paragraphs you produced.

7.8 USING THE IDDL MODEL TO STRUCTURE PARAGRAPHS

LO 4

One of the advantages to working from an outline is that an outline allows you to reflect on the structure of your essay from a meta-perspective (i.e., an outline reveals the ways in which the various elements of an essay are related to one another). The second stage of the IDDL model asks you to **D**efine the problems locally (i.e., at the level of the paragraph or series of related paragraphs), using the arguable proposition to define the specific questions that need to be answered in order to demonstrate that your argument is reasonable. Those questions ought to provide you with some guidance when you're making decisions about your paragraph structure.

In the example below, we've broken the arguable proposition into a series of questions that need to be answered if the argument is to succeed. The answers to those questions will become either paragraphs or a series of related paragraphs in the final essay.

Introduction:
What is the arguable proposition?

> **Example:** *Students should not listen to music while studying because learning is a memory process, memory works best when individuals can attend to a single stimulus, and music introduces a competing stimulus to the material the student is studying.*

What is the claim?
- *Students should not listen to music while studying*

What is the causal connector?
- *because*

What are the reasons in support of the claim?
- *learning is a memory process*
- *memory works best when individuals can attend to a single stimulus*
- *music introduces a competing stimulus to the material the student is studying*

Identify the first local problem.
- How will you prove that learning is a memory process?

Identify the second local problem.
- How will you prove that memory works best when individuals can attend to a single stimulus?

Identify the third local problem.
- How will you prove that music introduces a competing stimulus to the material the student is studying?

Why would a reasonable person disagree?
- Are there any exceptions to the points you've made above?

Conclusion:
What must be proved?
- You must prove that *students should not listen to music while studying because learning is a memory process, memory works best when individuals can attend to a single stimulus, and music introduces a competing stimulus to the material the student is studying.*

In identifying the specific questions that need to be addressed in your essay, you also identify the natural units of the essay. You can use those units to guide your decision making when organizing your essay into paragraphs.

LO 3 7.9 MAKING WRITING DECISIONS ABOUT PARAGRAPHS

In the following chart, we've identified some of the considerations that are important when making decisions about constructing paragraphs. The questions at the end of the chart might help to guide you when you're working on your own essay.

Making Writing Decisions	About Constructing Paragraphs in Your Own Essay

What is the purpose of this writing decision?

Though paragraphs have a number of functions, the most important one in this context is the function of grouping ideas by a single unifying theme.

What is the effect of this writing decision?

Essays in which the paragraphs are well organized tend to be coherent and clear. The reader is able to recognize both the relationship of the information within the paragraph and the relevance of the paragraph to the essay itself.

What considerations inform this decision?

As we've mentioned before, writing, to some degree at least, is the act of imposing order on ideas. That is particularly true when organizing an essay into paragraph units. By identifying one particular idea as the controlling idea of a particular unit of meaning, paragraphs give that idea pre-eminence. Therefore, when making decisions about paragraphs, you need to think about the ideas on which the essay's argument stands.

Suggested strategy for making this decision.

The IDDL model allows you to think about paragraphs on the basis of their function within the overall structure of the essay. Identify the key elements that underpin your argument and organize the essay around them.

Questions to guide decision making in your own essay.

1. Look at the essay on which you are currently working. What is the argument, either implicit or explicit, that the essay is making?
2. What are the key points in that argument?
3. Looking at the first of those key points, ask yourself what needs to be proved or explored. What evidence might you offer to support the idea? In what ways will you explore the idea?
4. For each succeeding key point, repeat the process you followed above.
5. After drafting each paragraph, ask yourself whether (1) the paragraph is unified by a single, controlling idea, and (2) whether that single, controlling idea is clearly related to the essay's thesis.

7.10 CONCLUSION

In this chapter, we've reviewed some of the principles that ought to guide you when you're organizing your ideas into sentences and paragraphs. In each case, we tried to define the principle in relation to the effect it would have. By concentrating on the effect of the decisions you make as a writer, you will find that you're better able to manage those effects intentionally.

The decisions you make about composing sentences result in a corresponding change in effect. This allows you to alter the emphasis of a sentence by altering the sentence structure. As you come to master the different sentence structures, you are better able to introduce subtle adjustments of meaning. You can also use that understanding to introduce a variety of sentence structures to your essay, making it livelier and, thus, more pleasing to the reader. Similarly, by understanding the principle of paragraph organization, you are able to make decisions about the most effective way to foreground the ideas you think are important. If paragraphs are units of meaning that are governed by a single controlling idea, you ought to select and articulate those controlling ideas in such a way as to create units that serve the larger essay. At the end of the chapter, we returned again to the IDDL model, demonstrating the way in which it can be used to identify the key themes that you need to explore as you move from your thesis statement to your conclusion. That knowledge allows you to make better decisions about the controlling ideas that will anchor the various paragraphs and the ways in which those paragraphs will fit together.

MyCompLab®

How Do I Get a Better Grade?

Go to MyCompLab for additional help with your grammar, writing, and research skills. You will have access to a variety of exercises, instruction, and videos that will help you improve your basic skills and help you get a better grade.

✔•┤Practice   **Evaluation Worksheet for Sentences**

> The worksheet below is intended for you to use when thinking about sentences
> in your own essay writing. Use the questions to determine whether the decisions
> you're making are having the effect you intend.

An Evaluation Worksheet to Guide Decision Making When Constructing Sentences in Your Own Essay

1. Take out the essay on which you are currently working and look at the sentences in the first paragraph. Are the sentences complete (i.e., does each have a subject and a predicate)?

2. Look at sentences that express key ideas. It's critically important that you craft those sentences carefully. They establish the context for other sentences. Readers can often decipher meaning by reasoning inductively from the context, but the context must be clear.

3. Does each sentence convey its intended meaning precisely? Could the idea be expressed more clearly if you altered the structure of the sentence? Has the sentence become so long that it's unmanageable? In many cases, it's easier to draft a complex idea as a series of simple, declarative sentences and then link them.

4. Has the sentence emphasized the point you intended to make? Should you restructure the sentence to add greater emphasis to a particular idea?

5. Look at the way in which you've connected individual sentences to one another. Can you restructure the sentence to make the connection clearer?

6. Review the sentences in the paragraph for variety. Have you fallen into a monotonous pattern, beginning each sentence the same way and using the same sentence structure repeatedly? Can you introduce variety without compromising clarity?

Evaluation Worksheet for Paragraphs

 Practice

The worksheet below is intended for you to use when thinking about paragraphs in your own essay writing. Use the questions to determine whether the decisions you're making are having the effect you intend.

An Evaluation Worksheet to Guide Decision Making When Constructing Paragraphs in Your Own Essays

1. Take out the essay on which you are currently working.

2. Identify the thesis and arguable proposition. What is the claim that's being made? What reasons or evidence have you provided in support of the claim?

3. Select the first reason and use it to guide you when constructing the first paragraph or series of related paragraphs. What needs to be proven? What evidence do you have in support of that reason? Is the discussion of, and support for, the first reason so extensive that it cannot be managed in a single paragraph? If so, break the paragraph into a series of paragraphs, with each paragraph addressing one aspect of the first reason.

4. Review the draft of the paragraph. What is the controlling idea? Are there ideas in the paragraph that don't appear to be related to that idea? Can they be rephrased to make the relationship clearer? Do they belong in a different paragraph? Or do they belong in that sad pile of irrelevant ideas that ought never to have been included in the first place?

5. For each reason that you've offered in support of your argument, use the process you followed above.

6. Think about exceptions to the claim you made in your arguable proposition. Do you want to discuss the counter-argument to your position in a single paragraph? Though there is no hard and fast rule on this, many writers explore the counter-arguments in the penultimate (i.e., next-to-last) paragraph.

✓•⌐Practice   **Sentence Variety Peer-Review Worksheet**

Writer's Name: _____

Reviewer's Name: _____

1. Look at four or five key sentences in the essay and note them below.

   _____

   _____

2. Do the sentences appear to convey their meaning effectively? Are there any that should be modified to improve clarity or alter emphasis? Note those below.

   _____

   _____

3. Can you suggest ways in which any of the sentences could be modified to improve clarity or alter emphasis? While making your suggestions, explain why you think the sentence should be altered in the way you suggest.

   _____

   _____

4. Returning to your essay again, reread two paragraphs and ask yourself whether you've overused certain sentence structures. Can you suggest ways to introduce sentence variety while still maintaining the meaning of the sentences?

   _____

   _____

✓•⌐Practice   **Paragraph Peer-Review Worksheet**

Writer's Name: _____

Reviewer's Name: _____

Select two paragraphs to review and assess their effectiveness using the questions below.

<u>First Paragraph</u>

1. Identify the controlling idea of the first paragraph and note it below.

   _____

   _____

2. Are there sentences in the paragraph that don't appear to be related to the controlling idea? Note those sentences below.

_____

_____

3. Can the sentences that appear unrelated to the controlling idea be rephrased to make their relationship to the paragraph clearer? Rephrase them and record the revision below. Note the way in which your revision improves the paragraph.

_____

_____

4. If a sentence cannot be reworked to make it more relevant to the controlling idea, ask yourself whether (a) the sentence belongs in a different paragraph, or (b) it belongs in that sad pile of irrelevant ideas that ought never to have included in the first place. Explain the reasoning behind your decision below.

_____

_____

<u>Second Paragraph</u>

5. Identify the controlling idea of the second paragraph and note it below.

_____

_____

6. Are there sentences in the paragraph that do not appear to be related to the controlling idea? Note those sentences below.

_____

_____

7. Can the sentences that appear unrelated to the controlling idea be rephrased to make their relationship to the paragraph clearer? Rephrase them and record the revision below. Note the way in which your revision improves the paragraph.

_____

_____

CHAPTER 8

Introductory Paragraphs

Learning Objectives

At the completion of this chapter, you will be able to:

1. Identify the differences between the ways in which novice and experienced writers write introductions to academic essays.

2. Discuss the importance of using the introduction to familiarize the reader with the text.

3. Demonstrate the ability to establish a pattern of reasoning by connecting important ideas in the introduction.

4. Distinguish between effective and ineffective strategies for writing introductions.

8.1 INTRODUCTION

Writers often approach introductions with the same anxiety as they would approach the first few moments of a blind date. It's so hard to know what to say. If you give away too much information too soon, you'll have nothing to talk about over dinner. If, on the other hand, you say nothing at all or leap too quickly into a discussion that presumes a familiarity you don't yet share, well, you might be eating dinner alone. You're torn. You want to establish a sense of connection but you don't want to move too quickly. You want to make a good impression but don't want to establish expectations that you can't possibly meet. It's a challenge. There's no doubt about it.

As is often the case, we have good news and bad news. Bad news first. We can't help you with the blind date part. Nobody can. Blind dates are just awkward. On the other hand, we might be able to help with the writing of introductions. The trick is to focus less on you and more on the reader. What does the reader need to know? As we've said before and will say again, writing decisions should be driven by purpose, and the purpose of an introduction is to provide the reader with a means of entering the text. The introduction is a gateway of sorts, an orientation to an unfamiliar world. Regardless of the number of essays your readers have read before, they haven't read your essay (and, even if they have read your previous essays, they have not read this *particular* essay). They are strangers to the text you've created. The introduction is meant to make them comfortable.

In this chapter, we'll discuss some of the challenges in writing introductions and a number of strategies for addressing those challenges. As always, we'll be guided by this principle: the decisions you make as a writer should be informed with an understanding of the effect those decisions will have on the text.

8.2   UNDERSTANDING THE DIFFERENCE BETWEEN THE PRACTICE OF THE NOVICE WRITER AND THE PRACTICE OF THE EXPERIENCED WRITER

LO 1

Novice writers often write as if the reader is already familiar with the text. They fail to recognize that the intellectual movement into a text is similar to a movement into a foreign culture. In order for the reader to operate effectively in any particular text, the writer needs to provide a guide to the conventions that will be followed. One of the characteristics of novice writers is that they often drop information onto the page without explaining either its purpose or its relationship to other ideas. That is, they *list* ideas rather than using the introduction to indicate the important relationships between the ideas. In contrast, the experienced writer uses the introduction to establish the pattern of ideas that will give the essay its shape.

In the following chart, we've identified some of the differences between the kind of introductions that novice writers produce and the kind of introductions that more experienced writers produce. One of the principal differences is the degree to which experienced writes are guided by attention to the needs of the reader. They shape the text to their audience and purpose. In contrast, novice writers often write introductions as if the information *needs* no introduction.

An introduction ought to articulate the essay's argument clearly. Experienced writers use the introduction to create a means by which the reader might enter the text, thereby establishing the conventions that will be followed and identifying the formatting protocols that will be observed. They make connections between the major ideas of the essay and identify the pattern of organization the essay will follow.

Novice Writers	Experienced Writers
■ Require thought for procedural, or "mechanical," writing functions.	■ Have, to a significant degree, automated procedural functions.
■ Focus on error avoidance rather than meaning.	■ Focus on developing or refining meaning.
■ Begin writing without planning, and edit, if at all, for grammatical errors.	■ Invest time and energy in planning and reviewing.
■ *Focus on "knowledge telling" (i.e., relating all the information they have and can find on a topic, rather than exercising critical judgment to determine relevance).*	■ *Organize, and reorganize, essay structure to allow individual ideas to serve the overall purpose of the essay.*

LO 2, 3, 4   8.3   ORIENTING THE READER TO THE TEXT

Imagine that you've rented a motel room. You've probably been to motels before and have a general understanding of the sort of things you might reasonably expect to find in a motel room (e.g., there is always a Gideon Bible in the top drawer of the bedside table and a remote control on top of the television). There is, nonetheless, a period of adjustment. The general knowledge that you have of motel rooms allows you to predict that this motel room will have certain characteristics, but you still need to learn more about this motel room in particular before you're going to be truly comfortable. Readers entering a new text feel the same way. Your job as a writer is to tell them what kind of motel this is and where they might find the things they need.

The text is like the motel room. Some things are familiar to the reader, but some things are unique to this particular text. In introducing the reader to the textual environment, the writer is immersing the reader in a new environment, one in which the reader must rely on the writer for an orientation to the customs, the expectations, and the character of the textual world. Despite the fact that writers tend to regard the introduction as a poor cousin of the more sophisticated and substantial paragraphs to follow, no one enters the text except by way of the introduction. The introduction establishes the relationship between the writer and the reader, identifying the writing protocols that the writer will observe (e.g., Will the writer work from a distance, using the third-person voice, or will the writer presume a more intimate relationship? Will the writer appeal to emotion or the intellect?).

By providing an introduction that helps readers make a transition between their own world and the world of the text, the writer gives readers the tools they need to access the essay. In short, the introduction provides a means of entry to the essay, transporting readers to the place of the text.

8.3.1 Making Writing Decisions about Orienting the Reader to the Text

In large part, you're writing an introduction to provide readers with the information they need to operate effectively within the text. The decisions you make in that regard will be guided by your understanding of writing purpose and audience.

Use the following chart to evaluate the introductions in your own essay writing. Are your introductions providing the reader with a way into the text?

Making Writing Decisions	About Orienting the Reader to the Text in Your Own Essay Writing

What is the purpose of this writing decision?

The movement to a textual environment is always, to some degree, a movement to a foreign environment. However familiar a reader may be with the protocols of texts in general, each new text requires a process of orientation.

What is the effect of this writing decision?

The writer's job is to make the reader feel at home by providing the information necessary for the reader to understand the rules that govern this new environment. In short, the more a reader knows about the protocols a writer is observing and the pattern of organization that will follow, the sooner the reader becomes comfortable in the text.

What considerations inform this decision?

In order to write an effective introduction, the writer needs to be aware of the distance that exists between the audience and the text. The more familiar the writer assumes the audience to be with the ideas that will be expressed in the essay, the less explicit the introduction needs to be. On the other hand, if the writer assumes the audience to be largely unfamiliar with the substance of the essay, the writer needs to provide a more complete and explicit introduction.

Suggested strategies for making this decision.

Think about the purpose of the text. What does the reader need to know if he or she is to understand your purpose? What is the thesis? What are the supporting ideas? How are the ideas related? Explain to the reader why you're writing and how you intend to proceed through the essay.

Questions to guide decision making in your own essay.

1. To understand what we're saying about introductions, we want you to take the essay that you're working on right now and consider the effect your introduction might have on the reader.
2. How does your introduction establish the pattern your argument will follow (i.e., have you made it clear to the reader what you are arguing and on what basis)?
3. How have you indicated the academic writing conventions you will follow? For example, what kind of evidence will you use? Will you speak to the reader from the first person (*I*) or from the third person (*he, she, they*)?

8.3.2 Writing Exercise—Orienting the Reader to the Text

In the following example, the writer has listed information without clearly identifying the way in which the reader is meant to understand that information. You may notice how difficult it is to anticipate the pattern of reasoning that the writer will follow. Because the writer has failed to explain how the information is meant to be organized, you have no way of predicting the course the essay will take.

One of the purposes of an introduction is to provide the reader with an orientation to the text. Does this introduction provide you with the information you need to feel at home within the text?

Example of an Unsuccessful Attempt to Use the Introduction to Orient the Reader to the Text

Health care professionals today may lack the proper skills for cardiopulmonary resuscitation. The problem is that "poor knowledge and skill retention following cardiopulmonary resuscitation training for nursing and medical staff has been documented over the past 20 years" (Hamilton, 2005, p. 288). Most people do not have time to take a four-hour course to be trained. The recent forms of independent study are an effective way of learning and retaining the simple psychomotor skills necessary for cardiopulmonary resuscitation (CPR).

Draft a thesis statement that links the information in the example above.

_____

_____

Use your thesis statement to guide you as you rewrite the introduction.

_____

_____

How does the introduction you wrote improve upon the original?

_____

_____

LO 2, 3, 4

8.4 ESTABLISHING READER EXPECTATIONS

Readers operate more effectively when they know what to expect from a text. When you receive a letter from your grandmother, you wouldn't be surprised to find her express that kind of maternal concern about your well-being that you've always known her to express or surprised to find that she might offer you a small token of cash (without telling anyone; that's just the kind of grandmother she is). You would, however, be a little surprised to find that she was footnoting her observations about things that had happened in the hometown by citing the local newspaper. It's a different kind of communication. Similarly, if your friend were to text you a brief message that included a lengthy references page, well, let's be honest, you might start reviewing applicants to replace him or her as an acquaintance. Nobody needs that kind of formality in a text message. On the other hand, readers of academic writing don't expect the writer to display familiarity in tone or in diction. Readers of academic writing do expect that the writer will recognize the protocols of the academic writing situation.

Those protocols are important. Protocols, like page format and methods of citation, are a way of familiarizing the reader with the text. While novice writers might imagine that instructors assign a particular writing format (e.g., APA, MLA) casually, the format provides the reader with information about the organization of the page and of the various elements of the essay. In short, the format helps to orient readers to the text by telling them where to find the information they need.

8.4.1 Sample Showing the Way in Which Writers Can Establish Reader Expectations through the Introduction

As you read the following writing sample, pay particular attention to the way in which the writer establishes reader expectations and forecasts the direction the essay will follow.

Example of a Writer's Use of the Introduction to Establish Expectations

Health care professionals have learned through their previous experiences with infectious disease outbreaks the importance of learning proper hand hygiene practices. Use of disinfectants and learning the proper techniques of hand washing are critical in the fight to stop the spread of communicable diseases in a health care setting. In the past, patients contracted hospital-associated infections due to the lack of established hand hygiene regulations and the improper practices that health care professionals followed. For all health care workers, the importance of proper education regarding hand washing is necessary, as the cost of preventing the transmission of micro-organisms that cause infections in patients is much less than having to treat the possibility of an infection outbreak. The Centers for Disease Control and Prevention (CDC) are promoting a strategy that calls for regular use of alcohol-based hand rubs, antimicrobial soaps, or antiseptic hand washes by health care professionals after treating or being in contact with infected patients or their surroundings. With the enactment of this strategy, they can reduce the number of infection-causing micro-organisms that will be transmitted from health care professionals' hands to the patients (CDC, 2002).

> The opening sentence of the introduction provides a thematic link for the elements of the essay.

> The writer has provided the essential ideas of the argument that is to be made, and has linked them in an order that demonstrates their relationship to one another. This allows the reader to anticipate, or predict, elements of the emerging essay.

8.4.2 Making Writing Decisions about Establishing Reader Expectations

In academic writing, you manage reader expectations in two ways: (1) by operating within the rules and protocols of a particular genre or writing format (i.e., the format indicates the way in which the page will be laid out, how evidence or other reference material will be selected and introduced, and how citations and references will be recorded), and (2) by using the thesis statement and the introduction to guide the reader to expectations that are consistent with your writing purpose (i.e., you create reader expectations by telling the reader what you intend to do).

Use the following chart to evaluate the introductions in your own essay writing. How has your introduction established the expectations that will guide your reader?

Making Writing Decisions	About Establishing Reader Expectations in Your Own Essay Writing

What is the purpose of this writing decision?

In fairness to the reader the writer needs to establish expectations for the text early. In an academic essay, the writer suggests the argument that will be made and the basis on which it's being made.

What is the effect of this writing decision?

By establishing expectations, the writer indicates to the reader both the ideas and the pattern those ideas will follow. This allows the reader to anticipate the progression of ideas.

What considerations inform this decision?

As noted above, in the discussion of orienting the reader to the text, the most important consideration is the distance that the writer perceives to exist between the audience and the text. The less familiar the audience is assumed to be with the subject, the more explicit the writer must be in establishing expectations.

Suggested strategies for making this decision.

Establishing reader expectations allows the reader to predict the direction the essay will take. Think about the implicit logic of the essay. What is the logical order of ideas? How can you forecast that order to the reader? While literary writing is sometimes well served by the withholding of key information until the reader reaches a climactic moment in the work, that principle rarely works in academic writing.

Questions to guide decision making in your own essay.

1. Return again to the essay that you're working on right now to evaluate whether you have written your introduction in a way that allows the reader to anticipate the direction your essay will take.
2. How does your introduction create reader expectations (i.e., how have you indicated the major ideas you will explore and how have you connected those ideas)?
3. Are the expectations you've established consistent with your intentions? Have you promised something that you won't deliver?
4. Does the reader have the information that he or she needs to proceed into the essay? What is the principal argument you're making? What information will the reader require to follow that argument?

LO 2, 3, 4   # 8.5   CONNECTING IDEAS

The introduction provides you with an opportunity to establish a pattern of organization for the essay. The introduction is the point at which the writer identifies the principal themes of the essay and indicates the relationship between those themes. That relationship is the thing the reader came to see. The information you include in your essay is available from a number of different writers in a number of different places. The way in which you use that information—crafting a unique expression of your particular view on an issue or phenomenon—is the thing that makes your essay worth reading.

8.5.1 Parallel Lines vs. Vectors

Writing imposes order on ideas. It establishes the relationship from one idea to another, and it links them in a way that permits a reader to recognize a coherent pattern. The point at which you want the reader to understand how major ideas will relate to one another is at the beginning. The introduction also allows you to establish that coherence. Unfortunately, writers sometimes imagine that dumping tangentially related ideas on the page, relying on their proximity to one another to demonstrate the connection, is enough to establish a pattern. That generally doesn't work as well as you would think. Unlike simple life forms (those curious creatures that biologists report in classroom videos), ideas do not self-organize.

One of the common difficulties with introductory paragraphs is that they fail to connect the major ideas of the essay. Instead, ideas are presented independently. Each idea is permitted to chart its own course, with the writer hoping, perhaps, that it will meet the other ideas at some point in the future.

Here's why that won't happen. If you imagine each idea to represent a line of thought, travelling in a linear direction as lines generally do, that idea will travel to infinity on the course that you've plotted. Now you introduce a second idea, representing a second line of thought. As the first line of thought did, this line also travels to infinity on its plotted course. Without pretending a mastery of geometry that we don't have, we are relatively certain that lines travelling parallel to one another will never meet. On the one hand, parallel lines travelling to infinity without ever meeting is an extraordinarily interesting idea, and one that you might want to spend a carefree afternoon reflecting on. On the other hand, that same concept argues, fairly convincingly, against your ever achieving any kind of coherence in an essay. Instead, you might want to consider having those ideas converge in your introduction. The convergence of ideas creates a common vector, which allows the ideas to come together in a focused way.

8.5.2 Comparing Introductory Paragraphs in Which Ideas Run Parallel to Those in Which the Ideas Converge

In the first example that follows, the writer has *listed* ideas rather than *connecting* them. Notice that, in this approach, the reader is given little or no indication of the relationship between the ideas.

Example of Paragraph in Which Ideas Run Parallel

In this example, you may notice that the introduction provides information as if the information itself might make the writer's point. That is rarely the case. The writer needs to introduce the information in such a way as to demonstrate the purposeful relationship between the individual sentences.

Marijuana is the most commonly used illegal drug in Canada. Its usage has many negative side effects on the brain, such as memory loss, shortened attention span, decreased problem-solving skills, depression, and anxiety, all of which can affect a person's learning capabilities. The active ingredient in marijuana is called tetra-hydrocannabinol (more commonly known as THC), and when it enters the brain it attaches itself to sites called cannabinoid receptors. Some areas of the brain contain many more cannabinoid receptors, such as the hippocampus (a part of the brain that plays a large role in the process of memory and emotions) which means that they will be affected much more by the use of marijuana than most other parts of the brain.

In the following example, the writer has linked the ideas together to create a pattern of ideas that will provide the introduction, and the essay, with its structure.

Example of Paragraph in Which Ideas Converge

By concentrating, in the introduction on establishing a relationship between the ideas that govern the essay, the writer has established a pattern that will provide the essay with coherence and structure. This initial pattern assists the writer to sustain the logic of the argument throughout the essay.

Though marijuana is the most widely used illegal drug, its usage has many negative side effects, all of which can affect a person's learning capabilities. These include: memory loss, shortened attention span, decreased problem-solving skills, depression, and anxiety. The active ingredient in marijuana, tetrahydrocannabinol (more commonly known as THC), is the agent that leads to the user's feeling of euphoria. It operates by attaching itself to sites called cannabinoid receptors. Unfortunately, because some areas of the brain, such as the hippocampus (a part of the brain that plays a large role in the process of memory and emotions), contain a disproportionate number of cannabinoid receptors, these will be affected much more by the use of marijuana than most other parts of the brain.

8.5.3 Making Writing Decisions about Connecting Ideas in the Introduction

By connecting ideas in the introduction, the writer establishes the relationship between the important themes of the essay. In effect, the introduction becomes a blueprint for the entire essay, guiding the writer (and the reader) through the text that follows. The chart below lists some of the questions you need to consider when connecting ideas in your introduction.

Making Writing Decisions	About Connecting Ideas in the Introduction in Your Own Essay Writing

What is the purpose of this writing decision?

The purpose of an introduction is not simply to provide a *list* of the ideas that will follow. Rather, it is to provide an introduction to the ideas and to the relationship between those ideas. While reflecting on the effectiveness of a draft introduction, the writer is looking to see whether the ideas are introduced in a way that forecasts or reveals those relationships.

What is the effect of this writing decision?

A successful introduction provides the writer with a blueprint for the essay. The logical relationship of principal ideas that is first captured in the introduction serves to guide the writer in the struggle to maintain coherence in the emerging text.

What considerations inform this decision?

It's important to remember when drafting an introduction that ideas that run parallel generally fail to provide the reader with any understanding of the ideas' relevance. In order to indicate why a particular idea has been introduced, it's usually necessary to indicate that idea's logical relationship to the other ideas in the introduction.

Suggested strategy for making this decision.

Prepare for writing a draft of your introduction by identifying your arguable proposition. An arguable proposition is generally a statement that makes a claim and provides the reasons for that claim. The arguable proposition will generally identify the logical or associative connection between ideas in an essay. Allow that connection to guide you in constructing both your introduction and, subsequently, your essay.

Questions to guide decision making in your own essay.

1. Examine the introduction of the essay you're currently writing.
2. How have you linked the principal ideas of the introduction?
3. Think about your arguable proposition (Chapter 2) and ask yourself whether you've connected the ideas in the introduction in the same way that you connected them in the arguable proposition. Do the connections between ideas reflect the relationship you mean to establish? Is the causal relationship the one you intend?
4. If not, what steps can you take to make the relationship between the ideas clearer?

8.6 STRATEGIES FOR WRITING INTRODUCTIONS TO ACADEMIC ESSAYS

LO 2, 3, 4

The introduction provides you with an opportunity to identify your purpose for the reader. In an academic essay, this is perhaps more important than it might be in other forms of writing. You don't necessarily need a hook or meditative quotation to engage the reader. The audience for an academic essay is not usually skimming through competing forms of media, looking for the one that promises to entertain. In most cases, your audience has already chosen to read your essay.

Accordingly, academic writers operate differently than writers of fiction or newspaper articles. Unlike writers of fiction, academic writers don't hold readers in suspense until the final page. If there's a murder, academic writers are inclined to give up the name of the guilty party in the first page. If your reader is surprised when he or she arrives at the concluding paragraph, well, frankly, you've done something wrong. Academic writers also differ from writers of newspaper or magazine articles in their approach to introductions. Unlike writers of newspaper or magazine articles, academic writers assume that their readers have made some kind of commitment to the article or book in front of them. Academic writers are, therefore, less inclined to organize their essays using a pyramid structure that provides all the important details in a single paragraph. Instead, writers of academic essays use the introduction to sketch an outline of the essay and to point readers in the direction that the essay will take them. The writers identify the arguable proposition and, curiously enough, provide enough information that their readers can anticipate the conclusion. In fact, in academic writing, a good introduction is one that pretty much gives away the conclusion upfront so the readers know, from beginning to end, exactly what it is the writer is trying to achieve.

In the following chart, we've provided a short list of general principles for writing introductions. You'll notice that, in each case, the principle speaks both to the relationship between the writer and the reader and to the relationship between the introduction and the essay itself.

Principles for Writing Introductions in Your Own Essay Writing
Write a draft or provisional introduction before beginning the essay. The process of articulating ideas will provide a focus to main themes and assist in the writing of a well-structured essay. You can write a tentative introduction first and then return to it as the themes become clearer. Many writers find that they need to write some kind of introduction in order to get the writing process started.
Create a checklist for the introduction. The elements of a good introduction include: ■ An outline that gives form to the structure of the essay. ■ An arguable proposition that articulates and limits the scope of the essay. ■ A forecast or summary of the essay's content.
Use the introduction to forecast the various themes of the essay. The introductory outline serves as the map indicating the individual themes of the essay. As the readers arrive at the discussion of each theme, they should find that they understand its purpose. They should also find that they recognize the relevance of the information and understand its relationship to the surrounding text.

Principles that have no obvious application may be of little use to you. In the section that follows, you'll find a list of strategies based on the principles above.

1. Using the Introduction to Contextualize Your Thesis

In providing background information, you signal to the reader the way in which your thesis fits within a larger context. It's important to remember that representation of your context is meant to serve your writing purpose. It is not meant to *be* the writing purpose. As we will discuss in a later section ("Strategies to Avoid When Writing the Introduction in Your Own Essay"), you don't need an exhaustive review of the topic from the beginning of time.

Example 1

Thesis Statement:
Despite the superior dexterity and cognitive ability of primates, the capacity of dogs for deep attachments to humans is one of the reasons why dogs should continue to be considered the species of choice in service work.

Introductory Paragraph:
Due, perhaps, to a pack instinct that provided an evolutionary advantage in their develop-ment as a species, dogs have emerged as prime candidates for work as service animals. They

often appear to have a greater interest in serving the interests of those they protect than in their own well-being and have been known to risk injury or death to defend the individuals with whom they bond. Despite the superior dexterity and cognitive ability of primates, the capacity of dogs for deep attachments to humans is one of the reasons why dogs should continue to be considered the species of choice in service work.

In three relatively short sentences, the writer has established a context for the argument that will follow. Though the writer will need to elaborate further in the essay, he or she has indicated the general thesis of the essay (i.e., dogs are better service animals than primates) and the rationale for that thesis (i.e., the dog's instinctive capacity for loyalty to others in its social group makes it a better candidate for service than the more intelligent and dexterous primate). To some degree, the writer has also indicated a pattern of organization for the essay by establishing the comparison between one animal and the other.

Example 2

Thesis Statement:
The American government should not be sponsoring culls of the wild mustang population.

Introductory Paragraph:
The horse is a proud and noble animal. Horses have been around for hundreds of thousands of years, having emerged from a much smaller species. The horse is now large enough to provide transportation and to fulfill many duties on a farm. It is odd, therefore, that the American government is willing to permit regular culls of the wild mustang populations.

In this example, the writer has provided information but has not organized the information in such a way as to indicate its relevance. How does the horse's pride and nobility relate to its evolution? How does its evolution relate to its capacity for service on the farm? How does the utility of a farm horse relate to the fate of wild mustangs?

Writing Exercises

In each of the following exercises, write an introduction that provides a context for the thesis statement.

Exercise 1

 Practice

Thesis Statement:
The use of extended cargo vans should be limited to professional drivers because the vans pose different challenges than smaller vehicles, the general driving public is not trained to operate them, and cargo vans have been involved in a disproportionate number of accidents compared to regular vans.

Introductory Paragraph:

_____

_____

_____

✓• Practice

Exercise 2

Thesis Statement:

Household laundry rooms should be equipped with childproof locks because young children can become trapped in dryers, injured by running washing machines, or exposed to harmful chemicals.

Introductory Paragraph:

_____

_____

_____

2. Using the Introduction to Establish a Pattern of Organization   The introduction also serves to establish a pattern of organization for the essay. With that in mind, you can begin to draft your introduction by using the outline of the essay you're intending to write. The essay might evolve as you write (in which case, of course, you will modify the introduction), but the outline will allow you to write a provisional introduction.

Example I

Thesis Statement:
Playing violent video games can be dangerous to a child's development because they are too realistic, they can be addictive, and they can lead children to spend too much time alone.

Introductory Paragraph:
There have been a number of articles written about the effects of playing violent video games on a child's development. In the last ten years, video game playing has doubled in the eight to fourteen years age group. Some researchers (Howell, 2009; Burns, 2012) have discovered that children play video games on average three to four hours a day. This consumes a large part of a child's day, leaving no time for other hobbies. Many of the video games on the market today are violent video games. Playing violent video games can be dangerous to a child's development because they are too realistic, they can be addictive, and they can lead children to spend too much time alone.

- How does this paragraph forecast or establish the pattern of organization the essay might follow?
- Based on this paragraph, what themes will be discussed in the essay?
- What is the order in which those themes will be discussed?
- How will those themes be connected or related to one another?

Example 2

Thesis Statement:
New strategies need to be developed for addressing tobacco use by teenagers because it seems that the process of decision making by the youth operates on different principles than the principles that govern adult decision making.

Introductory Paragraph:

There has been a marked decrease in the number of adult smokers (aged 18–75) in the last five years (Marshall, 2012). However, there has been an increase in the number of young smokers (aged 10–17) over the same period. It appears that the anti-smoking advertisements may be effective with the adult population, but they are not working for the younger genera- tion. Ten years ago the incidence of teenage smokers had declined for the first time in twenty years but, since that one-year drop, the numbers have been steadily increasing again. It may be that youth, armed with their sense of invulnerability, do not see the dangers associated with tobacco use. New strategies need to be developed for addressing tobacco use by teenagers because it seems that the process of decision making by the youth operates on different prin- ciples than the principles that govern adult decision making.

- How does this paragraph forecast or establish the pattern of organization the essay might follow?
- Based on this paragraph, what themes will be discussed in the essay?
- What is the order in which those themes will be discussed?
- How will those themes be connected or related to one another?

Writing Exercises

In each of the exercises below, use the thesis statement to guide you as you write an introductory paragraph that establishes a pattern of organization for the essay.

Exercise 1

✔• Practice

Thesis Statement:

All public schools should provide age-appropriate safer sex education to familiarize younger children with inappropriate touching and to teach older students to avoid unwanted pregnancies and sexually transmitted diseases.

Introductory Paragraph:

_____

_____

_____

Exercise 2

✔• Practice

Thesis Statement:

Cyclists should be permitted to ride on the sidewalks because there is no room for them on roadways, drivers do not pay attention to bicycles, and nobody walks on sidewalks anymore.

Introductory Paragraph:

_____

_____

_____

3. Using the Thesis Statement to Organize the Introduction   The thesis statement usually signals the claim you're making. In many cases, it also identifies, explicitly or implicitly, the reasons for those claims. In short, it may contain your entire argument in one or two sentences. The introduction is meant to provide a context for the essay that will follow. Since the thesis statement serves as the statement of purpose for the essay, it follows that you can use it to guide you as you draft the introduction.

Below you will find some examples of introductions that have been written around their respective thesis statements. You'll notice that the thesis statement serves as the controlling idea in the paragraph and all other ideas refer to or derive from it.

Example 1

Thesis Statement:
The sale of cigarettes should be banned because smoking is a preventable cause of serious health problems like cancer, respiratory ailments, and periodontal disease.

Introductory Paragraph:
Despite three decades of governmental programs to discourage the use of cigarettes, the practice of smoking continues to result in health concerns for users of tobacco and rising costs for the health care system. There is little doubt of the health risks associated with smoking. It is implicated in the development of a number of different cancers, including lung and oesophagus cancers. It is a significant factor in the development of respiratory diseases and has increasingly been identified as a concern in matters of oral health. The current policy of employing "soft" deterrents (e.g., advertising campaigns and increased taxes on tobacco) to discourage the practice of smoking does not appear to be working quickly enough. The government needs to consider more drastic measures. The sale of cigarettes should be banned because smoking is a preventable cause of serious health problems like cancer, respiratory ailments, and periodontal disease.

- What is the effect of organizing the introduction around the thesis statement?
- Based on this introduction, what argument do you expect the writer to make?
- What themes will be discussed?
- How will those themes be organized?
- How does the writer signal the pattern of organization?

Example 2

Thesis Statement:
For the safety of motorists, pedestrians, and the cyclists themselves, cyclists who fail to observe traffic regulations should be subject to fines for their infractions.

Introductory Paragraph:
While the steady increase in the number of cyclists in North American cities has had a number of benefits, it has also brought some challenges. An alarming number of cyclists seem to be either unaware of, or indifferent to, the traffic regulations that govern the roads. Whether or not they are aware of their obligation to follow those regulations, they must be held to account. Their reckless habits are creating a hazardous situation for everyone. For the safety of motorists, pedestrians, and the cyclists themselves, cyclists who fail to observe traffic regulations should be subject to fines for their infractions.

- What is the effect of organizing the introduction around the thesis statement?
- Based on this introduction, what argument do you expect the writer to make?
- What themes will be discussed?
- How will those themes be organized?
- How does the writer signal the pattern of organization?

Writing Exercises

In each of the exercises below, use the thesis statement to draft an introductory paragraph.

Exercise 1

✓• Practice

Thesis statement:

Organic farming is a more responsible farming practice than factory farming because it employs fewer toxic chemicals, employs crop rotation rather than artificial nutrients to maintain the soil, and operates within the natural capacity of the land to produce reasonable yields.

Introductory Paragraph:

_____

_____

_____

Exercise 2

✓• Practice

Thesis Statement:

Schools should return to the use of mandatory school uniforms to establish equality between students, to ensure that student clothing is appropriate, and to discourage clothing that indicates affiliation with street gangs.

Introductory Paragraph:

_____

_____

_____

8.6.1 Strategies to Avoid

It's just as important to keep track of strategies that don't work as it is to become skilled in the use of those that do. You may have learned some of these strategies at different times from different instructors for different kinds of essays. The academic essay is not one of those essays. In academic essays, gimmicky introductions often have the effect of diminishing your authority with readers, who expect you to come to the point directly. That's why we encourage you to wrestle against the temptation to warm up the audience with an interesting quotation or anecdote. It's also why we suggest that you ignore the voice that tells you to contextualize your essay with a wide-ranging discussion of a similar phenomenon in the time of Napoleon. You're trying to guide your readers to a focus on your argument. You're not trying to distract them from it.

The following chart provides a short list of other strategies you might want to avoid.

Strategies to Avoid When Writing the Introduction in Your Own Essay
1.   The Attention-Grabbing Introduction Despite what many students have learned, the use of interesting but irrelevant facts or anecdotes to begin an introduction is not particularly effective. They create an expectation that writers rarely meet and often simply get in the way. Your essay is better than that. Clear, well-written introductions, which identify the purpose and scope of the argument being presented, do not require advertising gimmicks.
2.   The Bookend Introduction Writing ought to be governed by purpose rather than empty form. The bookend introduction contains several vague sentences that do not say much. Instead, they exist merely to satisfy the writer's requirement to provide an introduction. The introduction is not merely a formal requirement but a functional one.
3.   The Restated Question Introduction If the audience is limited to the individual who wrote the question, he or she is already aware of it. It's not necessary to state that which is already known. Like the *bookend introduction,* the *restated question introduction* should be judged on the basis of its utility. If it doesn't advance the meaning of the text, it's probably just taking up space.
4.   The Dictionary Introduction This introduction begins by giving the dictionary definition of one or more of the words in the assigned question. It's often intended to provide authority to an essay. There are a number of problems with the dictionary introduction: (1) contrary to what students believe, the dictionary is not a particularly authoritative source (i.e., dictionaries reflect common usage; they do not determine meaning); (2) dictionary definitions, while adequate as guides to word usage in general, lack the specificity required for academic writing; (3) the definition of particular terms may not, in fact, be relevant to the writer's thesis; and (4) the dictionary introduction has been used too often to be novel or interesting.
5.   The "Broad Perspective" Introduction This kind of introduction generally makes broad, sweeping statements about the relevance of this topic since the beginning of time. It is usually very general (similar to the bookend introduction) and fails to connect to the thesis.
6.   The "Book Report" Introduction This kind of introduction follows a pattern students may have used in high school, providing the name and author of the book being discussed and a brief summary of the text. In most cases, the book report introduction offers information that is either already familiar to the reader or irrelevant to the thesis.
7.   The Quotation Introduction The quotation introduction generally begins with a clever quotation from a long-dead sage about some aspect of the essay's thesis. Though essayists often used it in the past, the quotation introduction is rarely employed in academic essays.
8.   The Rhetorical Question Introduction Novice writers often resort to rhetorical questions in their introductions in an effort to engage the reader in their topic immediately. The use of questions in an academic essay is generally discouraged. Among other problems with this strategy, readers generally suspect that the writer already knows the answer to rhetorical questions. Don't toy with them. Rhetorical questions should be rephrased as statements.

These types of introductions might serve your purpose when you write in different genres, but they generally detract from your credibility when you're writing an academic essay. In Chapter 1, we discussed some of the differences between writing in high school and writing at college or university. This is one of those differences. Your audience has changed. You are now dealing with a reader who does not expect to spend a great deal of time waiting for an essay to begin. Your introduction ought to reflect your awareness of that reader.

Writing Exercises

In the following exercises, you will use the information in the examples to write more effective introductions. In each case, your goal is to reorganize the information to create a greater focus on the thesis and the relationship between ideas.

1. **The Attention-Grabbing Introduction**

Rewrite the examples below using a more objective tone.

Example 1

 Practice

Trusting the automobile industry to monitor safety standards is like asking a fox to watch the chickens! This is the worst idea ever! The automobile industry has never worried about the safety of its customers. The cases of the exploding Pintos and the Corollas with sticky accelerators prove that. Those events ought to convince the government that it must take on a larger role in overseeing car manufacturing. Currently, the government is considering a reduction in the number of engineers it employs to monitor the design and manufacture of automobiles in this country, arguing that it is more efficient to allow the industry to police itself. That policy is misguided. The government ought to maintain its current role because it has an obligation to its citizens and the cost of mistakes in automobile design is too great to bear. They could easily result in the deaths of young children.

Rewrite:

Practice

Example 2

It's a fact! In America today, 35.7 percent of the adult population is obese and at risk of early death due to heart disease, stroke, type 2 diabetes, and certain types of cancer. The costs to society are extreme. In 2008, medical costs associated with obesity in the United States were estimated to be $147 billion. The country could hire a lot of teachers with that money.

Rewrite:

2. The Bookend Introduction

Rewrite these examples using the information to create an introduction that uses a thesis statement to organize ideas.

Practice

Example 1

This essay will discuss the importance of effective teaching strategies in online courses. It will be organized in the following manner: it will begin with a discussion of teaching practices in general; this will be followed by a discussion of learning online; and, finally, the essay will end with a discussion of the way in which good teaching affects learning online. The thesis statement is: online courses should be designed to reflect good teaching practices.

Rewrite:

Practice

Example 2

In the essay that follows, I will discuss the importance of animal rights. If this is to be a just society, it must recognize the rights of all higher animals. I will have to explain what higher animals are and why they deserve greater protection than insects. I will also discuss the effect that ignoring this important issue will have. If animal rights are not protected, it will only be a matter of time before human rights are also undermined.

Rewrite:

3. The Restated Question Introduction

Rewrite the introduction, emphasizing the thesis rather than the assigned question.

Example 1

Practice

In this essay, we have been asked to explain why President Roosevelt may have delayed American participation in the Second World War. There are many reasons why the professor might have asked us to consider this. In this course, we have looked at public sentiment in America in the early days of the war and found that Americans did not think that they should have to return to the old country to fight European wars. This essay is intended to investigate that theme further.

Rewrite:

Example 2

Practice

"How did the Punic Wars serve to establish the Roman Empire?"

The Punic Wars served to establish the Roman Empire in a number of ways: (1) they eliminated Carthage as a rival to Rome, (2) they provided Rome with access to a growing number of colonies, and (3) they led to Rome creating a powerful navy. This essay will explore these points in greater detail.

Rewrite:

4. The Dictionary Introduction

Rewrite the following introductions focusing on the thesis statements rather than the definitions.

Example 1

Practice

Webster's Dictionary defines euthanasia as "the act or practice of killing or permitting the death of hopelessly sick or injured individuals (as persons or domestic animals) in a relatively painless way for reasons of mercy." If that is the case, it seems foolish to argue against it. As *Webster's* says, it is "relatively painless" and it is undertaken for "reasons of mercy." Mercy is defined as "compassionate treatment of those in distress." Euthanasia, then, is "the act or practice of killing or permitting the death of hopelessly sick or injured individuals (as persons or domestic animals) in a relatively painless way for reasons of mercy" and it is "compassionate treatment of those in distress." Therefore, euthanasia is a good policy.

Rewrite:

✓• Practice

Example 2

Naturopathy is a form of "a system of therapeutics in which neither surgical nor medicinal agents are used, with dependence being placed only on natural remedies" *(American Heritage Dictionary)*. If that is the case, it is difficult to understand why people have such a difficult time accepting it. Naturopathy should be considered as a reasonable approach to health care because it uses natural remedies rather than chemical agents and intrusive surgical interventions.

Rewrite:

5.   The Broad-Perspective Introduction

Rewrite the following introductions focusing specifically on the arguments being made.

✓• Practice

Example 1

Human beings have always engaged in warfare. Many of the earliest records depict battles between groups. There were wars recorded in the Bible, the Greek myths, the histories of Rome, as well as in the records of other cultures. It appears, therefore, that war is inevitable. The United Nations is a fading ideal that has been hijacked by national interests. Its peacekeeping missions are no longer effective and its development programs seem to have limited effect. Its primary goal of serving as a forum for nations to resolve conflicts without war is unrealistic. War will continue as it always has. It is time to revitalize the United Nations with a new mandate or to eliminate it altogether.

Rewrite:

Example 2

Practice

In the past, human beings relied on forms of transportation that allowed them to attend to a number of tasks at a time. It was possible to drive oxen without concentrating on the path ahead or to ride a horse while watching the countryside. These days, however, it is important to pay attention. The operation of an automobile is a much more difficult task. While it might have been possible to text while driving a team of horses, it is dangerous to do so behind the wheel of a car. Texting while driving an automobile should be banned because it requires drivers to take their hands off the steering wheel, to look away from the road, and to focus on something other than driving conditions.

Rewrite:

6. The "Book Report" Introduction

Rewrite the following introductions using the information to support a specific thesis.

Example 1

Practice

Catcher in the Rye was published in 1951 by J.D. Salinger. At one point, Salinger collaborated on a script for a film adaptation. It received critical acclaim when it was first published, but it has been banned in schools and libraries repeatedly. The novel discusses a number of themes that were considered to be uncomfortable by society. Salinger also wrote short stories that were published in the *New Yorker* magazine and other magazines. He later suppressed republication of any of the stories he considered to be inferior. Some of the reasons *Catcher in the Rye* was banned were Salinger's use of vulgar language, his challenges to authority, and anti-family statements. However, those are the very themes that made the book attractive to youth. It continues to be effective because it addresses the questions that intrigue teenagers: sexuality, rebellion, and authenticity.

Rewrite:

Practice

Example 2

Karl Marx wrote *Das Kapital* in a number of individual units. The first one was entitled *The Production Process of Capital* and was published in 1867. Marx argued that the economic system of his time was designed to exploit the working class. He also recast the discussion of economics in terms of social science. This led to the recognition that poverty might be a societal problem rather than a personal failing on the part of the poor. The two later volumes of the collective work, *The Circulation Process of Capital* and *The Overall Process of Capitalist Production,* were organized by Friedrich Engels from Marx's notes. Marx's theory became the competing economic model to capitalism in the twentieth century because it offered working classes an opportunity to advance in society, to organize themselves in collectives to challenge the power of the upper classes, and to understand poverty as a social phenomenon.

Rewrite:

7.   The Quotation Introduction

Rewrite each of the following introductions emphasizing the respective thesis rather than the quotation.

 Practice

Example 1

How many legs does a dog have if you call the tail a leg? Four. Calling a tail a leg doesn't make it a leg. (Abraham Lincoln)

The quotation from Abraham Lincoln makes a point that is very relevant to the thesis of this essay. He suggests that people who attempt to confuse an issue by redefining important terms are fooling nobody but themselves. Those who believe that they can eliminate the undue influence of Christian values from North American society by changing "Merry Christmas" to "Happy Holidays" are calling a tail a leg. If the governments of the United States and Canada are serious about creating pluralistic societies in which all citizens feel at home, they should either adopt policies that recognize the religious holidays of all major religions or eliminate the recognition of any of them. That is the meaning of the quotation by the "Great Liberator," Abraham Lincoln.

Rewrite:

Example 2

Buddha says that "Peace comes from within. Do not seek it without." Despite this, a number of people try to force their personal values of non-violence on the rest of society. They argue against armed intervention in despotic regimes. They argue against invasions of enemy states. If Buddha, who is recognized as a great advocate of peace, suggests that peace is an internal state and that individuals should not seek it in the external world, pacifists really have no grounds on which to stand. The use of force is justified in the interests of national security and defence of the weak.

Rewrite:

8. The Rhetorical Question Introduction

Rewrite the following introductions eliminating the rhetorical questions.

Example I

Has nobody noticed the increase in violent behaviour by children over the last decade? Can it really be a coincidence that the increase in violence has occurred during the same period as the increase in violent computer games? There are a number of studies that have indicated that children who are exposed to depictions of violence become desensitized to it. There are also studies that suggest that children who are permitted to spend hours alone playing these games tend to become indifferent to the need for contact with other human beings. What effect do parents expect that indifference to have on their children?

Rewrite:

Example 2

Do the public really need an extension of Sunday-shopping hours? With the shops open till 9 p.m. most evenings, are there really so many people out there who are unable to complete their shopping in six days? The government has argued that the current rules about shopping are outdated and no longer reflect the values or the lifestyles of the general public. The new policies have been welcomed by business leaders who believe that they will create new opportunities for commerce and new positions for those looking for work. Is there anyone who is surprised by the support from business leaders? On the other hand, a number of smaller shop owners have expressed concerns about their ability to compete in the new environment. Family groups and union representatives have also complained that the new policy will rob families of opportunities to spend time together.

Rewrite:

8.7   CONCLUSION

In this chapter, we've explored the importance of an effective introduction. It's important to craft the writing of the introduction carefully because the introduction establishes the relationship between the writer and the reader, identifying the writing protocols that will be observed and orienting the reader to the specific textual environment they have entered. Steer away from interesting but irrelevant anecdotes and other devices designed to artificially stimulate interest in the essay. The purpose of the introduction is to help readers make the transition from their own world to the world of the text. Your obligation as a writer is to give them the tools they need to navigate that transition.

In order to write an effective introduction, then, you need to know your audience. You need to ask yourself who you're writing for, what degree of familiarity they have with the subject, and what expectations they might bring to the essay. If you are to create an effective bridge between the everyday world and the textual world of your essay, you need to understand the reader's point of departure and you need to identify your point of entry. The strategies we've reviewed in this chapter are designed to help you do those things.

MyCompLab®

How Do I Get a Better Grade?

Go to MyCompLab for additional help with your grammar, writing, and research skills. You will have access to a variety of exercises, instruction, and videos that will help you improve your basic skills and help you get a better grade.

Exercises: Evaluating the Effectiveness of Introductions

Sample Introduction 1

✔ Practice

Discovering Human Cognition through Comparative Psychology

[1]Comparative animal psychology strives to gain a deeper understanding of the mental capacities of animals. While many animals, including magpies, dolphins, and dogs, display the capacity for complex mental operations, chimpanzees and other primates hold a particular interest for researchers due to the similarity between Homo sapiens and lower primates (Gramner, 1991; Nilson, 1972).[2] [3]Chimpanzees display a family resemblance that fascinates their kin (*Homo sapiens*), and scientists have been able to increasingly identify evidence of similarities between humans and chimp behaviour and skills, prompting many researchers to think about the "vagaries of evolution." According to Brown (2004), "despite profound differences in the two species, just a 1.23 percent difference in their genes separates Homo Sapiens from chimpanzees" (p. 133). [4]By observing the cognitive similarities between humans and chimpanzees, researchers hope to develop a more thorough understanding of animal cognition.

1 The writer begins by establishing a general context for the essay. The larger discussion of comparative psychology allows the reader to recognize the specific thesis of the essay within a larger body of work. In the first two sentences, the introduction provides the reader with enough information to begin to anticipate the discussion that will follow.

2 The citation indicates two things to the reader: (1) that this is an argument that will stand on evidence, and (2) that this paper will subscribe to the writing protocols of APA format.

3 The writer moves from the general to the specific, linking the ideas that have been introduced to form a pattern that will culminate in the thesis statement at the paragraph's end. The information that is being provided serves the overall purpose of the essay, rather than being dropped in for its own sake.

4 In the thesis statement, the writer brings all of the various elements together, synthesizing them into a coherent whole.

Writing Exercise

How effectively has the writer indicated the purpose for this essay?

_____

_____

How has the writer indicated the audience for this essay?

_____

_____

Based on the thesis statement, what order of themes or ideas do you expect the writer to follow?

_____

_____

Has the writer provided enough background information for the reader to understand the context of the thesis?

_____

_____

What other information should the writer have provided in the introduction?

_____

_____

How could the introduction be revised to make it more effective?

_____

_____

✓• Practice

Sample Introduction 2

In the past, fast food meant hamburgers and fries or greasy chicken. It is not unusual today, however, to walk into a fast-food restaurant and find healthy food choices on the menu. Fast-food giants like McDonald's and Burger King are working to rebrand themselves as restaurants rather than food on the go. McDonald's was the first of the large fast-food restaurants to make the move to healthier food, offering options like salads, yogurt, and lean meats. In recent years, they have even begun to challenge high-end coffee shops like Starbucks by offering specialty coffees. The shift in focus has led to an increase in revenue. Other fast-food places are scrambling to catch McDonald's with their own healthy food choices. McDonald's continues to be the most successful fast-food restaurant because it has a large menu choice, consistent products, and relatively low prices.

Writing Exercise

How effectively has the writer indicated the purpose for this essay?

_____

_____

How has the writer indicated the audience for this essay?

_____

_____

Based on the thesis statement, what order of themes or ideas do you expect the writer to follow?

_____

_____

Has the writer provided enough background information for the reader to understand the context of the thesis?

_____

_____

What other information could the writer have provided in the introduction?

_____

_____

How could the introduction be revised to make it more effective?

_____

_____

✔•—Practice   Sample Introduction 3

Marijuana is the drug of choice for many teenagers due, in part, to the mistaken belief that it is safe to use marijuana. While it is true that marijuana offers fewer immediate dangers than stimulants like cocaine or designer drugs like ecstasy, it is not without its own risks. It has a long-term effect on memory and affects drivers in many of the ways that other intoxicants do. The greatest risk, however, lies in its apparent safety. While cannabis, in and of itself, may pose relatively few risks to the casual user, it is often treated with more harmful substances. The prudent public policy, therefore, is to do one of two things: governments should either legalize the substance and regulate its production and sale or maintain the current ban and aggressively enforce it. The current strategy of ignoring the distribution of potentially harmful bags of treated cannabis is dangerous.

Writing Exercise

How effectively has the writer indicated the purpose for this essay?

_____

_____

How has the writer indicated the audience for this essay?

_____

_____

Based on the thesis statement, what order of themes or ideas do you expect the writer to follow?

_____

_____

Has the writer provided enough background information for the reader to understand the context of the thesis?

_____

_____

What other information could the writer have provided in the introduction?

_____

_____

How could the introduction be revised to make it more effective?

_____

_____

Sample Introduction 4

✓● Practice

The number of households with some kind of computer gaming device has risen dramatically in the last twenty years. Most homes, in fact, have more than one game system available for their children to use. Children may spend several hours a day lost in any number of digital gaming environments. Some of the games may be educational but an increasing number offer disturbingly violent scenarios in which children participate in point-of-view action that is aggressive and anti-social. There has been a great deal of debate recently about the effects of violent video games on children's development. The time for debate is over. It is clear that violent video games are not good for children's development because they can lead to an unhealthy tolerance for violence, a psychological dependency on stimulation, and the risk of alienation from friends and family.

Writing Exercise

How effectively has the writer indicated the purpose for this essay?

_____

_____

How has the writer indicated the audience for this essay?

_____

_____

Based on the thesis statement, what order of themes or ideas do you expect the writer to follow?

_____

_____

Has the writer provided enough background information for the reader to understand the context of the thesis?

_____

_____

What other information could the writer have provided in the introduction?

_____

_____

How could the introduction be revised to make it more effective?

_____

_____

✓• Practice   Sample Introduction 5

A new law has been proposed requiring cyclists of all ages to wear a certified helmet when riding a bicycle. The law was proposed by a woman whose husband died after being hit by a car when he was riding his bicycle without a helmet. She lobbied the government to get the law passed, believing it would save lives. However, there are many who oppose the law, arguing that it is an intrusion on personal liberty. There may be merit to both arguments. In order to balance the competing concerns of liberty and public safety, the law should be amended to ensure that children are required to wear helmets without imposing that same constraint on adult riders.

Writing Exercise

How effectively has the writer indicated the purpose for this essay?

_____

_____

How has the writer indicated the audience for this essay?

_____

_____

Based on the thesis statement, what order of themes or ideas do you expect the writer to follow?

_____

_____

Has the writer provided enough background information for the reader to understand the context of the thesis?

_____

_____

What other information could the writer have provided in the introduction?

_____

_____

How could the introduction be revised to make it more effective?

_____

_____

Introductory Paragraph Evaluation Worksheet

✓• Practice

The following chart provides a series of general questions for use in evaluating the introduction in your essay. Use the worksheet to ensure that you have written an introduction that allows your readers to know what to expect in the essay they are about to read.

An Evaluation Worksheet to Guide Decision Making for Introductions in Your Own Essay Writing

Review your essay and evaluate the introduction.

1. Have you begun your introduction with an interesting but irrelevant anecdote or definition? Get rid of it. It is not worthy of the essay you are about to write.

2. Does the introduction include a controlling thesis statement? Is the thesis statement sufficiently specific that the reader is able to understand both the topic and the context?

3. Does the introduction forecast the main ideas that will serve to amplify or develop the thesis?

4. Have the main ideas been introduced as individual or discrete entities, or have they been organized in such a way as to reveal the logical connection between the ideas?

5. Have you provided the reader with the information and pattern of organization necessary to orient the reader within the text? Does the introduction tell the reader what to expect in the essay that follows?

6. Have you provided enough information to orient the reader to the text? If your introduction is two or three sentences long, it probably has not provided enough information.

✓• Practice   ## Peer-Evaluation Worksheet for the Introduction

Title of the Essay: _____

Introduction Draft Submitted By: _____

Peer Evaluator: _____

Thesis Statement:

_____

_____

_____

_____

Based on your understanding of the essay's thesis, what evidence is needed to support the argument?

_____

_____

_____

How does the introduction establish the pattern the writer's essay argument will follow?

_____

_____

_____

_____

How has the writer identified the connections between the essay's principal ideas?

_____

_____

_____

_____

Are there ideas/assertions/comments in the introduction that seem irrelevant to the writer's thesis?

_____

_____

_____

_____

Based on your understanding of the thesis, what further information ought to be included in the introduction?

_____

_____

_____

_____

CHAPTER 9

Transitions

9.1   INTRODUCTION

The best way to explain transitions (okay, maybe it's not the best way, but the way we are going to use) is to give you an example from the realm of your everyday experience. Imagine that you and some friends are discussing a recent movie when one of your friends suddenly starts talking about a completely unrelated topic—the demotion of Pluto from planet status, for instance, which is, certainly, a topic that needs more discussion. Confused by the unexpected direction the conversation has taken, you shake your heads and go back to discussing the movie. The friend talking about Pluto didn't make a transition from the topic of the movie to the topic of Pluto. The same principle holds true with writing. If you abruptly shift from one idea to another, without giving the reader any indication of why you have done so, you leave the reader to make his or her own connections and those connections may not be consistent with your intentions. In this chapter, we explain why transitions matter, why certain transitions work the way they do in particular situations, and how to select the most effective transitional word or phrase.

In the section on academic writing, we identified our audience as one that expects to be convinced on the basis of evidence that we've arranged in such a way as to provide a logical train of thought. Effective transitions help you to create that logical train of thought. They also provide the organization and structure that characterizes the work of experienced writers. The purpose of transitions is to identify the relationship between ideas in a sentence or a paragraph, or the relationship between themes in an essay. Effective transitions provide coherence to the essay and advance the process of the argument. Transitions also serve the purpose of indicating to your readers how you're connecting your ideas to one another and, sometimes at least, back to the principal thesis.

It's important to remember, therefore, that you shouldn't use transitional words or phrases as ornaments or placeholders. They are better than that. They have a higher purpose. Transitional words were born to give us order. Because they imply a logical connection between words, they should be used for that purpose. Readers interpret transitions in that way. For instance, *however* implies a change or modification from the pattern that had been established in previous sentences. *Therefore,* on the other hand, implies that the current statement is making a claim on the basis of preceding statement(s). If the transition word or phrase you've chosen implies a logical connection between ideas that you don't intend, use another word. Transitional words or phrases, sadly, are not terribly important in their own right; they were born to serve the larger purpose of providing order between ideas.

9.2 UNDERSTANDING THE DIFFERENCE BETWEEN THE PRACTICE OF THE NOVICE WRITER AND THE PRACTICE OF THE EXPERIENCED WRITER

LO I

In order to acquire an understanding of the writing process that experienced writers follow, it's useful to identify the differences between the writing practices of novice writers and those of experienced writers. You've seen the following chart in previous chapters. In this instance, refer to the differences between the novice writer and the experienced writer in the areas of *error avoidance, grammatical errors, and knowledge telling.* Novice writers generally pay greater attention to mechanical writing functions and less attention to the development of meaning. By focusing on the integration of ideas through the use of transitions, as the experienced writers do, novice writers will be able to develop greater coherence in their writing.

Novice writers often forget that the purpose of the sentence is to contribute to a meaningful paragraph and that the purpose of the paragraph is to contribute to an essay. The organization of ideas is as important as the individual expression of those ideas. In our examination of transitions we're going to explore the way novice writers use transitions to connect their ideas. Because those writers

Novice Writers	Experienced Writers
■ *Require thought for procedural, or "mechanical," writing functions.*	■ *Have, to a significant degree, automated procedural functions.*
■ *Focus on error avoidance rather than meaning.*	■ *Focus on developing or refining meaning.*
■ Begin writing without planning, and edit, if at all, for grammatical errors.	■ Invest time and energy in planning and reviewing.
■ *Focus on "knowledge telling" (i.e., relating all the information they have and can find on a topic, rather than exercising critical judgment to determine relevance).*	■ *Organize, and reorganize, essay structure to allow individual ideas to serve the overall purpose of the essay.*

are concentrating on *error avoidance, grammatical errors,* and *knowledge telling,* they cannot concentrate to the same extent on the transitions between ideas. The problem is not that novice writers are incapable of understanding that it's important to link one idea to another; the problem is that they are too busy attending to more familiar writing decisions (like whether or not they are writing in the correct tense) to worry about problems like transitions.

Experienced writers have identified the development of meaning as the main goal of any writing situation, so they focus on larger questions of meaning, often at the expense of error avoidance. Novice writers may suppose that the text of experienced writers emerged error-free and syntactically sound. Not so much. In fact, most experienced writers assume that they will come back to edit text for correctness. However, in the development of the text, they will focus on the overall meaning.

9.2.1 Looking at the Effect of Transitions

Review the writing sample below and think about the way in which the information has been linked. Are the transitions effective or has the writer simply dumped information on the page, leaving readers to determine the relationship between the ideas?

Writing Sample
Marijuana is the most commonly used illicit drug in Canada. Its usage has many negative side effects on the brain such as memory loss, shortened attention span, decreased problem-solving skills, depression, and anxiety, all of which can affect a person's learning capabilities. The active ingredient in marijuana is called tetrahydrocannabinol (more commonly known as THC) and, when it enters the brain, it attaches itself to sites called cannabinoid receptors. Areas of the brain that contain many more cannabinoid receptors, such as the hippocampus (a part of the brain that plays a large role in the process of memory and emotions), will be affected much more by the use of marijuana than most other parts of the brain.

In the first two sentences, you will notice that there is no transition between the ideas. The first sentences states that *Marijuana is the most commonly used illicit drug in Canada.* The next sentence states that *Its usage has many negative side effects on the brain such as memory loss, shortened attention span, decreased problem-solving skills, depression, and anxiety, all of which can affect a person's learning capabilities.* The second sentence is related to the first in a general way but has no obvious connection to the assertion that marijuana is the most commonly used illicit drug. Readers are left to draw their own conclusions about the connections between the two sentences.

- Are the side effects caused because the drug is illegal?
- If marijuana was not illegal, would there still be side effects?
- How does marijuana being illegal affect a person's learning capabilities?
- How are the problems with learning associated with the fact that marijuana is illegal?
- If marijuana was legal, would the problems associated with learning capabilities be erased?

The reader can guess at the relationship but, in academic essays, that's not the reader's job.

How might you make the connection between the two sentences clearer for the reader? Rewrite the sentences to make the connection more clear.

_____

_____

Compare the following example to the example on the previous page, paying attention to the commentary on the margin of the page. It explains some of the decisions that have been made to provide the text with greater cohesion. For instance, you should notice that the revision includes a transition between the first and second sentence, making the connection between marijuana being illegal and the side effects of using marijuana clearer for the reader.

Revised Example of the Passage with Comments on the Use of Transitions

Marijuana is the most commonly used illicit drug in Canada. Despite its popularity, the drug has many negative side effects such as memory loss, shortened attention span, decreased problem-solving skills, depression, and anxiety, all of which can affect a person's learning capabilities. These side effects are caused by the active ingredient in marijuana, tetrahydrocannabinol (more commonly known as THC), which, when it enters the brain, attaches itself to sites called cannabinoid receptors. Areas of the brain that contain many more cannabinoid receptors, such as the hippocampus (a part of the brain that plays a large role in the process of memory and emotions), will be affected much more by the use of marijuana than most other parts of the brain.

The writer has begun the second sentence with a transition to identify the relationship between these two sentences.

The writer has made a transition between the negative effects and the active ingredient.

Here, the connection between the two sentences is implicit but relatively clear. The sentences are linked by a common theme.

Compare your revisions of the first example of the text to the revisions above. In what ways were your revisions similar?

_____

_____

In what ways were your revisions different?

_____

_____

How did the differences in the revisions affect the meaning of the text?

_____

_____

LO 2

9.3 TRANSITIONS AND ORGANIZATION IN LANGUAGE

In order to understand the role of transitions, we need to understand syntax. Syntax is an organizing principle that allows us to make sense of combinations of values or ideas by placing them in a particular order. This sounds much more complicated than it needs to be. In the following section, we're going to take a crack at explaining it in a brilliantly novel way. If that doesn't work, we'll try a more traditional approach.

9.3.1 Syntax and Language

Syntax is the ordering principle of language. In most languages, words alone do not convey meaning. It's necessary to place the words in a particular order to allow the reader to recognize the writer's intended meaning. Discussions of the purpose and effect of syntax can get very complicated, but we suspect that you'd prefer this one didn't. The examples below are intended to draw on concepts that are already familiar to you to demonstrate why syntax matters.

Understanding the Effect of Syntax on Writing (A Very Clever Analogy for Those Who Understand Computer Programming and a Useless Distraction for Those Who Do Not)

Explaining syntax is much easier than it used to be. Because computer programmers have borrowed the term and used it to explain the relationship between coding commands in computer code, and because students have become increasingly aware of how syntax works in computer code, we are able to use computer code as an analogy for syntax and language. Whenever you come across a problem in a computer operation in which the computer reports to you that there has been a syntax error, the problem the computer is identifying is its failure to understand what to do next. For example (this is a very simple example because we don't understand computer code nearly as well as we think we do), if you were to input two values (e.g., "3" and "4") without providing the computer with an operator (an operator is something like "+," "-," or "=" that describes the relationship between the two values), the computer would scratch its head, stare off into space, and finally confess that it did not understand.

Language works the same way. Within a sentence, syntax is a series of rules that allows us to link words meaningfully. The connections between sentences in a paragraph, or paragraphs in an essay, require a similar pattern of organization. If you don't provide the reader with a transition (which, in our example, provides the same function as an operator), the reader is unable to determine the relationship of one idea to another. It often results either in ambiguity (the reader doesn't know how to connect one idea to another) or error (the reader connects the ideas but connects them in a way that the writer did not intend).

9.3.2 Syntax and Language (A Less Complicated Explanation)

The example above works well for those who understand computer programming. For those who don't, there's an off chance that it may have confused the issue even more. Not to worry. The following example, which demonstrates the same principle in the context of language, requires no background in programming.

Syntax and Language: The Importance of Word Order in English
We're going to demonstrate the importance of syntax by providing a sentence in which syntax has failed: *sty the by chased the the was pig dog from.* Take a moment to try to decode the message.
The problem, of course, is that, while the words are familiar to you, you cannot derive the meaning of the sentence because the order does not permit you to understand who did what to whom. Though we may not know why, most of us recognize the importance of order in a sentence. We have learned, usually through a combination of formal education and linguistic immersion, to use a particular syntax to ensure that our audience is able to interpret our meaning. Without it, communication would be far more difficult.
On the other hand, when we do apply a recognized pattern of organization to the example above, the sentence becomes clear immediately: *The pig was chased from the sty by the dog.* The meaning emerges, not just from the words themselves, but from the order in which the words are received.

9.4 LINKING IDEAS WITHIN A PARAGRAPH   LO 2, 4

Because most of us internalized the fundamental syntactical rules of sentences long ago, we don't even notice that we are using them. You may wonder, then, why we are wasting your valuable time discussing it. A fair question. We want to suggest to you that you can apply the same general principle of pattern recognition to organizing ideas within a paragraph. If you don't provide readers with transitions that indicate the relationship of one sentence to another, they are left wondering whether the dog chased the pig, the pig chased the dog, or whether the sty chased both of them. Essentially, the transitional words serve to reflect the organization of the paragraph. They indicate the way in which the writer intends readers to put the ideas together.

Writing Exercise I

Read the paragraph below and evaluate the way in which the writer has linked the ideas, completing the short exercise that follows.

Example I

In today's hectic world, an increasing number of families are opting to eat out rather than sit down to the traditional family dinner. Fast food has become so common that some children do not even know what it means to have a home-cooked meal. With more families having two parents working outside the home, there is no one available to cook dinner for the children. Children have so many out-of-school activities that they do not spend much time at home anyway. The parents are constantly driving from one activity to another, *which* does not leave much time for home cooking. The problem with this lifestyle is that children are not getting their daily dose of the necessary vitamins. Most fast food does not contain enough nutrition to help keep bones strong and growing. Fast food is convenient but not necessarily healthy. Eating hamburgers and fries every day is a recipe for disaster in terms of health. Children are becoming more obese every year and, unless something changes, this trend will continue.

Has the writer made effective links between sentences in the paragraph? Choose two sentences from the paragraph and link them using a word or phrase that reflects the relationship between them.

_____

_____

Read the following revision of the paragraph, reflecting on the way in which transitions have been used to keep the ideas connected.

Example I—Rewrite I

In today's hectic world, an increasing number of families are opting to eat out rather than sit down to the traditional family dinner. *In fact,* fast food has become so common that some children do not even know what it means to have a home-cooked meal. *Because* so many families have two parents working outside the home, there is no one available to cook dinner for the children. *In addition,* children have so many out-of-school activities that they do not spend much time at home in any case. *This is further complicated* by the fact that parents are constantly driving from one activity to another, *which* does not leave much time for home cooking. The problem with this lifestyle is that children are not getting proper nutrition *because* most fast food does not contain the elements it needs to help keep bones strong and growing. Fast food is convenient but not necessarily healthy. In fact, some experts argue that eating nothing but hamburgers and fries on a daily basis is a recipe for disaster in terms of health. Children are becoming more obese every year and, unless something changes, this trend will continue.

What is the effect of adding transitional words or phrases to the passage?

_____

_____

Writing Exercise 2

Read the second example and reflect on the ways in which the ideas in the sentences could be connected more effectively. After doing so, revise the paragraph, making the changes necessary to improve the transitions between the sentences.

Example 2

The concept of marriage has changed a great deal over the past fifty years. In the past, those who got married tended to stay married. The institution of marriage has now changed to the extent that many people might have a number of ex-spouses. It is not unheard of for children to have six or more sets of grandparents and an endless assortment of stepmothers and stepfathers. Priorities shift with new relationships. Children can feel left out. It can get very confusing for children. Children are rarely consulted when a parent selects a partner, though the children are directly affected by the decision the parent makes. Children just have to make the best of a bad situation. Parents sometimes make decisions on the basis of their own needs and the needs of their new partners. It used to be that the welfare of the child came first, but that is a thing of the past.

Rewrite the paragraph, organizing it around a single controlling idea. Some sentences may have to be deleted or modified slightly to accord with the controlling idea that you develop.

Example 2—Rewrite 2

Compare your version of the rewrite to the rewrites of your classmates. How are they similar?

_____

_____

How are they different?

_____

_____

9.4.1 All Transitions Are Not Created Equal—A Writing Sample

In the writing sample that follows, the commentary on the side of the page is meant to foreground the *effect* of the transitions that have been used. Read the text, stopping at each of the points at which there is a discussion of the decisions that were made regarding transitional phrases. The commentary explains the purpose of the transition and its effect on the coherence of the essay. In short, the commentary shows that the transition is an integral part of the essay, providing a means of indicating the connection of one idea to another. By taking the time to understand the decisions that were made in the use of transitions in the writing sample model, you will gain a better understanding of the ways you might use transitions in your own essays. Remember that the effective use of a transition will signal to your reader your intended connection between ideas. As we mentioned before, transitions serve a higher purpose; they are never meant to serve as placeholders.

Transitions Writing Sample

The first sentence establishes a controlling idea.

"Even more" ties new information to ideas that had been discussed previously with a phrase that explains the relationship of the new information to the previous information.

This phrase refers back to the controlling idea of the paragraph

This sentence establishes a controlling idea for the second half of the paragraph.

"Rather than" indicates a distinction that is being made in the sentence.

In one study that focused on college students and the way in which college norms and religion affected alcohol consumption (Perkins, 1985), the researcher found that peer pressure was the most important factor in determining drinking behaviours. Even more than was the case with adolescents, college students reported that the values held by significant peers, rather than the values held by parents, were the primary influence on their decisions about drinking. Perkins (1985) also noted that religious background had an effect on decision-making. Three main religions were considered in this study: Judaism, Catholicism, and Christians from the American South. The Jews in this study tended to consume less alcohol at the beginning of college, but eventually their drinking habits increased to fit the immediate campus norms. Nonetheless, it was found that Jews generally drank less than Catholics. The Christians from the American South, whose belief in the human body as God's temple generally encouraged them to refrain from alcohol, were generally least likely to consume alcohol.

In the example above, the writer has led the reader through the text by connecting the ideas in one sentence to the ideas in the next. On some occasions, the connections are direct and overt (e.g., the phrase *Perkins (1985) also noted* is used to indicate that an idea is being continued from the previous sentence), while, at other times, the connection is more subtle (e.g., the phrase *The Jews in this study tended to consume less alcohol at the beginning of college* is linked thematically to the rest of the paragraph and relies on its place in the paragraph to contextualize its meaning).

9.4.2 Making Writing Decisions about Transitions within Paragraphs

The decisions you make about the transitions you use will always be guided by purpose. The following chart provides a series of questions that you can use to evaluate the use of transitions within paragraphs in your own essay writing.

Making Writing Decisions	About Transitions within Paragraphs in Your Own Essay Writing

What is the purpose of this writing decision?

The cohesion of a paragraph depends upon its organization. The effective use of transitions allows a writer to establish organizational patterns.

What is the effect of this writing decision?

Often, novice writers attempt to develop paragraphs by simply dumping information on the page, as if the information might magically arrange itself into something meaningful. It won't. Good writing is characterized by an organizational structure that serves an obvious purpose. The links between ideas in a paragraph reflect that organization.

What considerations inform this decision?

In order to select the proper transitional word or phrase, writers need first to understand the way in which the reader is meant to construct meaning. In essence, writers need to know what the relationship between ideas is, which idea governs the others, and whether a second idea is meant to add to the first or to qualify it.

Suggested strategies for making this decision.

Identify the idea that governs the paragraph and use that idea to determine the way that the sentences ought to be linked. What is the overall purpose of the paragraph? Have the sentences been linked in a way that serves that purpose? Linking sentences without considering their function within the paragraph will not help the paragraph as much as you might think.

Questions to guide decision making in your own essay.

1. To understand what we are saying about transitions within paragraphs, we want you to take the essay that you are working on right now and choose one of the paragraphs. Read the paragraph over and assess the relationship between one sentence and the next.
2. What is the connection between the two sentences? Does the second sentence further the point that the previous sentence made? Use a transition that reflects that connection (e.g., *additionally, again*).
3. If there is no connection between the sentences, well, there ought to be. If you're unable to connect the sentences logically, you may need to move one of the ideas to another paragraph.
4. Looking at the same paragraph, ask yourself whether the transitions between the sentences work together to develop the paragraph's main idea. How have the ideas linked together to make a single point?
5. If you find that the transitions are not working to make the point you intend to make, refer to the transitions chart that lies ahead in section 9.6 to find a word or phrase that allows you to make the intended connection clearer.
6. Work through the rest of your essay, using the questions above to ensure that you are making connections between the ideas in the paragraph.

LO 2, 4

9.5   LINKING PARAGRAPHS WITHIN AN ESSAY

Similarly (you'll notice that we're using the word *similarly* to indicate that we expect the reader to understand that we are continuing with the same idea), transitional words can be used to connect one paragraph to another, thereby providing a structure to the essay. By using words or phrases that guide the reader in the interpretation of the connection between paragraphs, the writer guides the reader to the intended construction of the overall meaning of the essay.

It's important to remember that transitions should reflect the organizational pattern of the essay. In most cases, even the best transitions cannot rescue an essay that is incoherent to begin with. As we've mentioned, the use of an organizing model like the IDDL model will help you to arrange the paragraphs in such a way as to ensure that they can be linked effectively.

9.5.1 Making Writing Decisions about Transitions between Paragraphs in an Essay

Transitions are often used at the beginning of the new paragraph to indicate the way in which the themes of the new paragraph are connected to the themes of the previous paragraph. There are many possible relationships that can exist between sentences, paragraphs, and ideas. It's your job, as the writer, to indicate the way in which you intend the elements to be connected. If, for instance, you're intending to indicate that you're summarizing a particular section of the essay or the essay itself, you might use words such as *finally, in a word, in brief, in conclusion, in the end, in the final analysis, on the whole, thus,* and *to conclude* (you can refer to the table later in the chapter for a list of transition words for specific purposes).

The following chart provides a series of questions that you can use to evaluate the use of transitions between paragraphs in your own essay writing. Consult it to guide your reflections on the use of transitions between paragraphs.

Making Writing Decisions	About Transitions between Paragraphs in Your Own Essay Writing

What is the purpose of this writing decision?

One of the principles that we return to often in this text is the idea that writing works, in part, by imposing order on ideas. Clever ideas are not enough. In order for writing to be meaningful it needs to be guided by an awareness of the relationship of one idea to another. That, in brief, is the function that transitions serve at the level of the essay and at the level of the paragraph.

What is the effect of this writing decision?

Clear identification of the way in which one paragraph is connected to another provides the reader with an understanding of the relationship between the paragraphs.

What considerations inform this decision?

Just as there is a logic to the order of ideas within a sentence, so too is there a logic to the order of paragraphs within an essay. Generally, one paragraph will provide information that the succeeding paragraph will rely on, and, in turn, the succeeding paragraph will provide a foundation for the one that follows it. Transitions simply reflect that logic.

Suggested strategies for making this decision.

Consider the various units of meaning (e.g., sentences, paragraphs). Should they be connected by a transition that suggests that one is to be added to the other (e.g., *additionally, also*) or a transition that suggests a change of direction (e.g., *however, on the other hand*)? Understand your purpose and allow that understanding to guide your selection of transitional words or phrases.

Questions to guide decision making in your own essay.

1. The transitions between paragraphs work in much the same way as the connections between sentences work within the paragraph. Return to your essay again and examine the way in which one paragraph has been connected to the next.

2. What is the relationship between the two paragraphs? Does the second paragraph further the point that the previous paragraph made? Use a transitional word or phrase that reflects that connection (e.g., *additionally, again*).

3. If there's no connection between the paragraphs, you might need to consider whether the paragraphs are organized in the right order. Think about the argument you're making. What purpose does each paragraph serve in that argument? By reflecting on the purpose of each paragraph in the essay, and on the relationship of each paragraph to the next in that larger argument, you should be able to determine the logical connection between the paragraphs.

Writing Exercise 3

✓• Practice

Read the following passage and answer the questions below.

Example 1—Transitions

Most people want to maintain a healthy body but do not know how to do so. The changes in recommendations for diet occur so quickly that it is difficult to keep up. Ten years ago, the inclusion of red meat in a diet was discouraged. In moderation, it is now considered an acceptable part of a diet. Similarly, butter and dairy products were once considered to be unhealthy. Now, dairy products are considered important components of a healthy diet. It may be that the answer to the question depends upon the nature of the question itself.

When the Atkins Diet became popular, carbohydrates were to be excluded, and protein was the key element in a good diet. It seems that every year there are new and different diets that are guaranteed to help people lose weight. Some of the latest diets on the market include ones that are low in fat, diets that require individuals to eat only grapefruit, or diets that require eating only cabbage soup. There are so many diets available and so many people who are willing to believe that there is a magic strategy for eliminating excess weight.

Some people who have problems controlling their food intake are willing to consider more radical measures to manage their weight. They opt for a particular stomach surgery during which surgeons place *lap bands* around the stomach to shrink its size. Another surgical method to help people lose weight is called gastric bypass surgery. In gastric bypass surgery, surgeons divide the stomach into two parts, artificially creating a sense of fullness. Dramatic weight loss has been attributed to these two surgical procedures.

Identify the transitions between the paragraphs.

_____

_____

In what ways are the transitions effective or ineffective?

_____

_____

Rewrite the sentences to make the transitions between the paragraphs more effective.

_____

_____

✓•─ Practice

Writing Exercise 4

Read the following the passage and answer the questions below.

Example 2—Transitions

There is an epidemic of obesity in the United States and Canada affecting individuals as young as six to those in their eighties. Many have tried to address the problem by limiting food intake. The problem, however, with trying to manage weight by managing food intake is that most people fail to recognize that it is not the volume of food but the kinds of food that cause weight gain. Over a period of ten years, Brown (2012) found that the foods most associated with weight gain were french fries, potato chips, sugary drinks, sweets, and refined grains. The foods most closely associated with weight loss were fruits, yogurt, nuts, and vegetables.

There is no single strategy for battling obesity. People look for quick fixes, attempting to limit their intake of food to one or two food groups. Some try to live on fruits and vegetables, while others shun carbohydrates, all in an effort to maintain a particular body weight. The problem with this approach is that the body does not always get the nutrition it needs.

In order to maintain a healthy weight, people should exercise more. The Centre for Good Health (2012) recommends that all adults get a minimum of three hours of moderate exercise per week if they are trying to maintain their current weight. If they are attempting to lose weight, they need four to five hours of vigorous exercise a week. People should also do weight-training exercises to maintain fitness and to help build lean muscle mass.

Identify the transitions between the paragraphs.

_____

_____

In what ways are the transitions effective or ineffective?

_____

_____

Rewrite the sentences to make the transitions between the paragraphs more effective.

_____

_____

9.6   TRANSITIONAL WORDS OR PHRASES   LO 3

Below, in the column in the middle, we have included a table of transitional words and phrases. In the column on the left, we have identified the purpose and effect of each transition. In the final column, on the right, we provide an example of the way in which a transition in this category might be used to clarify the relationship between two sentences. Remember that transitions are intended to provide your essay with a sense of structure and coherence. They are not meant to flesh out or dress up a sentence.

Intended Connection	Transitional Word or Phrase	Example
Similarity/Additional Support or Evidence ■ To compare, show agreement, or to add more information.	_also, in the same way, just as, so too, likewise, similarly, in like manner, analogous to, equally, in addition, as well as, comparably, identically, in common, further, furthermore, additionally, equally important, comparatively, correspondingly, moreover, again, also, besides, then, next, another_	Darwin believed that evolution progressed through a series of mutations that provided individual members of a species with a competitive advantage. _Moreover_, he believed that these changes within a species would, on occasion, result in new species emerging.
Exception/Contrast ■ To show opposition, limitations, contradictions, or an alternative view.	_but, however, in spite of, on the one hand . . . on the other hand, nevertheless, nonetheless, notwithstanding, whereas, on the contrary, by comparison, at the same time, rather, in contrast, on the contrary, still, yet, compared to, up against, although, conversely, meanwhile, even though, rather, alternatively, at the same time, instead, despite, otherwise, regardless_	Some have argued that Darwin's theory of evolution can also be applied to social change. _However_, the change mechanism that Darwin described does not translate to social change as easily as they might imagine.
Cause and Effect ■ To show causal relationships and consequences.	_accordingly, consequently, hence, so, therefore, thus, if/then, given that, so that, so as to, due to, in the event that, as long as, in order to, since, because of, as a result of, for this reason_	In the course of his travels, Darwin observed that different populations of the same species often show evidence of a common variation from the norm. _As a result of_ his observations, Darwin suggested that change is introduced to species when random variations prove to be advantageous.

(continued)

(continued)

Example/Emphasis ■ To show support for your argument.	*for example, for instance, namely, specifically, to illustrate, in other words, to put it differently, for one thing, notably, including, like, in fact, in general, in particular, in detail, for this reason, with attention to, to emphasize, to clarify, to explain, such as, frequently, significantly, another key point, to point out, with this in mind*	According to Darwin, not all variations resulted in evolutionary change. *For example,* variations that were neither advantageous nor harmful were likely to die out in a single generation.
Place/Position ■ To identify, restrict, limit, or qualify location.	*above, adjacent, below, beyond, here, in front, in back, nearby, there, in the middle, to the left/right, in the distance, next to, over, near, above, up, down, wherever, around, between, before, alongside, amid, among, beneath*	In time, fossil evidence seemed to confirm Darwin's general thesis. At the Earth's surface we find the skeletal remains of species that are familiar to us. *Below* that surface area, however, palaeontologists have found the remains of creatures that appear to have been the predecessors of the world's contemporary species.
Time/Sequence/Order ■ To show sequence or chronology of events.	*after, afterward, at last, before, currently, during, earlier, immediately, simultaneously, subsequently, then, at the present time, at the same time, to begin with, in due time, thereafter, first, second, third . . . next, then, finally, later, last, until, next, now, formerly, prior to, previously*	Darwin's travels were physically taxing, but he endured them stoutly. *Subsequently,* however, the strain of domestic life would prove too much for him and his health would begin to decline.
Conclusion/Summary ■ To indicate concluding statements or summaries, or to restate ideas.	*finally, in a word, in brief, in conclusion, in the end, in the final analysis, on the whole, thus, to conclude, to summarize, in sum, in summary, as can be seen, after all, by and large, in short, to sum up, overall, for the most part, as has been noted, given these points, all things considered, as has been shown*	Initially, it was believed that Darwin's *On the Origin of Species* might be too scandalous for the audience of his day. *In the end,* however, the book proved to be wildly popular.

It's important to note that the suggestions above are always guided by purpose. The test for any particular transitional word or phrase is this: Does the word allow the reader to recognize the intended relationship between the sentences or paragraphs it connects? No? Then find a different word.

For example, if you've constructed a paragraph that consists of a list of characteristics of a particular phenomenon, you might conclude with a phrase that summarizes the list (e.g., *finally, in summary*). You would not, however, conclude with a word like *therefore,* which indicates causality.

9.6.1 Making Writing Decisions about Selecting the Appropriate Transitional Word or Phrase

The purpose of a transitional word or phrase is to help connect ideas or groups of ideas. They are not meant to be used haphazardly, however, or to carry the load alone. In making your decisions about the use of transitions, you need to reflect on the relationship between the ideas you're bringing together and on the context in which they appear.

In the following chart, you will find a series of questions that you can use to guide your selection of the appropriate transitional word or phrase.

Making Writing Decisions	Selecting the Appropriate Transitional Word or Phrase to Use in Your Own Writing

What is the purpose of this writing decision?

The selection of the appropriate transitional word or phrase is intended to provide a piece of writing with structure.

What is the effect of this writing decision?

The right transition allows the reader to recognize the way in which sentences, paragraphs, and ideas are connected to one another. The wrong transition leads the reader to assume a connection between sentences, paragraphs, and ideas that the writer did not intend.

What considerations inform this decision?

Choosing a transitional word or phrase requires that the writer think about the connection that is intended.

Suggested strategies for making this decision.

The previous chart facilitates that process by providing a bank of transitional terms with their corresponding purposes.

Questions to guide decision making in your own essay.

1. Looking at a pair of sentences or paragraphs in your own essay, think about the connection you intend to make between them. Find that connection in the previous chart.
2. Select a word or phrase from the corresponding box in that chart.
3. If there is no word that properly captures the connection you intend, select the word that most closely corresponds with your meaning and look it up in a thesaurus.

Writing Exercise 5

In the following exercise, you have an opportunity to practise connecting pairs of sentences using transitions. As always, bear in mind that the transitional word or phrase you choose ought to reflect the intended relationship between the sentences.

Create two original sentences and link them logically, using the transitions provided.

Because

_____

_____

Therefore

_____

_____

However

_____

_____

Nevertheless

_____

_____

But

_____

_____

So

_____

_____

Meanwhile

_____

_____

As a result

_____

_____

Consequently

_____

_____

In summary

_____

_____

9.7 FINALLY, A NOTE ON TRANSITIONS AND STYLE . . . (OR, WHY PEOPLE TELL YOU NOT TO USE TRANSITIONS LIKE *FINALLY*)

LO 1, 3

By the way, you probably shouldn't use transitions like *finally* in your final drafts. In fact, you may be told that you shouldn't use a number of the more obvious transitional phrases we've discussed. In time, writers should learn to signal their transitions *implicitly,* using the text to smoothly effect the transition rather than simply dropping in a transition word to announce it.

Though style is a matter of convention and is, therefore, more difficult to explain by reference to absolute rules, it is not entirely unimportant. Stylistic expectations emerge from the conventions of the linguistic community in which you're operating. Language works because we agree to follow those conventions (e.g., we agree to a common definition of words). If you think that cultural conventions don't matter, try sunbathing in the nude at a church picnic. In many cases, you might have an easier time of that than you would of convincing traditional grammarians that it's acceptable to end a sentence with a preposition.

Therefore (did you notice the transition there?), we suggest that you use the explicit transitions we've suggested while you are writing drafts. These will ensure that you are aware of the connections you are making between ideas (or, perhaps, ensure that you are aware that you've failed to make a connection). Depending on the writing situation and/or the stylistic preferences of your audience, you may choose to replace your connecting words with more subtle transitions during the revision stage.

9.8 CONCLUSION

Transition words or phrases identify the relationship between words, sentences, and paragraphs. Transition words provide paragraphs and essays with unity and coherence, assisting the writer to work toward the ultimate purpose of the writing exercise: the development of meaning. There are a number of different transition words that can signal specific connections between ideas. There are words to signal similarity, contrast, cause and effect, place or position, time, sequence or order, and conclusion or summary. The type of transition you choose ought to reflect the logical connection you intend to make between your ideas. An understanding of transitions allows writers to connect sentences and paragraphs together to advance the development of an essay. The effective use of transition words or phrases also provides the essay with coherence. It's important to remember, however, that effective transitions are those that you use to guide or reflect the logic of the essay. You shouldn't use them simply to fill space. It's also useful to remember that it's much easier to employ transitions successfully in a text that has already been organized into coherent groups of ideas.

MyCompLab®

How Do I Get a Better Grade?

Go to MyCompLab for additional help with your grammar, writing, and research skills. You will have access to a variety of exercises, instruction, and videos that will help you improve your basic skills and help you get a better grade.

Sample Essay I

Putting It All Together

Throughout the chapter, we've examined the effect that the use of transitions has on the cohesion of a text. While we have attempted to explain why one transition may be more effective than another, writing does not come with precise formulas (we recognize that life would be a lot easier if it did). In this final essay, we want you to notice that using transitions requires you to make a decision about the use of transitions on the basis of the effect they have on the cohesion of the text. Does each transition provide the reader with a means of connecting ideas in the way that you intended? Yes? Then it works. If it doesn't, or if it does so but not clearly, you need to find a way of connecting the ideas more clearly.

Discovering Human Cognition through Comparative Psychology

Comparative psychology strives to gain a deeper understanding of the mental capacities of animals. While many animals—including magpies, dolphins, and dogs—display the capacity for complex mental operations, chimpanzees and other primates hold a particular interest for researchers due to the similarity between *Homo sapiens* and lower primates (Gramner, 1991; Nilson, 1972). Chimpanzees display a family resemblance that fascinates their kin (*Homo sapiens*), and scientists have been able to increasingly identify evidence of similarities between human and chimp behaviour and skills, prompting many researchers to think about the "vagaries of evolution." According to Brown (2004), "despite profound differences in the two species, just a 1.23 percent difference in their genes separates Homo Sapiens from chimpanzees" (p. 133). By observing the cognitive similarities between humans and chimpanzees, researchers hope to develop a more thorough understanding of animal cognition.[1]

In order to[2] gain a deeper understanding of how animals learn and think, Orowitz (2004) studied the problem-solving capacity of chimpanzees and found that it closely mapped to the problem-solving processes of *Homo sapiens*. Norris (1999) also found a similarity between the reasoning patterns of the two species. In Norris's research (1999), a chimp named Alladin was given the challenge of getting a piece of fruit that was out of his reach. Nearby, there were two sticks: (1) a short stick that was within reach, and (2) a longer stick that was well beyond reach. [3]After several failed attempts to reach the fruit, Alladin realized that he could use the short stick to retrieve the longer stick, and use the longer stick to reach the fruit. The chimp's actions suggested the capacity to work through a multi-stage problem with no apparent training. That capacity to reason appeared to be innate.

In addition to Norris's work (1999) with Alladin, there have been a number of studies with apes, chimpanzees, and gorillas that have revealed their ability to use natural tools such as sticks and other objects to accomplish tasks and acquire goods. This[4] is commonly referred to as functional fixedness, a capacity through which animals select appropriate branches or stones to use as hammers in cracking nuts (Better, 1996). Chimps have also[5] been observed breaking off reeds or sticks, stripping them of their twigs and leaves, and carrying them to termite mounds to "fish" for termites. When observing animals in a natural environment, researchers have found that chimpanzees display sophisticated abilities to select different objects as tools (e.g., heavy sticks to puncture holes, light flexible sticks to use for fishing). In fact, researchers have also found that there are forty-nine local customs related to chimpanzee tool use, grooming, and courtship (Grant, Penny, & Gordski, 2009).

[6]Scientists have noted that, in all primates, the left hemisphere of the brain records rules based on experience, while the right hemisphere avoids rules in order to detect details and unique features that allow it to decide what is familiar and what is novel. This dichotomy is true for both human and non-human animals, which likely reflects the evolutionary origins of the underlying brain mechanisms. Researchers speculate that

1 The last sentence of the introduction provides one half of the thematic link between the introduction and the first paragraph by making a general statement that will be answered by the more specific first line of the first body paragraph. Rather than using an explicit transitional word or phrase, the writer has made the connection implicitly.

2 The writer uses the phrase "In order to" to indicate that the information to follow will begin to demonstrate the first aspect of the general claim of the last sentence of the introduction.

3 The writer connects this sentence to the previous sentence by expanding on the principal action of the previous sentence (i.e., the attempts to reach the fruit).

4 When used carefully, gestural words like "this" or "that" connect ideas by pointing, textually, to a nearby noun or idea. On the other hand, when they are used carelessly, gestural words point vaguely, leaving the reader to guess what the referent is.

5 In this phrase, "also" indicates that the writer is furthering an idea that has already been introduced.

6 While this sentence has an implicit connection to the previous paragraph, it is not immediately clear what that connection is. The writer might have chosen to make the relationship more explicit with a transitional word or phrase. For example, the writer might have chosen to open the paragraph with a statement like the following: *The use of tools testifies to certain thinking processes and those processes generally require particular brain structures.*

7 Words like "although" indicate that an idea is being (or, in this case, is about to be) qualified in some way.

8 Again, the absence of a clear transition leaves the reader guessing how this paragraph relates to the text around it. The writer might have introduced the paragraph with a sentence that explained how the Theory of Mind connected to the previous paragraph. For example, the writer might have begun with a sentence like the following: *The capacity for self-awareness is related to what has been called the Theory of Mind.*

9 The use of the word "also" indicates that this idea is meant to be understood as a further development of the preceding statement.

10 This sentence indicates that there will be a change in direction in the essay. The word "Although" affirms the idea it refers to, while simultaneously suggesting that idea is about to be qualified or limited in its application. It allows the writer to introduce a competing idea.

the underlying brain structures that contribute to commonality between human and non-human primates in problem solving and rule making also apply to primal language capacities. Hauser (2000) argued that "animals have interesting thoughts, but the only way they can convey them is by grunts, shrieks, and other vocalizations, and by gestures." Hauser suggested that these grunts and shrieks operate as a form of language among non-human primates.

Although[7] Flowman and Brown (1997) have suggested that the mental capacity of most non-human primates is approximately equivalent to a two-year-old child, non-human primates have been observed practising sign language. University of Nevada researchers Gardner and Gardner (1995) successfully taught sign language to a chimpanzee named Washoe. By the time of her death at forty-two, she could use about 250 distinctive American Sign Language signs, as measured by the Schrier Research Laboratory. Remarkably, Washoe was also able to teach another chimpanzee, Loulis, to use sign language without any human intervention, marking the first animal-to-animal transfer of human language. Although chimpanzees do not have the same facility of language as humans, their ability to think and communicate indicates an impressive level of intelligence.

[8]"Theory of Mind" is a term that is used to refer to a person's ideas about their own and others' mental states. Chimpanzees and orangutans have been observed using mirrors to inspect themselves and touching coloured spots that a researcher has dabbed on their faces. Chimps and baboons have also[9] been observed using deception. In one such example, a young baboon feigns having been attacked to have the mother drive away competing baboons from their food. These actions indicate that primates are capable of self-recognition and of understanding others' perceptions of a given situation.

[10]Although these feats are impressive, there are also significant differences to be observed when comparing animal to human intelligence. According to Hauser (2000), animals have "laser beam" intelligence, by which he means that, although non-human primates can find a specific solution to solve a specific problem, these solutions cannot be applied to new situations or to solve different kinds of problems. That is, although chimpanzees may be favourably compared to other animals when displaying the ability to construct tools, they generally lack the "floodlight" cognitive capacity that allows *Homo sapiens* to use existing knowledge in new ways and to apply the solution of one problem to another situation.

[11]Comparative psychologists continue to pursue their quest to discover whether animal intelligence operates the same way that human intelligence does. [12]Some argue that non-human primates use strategies similar to humans, providing some of the closest human–animal similarities in performance ever reported in the comparative literature. In addition, scientists have noted a similarity in the cognitive functioning of all primates, with the two hemispheres differentiating between tasks in similar ways. [13]Some skeptics continue to doubt that the cognitive patterns of lower primates map to human intelligence, arguing that the lower primates cannot plan, conceptualize, show compassion, or use language. [14]However, this runs contrary to research provided by other animal researchers that demonstrates strong evidence that many animals, especially non-human primates, exhibit insight, show family loyalty, communicate with one another, display altruism, transmit cultural patterns across generations, and comprehend the syntax of human speech. While there may be significant differences between the thinking patterns of the species, current research suggests that the similarities imply a commonality that is significant enough to permit study by analogy.

11 Again, the transition could have been clearer, though there is an implicit transition.

12 "Some argue" separates the larger group into two competing camps. It allows the reader to anticipate that there will be a corresponding group later in the paragraph.

13 "Some skeptics" is the corresponding group to "Some argue."

14 "However" represents a change in direction.

Sample Essay 2

In this exercise, you will evaluate the essay below, thinking about the degree to which the connections within the paragraphs and between the paragraphs are effective.

To Vaccinate or Not?

In the early nineties, a story arose in the media claiming that the practice of vaccinating children could lead to the development of autism. There was little science to support the claim, but there was an actress who maintained that her son developed autism after having been vaccinated. The word of a single individual with no medical training set off a firestorm of protest from parents who subsequently refused to have their children vaccinated. These parents stated that the risk of their respective children developing autism was too great and that they would rather take their chances with their children developing diseases such as whooping cough, measles, mumps, rubella, and polio.

In 1998, a respected journal of medicine published an article arguing that there was no scientific evidence to support the believed link between vaccinations and autism. Many believed that the article would be enough to convince the parents who had been worried to return to the vaccination program. That has not proven to be the case. There are still parents who believe that vaccinations can cause autism. The effect of those decisions are starting to be felt around the world as more children come down with diseases such as measles, mumps, and whooping cough. In effect, diseases that were once thought to have been eradicated in developed countries are re-establishing themselves.

The number of children who have not had their vaccinations or who have missed booster shots is not large, but it is substantial enough to cause a change in some medical practices. Some physicians are refusing to treat patients who have not had their vaccinations. They point to the need to protect their other patients. Physicians say that patients who are at risk include patients who suffer from autoimmune diseases and babies who do not have the necessary immunity to fight infections. These physicians worry that, if some individuals do not get vaccinated and become infected, the few will infect the many.

There are a growing number of physicians, especially pediatricians, who have instituted the new policy. According to the regulating body of the American Academy of Pediatricians, the number of physicians who are turning away patients or asking patients to leave has risen by 10 percent over the past five years. The official position of the AAP is that the decision to ask patients to leave should be seen as a last resort by physicians. The academy is worried that, in turning unvaccinated patients away, physicians are leaving the children with no medical care. The ones who should be the most concerned, the parents, do not seem to share the concerns of the medical community. Despite the evidence that demonstrates there is no link between autism and vaccinations, some parents stubbornly cling to the myth to the detriment of their own children.

What is the controlling idea or thesis of this article?

_____

_____

Are the links between ideas within each paragraph clear? Identify specific points at which you could make the connections between sentences clearer.

_____

_____

Are the links between paragraphs clear?

_____

_____

What transitions could you use to make the connection between paragraphs clearer?

_____

_____

Transitions Evaluation Worksheet

The following chart provides a series of general questions for use in evaluating the transitions and connections that you make in your writing. Use the worksheet to review your essay and evaluate the transitions.

A Transition Evaluation Worksheet to Guide Decision Making in Your Own Essay Writing

1. Review the first paragraph after the introduction. What is the subtopic or major idea controlling that paragraph? How does that idea support the essay's thesis?

   a. Examine the sentences in the paragraph. Is there a logical connection between the sentences?

   b. In what way have you identified the connection between one sentence and the next? (Examine each pair of sentences.) Do the transitions allow the reader to follow your reasoning?

   c. In what way have you identified the connection between each sentence and the subtopic? Do the transitions allow the reader to follow your reasoning?

   d. In what way is each sentence linked to the subtopic you identified for the paragraph?

(continued)

(continued)

2. Review each succeeding paragraph in the same way to ensure that the paragraph is coherent (i.e., that the ideas are linked to the subtopic and to each other).

   a. Examine the last sentence of each preceding paragraph and the first sentence of the next paragraph to ensure that each paragraph is linked to both the preceding paragraph and the following paragraph.

   b. How is each paragraph connected to the main paragraph?

3. Look at the relationship of one paragraph to the next.

   a. Does each succeeding paragraph add to or amplify the sentiments of the preceding paragraph? Does it counter the ideas? Does it change direction? Does it derive a conclusion on the basis of the preceding paragraph? What transition words or phrases should you use to indicate the connection?

   b. How have you indicated the relationship of each paragraph to the essay's main thesis? How do we make a connection back to the main point of the essay?

✔●─┤Practice   **Peer-Review Worksheet for Transitions**

Essay Written By: _____

Peer Reviewer: _____

Introductory Paragraph:

What is the thesis statement?

_____

_____

What are the supporting ideas?

_____

_____

How has the writer indicated the relationship between the thesis statement and the supporting ideas?

_____

_____

How has the writer indicated the relationship between each of the supporting ideas?

_____

_____

Paragraph 1:

How has the writer indicated the relationship between this paragraph and the general thesis of the essay?

_____

_____

How has the writer indicated the relationship between each of the paragraph's key ideas?

_____

_____

How has the writer indicated the logical relationship between this paragraph and the next one?

_____

_____

Paragraph 2:

How has the writer indicated the relationship between this paragraph and the general thesis of the essay?

_____

_____

How has the writer indicated the relationship between each of the paragraph's key ideas?

_____

_____

How has the writer indicated the logical relationship between this paragraph and the next one?

_____

_____

Paragraph 3:

How has the writer indicated the relationship between this paragraph and the general thesis of the essay?

_____

_____

How has the writer indicated the relationship between each of the paragraph's key ideas?

_____

_____

(*continued*)

(continued)

How has the writer indicated the logical relationship between this paragraph and the next one?

_____

_____

For each succeeding paragraph:

How has the writer indicated the relationship between this paragraph and the general thesis of the essay?

_____

_____

How has the writer indicated the relationship between each of the paragraph's key ideas?

_____

_____

How has the writer indicated the logical relationship between this paragraph and the next one?

_____

_____

Concluding Paragraph:

How has the writer indicated the relationship between the introductory paragraph and the concluding paragraph?

_____

_____

How has the writer indicated the relationship between each of the main ideas of the essay?

_____

_____

How does the pattern established above correspond with the pattern of reasoning that was used throughout the essay?

_____

_____

Conclusions

CHAPTER 10

Learning Objectives

At the completion of this chapter, you will be able to:

1. Identify the differences between the ways in which novice and experienced writers write conclusions for academic essays.
2. Explain the ways in which the conclusion can be used to answer the expectations that were raised in the introduction.
3. Demonstrate the ability to connect important ideas in the conclusion.
4. Distinguish between effective and ineffective strategies for writing conclusions.

10.1 INTRODUCTION

Just as the introduction allowed you to orient the reader to the text, the conclusion allows you to ensure that the reader leaves the text understanding what you meant to say. The conclusion is like a trial lawyer's final summation: it allows you to remind your audience of the evidence they have seen but it also provides you with an opportunity to supply the reader with an interpretation of that evidence. That is, you have an opportunity to say what the evidence is and what the evidence means.

Like the introduction, the conclusion can be difficult to write. It's useful to remember its purpose: the conclusion is designed to provide the reader with a concise summation of the argument and a brief review of the way in which the evidence that you've presented leads to a particular conclusion. Just as the introduction provided a bridge into the essay, creating a context for the argument you're presenting, the conclusion provides a bridge back to the world beyond the essay. In addition, the conclusion assists the reader in the process of integrating the individual elements of the essay into a unified whole. The conclusion provides you with a final opportunity to argue for a particular interpretation of the evidence. It also provides an opportunity to explain, again, why the question that you're investigating is worthy of concern. In addition, the conclusion might identify the larger concerns that emerge from your findings, inviting the reader to consider the implications of the argument or to consider the questions that emerge from the argument. The conclusion pushes beyond the immediate boundaries of the essay, allowing the reader to consider broader issues, make new connections, and elaborate on the significance of your findings.

Though you've connected your ideas internally, ensuring that each paragraph is coherent and that there is a general coherence to the essay, and though you have maintained a coherent argument from the beginning, ensuring that your transitions have indicated how each idea is meant to relate to the others, you, nonetheless, need to explain to readers what the textual experience they've just undergone means. Information doesn't necessarily mean anything. Data does not necessarily mean anything. It's only when the writer draws the individual pieces together and identifies the conclusions that he or she has drawn that the essay can be said to have arrived at its purpose. Readers can still disagree, but the writer is obliged to let them know what they are disagreeing with.

LO 1, 4

10.2 UNDERSTANDING THE DIFFERENCE BETWEEN THE PRACTICE OF THE NOVICE WRITER AND THE PRACTICE OF THE EXPERIENCED WRITER

In order to acquire an understanding of the writing process that experienced writers follow, it's useful to identify the differences between the writing practices of novice writers and those of experienced writers. You've seen the following chart in previous chapters. In this instance, refer to the differences between the novice writer and the experienced writer in the areas of *error avoidance, grammatical errors, and knowledge telling*. Novice writers are generally paying greater attention to mechanical writing functions and less attention to the development of meaning. By focusing on the integration of ideas through the use of transitions, as the experienced writers do, novice writers will be able to develop greater coherence in their writing.

Novice Writers	Experienced Writers
■ *Require thought for procedural, or "mechanical," writing functions.*	■ *Have, to a significant degree, automated procedural functions.*
■ *Focus on error avoidance rather than meaning.*	■ *Focus on developing or refining meaning;*
■ *Begin writing without planning, and edit, if at all, for grammatical errors.*	■ *Invest time and energy in planning and reviewing;*
■ *Focus on "knowledge telling" (i.e., relating all the information they have and can find on a topic, rather than exercising critical judgment to determine relevance).*	■ *Organize, and reorganize, essay structure to allow individual ideas to serve the overall purpose of the essay.*

Novice writers imagine that the conclusion is a formal requirement rather than a practical one. That is, novice writers often write a conclusion because they are obliged to do so rather than writing a conclusion because they feel it satisfies some practical purpose. The effect of such a strategy for writing conclusions is that the writers don't genuinely intend to provide any new information or new strategy for interpreting information. They're writing a conclusion because it would be impolite to send readers off without saying good-bye.

The experienced writer, on the other hand, recognizes the conclusion to be an essential element of the essay. It provides shape, answering many of the questions raised in the introduction without simply rewriting the introduction (you never simply rewrite the introduction; if the reader wanted to read the introduction again, and it's very difficult to see why that might be the case, the reader could go back to the introduction). Experienced writers regard the conclusion as an opportunity to explore what they've already said in their essays, to test the limits of what they've proven, and to survey the consequences of what they've proven.

The fundamental difference between the conclusion that a novice might write and the one a more experienced writer might write is that the more experienced writer is likely to provide a conclusion that is driven by purpose. Unlike the awkward good-bye of the novice writer, undertaken without any real sense of what he or she is meaning to say but informed with an urgent need to say something, the experienced writer uses the conclusion to ensure that the reader is not leaving without a proper understanding of the text or some sense of what the value of that text might be in the world to which the reader returns.

10.2.1 Differences between Effective and Ineffective Conclusions

There are certain features that characterize effective conclusions and those conclusions that are, well, less effective. Those differences generally emerge from the different decisions writers make about their conclusions. The following chart identifies some of those decisions.

Characteristics of Writers of Effective Conclusions	Characteristics of Writers of Less Effective Conclusions
Writers use the conclusion to synthesize ideas, to summarize the essay, and to highlight points of particular importance.	Writers restate the introduction, using both the introduction and the conclusion as bookends to the essay.
Writers use conclusions to complete the argument they've made throughout the essay. They do not use conclusions to introduce an argument that they forgot to make earlier.	While they are writing their conclusions, writers discover ideas that they should have included earlier. Because the thought of revising the entire essay is daunting, they try instead to sneak the idea into the conclusion, hoping that the reader won't notice (the reader usually notices).
Writers craft conclusions that remain true to the tone that has characterized the essay. The conclusion doesn't rise to a higher level of urgency or generalize beyond the scope that has already been established in the essay.	Writers use the conclusion to indulge in excessively grand statements, seeking to inspire passion in their reader rather than understanding. Rather than writing a conclusion that speaks precisely to the essay it concludes, they use it as a forum for editorializing or rabble-rousing.
Writers think of the conclusion as an integral part of the essay and present their argument in a concise fashion. They send their readers away with a brief but comprehensive statement of the argument.	Writers think of the conclusion as being a formal requirement in the essay-writing process. More good manners than good writing. They see it as a prescribed add-on, satisfying a tired formula for essay writing and, thus, fail to recognize the important function the conclusion serves.

10.2.2 Example of Effective and Less Effective Conclusions

In the following example of a less effective conclusion, the writer seems to force a conclusion on the essay, using a series of provocative statements to appeal to the reader's emotion. The series of statements are united in theme but lack coherence.

Example of a Less Effective Conclusion

This conclusion begins with a statement that is so general as to seem purposeless. It says nothing specific about the paper about which it speaks.

It may be unnecessary to state what the paper's point has been. If the reader has not recognized that point, it may not help to identify it in the conclusion.

The writer seems to be moving from one rhetorical form (the argumentative essay) to another (an appeal to emotion).

Again, the personal appeal seems to add little information. Instead, it seems to plead for a conclusion that has not been justified by the evidence.

The final sentence of the essay resorts to a sentimental appeal to the reader.

Teen pregnancy has an effect on both the teens and their loved ones. The point of this paper has been to prove that preventing teenagers from having sex is no longer in the hands of parents or anyone but the teens themselves. Teenagers are starting to have sex at a younger age and there is nothing more a parent or anyone else can do to stop it. Instead of focusing on preventing teenagers from doing it, focus on letting them do it in a safe way and with respect for parents and themselves. Preach to them not about how bad having sex is or how it is not their time but teach them to be respectful about it and especially safe. If support is given, teenagers will be more willing to ask for help. In addition, they are more likely to have the knowledge of safe sex practices and more likely to concentrate on avoiding pregnancy rather than worrying about being discovered by parents. Teenagers are not as crazy as they are made out to be. Give them a chance; remember, we were all young once.

In the following example of a more effective conclusion, the writer demonstrates how the ideas that emerge from the essay come together to form a logical argument. The conclusion clearly identifies the relationship between the ideas, and suggests the only logical reasoning that can be drawn from the argument.

Example of More Effective Conclusion

This paper has explored the proposition that the only effective strategy for reducing the rate of teen pregnancy is one that addresses the teen as the decision maker. Despite the best attempts of parents and educators, teens are continuing to experiment with sex at younger and younger ages. The decision, clearly, is one that resides with the teens themselves. Instead of investing in failed strategies that rely exclusively on abstinence, there ought to be a program that focuses on teaching teens to engage in safer sex practices, with respect for themselves and for parental values. There is no evidence that preaching to teens about the morality of premarital sex is effective, but there is evidence to support the effectiveness of frank discussions about contraception and family values. If the purpose of interventions by parents and educators is to avoid teen pregnancy, it seems that the best strategy is one that empowers teens to make good decisions.

In the opening sentence of this conclusion, the writer returns to the thesis that has guided the essay. The reminder of the thesis prepares the reader for the synthesis of the argument that is to follow.

In these two sentences, the writer reminds the reader of the dilemma that has been explored in the essay.

10.3 ENSURING THAT READER EXPECTATIONS HAVE BEEN MET

LO 2

In the introduction, you worked to establish expectations that informed your reader of the purpose of your essay. In establishing those expectations, you allowed your reader to anticipate the direction the essay would follow and encouraged the reader to make certain predictions. Over the course of the essay, with broad strokes, you attempted to meet those expectations with the essay as it emerged. Each stage of the essay was a response to the expectations you'd engendered earlier, though those responses may have been more implicit than explicit. In the conclusion, you have an opportunity to ensure (1) that you've met each of the expectations you established previously, and (2) that you've shown your reader the way in which the expectations have been met. The conclusion allows you to explicitly identify both the various elements of your argument and the way in which those elements come together to make your case.

The writer synthesizes the competing ideas of the essay, arriving at a conclusion that appears to resolve the opposition between the ideas.

The writer concludes by identifying the way in which the proposed solution satisfies the purpose that was stated at the beginning of the essay.

10.3.1 Writing Sample in Which the Writer Uses the Conclusion to Ensure That Expectations Have Been Met

In the following example, the writer has drawn the various elements of the essay together in a brief restatement of the argument. We're not suggesting that you cut and paste the introduction, but rather that you review the expectations you established in your introduction, that you think about the way in which you satisfied those expectations over the course of the essay, and that you ensure that you have clearly identified the way in which those realized expectations lead the reader to a particular conclusion.

The writer begins the concluding paragraph by reviewing the claims that have been made.

The writer reminds the reader of the limits to his or her claims.

The writer lists some of the rival explanations that the essay has explored.

Example of a Writer's Use of the Conclusion to Ensure that Expectations Have Been Met

In conclusion, young adults are likely to begin cigarette smoking if (i) they are raised in an environment of smokers, (ii) they are in a relationship with a smoker, or (iii) they are pressured by peers to begin smoking. That is, many young adults begin smoking in situations in which smoking has been normalized. However, mere association with smokers is not enough to explain the decision to begin smoking. Other factors must be considered, including advertising from tobacco companies that is geared at the young through billboards and magazines, and advertising in lower-income neighbourhoods. Additional steps, such as the ones mentioned in this essay, should be considered in evaluating why smoking is still so prevalent in society in spite of the current campaigns to eliminate it.

Writing Exercise

Read the following examples and reflect on the effectiveness of the conclusion that is being offered.

✔•⎯Practice

Example 1

Topic:

Current State of Health among Children

Theis:

Children in North America have become less healthy over the past decade, with more overweight children than there were ten years ago, more children eating fast food than before, and fewer children getting adequate daily exercise.

Conclusion:

Children should not rely on video games to keep themselves entertained.

Is this conclusion effective? Why or why not?

_____

_____

What conclusion were you expecting?

_____

_____

Why did you have that expectation?

_____

_____

Example 2

✓•─Practice

Topic:

Current State of Health among Children

Thesis:

Children in North America have become less healthy over the past decade, with more overweight children than there were ten years ago, more children eating fast food than before, and fewer children getting adequate daily exercise.

Conclusion:

Parents should ensure that their children are physically active at least one hour each day. This can involve walking, cycling, or any other form of exercise that gets children moving.

Is this conclusion effective? Why or why not?

_____

_____

What conclusion were you expecting?

_____

_____

Why did you have that expectation?

_____

_____

Example 3

✓•─Practice

Topic:

Bicycle Safety

Thesis:

To avoid collisions with automobiles, pedestrians, and inanimate objects, bicyclists should learn to take responsibility for their own safety and follow the rules of the road.

Conclusion:

As summer approaches, there will be more bicyclists on the road. Drivers must watch for cyclists because they have as much right to be on the road as a vehicle.

Is this conclusion effective? Why or why not?

_____

_____

What conclusion were you expecting?

_____

_____

Why did you have that expectation?

_____

_____

Practice

Example 4

Topic:

Bicycle Safety

Thesis Statement:

To avoid collisions with automobiles, pedestrians, and inanimate objects, bicyclists should learn to take responsibility for their own safety and follow the rules of the road.

Conclusion:

With summer approaching, there will be more bicyclists sharing the road with motor vehicles. Bicyclists should keep in mind that there are certain safety precautions they can take to minimize injury to themselves or others.

Is this conclusion effective? Why or why not?

_____

_____

What conclusion were you expecting?

_____

_____

Why did you have that expectation?

_____

_____

Practice

Example 5

Topic:

Legalization of Marijuana

Thesis Statement:

Marijuana should not be legalized because marijuana can damage specific brain functions, can cause health problems, and can jeopardize the safety of others.

Conclusion:

Marijuana may be harmful but it should be legalized for the use of people who are in chronic pain.

Is this conclusion effective? Why or why not?

_____

_____

What conclusion were you expecting?

_____

_____

Why did you have that expectation?

_____

_____

Example 6

✔• Practice

Topic:

Legalization of Marijuana

Thesis Statement:

Marijuana should not be legalized because marijuana can damage specific brain functions, can cause health problems, and can jeopardize the safety of others.

Conclusion:

While some people think that smoking marijuana is harmless, research has shown that even small amounts of marijuana over time can have lasting effects on an individual's health. Smoking marijuana can also impair an individual's judgment, which can adversely impact others. People who smoke marijuana cause accidents due to their poor judgment and propensity for risk-taking.

Is this conclusion effective? Why or why not?

_____

_____

What conclusion were you expecting?

_____

_____

Why did you have that expectation?

_____

_____

Example 7

✔• Practice

Topic:

Global Warming

Thesis:

The threat of global warming has been exaggerated by scientists who are only manufacturing a crisis to keep their jobs. Weather is cyclical and there have been other instances of weather cycles.

Conclusion:

Governments should reduce funding to global warming research because the crisis has been manu-factured by scientists who are worried about job security.

Is this conclusion effective? Why or why not?

_____

_____

What conclusion were you expecting?

_____

_____

Why did you have that expectation?

_____

_____

✓●—Practice

Example 8

Topic:

Global Warming

Thesis:

The threat of global warming has been exaggerated by scientists who are only manufacturing a crisis to keep their jobs. Weather is cyclical and there have been other instances of weather cycles.

Conclusion:

The history of weather on Earth has been characterized by peaks and valleys in temperature. A study of weather patterns shows that the Earth warms at certain times and cools at other times. This is nature's way of resetting Earth's thermostat.

Is this conclusion effective? Why or why not?

_____

_____

What conclusion were you expecting?

_____

_____

Why did you have that expectation?

_____

_____

Example 9

Topic:

Dogs and Licences

Thesis Statement:

There should not be a bylaw requiring dogs in the city to be licensed because some dogs are always kept in yards, some dogs are too old to roam, and some dogs have microchips in their ears that can be used to track them.

Conclusion:

The city is just looking to make money by requiring all owners to purchase a licence for their dogs. There is no need to have a dog licensed unless the dog is regularly on the street alone.

Is this conclusion effective? Why or why not?

_____

_____

What conclusion were you expecting?

_____

_____

Why did you have that expectation?

_____

_____

Example 10

Topic:

Dogs and Licences

Thesis Statement:

There should not be a bylaw requiring dogs in the city to be licensed because some dogs are always kept in yards, some dogs are too old to roam, and some dogs have microchips in their ears that can be used to track them.

Conclusion:

Dog owners should be free to make their own decision as to whether to purchase a licence for their animal. The city states that if dogs are lost, a licence will help reunite them with their owners. However, most dogs now have computer chips in their ears that facilitate identification without needless yearly licence renewals.

Is this conclusion effective? Why or why not?

_____

_____

What conclusion were you expecting?

_____

_____

Why did you have that expectation?

_____

_____

10.3.2 Making Writing Decisions about Satisfying Reader Expectations

As you were reading over the examples in the last section, you were making decisions about the effectiveness of the conclusions. You were judging whether the conclusions satisfied the expectations you had developed on the basis of the thesis statements. These are the kinds of decisions you will make when you are writing your own essays (once again, it is a metacognitive practice). By reflecting on the characteristics of the conclusions you found effective and comparing those to the ones that were less effective, you will develop the understanding you need to monitor your own work.

The following chart is designed to help you to evaluate your own conclusion. In your introduction, you make certain promises to the reader. Use the questions at the bottom of the chart to ensure that you keep them.

Making Writing Decisions	About Ensuring that You Have Met Reader Expectations in Your Own Essay Writing

What is the purpose of this writing decision?

Addressing reader expectations served to provide readers with the opportunity to forecast the text that would follow. It allowed readers to predict ideas in advance. Ensuring that those expectations have been met provides the essay with a sense of cohesion and closure.

What is the effect of this writing decision?

If the writer has established reader expectations, the writer has an obligation to meet those expectations. Failure to do so leaves the reader with a sense that the text is incomplete.

What considerations inform this decision?

Every expectation that you establish with your reader early in the essay is an unfinished action. It is a question without an answer. Until you close that action, providing each expectation with a satisfying conclusion, you leave the reader in anticipation or confusion. The expectation is a debt. By the end of the essay, the expectation is a debt that you must repay.

Suggested strategies for making this decision.

In order to ensure that you've met the reader's expectations, return to the introduction to take an inventory of the expectations you established. What did you indicate to the reader that he or she might reasonably come to expect of the essay? For each of the expectations that you identify, ensure that there is some answering action in the essay.

Questions to guide decision making in your own essay.

1. A good conclusion clarifies the subject of an essay for its reader. Read over your conclusion again. Does it convey the message you expected it to convey? Does it lead the reader to the understanding you intended?

2. Does the argument of the essay guide the reader to the conclusion? If not, rework the conclusion. The conclusion is perhaps the most important part of your essay because you have only one chance to tie up all the arguments into one concise package. Don't waste this opportunity by throwing in everything you can think of about the topic. That never works.

10.3.3 Writing Sample Showing the Use of the Conclusion to Provide Closure

In the writing sample below, you will see that the writer has drawn the ideas together to create a single, unified theme. By doing so, the writer has provided a brief summation of the argument that the essay has explored in detail. The conclusion reminds the reader of the way the individual elements of the essay were intended to fit together.

Example of a Conclusion that Brings Closure to the Text

In learning through experience, students escape the old dichotomy between the masters (i.e., those who know) and the pupils (i.e., those on whom learning is bestowed). The concept of "inexperience" replaces the concept of "ignorance," and the process of education emerges as one in which students *come to an understanding* rather than simply receive information. Experiential learning has been recognized as an efficient mode of education, with the pace of learning being accelerated through the reinforcement of concepts through application. The days of learning through passive reading and memorizing belong to the past. It is time for hands-on learning that can be applied in real-world situations.

> In this conclusion, the writer has worked to answer the principal questions that were raised in the essay: (1) What is the best way to learn? (2) Why is it the best way to learn? and (3) What are the implications of this argument to the world beyond the essay?

10.3.4 Making Writing Decisions about Providing Closure to the Text

One of the important functions the conclusion serves is the provision of closure to the text. It's possible, of course, to end an essay without including a conclusion. You just stop writing. There are a couple of problems with that strategy: (1) it seems impolite, much like walking away from a conversation without saying goodbye, and (2) it leaves your readers without your guidance as they exit the text and attempt to pull the strands of your argument together.

You can use the following chart to guide you as you reflect upon the degree to which you've provided closure to your own essay. As you're reviewing the chart, think about the conclusions you've written.

Making Writing Decisions	About Providing Closure to the Text in Your Own Essay Writing

What is the purpose of this writing decision?

Just as the reader requires guidance into the text, the reader also requires a bridge back to the world beyond the text.

What is the effect of this writing decision?

A well-written conclusion provides the reader with a sense of closure to the ideas and the argument that have been expressed.

What considerations inform this decision?

In order to provide the reader with a sense of closure, the writer must ensure that all questions raised in the text have been addressed, if not answered, and that the ideas have been synthesized to create a coherent whole.

Suggested strategies for making this decision.

In the introduction, the writer identified the pattern of ideas that he or she would be exploring in the text. When looking at the conclusion, reflect upon that pattern. Is the pattern of ideas that were introduced at the beginning of the essay still operating at the end? Has the writer provided a rationale for both the argument and the importance of that argument? Just as importantly, has the writer provided an explanation for the significance of the argument in the world beyond the text?

Questions to guide decision making in your own essay.

1. Read your conclusion. Does the conclusion answer the questions you raised in your introduction? Remember, you are not restating your introduction, but you need to ensure that the conclusion is consistent with the introduction. There has to be a kind of agreement between the two. If there isn't, go back and rework the conclusion until the introduction and the conclusion align.

2. Now, go back and read the entire essay. Make a list of all the questions that were raised in the text. Review your conclusion. Have you addressed the questions that emerged in the essay? If not, return to your conclusion and ensure that you do.

3. Does your conclusion leave your reader wanting to know more about your topic? A good conclusion will provide the reader with a bridge to the argument outside the essay. How have you guided the reader to make connections between your specific argument and the world beyond the essay? Have you discussed the implications of your argument? Have you suggested ways in which the specific argument might be relevant to the reader?

LO 3, 4

10.4 ENSURING THAT ALL IDEAS HAVE BEEN SYNTHESIZED

Writing is, in part, the act of creating order. One of the characteristics of inexperienced writers is that they often introduce ideas either without explaining the significance of those ideas or without explaining the way in which the various ideas work together to develop a larger theme. While you ought to be working toward a synthesis of ideas throughout the essay, the conclusion provides an opportunity to weave the various threads of the essay together to create a unified whole.

Writing Sample I

An example of a conclusion in which the writer synthesized main ideas

Although there is much evidence that addiction is related to genetic factors, it still appears that rates of alcoholism may be affected by environmental factors, such as the influence of peers, domestic home life, and moral values. That is, the research has clearly established that environment plays some part in the onset of the disease. As this research further develops, it will lead both to new strategies for managing the factors that are controllable (i.e., environmental factors) and to new ways of identifying the factors that can be influenced only by medication or gene therapy. In this way, therapists will develop a more flexible toolkit for addressing alcoholism and other debilitating addictions.

> In the first sentence of the conclusion, the writer has defined the relationship between the two competing ideas of the essay.

> In this sentence, the writer reminds the reader of the particular aspect of the complex relationship that has been explored in the essay.

> Finally, the writer demonstrates the way in which the various ideas have been synthesized as a single statement.

Writing Exercise

When a writer has successfully synthesized an essay in the conclusion, the reader ought to be able to reconstruct the principal structure of the essay from the conclusion alone. Review the conclusion below and answer the questions that follow to determine whether you think the essence of the essay has been woven into a unified whole.

Writing Sample 2

An example of a conclusion in which the writer has failed to synthesize main ideas.

People of all ages should wear bicycle helmets when they are riding because helmets can save lives. A car that weighs over two thousand pounds cannot stop immediately. If a cyclist suddenly crosses the path of the vehicle, the vehicle will not be able to stop and the cyclist will be hit. Cyclists have no real protection when they are riding and often hit their heads on the pavement as they fall. Do you know what happens to a head that hits the pavement? It smashes like a watermelon. If the cyclist is wearing a helmet, the helmet can help to cushion the blow. Cyclists might still be hurt but at least they will have their heads intact. On the other hand, helmets can be uncomfortable. Many people say that helmets are too hot to wear in the summer. Adults often claim that they do not see a need to wear helmets themselves although they are in favour of making helmets mandatory for children. Perhaps adults should have the right to decide whether they want to wear bicycle helmets or not. Therefore, helmets should not be mandatory for adults.

How does this conclusion indicate the thesis of the essay?

_____

_____

_____

How does this conclusion indicate the writer's position on the issue? Can you identify the writer's arguable proposition?

_____

_____

How does this conclusion reflect the essay's pattern of organization?

_____

_____

If this was your conclusion, what could you have done differently that would have synthesized the main points more clearly? Try rewriting the conclusion here.

_____

_____

10.4.1 Making Writing Decisions to Ensure That All Ideas Have Been Synthesized

The unique expression of ideas that emerges from each writer derives, in large part, not from the ideas themselves (most of which, frankly, are not new), but from the novel way in which the writer has ordered and connected those ideas. It's important to remember, however, that the way in which the ideas are woven together should be determined by the argument they serve. Use the following chart to ensure that you've organized your ideas to create the argumentative structure you intend to make.

Making Writing Decisions	About Ensuring All Ideas Have Been Synthesized in Your Own Essay Writing

What is the purpose of this writing decision?

Among its other functions, language imposes order. It brings ideas together to form a coherent whole. One of the consistent differences between novice and experienced writers is the degree to which they have woven ideas together to serve a unified purpose.

What is the effect of this writing decision?

If novice writing is sometimes characterized by the appearance of information being randomly dumped on a page, the work of experienced writers more often demonstrates a pattern in which all ideas have been brought together. This cohesion allows the reader to understand the relationship between the diverse ideas in the text.

What considerations inform this decision?

In order to synthesize the different ideas in the text, the writer needs to be aware of the relationship between those ideas. Which ideas are the controlling ideas? Which ideas are subordinate to those controlling ideas? What is the relationship between those subordinate ideas?

Suggested strategies for making this decision.

Think about the purpose of the text. Think about the logical order of ideas. Which idea needs to be discussed first? What is the logical relationship of that idea to the next?

Questions to guide decision making in your own essay.

1. Once more, return to your essay and read the conclusion. In this reading, you're looking to see whether you've ordered your ideas logically and consistently.
   a. Does the pattern of ideas in your conclusion match the pattern of ideas in the essay?
   b. Have you made a connection between the ideas or did you just write them down in the order you thought of them?
   c. Is there a logical order to your points?
   d. Is the order of ideas consistent with their relevance to the argument?

2. If the answer to any of the questions above is no, rewrite the conclusion to ensure that you've connected the ideas in the way that you had intended.

10.5 WRITING STRATEGIES FOR WRITING CONCLUSIONS   LO 3, 4

Conclusions, quite simply, ought to make sense. They ought to synthesize main ideas and provide closure to the text. They ought to help the reader understand the way in which the individual pieces fit together and they ought to help guide the reader so that he or she finishes reading the text with a clear understanding of the argument.

In this section, we identify some strategies you can use for organizing the conclusions you will write in your essays.

10.5.1 The Summary Statement

One of the strategies you can apply to great effect when writing your conclusion is to use a summary statement. A summary statement packages the argument you've made and helps the reader to focus on the main themes that you discussed in the body of the essay. However tempting it might be to cut and paste your introduction to the end of the essay, a summary statement demands a little more than that. It should capture the essence of the essay by focusing on the relationship between the main ideas in the essay.

The summary statement is an effective way of beginning the conclusion to an academic essay.

Writing Exercises

In the following section, you will find three examples of summaries, followed by seven exercises in which you will write summary statements using the information you find in the thesis statements.

✓•─Practice

Example 1

Thesis Statement:

There is an obesity epidemic among children because they do not get enough exercise, they eat unhealthy foods, and they drink high-calorie sugary drinks.

Summary Statement:

Unhealthy food choices such as fast food, high-calorie sugary drinks, and a lack of exercise, have all contributed to the obesity problem in children.

✓•─Practice

Example 2

Thesis Statement:

Bicycle helmets should be mandatory for people of all ages because helmets reduce head injuries, helmets cushion the head during a fall, and helmets protect the rider's face from being scraped on the road.

Summary Statement:

Bicycle helmets are not just for children and should be worn by people of all ages because of the overall safety features of the helmet.

✓•─Practice

Example 3

Thesis Statement:

Organic farming is a more environmentally responsible practice than factory farming because it uses fewer harmful chemicals, employs crop rotation to maintain the vitality of the soil, and contributes less to the contamination of groundwater.

Summary Statement:

The practices of using fewer chemicals on fields, allowing fields to recover between plantings, and reducing the amount of water pollution have all contributed to making organic farming more environmentally friendly than factory farming.

✓•─Practice

Example 4

Thesis Statement:

Video games are harmful to children's development because they are addictive, they can increase violent tendencies, and they can contribute to children's isolation from family and friends.

Summary Statement:

Use the information in the thesis statement to draft a summary statement.

_____

_____

_____

Example 5

Thesis Statement:

The euro zone is in danger of collapse because of an increase in debt among some member nations, the increasing reluctance of nations like Germany to support failing economies, and international concerns about the viability of the European Union.

Summary Statement:

Use the information in the thesis statement to draft a summary statement.

_____

_____

Example 6

Thesis Statement:

The ban on sales of cigarettes to teens should be more strictly enforced because teens are the most likely segment of the population to begin smoking, they are more prone to peer pressure, and they are less likely than adults to consider long-term consequences.

Summary Statement:

Use the information in the thesis statement to draft a summary statement.

_____

_____

Example 7

Practice

Thesis Statement:

The practice of using cell phones while driving should be strictly prohibited because it requires drivers to focus on multiple tasks and it often results in drivers removing their hands from their steering wheels.

Summary Statement:

Use the information in the thesis statement to draft a summary statement.

_____

_____

Example 8

Thesis Statement:

School uniforms should be mandatory because they diminish the competition among students, they allow students to dress in the morning without the distraction of having to choose their clothes, and they create a sense of commonality among the student body.

Summary Statement:

Use the information in the thesis statement to draft a summary statement.

_____

_____

✓● Practice

Example 9

Thesis Statement:

Dogs are better pets than cats because dogs are loyal, they interact with owners to a greater extent, and they have an innate capacity for forming packs or family units.

Summary Statement:

Use the information in the thesis statement to draft a summary statement.

_____

_____

✓● Practice

Example 10

Thesis Statement:

Many people prefer to own cats rather than dogs because cats are more self-sufficient, do not have to be walked, and are cheaper to own.

Summary Statement:

Use the information in the thesis statement to draft a summary statement.

_____

_____

The following chart provides a short list of effective strategies for writing conclusions.

Other Strategies for Writing Conclusions in Your Own Essays
Challenge the essay.   If it seems that the conclusion is saying nothing new or interesting, return briefly to the essay itself. Why does it matter? Why should anybody care? The answers to those questions ought to provide the beginning of the conclusion.
Synthesize the essay.   Draw the main ideas together. The purpose of the conclusion is to provide the reader with an understanding of the relationship between the information.

Identify what has been discovered in the process of writing the essay and what has yet to be proved. The conclusion is a conclusion to the essay. It does not need to be the final word on the subject. Use the conclusion to contextualize the findings.
Highlight the significance of the thesis. The conclusion provides an opportunity to remind the reader of the importance of the ideas you've discussed (within reason, of course; don't overstate the significance of a mundane idea).
Draw inferences and explore the consequences of the argument. Discuss the implications of the conclusions. What new questions arise from the essay?
Offer suggestions for further action. Does the conclusion suggest actions that ought to be pursued in the world beyond the essay? Explore those possibilities.

10.6 STRATEGIES TO AVOID WHEN WRITING CONCLUSIONS

LO 4

There are three categories of conclusions you ought to avoid: (1) conclusions in which you scramble to cover all the ideas you forgot to mention in the essay, (2) conclusions in which you end by restating everything you've already said, and (3) conclusions in which you abandon any pretense of objectivity and emote all over the page. The first strategy testifies to a lack of planning, the second to a failure of imagination, and the third, well, the third is the textual equivalent of suddenly switching to a foreign language at the end of the essay. However much fun it may be to write those kinds of conclusions, they confuse people.

The chart below includes a number of other strategies you may want to avoid.

Strategies to Avoid When Writing Conclusions in Your Own Essays
Don't state the thesis for the first time in the conclusion and don't introduce a new idea or subtopic in the conclusion.
Don't simply restate or rephrase the thesis statement without making any substantive changes.
Don't make sentimental, emotional appeals that are out of character with the rest of an analytic paper.
Don't indulge in rhetorical excess.
Don't introduce evidence, quotations, or statistics that you should have used in the body of the paper.
Don't focus on minor points.
Don't apologize for your view by stating that you might not be an expert or this is only your opinion.
Don't begin with an unnecessary, overused phrase such as "in conclusion," "in summary," or "in closing." In written communications, such phrases are usually unnecessary. The reader is aware that the essay is coming to a close.

10.7 CONCLUSION

Like the introduction to an essay, the conclusion is an element that rarely receives its due. In many cases, writers tack on a conclusion out of a sense of obligation, stringing together a series of empty phrases in an attempt to fill an empty space and escape from the text without saying anything. That's not a conclusion. A conclusion is meant to provide the reader with an understanding of the essay's purpose and to synthesize the individual elements of the essay into a unified whole. It allows you to justify your own interpretation of the evidence, to identify alternative explanations that are worthy of consideration, and to recognize issues that are yet to be investigated. If your conclusion is effective, it should send the reader back into the world believing that you've satisfied the expectations you established throughout the essay and that the argument you offer is a reasonable one.

MyCompLab®

How Do I Get a Better Grade?

Go to MyCompLab for additional help with your
grammar, writing, and research skills. You will have access to a variety of
exercises, instruction, and videos that will help you improve your basic
skills and help you get a better grade.

Sample Essay

Putting It All Together

In this chapter, we've discussed the function of the conclusion and identified some of the questions a writer needs to consider when writing the conclusion. It's just not as easy as it looks. In the writing sample below, we've included the complete essay to demonstrate the degree to which the conclusion emerges from the essay. In the notes that appear in the margin, we've identified the main ideas of the essay. You will notice that the conclusion draws these ideas together and explains the significance and importance of each. The conclusion restates the argument briefly, demonstrating the way in which the evidence serves to establish the essay's main thesis as a reasonable proposition.

After reading the sample essay and the annotations in the margin, answer the questions that follow the essay.

Discovering Human Cognition through Comparative Psychology

[1]Comparative psychology strives to gain a deeper understanding of the mental capacities of animals. While many animals—including magpies, dolphins, and dogs—display the capacity for complex mental operations, chimpanzees and other primates hold a particular interest for researchers due to the similarity between *Homo sapiens* and lower primates (Gramner, 1991; Nilson, 1972). Chimpanzees display a family resemblance that fascinates their kin (*Homo sapiens*), and scientists have been able to increasingly identify evidence of similarities between human and chimpanzee behaviour and skills, prompting many researchers to think about the "vagaries of evolution." According to Brown (2004), "despite profound differences in the two species, just a 1.23 percent difference in their genes separates Homo Sapiens from chimpanzees" (p. 133). By observing the cognitive similarities between humans and chimpanzees, researchers hope to develop a more thorough understanding of animal cognition.[2]

[3]In order to gain a deeper understanding of how animals learn and think, Orowitz (2004) studied the problem-solving capacity of chimpanzees and found that it closely mapped to the problem-solving processes of *Homo sapiens*. Norris (1999) also found a similarity between the reasoning patterns of the two species. In Norris's research (1999), a chimp named Alladin was given the challenge of getting a piece of fruit that was out of his reach. Nearby, there were two sticks: (1) a short stick that was within reach, and (2) a longer stick that was well beyond reach. After several failed attempts to reach the fruit, Alladin realized that he could use the short stick to retrieve the longer stick, and use the longer stick to reach the fruit. The chimp's actions suggested the capacity to work through a multi-stage problem with no apparent training. That capacity to reason appeared to be innate.

[4]In addition to Norris's work (1999) with Alladin, there have been a number of studies with apes, chimpanzees, and gorillas that have revealed their ability to use natural tools such as sticks and other objects to accomplish tasks and acquire goods. This is commonly referred to as functional fixedness, a capacity through which animals select appropriate branches or stones to use as hammers in cracking nuts (Better, 1996). Chimps have also been observed breaking off reeds or sticks, stripping them of their twigs and leaves, and carrying them to termite mounds to "fish" for termites. When observing animals in a natural environment,

1 The introduction serves to establish the organizational structure of the essay. It provides the reader with the information necessary to anticipate both the main ideas of the essay that follow and the relationship between those ideas.

2 Each of the paragraphs follows a specific aspect of the argument in greater depth. Each of these will need to be drawn together in the conclusion.

3 Paragraph 2 explores the inventive abilities of lower primates.

4 Paragraph 3 further explores the tool-making abilities of lower primates.

researchers have found that chimpanzees display sophisticated abilities to select different objects as tools (e.g., heavy sticks to puncture holes, light flexible sticks to use for fishing). In fact, researchers have also found that there are thirty-nine local customs related to chimpanzee tool use, grooming, and courtship (Grant, Penny, & Gordski, 2009).

5 Paragraph 4 identifies a theoretical basis for the perceived similarities between humans and non-human primates.

[5]Scientists have noted that, in all primates, the left hemisphere of the brain records rules based on experience while the right hemisphere avoids rules in order to detect details and unique features that allow it to decide what is familiar and what is novel. This dichotomy is true for both human and non-human animals, which likely reflects the evolutionary origins of the underlying brain mechanisms. Researchers speculate that the underlying brain structures that contribute to commonality between human and non-human primates in problem solving and rule making also apply to primal language capacities. Hauser (2000) argued that "animals have interesting thoughts, but the only way they can convey them is by grunts, shrieks, and other vocalizations, and by gestures." Hauser suggested that these grunts and shrieks operate as a form of language among non-human primates.

6 Paragraph 5 further explores the similarities between the species in terms of language abilities.

[6]Although Flowman and Brown (1997) have suggested that the mental capacity of most non-human primates is approximately equivalent to a two-year-old child, non-human primates have been observed practising sign language. University of Nevada researchers Gardner and Gardner (1995) successfully taught sign language to a chimpanzee named Washoe. By the time of her death at forty-two, she could use about 250 distinctive American Sign Language signs, as measured by the Schrier Research Laboratory. Remarkably, Washoe was also able to teach another chimpanzee, Loulis, to use sign language without any human intervention, marking the first animal-to-animal transfer of human language. Although chimpanzees do not have the same facility of language as humans, their ability to think and communicate indicates an impressive level of intelligence.

7 Paragraph 6 further explores the commonality between lower primates and humans by identifying the common capacity for self-awareness and deception.

[7]"Theory of Mind" is a term that is used to refer to a person's ideas about their own and others' mental states. Chimpanzees and orangutans have been observed using mirrors to inspect themselves and touching coloured spots that a researcher has dabbed on their faces. Chimps and baboons have also been observed using deception. In one such example, a young baboon feigns having been attacked to have the mother drive away competing baboons from their food. These actions indicate that primates are capable of self-recognition and of understanding others' perceptions of a given situation.

[8]Although these feats are impressive, there are also significant differences to be observed when comparing animal to human intelligence. According to Hauser (2000), animals have "laser beam" intelligence, by which he means that, although non-human primates can find a specific solution to solve a specific problem, these solutions cannot be applied to new situations or to solve different kinds of problems. That is, although chimpanzees may be favourably compared to other animals when displaying the ability to construct tools, they generally lack the "floodlight" cognitive capacity that allows *Homo sapiens* to use existing knowledge in new ways and to apply the solution of one problem to another situation.

[9]Comparative psychologists continue to pursue their quest to discover whether animal intelligence operates the same way that human intelligence does. [10]Some argue that non-human primates use strategies similar to humans, providing some of the closest human–animal similarities in performance ever reported in the comparative literature. [11]In addition, scientists have noted a similarity in the cognitive functioning of all primates, with the two hemispheres differentiating between tasks in similar ways. [12]Some skeptics continue to doubt that the cognitive patterns of lower primates map to human intelligence, arguing that the lower primates cannot plan, conceptualize, show compassion, or use language. However, this runs contrary to research provided by other animal researchers that demonstrates strong evidence that many animals, especially non-human primates, exhibit insight, show family loyalty, communicate with one another, display altruism, transmit cultural patterns across generations, and comprehend the syntax of human speech. While there may be significant differences between the thinking patterns of the species, current research indicates that the similarities suggest a commonality that is significant enough to permit study by analogy.[13]

8 Paragraph 7 acknowledges the significant dissimilarities between the cognitive abilities of the species.

9 The first sentence of the conclusion returns to the central question of the essay.

10 The second sentence draws together the cultural similarities into a single, coherent statement. This economical synthesis of ideas begins to link the paragraphs together.

11 This sentence similarly notes the biological similarities the essay has discussed.

12 The conclusion also acknowledges rival views.

13 The final sentence returns the reader to the world beyond the text, with a summary that captures the general themes of the essay.

Writing Exercise

✓ ● **Practice**

What is the thesis of the essay?

_____

_____

What expectations are established in the introduction?

_____

_____

What is the organizational pattern that is established in the introduction (i.e., how does the introduction indicate the way in which the argument of the essay will be organized)?

_____

_____

To what extent does the conclusion mirror the organizational pattern of the introduction and the essay?

_____

_____

Does the conclusion provide a summary statement? If so, record it below. If a summary statement is not provided, what might the summary statement have said?

_____

_____

Does the conclusion include any important themes that had not been mentioned in the essay? If so, what are they?

_____

_____

Do you feel that the conclusion provided the essay with a sense of closure? Why or why not?

_____

_____

✔•⌐Practice   **Evaluation Worksheet**

The following chart provides a series of general questions for use in evaluating the conclusion in your essay. Use the worksheet to ensure that you've written a conclusion that summarizes, and brings closure to, your essay.

An Evaluation Worksheet to Guide Decision Making When You Write Your Own Conclusions

Review your essay and evaluate the conclusion.

1. Does the conclusion agree with the principal thesis of the essay? Have you introduced ideas or arguments that were not discussed in the essay?

2. Does the conclusion reflect the structure of the essay?

    a. Has your conclusion articulated the argument you were attempting to make, by organizing the ideas in such a way as to establish the relationship between main ideas and subordinate points?

3. Review your conclusion in relation to your purpose.

    a. Has the essay reflected that purpose or are you attempting to use the conclusion to answer questions that you failed to make in the essay itself?

4. Is the conclusion consistent with the tone of the essay?

    a. Have you used the conclusion to editorialize beyond the scope and purpose of the essay?

    b. Have you used the conclusion to indulge in brilliant but irrelevant rhetorical excess? (If so, cut it out and post it on a bulletin board; you may not want to waste it, but it certainly doesn't belong in your essay.)

5. The conclusion provides you with your last chance to speak to your readers. Have you written the conclusion clearly enough that the message they take away is the message you intended to deliver?

Peer-Evaluation Worksheet for the Conclusion ✔—Practice

Title of the Essay: _____

Draft of Conclusion Submitted By: _____

Peer Evaluator: _____

Based on your understanding of the essay's introduction, what expectations did the writer establish in the introduction?

_____

_____

How has the writer addressed those expectations in the conclusion?

_____

_____

(continued)

(continued)

How has the writer connected the essay's principal ideas in the conclusion?

_____

_____

_____

Does the pattern of reasoning in the conclusion reflect the pattern of reasoning that was used throughout the essay? If not, in what way is it different?

_____

_____

_____

What ideas/assertions/comments in the conclusion seem irrelevant, or appear to introduce themes that were not addressed in the essay?

_____

_____

_____

Is the tone of the conclusion consistent with the tone of the essay? If not, in what way has it changed?

_____

_____

_____

What further information, if any, ought to be added to the conclusion?

_____

_____

_____

Recursivity and Revision

11.1 INTRODUCTION

You know those writers who wake up one morning with an idea fully formed, sit down at the computer, and pour out a twenty-five-page treatise on some obscure topic without pausing a moment to reflect on the emerging text or to reconsider the decisions that informed the writing process? It's annoying, isn't it? Just doesn't seem fair.

It doesn't happen. Or, if it does, it happens so rarely as to register as never happening. Most experienced writers reflect on their respective writing processes constantly, continuously evaluating the effect of the decisions they've made, and wrestling against the growing influence of the emerging text (below, we'll discuss the conflict between a writer's intentions and the stubborn reluctance of the emerging text to meet those intentions). In Chapter 1, we discussed the curious relationship between the writing process and the finished essay. The writing process is often tentative (i.e., the writer experiments with his or her translation of an idea into text) and usually recursive (i.e., the writer moves forward, writing text, and, then, circles back to ensure that the new section aligns properly with the text that has preceded it). The finished essay, if successful, is generally characterized by linearity, with individual ideas carefully orchestrated to serve the larger purpose of the essay. In this chapter, we review the practice of revision, distinguishing it from editing—the process with which it's often confused—and discussing some strategies for revising at different stages in the essay-writing process.

LO 1   11.2   DIFFERENCES BETWEEN NOVICE AND EXPERIENCED WRITERS IN THE PROCESS OF REVISION

One of the practices that distinguishes the writing practices of novice writers from those of experienced writers is the degree to which the writer monitors the emerging text for coherence, clarity, and correspondence to purpose. Because the experienced writer is intent on *developing or refining meaning*, the experienced writer orchestrates the various ideas of an essay to serve a larger goal, *organizing, and reorganizing, essay structure to allow individual ideas to serve the overall purpose of the essay*. In contrast, the novice writer, who often *focuses on error avoidance rather than the development of meaning*, tends to focus on *knowledge telling*, relating and reporting information without identifying its relevance and without integrating it into the larger structure of the essay. Novice writers tend to make changes to the surface elements of their essays. That is, they pay attention to grammatical errors, sentence construction, and formatting errors, because those problems are often easiest to identify.

In the chart below, you'll notice some of the key differences between novice and experienced writers in their respective revision processes.

Novice Writers	Experienced Writers
■ Require thought for procedural, or "mechanical," writing functions.	■ Have, to a significant degree, automated procedural functions.
■ *Focus on error avoidance rather than meaning.*	■ *Focus on developing or refining meaning.*
■ Begin writing without planning, and edit, if at all, for grammatical errors.	■ Invest time and energy in planning and reviewing.
■ *Focus on "knowledge telling" (i.e., relating all the information they have and can find on a topic, rather than exercising critical judgment to determine relevance).*	■ *Organize, and reorganize, essay structure to allow individual ideas to serve the overall purpose of the essay.*

Novice writers sometimes have problems with the revision process because they lack the necessary revision strategies to make meaningful changes to their essays. Expert writers tend to have a repertoire of strategies that they can use when they revise their essays.

11.3 THE DIFFERENCE BETWEEN REVISION AND EDITING

LO 2

Despite the apparent similarity between the two processes, there is a profound difference between editing and revising. In Chapter 13, you'll find strategies for editing and proofreading your essay. Chapter 13 is exactly where you might expect to find such information. It's near the end of the textbook, with the location providing a metaphoric hint to the function the information will serve in the process of writing. Editing provides a final opportunity for writers to dust the essay off and give it a nice shine. It's a kind of quality-control process, ensuring that every essay that leaves the shop has been checked for surface defects.

Revision is different. Though proofreading may be part of the revision process, it's not the principal focus. Revision is an integral and ongoing part of composition, a monitoring of the emerging text to ensure that there's a correspondence between your intentions for the essay and the text as it appears on the page. Recursivity, the practice of circling back to earlier stages of the essay, allows you to make adjustments as you write; this is where you refine and adjust each element of the essay to bring the various parts into alignment. The revision process may cause you to adjust your thesis statement to accord with new insights that have emerged in the writing process, or to rephrase a particular paragraph to bring it back into line with the thesis statement. It may lead you to reflect upon the evidence you've used to support your thesis or to reorganize a paragraph for greater internal unity and cohesion. It may even cause you to restructure the essay entirely, fundamentally altering the shape of the argument, to ensure that your reader is able to follow the development of your ideas. The commitment to an ongoing process of revision—the rethinking and reshaping of an essay—constitutes one of the most significant differences between experienced writers and others.

The chart below identifies some of the important differences between the processes of revising and editing. Because both are active processes, we've phrased the differences as questions about the different actions each requires.

Process of Revising	Process of Editing
■ Have you clearly identified your audience? ■ Have you read to verify that your purpose for writing is clear to the reader? ■ Have you written a thesis that clearly articulates and limits the scope of your essay?	■ Have you run the spell-check program in your word processor? ■ Have you read your essay carefully, checking for incorrect words that you've spelled correctly (e.g., homonyms)? ■ Have you monitored for mistakes in tense?

(continued)

(continued)

- Have you monitored the emerging text to ensure that the essay continues to correspond with the thesis statement?
- If the essence of the thesis statement and the essence of the essay have drifted apart, have you reworked one or both to bring the two into alignment?
- Have you checked to ensure that your essay has a clear introduction, body, and conclusion?
- Have you checked to see that the organization of paragraphs in your essay matches the pattern of organization forecast by the thesis statement?
- Have you continued to evaluate the overall organization and structure of the essay?
- Have you monitored the development of ideas in each paragraph, ensuring that each is governed by a single controlling idea?
- Have you made effective decisions about paragraph breaks, dividing paragraphs with too many ideas into two or more separate paragraphs?
- Have you used transitional words or phrases to create a logical progression through the essay?
- Have you ensured that you've supplied the evidence necessary to substantiate your claims and deleted information that isn't relevant?
- Have you integrated external content in the essay effectively, ensuring that it serves the essay's overall purpose?
- Have you monitored the balance between quotations, paraphrases, and summaries, and your own interpretations and analysis?
- Have you maintained the degree of objectivity that is appropriate to the writing conventions you're using (e.g., APA, MLA, *Chicago*)?
- Have you addressed competing views of the subject and represented those alternative views fairly? Have you monitored for surface errors like spelling and punctuation?

- Have you monitored for grammar and common usage mistakes (e.g., run-on sentences, sentence fragments, subject–verb agreement, pronoun agreement, plurals and possessives)?
- Have you monitored your sentences to ensure that you're maintaining an active voice?
- Have you monitored the text for typing errors (e.g., unnecessary or repeated words or missed words)?
- Have you checked for repetition to ensure that each paragraph begins with a different word, to prevent all of your paragraphs from looking the same?
- Have you monitored the text for slang and contractions?
- Have you monitored the text for adherence to formatting requirements (e.g., citations, page format, tense)?

11.4 WRESTLING WITH THE EMERGING TEXT

Oddly enough, one of the greatest challenges writers face is the damaging inflexibility of their own texts. You would think that your own essay might show you a little respect, but that is rarely the case. As a writer, you exercise the greatest control of the shape of your work at the outset. In the planning stage, you (1) define your purpose, (2) anticipate your audience, (3) shape your argument, and (4) begin, usually with equal measures of optimism and fear, to draft your essay. Unfortunately, in translating your ideas from ingenious concept to lowly text, something happens. The expression of ideas fails to meet your intention. Your ability to manage complex intellectual structures seems to slip away. The essay, so far from politely following the plan, like a well-behaved retriever on a leash, behaves instead like a crazed terrier puppy, intent on following some inner voice that only terriers understand. And the further you proceed with the essay, the more like a terrier it becomes, headstrong and unruly.

It's not your imagination. That is, in fact, often the nature of writing. As the act of composition progresses, the text begins to exert ever greater control. The things you've already said dictate the things you can say subsequently. And the further you proceed in the process, the greater the constraint that the things you've written will exercise over the choices you can make. Revision, therefore, may include your returning to an earlier point in the essay to rework and reword an idea. It may involve a reorganization of material within a paragraph or a reordering of a series of paragraphs. Sometimes, revision of an essay that is not working the way you had intended may even require that you start over. In most cases, the closer you are to the beginning of an essay, the greater the flexibility you enjoy. If you're struggling with an essay that won't behave itself, return to a stage at which you have greater control.

11.5 THINGS TO CONSIDER WHILE REVISING

Revision provides you with an opportunity to reflect upon the structure and organization of your essay to ensure that the underlying foundation is serving the development of meaning. It also allows you to consider whether the way in which you have expressed your ideas clearly reflects your intentions and whether you've been ruthless enough in cutting away ideas and sentences that serve no real purpose in the essay apart from adding to the word count. It's important to avoid becoming too attached to every word, sentence, or paragraph you write. You need to remember that the elements of the essay are meant to serve the larger whole and that, brilliant or not, some of your best lines will end up on the cutting-room floor. It's one of the great tragedies of writing. Revision is a process of change, involving the deletion of great thoughts that don't work, the addition of pedestrian but necessary facts or explanations, and the reworking of sections of text that don't make sense to anyone but you. Sometimes it helps to wait a few days before you undertake the final revision. It's always harder to revise while you're still emotionally involved with the essay.

The questions in the following chart are designed to guide you as you work through the process of revision.

General Questions to Guide Revision
■ Is the thesis statement of the essay clearly articulated? 　1. Is the purpose of the essay clear? 　2. Is the nature of the argument clear?
■ Does the topic sentence of each paragraph reflect a clear connection to the controlling thesis of the essay? Does it reflect a relationship to the preceding paragraph?
■ Are the individual paragraphs internally coherent? Is each paragraph governed by a single controlling idea? Are the ideas in each of the paragraphs well developed?
■ Are there paragraphs that are not relevant to the overarching argument of the essay? Are there ideas or sentences that are not relevant to the paragraph? If so, no matter how clever they are or how elegantly you've expressed them, they have to go (if they are too valuable to lose, they can be posted on a bulletin board or added to a blog; irrelevant utterances of genius have no place in the essay).
■ Are there statements for which there is no evidence? If so, either find the evidence or take them out. Unsubstantiated claims serve no useful purpose. In academic writing, an argumentative essay stands on evidence.
■ Are the paragraphs organized in a pattern that is consistent with the argument? Does each paragraph build on the previous one?
■ Have you acknowledged reasonable challenges to the argument? Have you answered counter-arguments? However tempting it might be to ignore valid objections, the failure to address those objections weakens the argument.
■ Is the general thesis of the essay worthy of argument? Is there an argument to be made? Would anyone argue against the proposition?
■ Is the tone of the essay appropriate? Emotional appeals and rhetorical excess are generally avoided in academic writing.

LO 3   11.6   REVISING THE THESIS STATEMENT AND INTRODUCTION

One of the questions that ought to guide you as you're revising your essay is this one: Am I satisfying my writing purpose? That question is easier to answer if you *have* a purpose for writing (and a purpose beyond the utilitarian one of "Someone told me to write an essay"). A clearly defined thesis statement—one that includes an arguable proposition—provides a benchmark against which to judge the degree to which the emerging essay is satisfying your intentions. It identifies the claims you're making and the reasons, or evidence, you intend to offer in support of those claims. It also suggests a blueprint for the essay itself. As the writing process progresses, the introduction in general, and the thesis statement in particular, serve as the basis for the monitoring of the development of the essay. By comparing the emerging text to your stated purpose, you are able to determine whether you have strayed from the path you intended to follow. One of the advantages of the IDDL model is that it allows you to extract from the thesis statement the themes you intend to explore and to use those themes to anchor the outline of the essay. It's important, then, that you begin with a thesis statement and introduction that provides you, and your reader, with a sense of the direction the essay will follow.

Practice Exercise 1

✓•─ Practice

Read the following introductory paragraph and ask yourself whether the thesis statement and introduction provide enough guidance to allow you to effectively monitor the emerging text. Ask yourself, in addition, whether the introduction would permit your reader to anticipate the principal elements of the argument you are about to make.

> Cell phone use has increased exponentially in the last several years, especially with people in the 16–30 age group. It is not unusual to see young people talking on their cell phones while walking on the street, while going to the movies, while eating in restaurants, and while driving their vehicles. The rise in the number of people who talk while driving has also led to a rise in the number of accidents attributed to hand-held cell phone use. It is easy for drivers to become distracted when they are talking and driving; driving is a difficult task that requires concentration on the part of drivers to keep track of what is going on around them. They have to pay attention to other drivers, cyclists, and pedestrians. A moment of inattention can lead to an accident. Statistics released by the police association show that 40 percent of all vehicle accidents are attributed to cell phone use by young drivers (Brown, 2010).

Having read the paragraph, respond to these questions:

1. What is the topic of the essay? List all possible topics.

   _____

   _____

2. What would you identify as the thesis statement for this essay?

   _____

   _____

3. How could you rewrite the paragraph to provide it with a clearer thesis statement? Write it out now.

   _____

   _____

   In the example above, it's very difficult to determine the thesis of the essay. It could be any one of a number of things:

1. It could be about young drivers (ages 16–30) and cell phone use.
2. It could be about the dangers of driving and talking on a cell phone.
3. It could be about the dangers that drivers who talk on their cell phones pose to other drivers, cyclists, and pedestrians.
4. It could be about the problems caused by drivers who get distracted while driving.
5. It could be about drivers who talk on their cell phones and cause accidents.

The problem with the example above is that it fails to foreground a controlling thesis for the essay. It may be the case that the writer will discuss all of the points that are listed. Without a thesis statement that identifies the relationship of one idea to the next, however, it is difficult to determine what the focus of the essay will be.

Now, read the same paragraph below, with a clearly articulated thesis statement.

> The use of cell phones by drivers should be banned because it is a dangerous distraction for all drivers, it leads to a higher rate of accidents, and it poses a particular risk for younger drivers. Drivers have reported that the distraction of their respective cell phone conversations led them to lose track of events outside their vehicles and that this lack of attention contributed to driving difficulties ranging from the failure to attend to changes in traffic flow to the failure to notice other vehicles or pedestrians. A number of studies have identified cell phone usage as a contributing factor in accidents. Although the use of a cell phone while driving is problematic for all drivers, it poses a particular risk for younger drivers. Some statistics indicate that approximately 40 percent of all vehicle accidents are attributed to young drivers who were talking on their cell phones while driving (Brown, 2010).

The thesis of the paragraph should be easier to recognize now (*The use of cell phones by drivers should be banned because it is a dangerous distraction for all drivers, it leads to a higher rate of accidents, and it poses a particular risk for younger drivers*). By subordinating some of the ideas to a single controlling thesis, the relationship between the various themes becomes more obvious. The first example contained a number of ideas that were tangentially related, but it failed to provide any indication of the specific purpose the information would serve. It was, as is often the case in unsuccessful essays, an information dump, or mere list of assertions or facts with no obvious point or purpose. The second example, which included many of the same ideas, used a thesis statement to give order to the information, and then effectively linked the ideas to correspond to the thesis statement.

✓•┤Practice

Practice Exercise 2

Read over the following introductory paragraph and ask yourself whether the thesis statement and introduction would allow you to effectively monitor the emerging text and allow your reader to anticipate the principal elements of the argument you are about to make.

Despite the dangers attributed to smoking, young people between the ages of twelve and eighteen continue to smoke. It appears that the warnings printed on the side of cigarette packages do not deter young people from beginning to smoke or from continuing to smoke. Similarly, the advertisements on television showing people in the final stages of either cancer or emphysema also do not appear to have any noticeable effect on the number of teens who smoke. Statistics have shown that the influence of parents is one of the main factors that determine if a child will begin smoking (Puffer, 2010). Puffer (2010) observed that teens are 60 percent more likely to begin smoking if one or both of their parents are smokers. Of course, there is also one other factor that cannot be ignored and that is the influence that peer pressure exerts on teens to begin smoking. Puffer (2010) reported that teens who have friends who are smokers are 30 percent more likely to become smokers.

After reading the paragraph, respond to the following questions.

1. What would you identify as the thesis of this essay?

    _____

    _____

2. Is the thesis statement sufficiently clear? Identify the ways in which the thesis statement could be improved.

    _____

    _____

3. How did the writer introduce you to the thesis?

    _____

    _____

4. What were the main points of the writer's argument?

    _____

    _____

5. If you were reading this essay, what would you expect the author to discuss in the body of the essay?

    _____

    _____

6. Compare the paragraph in Practice Exercise 1 to the paragraph in Practice Exercise 2. Which one better prepared you to anticipate the essay that would follow? What was the difference?

    _____

    _____

11.6.1 Thinking about Revisions: Thesis Statement and Introduction

The following chart provides some guidelines that you can follow when you are revising your thesis statement and introduction. Use the questions at the end of the chart to guide your decision making.

Making Writing Decisions	About Revising Your Thesis Statement and Introduction

What is the purpose of this writing decision?

The thesis statement and introduction should articulate and limit the scope of your essay. Reflecting on your purpose in writing, and ensuring that your thesis statement corresponds to that purpose, provides you with direction in the composition process.

What is the effect of this writing decision?

A clear and specific thesis statement serves as a mental benchmark against which to measure the relevance and effectiveness of various aspects of the essay as you compose them. It becomes the basis for many of the other decisions you will make while revising.

What considerations inform this decision?

In order to be effective, a thesis statement (and, to a lesser extent, the introduction) ought to be specific enough that it allows you to distinguish between the ideas that need to be included in the essay and the ideas that, however interesting, do not belong.

Suggested strategies for making this decision.

Think about the argument you intend to make. Ask yourself whether your thesis statement clearly and completely forecasts the basis for that argument.

Questions to guide decision making in your own essay.

1. What is the specific argument you are making? Does your thesis statement reflect that argument?
2. In what way does the thesis statement clearly articulate and limit the scope of your argument? How could you express the thesis more clearly?
3. Does the introductory paragraph forecast the order or pattern the argument will follow? Does that order make sense? Have you included information that serves no purpose?
4. What argument would your reader predict on the basis of your thesis statement and introduction? Is that the argument you intend to make? If not, you need to alter the introduction.
5. What outline emerges from the introduction? Is that the outline you intend to follow? Could you write the essay you intend to write using the introduction as a guide?

LO 3, 4 ## 11.7 REVISING YOUR PARAGRAPHS

If you used the IDDL model to craft an outline, the relationship of the individual paragraphs—both to one another and to the larger essay—should be obvious to you. The process of revision allows you to reflect on the effectiveness of the organizational pattern as you write. If you find that your intended organizational pattern isn't working or that a different organizational pattern would work more effectively, the IDDL model also permits you to experiment with alternative arrangements. One of the advantages of the model is that it foregrounds the structure of the essay. By attending to that structure, you are more likely to develop an essay that is coherent.

Having developed a pattern of organization that serves the essay well, it's useful to examine each of the paragraphs of your essay individually. Internal coherence in a paragraph derives from the degree to which the paragraph is governed by a single controlling idea. Though a paragraph might comprise a number of important themes, those themes ought to be organized around one larger idea that provides unity.

Writing Example

Read over the following paragraphs, guided by two of the principles that were discussed above (i.e., [1] revision allows you to ensure that the paragraphs are organized in a way that serves the larger essay structure, and [2] revision allows you to reorder and rephrase sentences within a paragraph to maintain internal coherence).

Reflect on the decisions you would make if you were revising the paragraphs in this brief essay. In this example, you should be paying particular attention to the essay structure and the degree to which the writer has identified the relationship of the individual ideas to the essay's controlling thesis and to one another.

Sample Essay

[1]Talking on cell phones while driving has become quite common, especially among the 16–30 age group. When talking on their cell phone, drivers become distracted and do not pay attention to what is happening around them. There have been many car accidents reported recently in which the cause of the accident is attributed to cell phone usage (Howard, 2011). Drivers frequently say that they were either looking at their cell phones and glanced up just in time to see the car they eventually hit, or they were so busy listening to the caller that they failed to see the vehicle before they hit it.

[2]It is very dangerous to talk and drive. Statistics released through the police department said that 40 percent of the minor accidents reported

1 This paragraph contains information, but has no clear thesis. Though the reader may be able to work out, inductively, an implied purpose to the paragraph, that purpose is not clear.

2 Again, although this paragraph is composed of information that might be relevant, the purpose of the paragraph is not clear. You will also notice that there is no transition between this paragraph and the one that precedes it and, thus, no obvious indication of the relationship between the two.

3 Although this paragraph contains information that is tangentially relevant to the implied thesis, it seems to have moved the essay in an unexpected direction.

4 In general, you should notice that the essay comprises a series of paragraphs that, though related by topic, have no controlling thesis. Similarly, though each of the individual paragraphs revolves around a distinct aspect of the topic, they could each be improved by a clearer statement of purpose.

in Winnipeg in the last year could be attributed to driver inattention due to cell phone usage. Despite the recent advertisements to discourage the practice, many motorists still use their cell phones when driving.

³Even hands-free cell phone devices such as Bluetooths can lead to driver inattention. Just because the driver's hands are free does not mean that his or her mind is free from distraction. Many drivers find it difficult to talk and drive. The only solution is to ban cell phones altogether, although there are some people who argue that one should not talk to passengers or listen to the radio either, as those practices can be distracting too.[4]

1 This is the introductory paragraph that we revised in Practice Exercise 1. It provides an introduction to the pattern of reasoning the essay will follow.

2 Rearranging the order of the paragraphs to correspond with the order of points as they were listed in the introduction makes the short essay easier to follow.

3 The topic sentence of the paragraph links back to the general thesis of the essay (i.e., *The use of cell phones by drivers should be banned because it is a dangerous distraction for all drivers*").

4 The sentences of the paragraph have been reorganized to serve the identified purpose of the paragraph (as it is identified in the topic sentence), and, by extension, the larger essay.

5 Again, the topic sentence makes the relationship between this paragraph and the general thesis clear.

6 The relationship of this sentence to the paragraph is rendered clearer by the addition of "young drivers" as the subject of the sentence.

7 By identifying that "younger drivers" were the specific focus of the research, the writer indicates their relevance to the paragraph.

Revised Sample Essay

¹The use of cell phones by drivers should be banned because it is a dangerous distraction for all drivers, it leads to a higher rate of accidents, and it poses a particular risk for younger drivers. Drivers have reported that the distraction of their respective cell phone conversations led them to lose track of events outside their vehicles and that this lack of attention contributed to driving difficulties ranging from the failure to attend to changes in traffic flow to the failure to notice other vehicles or pedestrians. A number of studies have identified cell phone usage as a contributing factor in accidents. Although the use of a cell phone while driving is problematic for all drivers, it poses a particular risk for younger drivers. Some statistics indicate that approximately 40 percent of all vehicle accidents are attributed to young drivers who were talking on their cell phones while driving.

²There is considerable evidence to support the view that the use of cell phones poses a significant risk for drivers. ³Statistics released through the Winnipeg Police Department indicated that 40 percent of the minor accidents reported in Winnipeg in the last year could be attributed to driver inattention due to cell phone usage. ⁴Despite the recent campaigns discouraging the practice, many motorists still use their cell phones when driving.

⁵The use of cell phones while driving is particularly prevalent among the 16–30 age group. ⁶As with other drivers, young drivers become distracted and do not pay attention to what is happening around them when they are talking on their cell phones. ⁷Research has shown that 40 percent

of car accidents by younger drivers can be attributed to cell phone usage (Howard, 2011). Drivers frequently say that they were either looking at their cell phones and glanced up just in time to see the car they eventually hit, or they were so busy listening to the caller that they failed to see the vehicle before they hit it.

[8]~~Even cell phone devices such as Bluetooths can lead to driver inattention. Just because one's hands are free does not mean one's mind is free from distraction. Many drivers find it difficult to talk and drive. The only solution is to ban cell phones altogether, although there are some people who argue that one should not talk to passengers or listen to the radio either as those practices can also be distracting too.~~

8 This paragraph, which introduces ideas that were not anticipated in the introduction, is problematic because it departs from the pattern of ideas the reader had been led to expect. It can be dealt with in one of two ways: the writer can return to the introduction and integrate the ideas or the writer can delete the paragraph. Because the paragraph itself lacked unity or focus, we chose to delete it.

11.7.1 Thinking about Revising Your Paragraphs

In the chart below, you will find questions to guide you as you revise your paragraphs.

Making Writing Decisions | About Revising Your Paragraphs

What is the purpose of this writing decision?

Paragraphs are units of meaning. They are the blocks of ideas a writer uses to construct the larger essay. In order to function in that way, they need to be unified by their respective themes. The organization of the paragraphs within the larger essay is meant to be guided by, and to reflect, the structure of the essay's argument.

What is the effect of this writing decision?

By organizing each paragraph around a single controlling idea, a writer is able to identify the relationship between the individual ideas. Similarly, by organizing paragraphs logically, the writer is able to use the pattern to reflect the logic of the essay.

What considerations inform this decision?

Revision is guided by a writer's understanding of purpose. When monitoring the emerging text, then, it is important that the translation of ideas into sentences, sentences into paragraphs, and paragraphs into an essay be measured against a well-defined thesis.

Suggested strategies for making this decision.

Identify the argument that is reflected, explicitly or implicitly, in the thesis statement. A well-crafted thesis statement provides the essential argument from which an essay emerges. In addition, the use of the IDDL model provides a visual representation of the argument, foregrounding the relationship of the individual parts to the whole and enhancing a writer's ability to recognize the effect of proposed changes.

Questions to guide decision making in your own essay.

1. Look at the draft of the essay on which you are currently working. Is the thesis statement clear enough that you can use it to guide you in writing, and revising, the essay? Does it identify an arguable proposition?
2. What reasons have you supplied in support of the proposition? How have you indicated the relationship of those reasons to the proposition?
3. How does the introduction forecast the route the essay will follow? In what way do you indicate the pattern of reasoning you intend to use?
4. What is the logical order of the ideas you intend to explore? Does the introduction reflect that order?
5. Do the paragraphs follow the order of ideas you forecast in the introduction? Does that order continue to make sense as you write? Do you need to circle back to modify the order? Do you need to circle back to modify the thesis statement?
6. Look at each of the paragraphs individually. How have you indicated the purpose of the paragraph to the reader? Does that purpose correspond with the essay's general thesis?
7. Does the topic sentence of each paragraph provide unity to the paragraph? Is it specific enough to limit the scope of the paragraph? Are the individual ideas in the paragraph subordinated to the controlling idea?
8. Is there a clear relationship between the idea that is expressed in the topic sentence of the paragraph and the general thesis of the essay?
9. How have you identified the relationship between one paragraph and the next?
10. Is the essay moving toward the conclusion that was anticipated in the introduction? Are you continuing to circle back to ensure that there is an observable and comprehensible structure to the essay?

11.8   MONITORING YOUR WORD CHOICE

LO 1, 3, 4

Word choice is about precision, selecting the word that conveys your meaning clearly, even while it reflects your awareness of audience and reader expectation. By monitoring your essay for word-level clarity, wordiness, and colloquialisms or clichés, you are able to determine whether the language you are using is both effective and appropriate to the genre in which you are writing. As is often the case in the process of revision, it's a mistake to attempt to wrestle a word you *like* into a sentence that rejects it. It usually takes more time to save words or phrases from your first attempt at articulating an idea than it does to abandon the sentence and try again. You can't fall in love with your own work. Diction, like essay structure, serves meaning.

While academic writing generally requires a certain degree of formality, it doesn't require that you abandon the language you know and love for a specialized jargon with which you are unfamiliar. The problem with adopting an idiom that's not your own is that it rarely works. You end up using words you don't know and using them incorrectly.

Example: "The physics professor was monogamous in his delivery and his students were bored."
It may be the case that the professor was married to the same type of delivery over the years, but it's more likely the writer meant to say *He was monotonous in his delivery and his students were bored.* In the second version of the sentence, the writer

is conveying the message that the professor lectured in a tone that did not change. There was no variety in pitch or intonation.

Finally, a note about thesaurus use. The thesaurus is meant to help you to find the right word amid a group of synonyms. Not the biggest word. Not the prettiest word. Not the most Latinate word. The right word. A good idea doesn't need to be wrapped in pretty clothes to stand out. A good idea wants only to be articulated precisely. (PS: Thesauri list synonyms. Synonyms are not textual clones. A synonym is a word that is related to another word of similar meaning, but synonyms are not always interchangeable. Just so you know.)

Practice Exercise 3

Review the following paragraph, paying particular attention to the underlined words. Ask yourself whether you can think of another word that could be used in place of the underlined word. Reflect on the effect of that word change. At the same time, look to see whether you can find words or phrases that are not needed in a sentence. See whether you can improve the clarity of the sentence or paragraph by deleting words that seem to have no real function.

Cell phones are such a <u>huge</u> <u>part</u> of the social fabric of society now that it is <u>hard</u> to imagine a time when the only way to communicate with someone was to either visit them or call them on an old-fashioned <u>landline</u>. In those early days before cell phones, people were <u>not available</u> to other people twenty-four hours a day like they are now. Now, it is not unusual to see people of all ages with their hands <u>held up</u> to their ears <u>holding</u> cell phones. Cell phone use has gotten out of hand in today's society. Everywhere you go, you see people talking on their cell phones. One sees people talking on their cell phones everywhere: at doctor's offices, at the grocery store, in a movie, at a play, in school, and in restaurants. For some people, they cannot remember a time before the cell phone since they have grown up with the device.

Remember that decisions about word choice, or diction, are not always dictated by rules of grammar or by syntactical need (i.e., it's not always the case that a questionable word choice will render a sentence incomprehensible). In many cases, those decisions will be governed by context, genre, and audience.

Look at the revised paragraph and reflect on the effect that the revisions might have.

Cell phones are such a [1]<u>huge</u> <u>part</u> of the [2]social fabric of society now that it is [3]<u>hard</u> to imagine a time when the only way to communicate with [4]someone was either to visit them or to call them on an [5]old-fashioned [6]<u>landline</u>. [7]In those early days before cell phones, people were not available [8]to other people twenty-four hours a day like they are now. [9]Now, it is not unusual to see [10]people of all ages [11]with their hands <u>held up</u> to their ears <u>holding</u> a cell phone. One sees people talking on their cell phones everywhere: at doctor's offices, grocery stores, movies, and plays, in schools, and in restaurants. [12]For some people, they cannot remember a time before the cell phone <u>since</u> they have grown up with the <u>device</u>.

1 You could change the sentence to read: "Cell phones are such an important part of the social fabric of society now..." Or "Cell phones have come to represent..."
2 This is both a cliché and redundant. The sentence could be changed to read: "Cell phones have become such an important part of society today that it is . . . "
3 Though "hard" is metaphorically accurate, it could be replaced with the word "difficult."
4 Replace with the more exact "an individual."
5 The context renders "old-fashioned" redundant. The word is also informal and imprecise.
6 This word seems too informal for academic writing. You could say "or call them on a traditional telephone."
7 This phrase is informal and imprecise. It is also unnecessary. You could say "Before cell phones became common."
8 This phrase is redundant.
9 In this context, the word "now" suggests a conversational tone that is usually discouraged in academic writing.
10 This is a cliché that has lost all power. It should be replaced with a clearer representation of the writer's intention.
11 This clause might be more economically phrased as "with their cell phones to their ears."
12 This sentence might be rephrased more sparingly as "Because so many have grown up with the device, many people cannot remember a time before the cell phone."

11.9   REVISING USING THE IDDL MODEL

The purpose of the IDDL model is to provide a structural model for essay writing, which creates a visual representation that allows you both to conceive of your essay in its entirety and to focus on specific aspects of the essay in isolation. It also provides a means by which to monitor the emerging essay and to revise systematically. Because the model allows you to reflect on the overall structure of the essay, recognizing the complex interrelationship of the various components to one another and to the larger theme of the essay, it also allows you to identify the point at which the logic of the essay has failed and to predict the effect that potential revisions might have.

We'll use the following example to show the way in which you can compose your essay, using the IDDL model, and then, subsequently, reflect back upon the worksheet to ensure that your argument is coherent and clear, with each of the individual parts of the essay functioning both internally (e.g., paragraphs demonstrating an internal consistency) and as part of the larger structure (e.g., paragraphs demonstrating a logical connection to the general thesis of the essay).

I. Essay Draft Using the IDDL Model
Introductory Paragraph
■ **Thesis Statement:** *The use of a cell phone while operating a car introduces an unnecessary distraction.*
Drivers who use cell phones while operating vehicles can become distracted from the emerging conditions on the road. When operating a vehicle, drivers need to focus on those emerging conditions and focus is difficult while one is also operating a cell phone. It is always challenging for individuals to divide attention between two competing activities. The use of a cell phone while operating a car introduces an unnecessary distraction.
Section 1
■ **Subthesis:** *The use of cell phones by drivers should be banned because it is a dangerous distraction for all drivers.*
Using a cell phone while driving can lead a driver to unnecessary collisions due to driver inattention. Drivers cannot pay attention to the road because their attention is divided between the cell phone conversation and conditions on the road. This can result in drivers colliding with other cars, pedestrians, bicyclists, animals, and fences. The result of such collisions can be that drivers injure themselves, their passengers, other drivers, pedestrians, cyclists, or animals.
Section 2
■ **Transition from Paragraph 1**
■ **Subthesis:** *The use of cell phones while driving can also cause drivers' reaction times to be compromised.*
The use of cell phones while driving can also cause drivers' reaction times to be compromised. When talking on a cell phone, drivers shift their attention between the conversation and the traffic around them and, thus, often do not have time to react to emerging conditions. They often rear-end cars that are stopped at stoplights because

they are not aware that other vehicles have stopped. They can also overlook small children who might dash out into the street, sometimes causing injury or even death. Drivers using cell phones have been known to hit individuals in road-repair crews because they did not notice the signs that signalled roadwork ahead, did not notice signs calling for reduced speed, and did not notice flag persons who were attempting to slow the traffic. Even answering a ringing cell phone can cause problems. When drivers reach for the cell phone, they usually take their eyes off the road briefly. Even if they look away only for a couple of seconds, however, they can run off the road or collide with the traffic around them.

Counter-argument

While some have argued that many drivers are able to manage the challenge of multiple stimuli, they have primarily cited the examples of professional race car drivers as evidence. Whether or not it is a good practice for professional race car drivers to use cell phones while driving is largely beside the point. Most people are not professional race car drivers and if the government decides to include a provision to exclude those that are, it would have relatively little effect on the rest of the driving public.

Conclusion

It is clear that the practice of using cell phones while driving is dangerous. It requires that drivers attend to too many tasks at one time, robbing each of the attention it requires. Because a driver is unable to manage multiple tasks at once, the driver should choose to do one or the other. That is, drivers should either drive their cars or stop to talk on the phone. It is dangerous to attempt to do both at once.

One of the advantages to using models like the IDDL model is that it foregrounds the structure of your essay, separating the individual components and allowing you to work on each separately. You can examine each of the sections independently to ensure that the paragraphs or groups of paragraphs are coherent. Because the model reflects the fundamental structure of the essay, it allows you to monitor the text as it emerges and to think about ways in which the structure could be modified to make your argument more effectively.

The chart below can be used as a guide for revising the previous essay draft.

2. Revision of the Essay Using the IDDL Model
Topic: Cell Phones
Introduction
1. Have you identified the controlling thesis of the essay?
2. Have you identified the individual points, or subtopics, that you will discuss in the course of your exploration of the controlling thesis?
3. Reflect on each of the individual points or subtopics. In what way is each related to the controlling thesis?
4. In what way does each contribute to your exploration of the thesis?
5. Does the organization of the introduction provide a pattern that you can use to structure the essay?

(continued)

(continued)

Section 1

- **Subthesis:** *The use of cell phones by drivers should be banned because it is a dangerous distraction for all drivers.*

1. What is the relationship of this paragraph, or series of related paragraphs, to the introduction?
2. Has the subtheme been articulated clearly enough that you are able to identify the information you need either to substantiate the claim or to explore the subtopic thoroughly?
3. How can you justify the claim you are making most effectively? Do you require evidence from science or social science? Do you require scholarly opinion?
4. What question lies at the heart of the subtheme? Has each paragraph in this section been organized around that subtheme? Does each paragraph in this section reflect the pattern of reasoning that derives from the arguable thesis?
5. Are the paragraphs arranged logically? Are you leading your reader from one point to another in a way that is consistent with the argument you are making?
6. Have you indicated the relationship of one paragraph to another using transitional words or phrases?

Section 2

- **Transition from Paragraph 1**
- **Subthesis (paragraph topic sentence):** *The use of cell phones by drivers should be banned because it leads to a higher rate of accidents.*

1. What is the relationship of this paragraph, or series of related paragraphs, to the introduction?
2. Has the subtheme been articulated clearly enough that you are able to identify the information you need either to substantiate the claim or to explore the subtopic thoroughly?
3. How can you justify the claim you are making most effectively? Do you require evidence from science or social science? Do you require scholarly opinion?
4. What question lies at the heart of the subtheme? Has each paragraph in this section been organized around that subtheme? Does each paragraph in this section reflect the pattern of reasoning that derives from the arguable thesis?
5. Are the paragraphs arranged logically? Are you leading your reader from one point to another in a way that is consistent with the argument you are making?
6. Have you indicated the relationship of one paragraph to another using transitional words or phrases?

Section 3

- **Transition from paragraph 2**
- **Subthesis (paragraph topic sentence):** *The use of cell phones by drivers should be banned because it is a particular risk for younger drivers.*

1. What is the relationship of this paragraph, or series of related paragraphs, to the introduction?
2. Has the subtheme been articulated clearly enough that you are able to identify the information you need either to substantiate the claim or to explore the subtopic thoroughly?
3. How can you justify the claim you are making most effectively? Do you require evidence from science or social science? Do you require scholarly opinion?
4. What question lies at the heart of the subtheme? Has each paragraph in this section been organized around that subtheme? Does each paragraph in this section reflect the pattern of reasoning that derives from the arguable thesis?
5. Are the paragraphs arranged logically? Are you leading your reader from one point to another in a way that is consistent with the argument you are making?
6. Have you indicated the relationship of one paragraph to another using transitional words or phrases?

Counter-argument
1. Does your investigation of the subtopic demand that you recognize some limits to the claim you are making?
2. What are those limits? Academic writing embraces, rather than retreats from, nuanced discussions of complex ideas. That kind of subtlety requires that you acknowledge the counter-argument (i.e., the opposing view) to your position.
3. How can you integrate opposing ideas without appearing to argue against yourself?

Conclusion
- **Review the question under consideration.**
- **Demonstrate the ways in which evidence has led to specific conclusions.**
- **Acknowledge continuing challenges to the position.**
- **Identify further areas for research or exploration.**

11.10 SOME FINAL THOUGHTS ABOUT REVISION

LO 1, 2, 3, 4

In the box below, we include a series of questions and answers about the revision process. They are meant to pull together some of the principles we've reviewed in our discussion of revising.

1. Is revising just checking for grammar, punctuation, spelling, etc.?
There is a profound difference between revising (ensuring that your ideas and your argument remain coherent) and editing. Experienced writers tend to focus on the first while novice writers focus on the latter. As we have mentioned before (and will mention again), good grammar makes a good essay better but does not make a bad essay good. The process of revising is a process of organizing, and reorganizing, material to ensure that the essay is guided by purpose and is working toward that purpose. In most cases, revision is an ongoing process. If you learn nothing else from this book, please understand that focusing on development of meaning and organization of ideas will improve your writing.

2. What kinds of things should I be looking for when I revise?
When you are revising, you are looking for any occasion when the logic of your essay fails. If one idea does not lead to another or if a group of ideas has been littered across the page without any obvious purpose, those ideas are obstructing your development of meaning.

3. Should I add more material when I am revising? Delete some?
The answer is either or both, as necessary. It's always better to have too much information rather than too little. You can delete what you don't need during revision. The answer, however, will always depend on the degree to which the essay is succeeding in its purpose. If you have not clearly established your claim or developed your idea, you need more material. If the volume of material is obscuring your purpose, you need to delete or reorganize it.

4. I think I have to reorganize now that I reread the essay. Should I do that?
As we have mentioned, writing is recursive. In order to develop an essay, you move forward, working with a provisional plan. As soon as that plan ceases to serve your purpose, you give it a quick hug, promise you'll call it tomorrow, and move on. Again, in

(*continued*)

(*continued*)

comparing novice writers to experienced writers, researchers have found that novice writers are more likely to correct grammatical mistakes than to reorganize for meaning. We suggest that you revise structure whenever the structure fails to serve your purpose. In short, whenever you see that the logic and organization of your essay has led it away from its principal purpose, revise to correct its course.

5. Are my paragraphs coherent and clearly written?
The test for coherence in a paragraph is very much like the test for coherence in an essay. Identify the principal theme or organizing idea of the paragraph. Are there ideas or statements that are not related to that idea? If so, they must either be integrated into the paragraph by expanding the principal theme or they have to go. The second question to ask yourself is whether the various statements of the paragraph have been organized in such a way as to make their purpose clear. Do you need transition words to link some of those statements? Is it clear how each of the sentences serves the principal theme of the paragraph?

6. I love a certain line but am not sure where to put it. How can I tell whether it belongs?
The saddest moment in any writing situation occurs when you recognize that your best sentence does not serve the overall purpose of the paragraph or the essay. You have to learn to be ruthless. If it is not relevant, sacrificing the essay to save the sentence is a bad bargain.

7. Can I get someone else to read my paper for me to see if it makes sense?
This is always a good idea. Often, when we are writing, the connections between ideas are apparent to us because we know what it is that we are trying to say. The advantage of having a second reader is that the second reader does not have access to the implicit information that you failed to include in the essay. Therefore, the gaps in the logic will be more apparent to the second reader.

8. Is revision really that important? I often don't have the time to rewrite. What can I do?
Start earlier. It is much easier than you think to recognize an essay that was written at the last minute. In most cases, that essay announces itself by the failure of its internal logic. It's very difficult to write well without taking the time to plan, to write, and to rewrite.

However, if you insist on writing papers at the last minute, at the very least you ought to show your reader the courtesy of planning the paper in advance. By using the IDDL model to organize your thoughts, you will have an opportunity to organize the major ideas of the paper before starting rather than having them occur to you at the last minute.

9. My friend writes like she talks. Is that something I should be trying for as well?
That depends. How well do you talk? In most cases, the voice you use while writing is different from the voice you use while speaking for two important reasons: (1) the language is generally more formal because the writing situation is generally more formal, and (2) in speech, we often use non-verbal means to communicate ideas or to support ideas. Because we are geographically and temporally separated from our audience when we're writing, it is usually necessary to provide more explicit explanations of the connections between our ideas.

10. Should I use a thesaurus when revising to vary my word choices?
The purpose of a thesaurus is to assist you in your search for the right word. If you cannot control your urge to insert synonyms—which you may or may not understand—simply to satisfy your appetite for variety, get rid of your thesaurus. The principle for selecting a word ought always to be this: Does the word accurately reflect my meaning?

11.11 CONCLUSION

Revision is one of the most important processes in writing. It allows you to correct the direction of an essay that has wandered from its purpose and has begun to stroll aimlessly through a topic. By monitoring the text as it emerges, and circling back to correct the alignment of the ideas you're exploring, you are able to maintain a pattern of organization that ensures the sentences in a paragraph, or paragraphs, operate in harmony to serve a single thesis. Information without pattern does not lead to an essay. Rather, your essay stands or falls in direct relation to your ability to meld the individual components into a coherent whole. The process of revision allows you to do that.

MyCompLab®

How Do I Get a Better Grade?

Go to MyCompLab for additional help with your grammar, writing, and research skills. You will have access to a variety of exercises, instruction, and videos that will help you improve your basic skills and help you get a better grade.

Sample Essay for Revising

Read the following essay and reflect on the ways you might revise it. Think about the principles of revising that have been discussed in this chapter.

Topic: *The Danger of Cigarette Usage and the Power of Addiction*

Thesis Statement: *Despite the evidence that smoking can lead to preventable health problems, can lead to premature death, and can affect non-smokers who are exposed to second-hand smoke, the practice continues due to the powerful effect of nicotine.*

Despite the evidence that smoking can lead to preventable health problems, can lead to premature death, and can affect non-smokers who are exposed to second-hand smoke, the practice continues due to the powerful effect of nicotine. Cigarettes contain more than four thousand different chemicals, with at least four hundred of the chemicals being considered toxic or poisonous (Black, 2012). Some of the chemicals found in cigarettes include not only nicotine and tar but also substances like DDT, carbon monoxide, formaldehyde, hydrogen cyanide, ammonia, and arsenic. These are the same toxins that can be found in rat poison, nail polish remover, and some types of wood varnish. Despite the widespread knowledge that tobacco contains harmful chemicals, people still continue to smoke. Having begun smoking, most are quickly hooked on the extremely potent chemical nicotine (Blue, 2008). Nicotine affects both the brain and the nervous system, providing an effect that usually becomes addictive.

Nicotine acts on the brain like any other addictive drug (Gold, 2010). It provides the smoker with a feeling of euphoria that soon becomes habit-forming. Smokers need to continue to smoke in order to maintain the feeling of enjoyment that smoking provides. Some people smoke two or three packages of cigarettes daily (Gold, 2010). The pleasant feeling that smoking provides wears off rather quickly, which is one of the reasons that smokers tend to increase the number of cigarettes they smoke, some to the extent that they are smoking almost continuously to maintain the sense of pleasure. When a smoker inhales nicotine, the lungs allow the nicotine to get into the bloodstream almost instantly. The smoker then feels the hit the nicotine gives them in their bloodstream. This is the cause of the smoker's addiction.

Smokers have shorter lifespans. On average, a smoker will die fifteen to twenty years before a non-smoker (Blue, 2009). Smoking causes premature aging due to the chemicals that go into the body. The chemicals damage organs due to their toxicity and, as has been previously noted, smoking leads to many health risks that can lead to premature death. In addition, because some of the chemicals are released through the skin, they can cause the skin to age prematurely. Nicotine and tar also stain teeth, and can cause a condition called halitosis or chronic bad breath. Many smokers think they can mask bad breath by using mouthwash or brushing their teeth, but those measures are rarely successful.

Some people argue that the public obsession with smoking cessation is unreasonable because there are many other factors that can contribute to a shortened lifespan. These individuals cite obesity and lack of exercise as two factors that can reduce a person's life expectancy (Green, 2009). They point to other factors that can also decrease the length of time people will live. If people live in a city, their life expectancy is reduced due to pollution and crime. Some people might engage in risky behaviours such as riding a motorcycle, bungee jumping, or rock climbing, which could all lead to a lower life expectancy. In addition, if people work in an industrial job, they could also have a shorter lifespan. People engage in many risky behaviours. Smoking is just one of the group.

Cigarettes are known to be the cause of many health problems, including eleven different types of cancer. Smoking is a leading cause of cancers such as lung, bladder, esophageal, oral, throat, cervical, kidney, stomach, and pancreatic. Smoking is also implicated in other diseases, such as chronic lung and pulmonary diseases, heart disease, stroke, aneurysms, leukemia, cataracts, and pneumonia. Smoking can also cause diabetes, and if a person is already a diabetic, smoking increases the risk of complications like blindness, kidney disease, heart disease, and stroke.

The knowledge that smoking can cause cancer does not stop people from smoking. Nor do the advertisements on television or on posters depicting black lungs caused by tar deposits, or the personal testimonials from people who cannot breathe without an oxygen tank. None of these tactics have deterred people from either continuing to smoke or beginning to smoke. It is hard to believe that children still view smoking as an adult thing to do and are influenced by the adults in their lives (Brown, 2009). If children have parents or guardians who smoke, they are more likely to take up the habit themselves (Brown, 2009).

Smoking does not only affect the smoker. Smoking is also a hazard to bystanders who come in contact with smokers. Smokers put their loved ones in danger every time they decide to light up a cigarette. Children of smokers often suffer from health problems caused by second-hand smoke. Some of the problems caused by smoking include ear infections, breathing problems, chronic bronchitis, and asthma. The medical costs of treating patients who are affected by second-hand smoke are in the billions (Gold, 2010). Smokers might think that they are harming only themselves, but the statistics prove otherwise.

Smoking is a dangerous habit that is hard to break. Though smokers understand the risks associated with smoking, they are either unwilling or unable to quit. They understand that smoking can cause health issues and might lead to premature death, but these are risks that they are willing to take. Even the knowledge that second-hand smoke can harm their loved ones and can cause health issues for their children is not enough to motivate them to stop. When confronted with the knowledge that their smoking habit could cause their children to start smoking, they still do not quit smoking. Many smokers understand that they should quit smoking, but nicotine is such a powerful drug and produces such a feeling of pleasure that they are unable to do so. People who smoke understand the dangers of smoking but make the choice to continue despite the evidence presented.

✓●─▕**Practice**   Read the essay again, looking at some of the ways in which you could improve the essay through revision. Use the questions below to guide you.

1. How does the thesis statement identify a specific claim?

_____

_____

2. Does the thesis statement provide the reasons for that claim? What are the reasons?

_____

_____

3. How does the thesis statement limit the scope of the essay?

_____

_____

4. Review the introduction. How does it forecast the principal themes the essay will explore? In what way does the introduction identify the pattern of reasoning the essay will follow?

_____

_____

5. Looking at the essay structure, ask yourself whether the paragraphs are arranged in accordance with the pattern that was established in the introduction. Does the pattern work? Is the order of the

paragraphs logical? Does the pattern of reasoning lead your reader from the introduction to the conclusion?

_____

_____

6. Do the transitions between paragraphs reflect the logic of the essay? Is there a way in which you might make that pattern of reasoning more obvious to your reader?

_____

_____

7. Read each paragraph, one at a time. Is each paragraph organized around a single controlling theme? Are the relationships between the individual ideas in each paragraph clear?

_____

_____

8. Is the tone of the essay consistent? Is the language appropriate for an academic essay?

_____

_____

9. Review the conclusion. Have the individual themes of the essay led to the conclusion? Is there any aspect of the conclusion that wasn't thoroughly explored previously in the essay? Looking back, from the conclusion to the introduction, ask yourself whether there is a clear path from one to the other.

_____

_____

Evaluation Worksheet for Revision

 Practice

The following chart provides a series of general questions to guide your revision process. It is important to remember, however, that the decisions you make in revision will derive, ultimately, from your understanding of the argument you intend to make.

An Evaluation Worksheet to Guide You in Revising Your Own Essay Writing

1. **Turn to the essay on which you're currently working and examine the thesis statement. Does the statement identify a specific claim? Does it identify the reasons for that claim? How does the thesis statement limit the scope of the essay?**

(continued)

(continued)

2. Review the introduction. How does it forecast the principal themes the essay will explore? In what way does the introduction identify the pattern of reasoning the essay will follow?

3. Looking at the essay structure, ask yourself whether the paragraphs are arranged in accordance with the pattern that was established in the introduction. Does the pattern work? Is the order of the paragraphs logical? Does the pattern of reasoning lead your reader from the introduction to the conclusion?

4. Do the transitions between paragraphs reflect the logic of the essay? Is there a way in which you might make that pattern of reasoning more obvious to your reader?

5. Read each paragraph, one at a time. Is each paragraph organized around a single controlling theme? Are the relationships between the individual ideas in each paragraph clear?

6. Review your conclusion. Have the individual themes of the essay led to the conclusion? Is there any aspect of the conclusion that wasn't thoroughly explored previously in the essay? Looking back, from the conclusion to the introduction, ask yourself whether there is a clear path from one to the other.

✓• Practice   **Peer-Review Sheet for Revision**

Essay Written By: _____

Peer Reviewer: _____

Please focus on the larger questions of structure and reasoning (i.e., argument).

a. In what way does the thesis statement articulate the argument and limit the scope of the essay?

_____

_____

b. How does the introduction establish the pattern of reasoning that will be used in the essay?

_____

_____

c. What is the key argument of paragraph 1? What evidence is provided that supports the argument? How does paragraph 1 serve the general purpose of the essay?

_____

_____

d. What is the key argument of paragraph 2? What evidence is provided that supports the argument? How does paragraph 2 serve the general purpose of the essay?

_____

_____

e. What is the key argument of paragraph 3? What evidence is provided that supports the argument? How does paragraph 3 serve the general purpose of the essay?

_____

_____

_____

f. What is the key argument of paragraph 4? What evidence is provided that supports the argument? How does paragraph 4 serve the general purpose of the essay?

_____

_____

_____

g. What is the key argument of paragraph 5? What evidence is provided that supports the argument? How does paragraph 5 serve the general purpose of the essay?

_____

_____

_____

h. What is the key argument of paragraph 6? What evidence is provided that supports the argument? How does paragraph 6 serve the general purpose of the essay?

_____

_____

i. How has the possibility of alternative views been addressed?

_____

_____

j. How does the conclusion provide closure to the text?

_____

_____

The Writing and Revision Stage

In the first section of the text, we discussed the planning stage of the writing process, a stage during which you created a writing space that reflected your purpose. The decision you make about the purpose of your essay assists you in inscribing the writing space with a general form for your essay, a form that demonstrates your awareness of the reader's expectation of a logical progression of ideas, and your understanding that the information you provide needs to contribute to the realization of the essay's purpose. The degree of writing efficiency in the writing and revision stage of the process depends on the degree to which you were able to precisely articulate your writing purpose in the first stage.

In the writing and revision stage, you've begun to translate your purpose into textual form, recognizing that each element of the essay will be governed by the essay's thesis. You're aware that the ideas you're exploring, and the information you're employing, must serve that thesis, and that the structure of the essay must reflect the pattern of organization embodied in the thesis. There is a rhetorical principle that derives from your commitment to that organizational pattern. The principle is called coherence, and it requires that paragraphs within an essay, and the ideas that comprise each paragraph, be connected in a way that allows the reader to follow the writer's development of meaning.

In the following pages, we provide brief synopses of Chapters 7 through 11, with a series of questions to guide your reflections on the effect of the concepts discussed in each chapter. Though each chapter is discussed in isolation, the five chapters are united by a single principle: the advice offered in each chapter is designed to remind you that you should make every writing decision with an understanding of its effect on the essay as a whole.

CHAPTER 7: THINKING IN MEANINGFUL UNITS

In Chapter 7, we reviewed some general rules about sentences and paragraphs. We did not, admittedly, provide a tutorial on sentence construction. Our purpose, instead, was to encourage you to think of the effect that your sentences would have on the reader (we don't mean to suggest that the mechanics of writing sentences are unimportant, but only that this text has a different focus; there are many excellent resources on sentence construction already available). We had a similar purpose in the discussion of paragraph construction. In focusing on the importance of unity in paragraphs, our principal purpose was to foreground the effect that decisions about paragraph development might have on both the larger essay and the reader.

Thinking about Sentences

1. Why is it important to understand the construction of a sentence on the basis of the effect the sentence will have on the reader?
2. Why is it important to understand the construction of a sentence on the basis of the effect the sentence has on the surrounding text?
3. Beyond grammatical correctness, what do you need to consider when drafting a sentence?
4. What effect does the understanding of sentence construction as a decision-making process have on your understanding of writing?

Thinking about Paragraphs

1. What is the effect of structuring a paragraph around a single unifying theme?
2. How will you connect all ideas in a paragraph to that theme?
3. How will you identify the relationship between ideas in a paragraph to ensure coherence?
4. What factors must you consider when making the decision to introduce a paragraph break? In effect, how do you know when one paragraph ought to broken into two paragraphs?
5. What effect does the understanding of paragraph construction as a decision-making process have on your understanding of writing?

CHAPTER 8: INTRODUCTORY PARAGRAPHS

In the discussion of introductory paragraphs, we reflected on the profound effect that introductions have on essays. The introductory paragraph is not meant to provide you with space for unrelated anecdotes, or to permit you to reflect, generally, on your topic. The introductory paragraph serves to provide your reader with a concise articulation of your thesis, the basis on which you will argue for your thesis, and the pattern of reasoning you will follow in your essay. It ought to establish expectations for the reader, and orient the reader to the conventions that you follow in the text.

Understanding the Effect of the Introductory Paragraph

1. What purpose(s) does an introduction serve?
2. How does an introduction achieve that/those purpose(s)?
3. How would you characterize the difference between an effective introduction and an ineffective introduction?
4. How does the genre of the essay affect your understanding of the characteristics of an effective introduction?

Thinking about Drafting an Effective Introduction

1. How does the introduction articulate, and limit, the focus of the essay?
2. How will you identify the relationship between the thesis and the supporting ideas?
3. How will you use the introduction to identify the organizational pattern of the essay?
4. What principle will you use to determine whether you ought to include a particular idea, assertion, or anecdote in the introduction?

CHAPTER 9: TRANSITIONS

In the discussion of transitions, we discussed the effect that transitions have on the coherence of your essay. Writing is the act of imposing order on ideas, creating a structure in which all ideas are arranged to serve the larger purpose of the paragraph, and, ultimately, the essay. Effective transitions are an economical way of establishing relationships between ideas, because they reflect the intended connection without unnecessary explanation.

Understanding the Effect of Transitions
1. What is the effect of using successful transitions in an essay?
2. How do successful transitions achieve their effect?
3. What are the characteristic differences between novice and experienced writers in the use of transitions?
4. Which of the two writing processes do you follow most closely?
5. How can you alter your writing process to move closer to the writing process of experienced writers?
6. What specific decisions do you have to approach differently?
7. How are you going to change your decision-making process to effect that change?
Thinking about Using Transitions Effectively
1. What principles guide you when you are thinking about using a transition to connect two sentences?
2. How do you identify the relationship between sentences?
3. How do you choose a transitional word or phrase to reflect that relationship?
4. What principles guide you when you are thinking about using a transition to connect two paragraphs?
5. How do you identify the relationship between paragraphs?
6. How do you choose a transitional word or phrase to reflect that relationship?

CHAPTER 10: CONCLUSIONS

As is the case with introductory paragraphs, the concluding paragraphs of essays often suffer from (1) a sudden shift in tone, with writers indulging themselves in hyperbole, and (2) a marked departure from the purpose that guided the essay. The purpose of the concluding paragraph is not to make claims that haven't been supported in the essay, to overstate the importance of your topic, or to slip in content that you forgot to mention previously. An effective conclusion is one that allows you to concisely summarize the argument you've made, humbly acknowledging its limitations, and, equally humbly, noting its significance.

Understanding the Effect of the Concluding Paragraph
1. What purpose(s) does the conclusion serve?
2. How does the conclusion achieve that/those purpose(s)?
3. How would you characterize the differences between an effective conclusion and an ineffective conclusion?

Thinking about Drafting an Effective Conclusion

1. How can you use the conclusion to provide the reader with a sense of completion?
2. How will you ensure that the reader's expectations have been met?
3. How will you link the ideas in the conclusion to reflect the organizational pattern of the essay?
4. How will you ensure that you are not overstating the significance of the argument?
5. Writers sometimes lose their way in the drafting of their conclusions, shifting from the position of careful analysis that characterized their essays to a position of passionate advocacy in the conclusion. How will you monitor the tone of the conclusion to ensure that it's consistent with the tone of the essay?

CHAPTER 11: RECURSIVITY AND REVISION

The process of writing is, at times, a messy business, with great intentions occasionally stumbling into chaotic confusion during the writing and revision stage. The value of your metacognitive understanding of writing is that you're aware of your intended purpose, you're monitoring your progress to determine the degree to which the emerging text is satisfying that purpose, and you're willing to circle back to revise your draft to ensure that it continues to progress logically from one stage to another, guiding the reader from the introduction to the conclusion. The commitment to revision is one of the characteristics of experienced writers.

Differences between Novice Writers and Experienced Writers in the Understanding of the Role of Recursivity in the Process of Writing

1. What is the effect of recursivity in the writing process?
2. What are the characteristic differences between the recursive practices of novice and experienced writers?
3. Which of the two writing practices do you follow most closely?
4. How can you alter your writing process to move closer to the writing practices of experienced writers?
5. What specific decisions do you have to approach differently?
6. How are you going to change your decision-making process to effect that change?

Recursivity and the Development of Meaning

1. What effect does recursivity have on the development of meaning?
2. How does recursivity achieve that effect?
3. How will you alter your writing process to ensure that you're monitoring, and revising, your essay effectively?

Recursivity and the Maintenance of Coherence in an Essay

1. What effect does recursivity have on the maintenance of coherence in your essay?
2. How does recursivity allow you to maintain coherence when you write an essay?
3. How will you alter your writing process to ensure that you are monitoring your essay to maintain coherence?

SECTION III: REVIEWING

CHAPTER 12

The Importance of Style and Format

Learning Objectives

At the completion of this chapter, you will be able to:

1. Identify the differences between the ways in which novice and experienced writers format their essays.
2. Distinguish between the three main writing styles (APA, MLA, *Chicago* style).
3. Use the three main writing styles (APA, MLA, *Chicago* style).

12.1   INTRODUCTION

Almost every essay you write in college or university will be expected to conform to a particular formatting convention. Those conventions will dictate the voice you use in the essay (i.e., first, second, or third person), the tense in which you write, the way in which you format your page, the citation method you use, and the convention you will follow when listing your references. Given the degree to which correctness in format is stressed, it may seem, in fact, that the formatting of your essay is as important as the content itself. It's not. It is, nevertheless, important. If you're told to use specific formatting guidelines, or you're told to follow a particular writing style, you should probably do so. A properly formatted paper is very much like an appropriately dressed candidate at a job interview: it doesn't guarantee that the essence beneath the form is worthwhile, but it does testify to the individual's ability to operate within the conventions that govern the discourse or situation. An appropriate concern about formatting will probably make your essay more successful; excessive concern about stylistic elements, on the other hand, may distract you from the process of writing itself.

Students often wonder why instructors place such importance on the styles of essays. That's a very good question. Good questions deserve thoughtful answers. In most cases, instructors emphasize the importance of format because formatting makes an essay easier to read and easier to understand. It offers the reader a familiar environment. However arbitrary those rules about spacing, margins, font type, and font size may appear, they are necessary if the reader is to successfully navigate the text. In addition, adhering to formatting rules ensures that you record all the essential information about your sources, including quotations and paraphrases (thus guarding against the charge of plagiarism).

In this chapter, we discuss the three most common writing styles that are used in college or university (i.e., APA, MLA, *Chicago*). We will not, however, list every specific rule and feature of each of the writing styles. There are two reasons for that decision: (1) writing styles change quite regularly, and, therefore, it makes more sense to teach you to use the conventions than it does to provide an inventory of rules that will change within a very few years, and (2) it's easier for you to acquire an understanding of the conventions strategically, with a focus on those that you will use most often, than it would be for you to attempt to understand all of them as though all of the conventions were equally important. We will also suggest a strategy for acquiring an understanding of a number of different conventions by comparing the key features of each style to the others.

12.2 UNDERSTANDING THE DIFFERENCE BETWEEN THE PRACTICE OF THE NOVICE WRITER AND THE PRACTICE OF THE EXPERIENCED WRITER   `LO 1`

12.2.1 Writing Conventions

Most experienced writers enjoy a couple of advantages over novice writers when it comes to the use of writing conventions: (1) experienced writers have worked with the writing conventions long enough that the process of formatting has become largely automated, and (2) experienced writers are usually writing in a single style, and thus have only to remember a single set of writing conventions. In the following chart, you'll notice that we have identified the principal difference between novice and experienced writers as being the degree to which the writers have internalized procedural knowledge (i.e., the understanding of *how* to do a particular thing).

12.2.2 Differences between the Novice Writer and the Experienced Writer

Unfortunately, internalizing procedural knowledge takes time, and the greater the volume of information that there is to internalize, the greater the length of time it takes.

Novice Writers	Experienced Writers
■ *Require thought for procedural, or "mechanical," writing functions.* ■ Focus on error avoidance rather than meaning. ■ Begin writing without planning, and edit, if at all, for grammatical errors. ■ Focus on "knowledge telling" (i.e., relating all the information they have and can find on a topic, rather than exercising critical judgment to determine relevance).	■ *Have, to a significant degree, automated procedural functions.* ■ Focus on developing or refining meaning. ■ Invest time and energy in planning and reviewing. ■ Organize, and reorganize, essay structure to allow individual ideas to serve the overall purpose of the essay.

In the following section, we discuss a different strategy for acquiring a working knowledge of writing conventions.

LO 2, 3   ## 12.3   A BRIEF COMPARISON OF THE THREE PRINCIPLE WRITING CONVENTIONS (APA, MLA, *CHICAGO*)

12.3.1 Chart of Similarities and Differences

In the chart below, we list major differences and similarities among the three principle writing conventions. As indicated in the previous section, the chart is not exhaustive. By focusing on these features, however, you are more likely to be able to attend to the most important elements of style without being distracted from your principal duty of developing a coherent essay.

	APA	MLA	*Chicago* Notes and Bibliography Style
Title Page	Title page required.	No title page required.	Only papers that are longer than 5 pages require a title page.
Font	12-point APA 6th ed., section 8.03, usually Times New Roman.	12-point, no clear preference for typeface, but Times New Roman recommended.	Times New Roman, 12-point for text and 10-point for notes.
Line Spacing	Double-space.	Double-space.	Double-space.
Writing Voice	Essays are generally written in third person. Reports of one's own research should be written in first person.	First person is accepted in MLA.	Generally, first or third person is used in *Chicago*.

Tense	Describe past events, procedures, and results in the past tense but use present tense to describe implications of the results and to present conclusions.	MLA uses present tense (e.g., Smith argues that . . . .).	*Chicago* style uses the present tense (e.g., Smith argues that . . . .).
Page Numbers	Number every page, starting with the title page. Do not change numbering systems through the text. APA asks for the page number to be set 1/2 inch down, at the right margin, and for the paper's title (or a short form of it) to be set in full capitals on the same line, starting at the left margin, to complete the running head.	Page numbers are required on every page, with numbers on all pages following consecutively in the upper right-hand corner, one-half inch from the top and flush with the right margin. (Note: Your instructor may ask that you omit the number on your first page. Always follow your instructor's guidelines.)	Page numbers on the pages that begin a major section, at the bottom centre of the page, ¾ inch from the edge. Other pages feature the page number on the upper-right corner, double-spaced above the text.
In-Text Citations or Notes	When citing a direct quotation, APA follows the author, year of publication, page number format (e.g., Brown, 2001, p. 234). When not citing a direct quotation follow the author, year of publication format (e.g., Brown, 2001).	When citing a direct quotation or when paraphrasing, MLA follows the author, page number format (e.g., Brown, 234). If the author's name is used in the text, then only the page number is included in the parentheses (e.g., Brown found that . . . [3]). Notice, that, unlike APA, there is no designation for page.	Footnotes or endnotes are used for citations. Footnotes in *Chicago* style generally include the author's name, the publication title, publication date, and publisher information (if being cited for the first time), and a page number.
Footnotes	No footnotes.	No footnotes. Use endnotes, if necessary. References in endnotes require a special style.	Footnotes begin on the bottom of the page of the referring citation, and are separated from the essay by a short horizontal line. Each footnote must begin on a new line, and the notes are usually single-spaced, with a blank line between notes.
Block Quotations	Longer quotations (40 words and longer) are formatted as block quotations. Block quotations are continuously indented from the left margin the same distance as a paragraph indent, and omit the quotation marks.	Longer quotations (4 lines of text or longer) are formatted as block quotations. Block quotations are continuously indented from the left margin the same distance as a paragraph indent, and omit the quotation marks.	Longer quotations (100 words or 8 lines of text) are formatted as block quotations. Block quotations are continuously indented from the left margin the same distance as a paragraph indent, and omit the quotation marks.

(continued)

(*continued*)

	APA	MLA	*Chicago Notes and Bibliography* Style
List of References	In APA, references are recorded on a References page. The References page comes at the end of the essay, and is placed on its own page. The heading "References" is centred on the page, and is not bolded, underlined, or capitalized. Only works that were cited in the essay are included on the References page.	In MLA, the list of references is referred to as either Works Cited or Bibliography. It comes at the end of the essay and is placed on a separate page from the essay itself. The heading is centred on the page and is not bolded, underlined, or capitalized. On a Works Cited page, you only include the sources that you used in your essay. If asked to produce a Bibliography, on the other hand, you list all the sources you consulted, regardless of whether you cited the sources in your essay or not.	The page is referred to as the Bibliography. A bibliography includes all materials that have been consulted in the preparation of the essay. It comes at the end of the paper, and is placed on a separate page from the essay. The heading is centred on the page and is not bolded, underlined, or capitalized.
Spacing in the List of References	References are double-spaced. Second and subsequent lines are indented five spaces.	Works Cited and Bibliography are both double-spaced. Second and subsequent lines are indented five spaces.	Bibliography is double-spaced. Second and subsequent lines are indented five spaces.
Authors' Names	References are cited alphabetically by the first author's last name. Only the initial(s) of the author's given name(s) are used in reference entries.	References are cited alphabetically by the first author's last name. The complete first name of the author is used in all reference entries.	References are cited alphabetically by the first author's last name. The complete first name of the author is used in all reference entries.

LO 2, 3   12.4   USING THE DIFFERENT WRITING STYLES

In this section, we take you through each of the three most common writing conventions used in university papers (i.e., APA, MLA, *Chicago*). In the chart above, we presented general guidelines for each of the styles so that you might be able to more easily compare the significant similarities and differences between them. In this section, we are going to review the different styles in greater detail. Remember that these are the most common features of the writing conventions only. It's important to consult you instructor for his or her specific requirements and a format style guide for the most current information on the respective formatting conventions.

12.4.1 APA Writing Conventions

The APA (American Psychological Association) style guide prescribes the writing conventions that are used most often in the social sciences (e.g., psychology, sociology, anthropology). APA is informed with an assumption that writers will argue directly from objectively verifiable evidence, and that the writer's role will be one of identifying the connection between the evidence and the conclusion. The APA style provides guidelines for formatting the essay as a whole, including directions for title pages, citation format, margins, and references lists.

12.4.1.1 APA Guidelines to Guide You as You Write Your Paper Here are some guidelines to keep in mind as you write your essay. Though the specific rules governing the format change frequently, these general principles have characterized the format for a relatively long time. (The full style is in the *Publication Manual of the American Psychological Association.*)

- Accounts of one's own research should be written in the first person.
- Use the past tense to describe past events and procedures (and their results) but use present tense to describe implications of the results and to present conclusions.
- Include reference citations in the body of the essay.
- Include a References page at the end of the essay.
- Type your essay, double-spaced, using standard-sized paper (8.5" × 11") with 1" margins on all sides. Writers are expected to use 10- to12-point Times New Roman font.
- Include a running head in the upper left-hand side of each page in full capitals starting at the left margin (to create a running head, type the first two or three words of the title of the paper).

12.4.1.2 In-Text Citations in APA In APA, in-text citations are made parenthetically, providing the reader with enough information to connect the information you're citing with the longer, and more complete, reference on the References page. The box below provides an example of an in-text citation.

There are two ways to cite in-text using APA formatting: (1) when citing an author that you've paraphrased, you use the author–year of publication format (e.g., Brown, 2011), and (2) when citing an author that you've quoted directly, you use the author–year of publication and page number format (e.g., Brown, 2011, p. 345).

12.4.1.3 Documenting Sources The expectation in APA is that writers will formally acknowledge any ideas or text that comes from an external source. The chart below indentifies some of the material you will need to cite.

- Direct quotations from books, articles, films, letters, emails, lectures, etc.
- Single words, short phrases, sentences, or longer passages that have been quoted from books, articles, etc.
- Ideas drawn from a source but presented in your own words.
- Paraphrases or summaries of books, journal articles, or pamphlets.
- Statistics.

You can use citations to serve a number of purposes:

1. To acknowledge the original source of the idea, phrase, or passage, and to guard against the charge that you are misrepresenting others' work as your own. Failure to cite constitutes plagiarism (i.e., the theft of others' ideas), which is, in an academic setting, a grave offence.
2. To allow the reader to find the idea or phrase in its original context. A properly formatted citation provides your reader with the list of sources you used so he or she can contextualize the information you provided.
3. To increase the authority of your own argument by drawing on the authority of your sources.
4. To acknowledge the source of external sources and to enhance the authority of your own argument.

It's usually a good idea to maintain an ongoing record of sources as you're gathering the information from journal articles, scholarly papers, etc. It's not recommended that you leave this step until you've finished your paper. There are few things more frustrating than having found a particularly effective piece of evidence and then having to delete the information because you cannot locate its source.

12.4.1.4 Principal Features of References Using APA Format   The following chart provides a guide to formatting references in APA.

Five Things to Know about Referencing in APA Format
1. For periodicals ■ Single-author example: Berndt, T. (2002). Friendship quality and social development. *Current Directions in Psychological Science, 11,* 7–10. The author's last name is first, followed by the first initial of the given name, followed by the year of publication in parentheses. The next item in the reference is the title of the article in which only the first word of the title is capitalized. The name of the journal is italicized, as is the volume number, and these are followed by the page numbers. Note that the journal name is written using uppercase and lowercase letters. ■ Multiple-authors example: Berndt, T., & Keefe, K. (1995). Friends' influence on adolescents' adjustment to school. *Child Development, 66,* 1212–1229.
2. For books ■ Single-author example: Berndt, T. (2002). *Friendship quality and social development.* New York, NY: Random House. ■ Multiple-author example: Brown, R., & Orange, R. (1991). *Friendship is a source of support for people who are experiencing difficulties in their lives.* New York, NY: House. The author's last name is first, followed by the initial of the author's given name, and then the date in parentheses. The name of the book is italicized, and is followed by the city and province or state (abbreviated) in which it is published, then the name of the publisher. Second and subsequent lines are always indented.
3. The references list is always alphabetized by the first author's last name.
4. All entries in the list are double-spaced.
5. Internet references include a link to the original site of the information: Smith, G. (2002). *Life in the city.* Retrieved from http://www.lifeinthecity.com

12.4.1.5 APA Formatting for Citing Articles with One Author In the following examples, we've provided a list of fictitious articles and the fictitious authors who wrote them. In the exercises that follow, you will format the information using the proper APA format for one author.

We will do the first one for you.

> George Brown. The Dangers of Cigarette Smoking. Journal of Medicine. July 2010. Volume 6, issue 4. Pages 36–60.
>
> **Correct APA Format**
>
> Brown, G. (2010). The dangers of cigarette smoking. *Journal of Medicine, 6(4)*, 36–60.

Notice that we put the author's last name first, followed by a comma, and then used only the initial of his first name followed by a period. This is followed by the date in parentheses followed by a period. The name of the journal is in italics, followed by a comma, the volume of the journal in italics, the issue in parentheses, a comma, the page numbers, followed by a period. Note that the page numbers appear without a page designation such as "p.," "pp.," or "page."

12.4.1.6 APA Formatting Examples for Articles with One Author

Format the following examples using the correct APA writing convention.

The Fall of the Euro by Bernard Gordonson. Journal of Economics, 2009. Volume 4, issue 2. Pages 40–50.

_____

_____

The Left Brain versus the Right Brain by Howard Strumboli. Educational Psychology, 2012. Volume 5, issue 6. Pages 34–46.

_____

_____

Video Games Are Harmful to a Child's Development by Henry Fordman. Gaming for Amateurs, 2011. Volume 1, issue 1. Pages 60–75.

_____

_____

Too Much Fast Food Is Bad for You by Ronald Kinship. The Journal of Healthy Living, 2012. Volume 7, issue 2. Pages 90–120.

_____

_____

The Link Between Heart Attacks and Smoking by Jennifer Cartwright. Journal of Medical Science, 2010. Volume 9, issue 1. Pages 29–49.

_____

_____

What Are the Risk Factors Associated with a Shorter Life-Span? By Kendra Quigley. Healthy Living, 2008. Volume 2, issue 2. Pages 45–60.

_____

_____

Fast Food Make-Over by Linda Garden. Journal of Healthy Lifestyle, 2010. Volume 4, issue 5. Pages 56–69.

_____

_____

The Dangers of Processed Food by Hannah Oak. Farm Life, 2011. Volume 3, issue 5. Pages 67–79.

_____

_____

Cell Phones Are a Hazard When Driving by Carter Ford. Car and Truck, 2010. Volume 6, issue 1. Pages 10–25.

_____

_____

The Dangers of Drinking and Driving by Georgina Stiff. Journal of Health, 2008. Volume 2, issue 4. Pages 15–30.

_____

_____

Reflect on the process you followed. Were you able to format the journal articles using the APA format? Learning to format is just a matter of practising. We imagine that, by the time you got to the last couple of examples, you found it much easier to do.

12.4.1.7 APA Examples for Articles with Two or More Authors   In the following examples, the names of articles and their author are presented. In this exercise, you will practise recording the information in the proper APA format for two or more authors. We've completed the first example for you to use as a guide.

Notice that we have indented the second line. You must always indent the second and subsequent lines in the references page.

George Brown and Brad Black. The Dangers of Cigarette Smoking. Journal of Medicine. July 2010. Volume 6, issue 4. Pages 36–60.

Correct APA Format

Brown, G., & Black, B. (2010). The dangers of cigarette smoking. *Journal of Medicine, 6(4),* 36–60.

Notice that the author's last name is recorded first, followed by a comma, and then an ampersand (i.e., the symbol for *and*). You only use the ampersand *inside* parentheses and on the references page. Otherwise, you write out the word *and.* After the ampersand, record the second author's name following the same format (i.e., last name first, followed by a comma, followed by the first initial of the first name, followed by a period). Follow this with the date in parentheses and a period. Then record the name of the journal, using italics, followed by a comma. The volume of the journal is also recorded in italics and followed by a comma. Record the page numbers next, followed by a period. Notice that the page numbers appear without a page designation like "p.," "pp.," or "page."

12.4.1.8 APA Formatting Exercise for Articles with Two Authors

Format the following examples using the correct APA format.

The Fall of the Euro by Bernard Gordonson and Brian Good. Journal of Economics, 2009. Volume 4, issue 2. Pages 40–50.

_____

_____

The Left Brain versus the Right Brain by Howard Strumboli and Hans Jorgensen. Educational Psychology, 2012. Volume 5, issue 6. Pages 34–46.

_____

_____

Video Games Are Harmful to a Child's Development by Henry Fordman and John Hollow. Gaming for Amateurs, 2011. Volume 1, issue 1. Pages 60–75.

_____

_____

Too Much Fast Food Is Bad for You by Ronald Kinship and Linda Collins. The Journal of Healthy Living, 2012. Volume 7, issue 2. Pages 90–120.

_____

_____

The Link Between Heart Attacks and Smoking by Jennifer Cartwright and Stephanie Jones. Journal of Medical Science, 2010. Volume 9, issue 1. Pages 29–49.

_____

_____

What Are the Risk Factors Associated with a Shorter Life-Span? By Kendra Quigley and Hannah Lost. Healthy Living, 2008. Volume 2, issue 2. Pages 45–60.

_____

_____

Fast Food Make-Over by Linda Garden and Jack Fromson. Journal of Healthy Lifestyle, 2010. Volume 4, issue 5. Pages 56–69.

_____

_____

The Dangers of Processed Food by Hannah Oak and Nicole Elm. Farm Life, 2011. Volume 3, issue 5. Pages 67–79.

_____

_____

Cell Phones Are a Hazard When Driving by Carter Ford and Henry Buick. Car and Truck, 2010. Volume 6, issue 1. Pages 10–25.

_____

_____

The Dangers of Drinking and Driving by Georgina Stiff and Kelsey Abstainer. Journal of Health, 2008. Volume 2, issue 4. Pages 15–30.

_____

_____

Review your work. Did you format the examples correctly? You may have found that, by the time you got to the last couple of examples, you were working without having to check the model we provided. Learning to format is largely a matter of practice.

12.4.1.9 APA Formatting for Books with One Author   In the next examples, you will practise the process of formatting references for books with a single author. As before, we do the first one for you and you can do the rest.

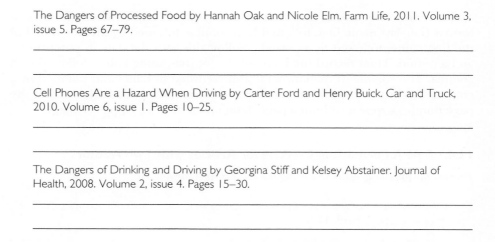

The Rise and Fall of Aspartame by Hugh Jordon. 2009. Rander Publishing, New York.

Correct APA Format

Jordon, H. (2009). *The rise and fall of aspartame.* New York, NY: Rander.

When you cite books in APA, you adhere to the following format: last name of the author, followed by a comma, followed by the first initial (only) of the author's first name, followed by a period. The initial of the writer's first name is followed by the year of publication in parentheses, which, in turn, are followed by a period. The name of the book is written in italics and only the first word is capitalized. The rest of the words are written in lower case. The title is followed by a period, the name of the city and province or state (abbreviated) in which the book was published, a colon, and the name of the publisher.

12.4.1.10 APA Formatting Examples for Citing Books with One Author

Format the following examples using the correct APA format.

Diet Foods That Prolong Life by Jerry Pacemaker. 2012. Houghtin Publishing, San Francisco.

_____

_____

Smoking Can Cause Cancer by Bob Cigar. 2007. Goone House, Atlanta, Georgia.

_____

_____

The Prime Suspect in Death by Eating by Bill McMurtry. 2006. Polson Incorporated, Philadelphia, Pennsylvania.

_____

_____

Romantic Movies and the Connection to Real Life Relationships by Susie Smart. 2011. House of Marvin. Georgetown, New Jersey.

_____

_____

Factory Farms versus Organic Farms by Jessie Track. 2010. Windswept Publishers. Savannah, Georgia.

_____

_____

Death by Pesticides by Lowell Fields. 2011. Tree Top Publishers. Columbus, Ohio.

_____

_____

Video Games Kill Brain Cells by Peter Edge. 2009. Overland Publishers. Minneapolis, Minnesota.

_____

_____

In Moderation Fast Food Is Not Harmful by Burt King. 2012. House of Honour. Boston, Massachusetts.

_____

_____

Factory Farmers Are Not the Bad Guys by Jim Cussins. 2008. Static Publishing. Seattle, Washington.

_____

_____

Cars Pollute the Atmosphere by Josie Developer. 2009. House of Iron. Los Angeles, California.

_____

_____

12.4.1.11 APA Formatting for Books with Two Authors In the examples below, you will be formatting a citation for a book with two authors. Again, we do the first one for you and you can do the rest.

The Rise and Fall of Aspartame by Hugh Jordon and Bob Hendrick. 2009. Rander and Rounder Publishing, New York.

Correct APA format

Jordon, H., & Hendrick, B. (2009). *The rise and fall of aspartame.* New York, NY: Rander and Rounder.

Notice that we have indented the second line.

When you cite books in APA, you begin with the last name of the author, followed by a comma, followed by the first initial (only) of the author's first name, followed by a period. This is followed by the year of publication in parentheses, which is followed by a period. The title of the book is written in italics and only the first word is capitalized. The rest of the words in the title are written in lowercase. The title is followed by a period. Finally, you note the name of the city and province or state (abbreviated) where the book was published, followed by a colon, and the name of the publisher.

12.4.1.12 APA Formatting Examples for Books with Two Authors

Format the following examples in the correct format for APA.

Diet Foods That Prolong Life by Jerry Pacemaker and Gerda Shunt. 2012. Houghtin Publishing, San Francisco.

_____

_____

Smoking Can Cause Cancer by Bob Cigar and Felicia Snuff. 2007. Goone House, Atlanta Georgia.

_____

_____

The Prime Suspect in Death by Eating by Bill McMurtry and Gord Hefty. 2006. Polson Incorporated, Philadelphia, Pennsylvania.

_____

_____

Romantic Movies and the Connection to Real Life Relationships by Susie Smart and Nancy Sharp. 2011. House of Marvin. Georgetown, New Jersey.

_____

_____

Factory Farms versus Organic Farms by Jessie Track and Felicia Fields. 2010. Windswept Publishers. Savannah, Georgia.

_____

_____

Death by Pesticides by Lowell Fields and Kevin Grain. 2011. Tree Top Publishers. Columbus, Ohio.

_____

_____

Video Games Kill Brain Cells by Peter Edge and Travis Green. 2009. Overland Publishers. Minneapolis, Minnesota.

In Moderation Fast Food Is Not Harmful by Burt King and Harry Prince. 2012. House of Honour. Boston, Massachusetts.

Factory Farmers Are Not the Bad Guys by Jim Cussins and Howard Johnson. 2008. Static Publishing. Seattle, Washington.

Cars Pollute the Atmosphere by Josie Developer and Sabrina Comfort. 2009. House of Iron. Los Angeles, California.

Example of paragraphs written in APA style   Notice the way in which the authors are cited in the text.

There was a time when smoking was not recognized as a danger to people or their health. Smoking was accepted as the norm and many adults smoked as a form of relaxation (Blue, 2008). Smoking was a "part of popular culture as was evidenced by the number of television shows, game shows, and talk shows that showed people smoking" (Blue, 2008, p. 34). Since the late 1970s, however, government regulations in the United States and Canada have prohibited the depiction of smoking among characters on television shows or guests who appear on game shows or talk shows. The change in attitude has arisen due to scientific studies that have proven "smoking cigarettes is dangerous to people and their health" (Brown, 2009, p. 24). Smoking cigarettes is harmful to people because smoking can lead to health problems, can affect people who are around smokers, and can lead to premature death.

Cigarette smoke contains more than four thousand different chemicals and at least four hundred of these are considered toxic or poisonous (Black, 2012). Black (2012) reported that the chemicals found in cigarettes include not only nicotine and tar, but also substances such as DDT, carbon monoxide, formaldehyde, hydrogen cyanide, ammonia, and arsenic, toxins that can be found in items such as rat poison, nail polish remover, and some types of wood varnish. Despite the widespread warnings that harmful chemicals are released in cigarette smoke, people still continue to smoke. This is a testament to the addictive nature of nicotine (Blue, 2008).

In this instance the name of the author and the year are provided to indicate that the author got the information from "Blue."

This reference is a direct quotation, so the author had to include the page number where the quotation was found.

Similarly, this is also a direct quotation, so once again the author included the page number.

In this instance, the author paraphrased the author "Black." In the first instance the citation comes at the end of the paraphrase and is, therefore, put in parentheses. The next sentence refers to a different statement in Black's work and so must cite Black once again.

Indicates a paraphrase, so just the author's name, "Blue," and the year of publication are required.

12.4.1.13 References Page in APA   In APA, the page of references is always placed on its own page and is called "References." The heading "References" is centred, but not underlined or bold. The individual reference entries are double-spaced, with the first line of the entry flush against the left margin and the second and subsequent lines indented. All authors are listed alphabetically by the first author's last name.

Use the model below to guide you when constructing a references page in APA.

Sample APA References Page

References

Brown, J. (2010). The fast food diet. *Journal of Healthy Eating 6,* 547–560.

Camelot, A. (2012). *Legends of King Arthur.* Boston, MA: Howard.

Hockman, T. (2009). Dangers of smoking. *Healthy Lifestyles 4,* 27–37.

Jordon, H., & Hendrick, B. (2009). *The rise and fall of aspartame.* New York, NY: Rander and Rounder.

Mandrick, G., Frinzand, H., & Burns, K. (2011). Video games are harmful to a child's development. *Parents 4,* 56–69.

Paulson, B. (2012). The effects of second-hand smoke. *Healthy Living,* 2, 8–48. Retrieved from http://www.healthyliving.com/articles/

Second and subsequent lines are indented.

Second and subsequent lines are indented.

LO 2, 3

12.5   COMPARING THE FORMATTING GUIDELINES OF APA TO MLA

In this section, you will find discussions of the key features of the MLA style format. By focusing on these general features, without worrying excessively about the formatting guidelines that emerge infrequently, you will be able to balance your obligation to conform to the conventions with your need to concentrate on how you orchestrate your argument and develop your ideas.

12.5.1   MLA Style of Formatting

The MLA (Modern Language Association) style of formatting is most commonly used in the liberal arts and humanities. As is the case with APA, MLA has certain specific guidelines for formatting essays. There are a number of similarities to the APA format in terms of the rationale for citation and for maintaining lists of references (e.g., acknowledging original sources and increasing the authority of one's own argument by attaching the authority of a scholar to it). One of the more significant differences lies in the degree to which interpretation of text is acceptable in essays and in the sources of evidence. Due to those differences, essays in the humanities often appear to admit the writer's opinion to a greater degree than do essays in the social sciences. That's not entirely the case. Writers in the humanities are still expected to make their arguments on the basis of some form of evidence.

12.5.2 General Principles to Guide You as You Write Your Paper in MLA

Here are some guidelines to keep in mind as you write your essay. These are some of the features of the MLA writing style.

- In MLA, you do not include a title page for the essay unless you've been specifically asked to do so.
- Write your essay using either the third person (e.g., *he, she, they*) or the first person (e.g., *I, we*).
- Write your essay using present tense to refer to present events and past tense to refer to past events.
- Include reference citations in the body of the essay.
- Type your essay, double-spaced, using standard-sized paper (8.5" × 11") with 1" margins on all sides. Writers are expected to use 12-point Times New Roman font.
- Include a "Works Cited" page at the end of the essay.

12.5.3 Guidelines for Referencing in MLA

Use the following chart to familiarize yourself with some of the more obvious features of referencing in MLA.

Five Characteristics of Referencing Using MLA Format

1. Use of Endnotes Page
   a. MLA recommends that all notes be listed on a separate page headed "Notes" (centred, no formatting).
   b. Use "Note" if there is only one note.
   c. The Notes page should appear before the "Works Cited" page. This is particularly important for papers that are being submitted for publication.
   d. You should list the notes themselves using consecutive Arabic numbers that correspond to the notation in the text.
   e. Double-space notes. Each endnote is indented five spaces; subsequent lines are flush with the left margin. Place a period and a space after each endnote number. Provide the appropriate note after the space.

2. Use of Footnotes (below the text body)
   a. When you need to format footnotes on the same page as the corresponding main text, begin footnotes four lines (two double-spaced lines) below the main text.

(*continued*)

(*continued*)

	b. Single-space footnotes. Each footnote is indented five spaces; subsequent lines are flush with the left margin. c. Place a period and a space after each footnote number. d. Provide the appropriate note after the space. e. Consult the *MLA Handbook for Writers of Research Papers* for more information.
3.	References are recorded on a **Works Cited** page.
4.	MLA style does not require the URLs of internet sources.
5.	MLA requires that you list the full name of the author or authors (e.g., Smith, George William).

12.5.4 MLA Formatting for Articles with One Author

The following examples deal with the names of articles and their authors. Practise recording the information in the proper MLA format with one author.

> George Brown. The Dangers of Cigarette Smoking. Journal of Medicine. July 2010. Volume 6, issue 4. Pages 36–60.
>
> **Correct MLA Format**
>
> Brown, George. "The Dangers of Smoking." *Journal of Medicine* 6.4 (2010): 36-60. Print.

In MLA formatting, you indicate the medium of publication.

To cite articles in the MLA format, you record the author's last name first, followed by a comma, followed by the author's full first name, followed by a period. The name of the article is identified by the use of quotation marks. Notice that the period goes inside the quotation marks. You then record the name of the journal in italics, followed by the volume and issue of the journal (no punctuation between the journal name and the volume). This is followed by the year in parentheses, followed by a colon, followed by the page numbers. Notice that the page numbers appear without a page designation such as "p.," "pp.," or "page." In MLA you have to indicate the medium of publication. In this case, we will say that the medium is print.

12.5.5 MLA Formatting Examples for Articles with One Author

Format the following examples using the proper MLA format.

The Fall of the Euro by Bernard Gordonson. Journal of Economics, 2009. Volume 4, issue 2. Pages 40–50.

_____

_____

The Left Brain versus the Right Brain by Howard Strumboli. Educational Psychology, 2012. Volume 5, issue 6. Pages 34–46.

_____

_____

Video Games Are Harmful to a Child's Development by Henry Fordman. Gaming for Amateurs, 2011. Volume 1, issue 1. Pages 60–75.

_____

_____

Too Much Fast Food Is Bad for You by Ronald Kinship. The Journal of Healthy Living, 2012. Volume 7, issue 2. Pages 90–120.

_____

_____

The Link Between Heart Attacks and Smoking by Jennifer Cartwright. Journal of Medical Science, 2010. Volume 9, issue 1. Pages 29–49.

_____

_____

What Are the Risk Factors Associated with a Shorter Life-Span? By Kendra Quigley. Healthy Living, 2008. Volume 2, issue 2. Pages 45–60.

_____

_____

Fast Food Make-Over by Linda Garden. Journal of Healthy Lifestyle, 2010. Volume 4, issue 5. Pages 56–69.

_____

_____

The Dangers of Processed Food by Hannah Oak. Farm Life, 2011. Volume 3, issue 5. Pages 67–79.

_____

_____

Cell Phones Are a Hazard When Driving by Carter Ford. Car and Truck, 2010. Volume 6, issue 1. Pages 10–25.

_____

_____

The Dangers of Drinking and Driving by Georgina Stiff. Journal of Health, 2008. Volume 2, issue 4. Pages 15–30.

_____

_____

12.5.6 MLA Formatting for Articles with Two Authors

The following examples deal with the names of articles and the authors. Format the information in proper MLA format for two or more authors.

> George Brown and Brad Black. The Dangers of Smoking. Journal of Medicine. July 2010. Volume 6, issue 4. Pages 36–60.
>
> **Correct MLA Format for Articles with Two Authors**
>
> Brown, George, and Brad Black. "The Dangers of Smoking." *Journal of Medicine* 6.4 (2010): 36-60. Print.
>
> **Correct MLA Format for Articles with Three Authors**
>
> Brown, George, Brad Black, and Bob Green. "The Dangers of Smoking." *Journal of Medicine* 6.4 (2010): 36-60. Print.

Remember to indent the second line.

Indent second lines

Notice that the first author's last name comes first, followed by a comma, and then the first author's first name, followed by a comma and the word "and," then the second author's full name, following this format: first name first, followed by the last name, followed by a period. It's important that you use the proper punctuation. The name of the article is in quotation marks. Notice that the period goes inside the quotation marks. This is followed by the name of the journal in italics, followed by the volume, a period, and then the issue of the journal, then the year of publication, and then a colon. The page numbers are followed by a period. Notice that the page numbers appear without a page designation such as "p.," "pp.," or "page." Finally, in MLA, you must indicate the medium in which the article was published (either print or Web).

12.5.7 MLA Formatting Examples for Articles with Two Authors

Format the following examples using MLA. In the examples, the medium will always be print.

The Fall of the Euro by Bernard Gordonson and Brian Good. Journal of Economics, 2009. Volume 4, issue 2. Pages 40–50.

_____

_____

The Left Brain versus the Right Brain by Howard Strumboli and Hans Jorgensen. Educational Psychology, 2012. Volume 5, issue 6. Pages 34–46.

_____

_____

Video Games Are Harmful to a Child's Development by Henry Fordman and John Hollow. Gaming for Amateurs, 2011. Volume 1, issue 1. Pages 60–75.

_____

_____

Too Much Fast Food Is Bad for You by Ronald Kinship and Linda Collins. The Journal of Healthy Living, 2012. Volume 7, issue 2. Pages 90–120.

_____

_____

The Link Between Heart Attacks and Smoking by Jennifer Cartwright and Stephanie Jones. Journal of Medical Science, 2010. Volume 9, issue 1. Pages 29–49.

_____

_____

What Are the Risk Factors Associated with a Shorter Life-Span? By Kendra Quigley and Hannah Lost. Healthy Living, 2008. Volume 2, issue 2. Pages 45–60.

_____

_____

Fast Food Make-Over by Linda Garden and Jack Fromson. Journal of Healthy Lifestyle, 2010. Volume 4, issue 5. Pages 56–69.

_____

_____

The Dangers of Processed Food by Hannah Oak and Nicole Elm. Farm Life, 2011. Volume 3, issue 5. Pages 67–79.

_____

_____

Cell Phones Are a Hazard When Driving by Carter Ford and Henry Buick. Car and Truck, 2010. Volume 6, issue 1. Pages 10–25.

_____

_____

The Dangers of Drinking and Driving by Georgina Stiff and Kelsey Abstainer. Journal of Health, 2008. Volume 2, issue 4. Pages 15–30.

_____

_____

12.5.8 MLA Format for Books with One Author

In the following examples, you will practise using MLA to format a citation for a book with one author.

The Rise and Fall of Aspartame by Hugh Jordon. 2009. Rander and Rounder Publishing, New York.

Correct MLA Format for One Author

Jordon, Hugh. *The Rise and Fall of Aspartame.* New York: Rander and Rounder, 2009. Print.

Indent second line of reference.

When you cite books in MLA, you begin with the last name of the author, followed by a comma, and then the full first of the author, followed by a period.

The name of the book is written in italics and the first letter of every major word is capitalized. The title of the book is followed by a period. This is followed by the name of the city in which the book was published, followed by a colon, the name of the publisher, followed by a comma, and finally the year. In MLA, you also have to indicate at the end the medium of publication. In this example the medium is print.

12.5.9   MLA Formatting Examples for Books with One Author

Format the following examples using the MLA format.

Diet Foods That Prolong Life by Jerry Pacemaker. 2012. Houghtin Publishing, San Francisco.

_____

_____

Smoking Can Cause Cancer by Bob Cigar. 2007. Goone House, Atlanta, Georgia.

_____

_____

The Prime Suspect in Death by Eating by Bill McMurtry. 2006. Polson Incorporated, Philadelphia, Pennsylvania.

_____

_____

Romantic Movies and the Connection to Real Life Relationships by Susie Smart. 2011. House of Marvin. Georgetown, New Jersey.

_____

_____

Factory Farms versus Organic Farms by Jessie Track. 2010. Windswept Publishers. Savannah, Georgia.

_____

_____

Death by Pesticides by Lowell Fields. 2011. Tree Top Publishers. Columbus, Ohio.

_____

_____

Video Games Kill Brain Cells by Peter Edge. 2009. Overland Publishers. Minneapolis, Minnesota.

_____

_____

In Moderation Fast Food Is Not Harmful by Burt King. 2012. House of Honour. Boston, Massachusetts.

_____

_____

Factory Farmers Are Not the Bad Guys by Jim Cussins. 2008. Static Publishing. Seattle, Washington.

_____

_____

Cars Pollute the Atmosphere by Josie Developer. 2009. House of Iron. Los Angeles, California.

_____

_____

12.5.10 MLA Format for Books with Two or More Authors

When you cite books in MLA that have two authors, you begin with the last name of the first author, followed by a comma, full first name of the first author, followed by a comma, followed by the "and," followed by the full first name of the second author, and followed by the last name of the second author. The name of the book is written in italics and the first letter of each word is capitalized. The title is followed by a period. This is followed by the name of the city in which the book was published, followed by a colon, and the name of the publisher, followed by a comma, followed by the year of publication. In MLA, you have to indicate the medium of publication. In the case of our examples, the medium is print. If you were to have retrieved the information online, the medium would be given as "Web."

In the following examples, you will practise formatting a book with two authors.

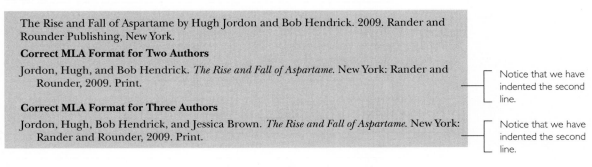

The Rise and Fall of Aspartame by Hugh Jordon and Bob Hendrick. 2009. Rander and Rounder Publishing, New York.

Correct MLA Format for Two Authors

Jordon, Hugh, and Bob Hendrick. *The Rise and Fall of Aspartame.* New York: Rander and Rounder, 2009. Print.

Notice that we have indented the second line.

Correct MLA Format for Three Authors

Jordon, Hugh, Bob Hendrick, and Jessica Brown. *The Rise and Fall of Aspartame.* New York: Rander and Rounder, 2009. Print.

Notice that we have indented the second line.

12.5.11 MLA Formatting Examples for Books with Two Authors

Using the MLA format, format the following examples using the proper form for books. For each of these examples, the medium of publication will be print.

Diet Foods That Prolong Life by Jerry Pacemaker and Gerda Shunt. 2012. Houghtin Publishing, San Francisco.

_____

_____

Smoking Can Cause Cancer by Bob Cigar and Felicia Snuff. 2007. Goone House, Atlanta, Georgia.

_____

_____

The Prime Suspect in Death by Eating by Bill McMurtry and Gord Hefty. 2006. Polson Incorporated, Philadelphia, Pennsylvania.

_____

_____

Romantic Movies and the Connection to Real Life Relationships by Susie Smart and Nancy Sharp. 2011. House of Marvin. Georgetown, New Jersey.

_____

_____

Factory Farms versus Organic Farms by Jessie Track and Felicia Fields. 2010. Windswept Publishers. Savannah, Georgia.

_____

_____

Death by Pesticides by Lowell Fields and Kevin Grain. 2011. Tree Top Publishers. Columbus, Ohio.

_____

_____

Video Games Kill Brain Cells by Peter Edge and Travis Green. 2009. Overland Publishers. Minneapolis, Minnesota.

_____

_____

In Moderation Fast Food Is Not Harmful by Burt King and Harry Prince. 2012. House of Honour. Boston, Massachusetts.

_____

Factory Farmers Are Not the Bad Guys by Jim Cussins and Howard Johnson. 2008. Static Publishing. Seattle, Washington.

_____

_____

Cars Pollute the Atmosphere by Josie Developer and Sabrina Comfort. 2009. House of Iron. Los Angeles, California.

_____

_____

12.5.12 Example of Paragraphs Written in MLA Style

Notice the way in which the authors are cited in the text.

> There was a time when smoking was not recognized as a danger to people or their health. Smoking was accepted as the norm and many adults smoked as a form of relaxation (Blue, 30). Smoking was a "part of popular culture as was evidenced by the number of television shows, game shows, and talk shows that showed people smoking" (Blue, 34). Since the late 1970s, however, government regulations in the United States and Canada have prohibited the depiction of smoking by characters on television shows or guests who appear on game shows or talk shows. This change in attitude reflects the findings of the many scientific studies that have proven "smoking cigarettes is dangerous to people and their health" (Brown, 24). Smoking cigarettes is harmful to people because smoking can lead to health problems, can affect people who are around smokers, and can lead to premature death.
>
> Cigarettes contain more than four thousand different chemicals and at least four hundred of these are considered toxic or poisonous (Black, 26). Black reports that the chemicals found in cigarettes include not only nicotine and tar but also substances such as DDT, carbon monoxide, formaldehyde, hydrogen cyanide, ammonia, and arsenic, toxins that can also be found in rat poison, nail polish remover, and some types of wood varnish. Despite the widespread warnings that harmful chemicals are released in cigarette smoke, people still continue to smoke. This is a testament to the addictive nature of nicotine (Blue, 38).

In MLA style, you just include the author's last name, with no date of publication.

When using a direct quotation, you include the author's name and the page number, but there is no page designation.

When using a direct quotation, you include the author's name and the page number, but there is no page designation.

In MLA style, you include the author's last name, but no date of publication.

In MLA style, you include the author's last name, but no date of publication.

12.5.13 References Page in MLA

In MLA, the page of references is always placed on its own page and is labelled "Works Cited." The title "Works Cited" is centred, but not underlined or bold. The individual reference entries are double-spaced, with the first line of the entry flush against the left margin and the second and subsequent lines indented. All authors are listed alphabetically by the first author's last name.

Use the model below to guide you when constructing a references page in MLA.

Sample MLA Works Cited Page

Works Cited

Brown, Jessica. "The Fast Food Diet." *Journal of Healthy Eating* 6.4 (2010): 547-60. Print.

Camelot, Arthur. *Legends of King Arthur*. Boston: Howard, 2012. Print.

Hockman, Tannis. "Dangers of Smoking." *Healthy Lifestyles* 4.4 (2009): 27-37. Print.

Jordon, Hugh, and Bob Hendrick. *The Rise and Fall of Aspartame*. New York: Rander, 2009. Print.

Mandrick, George, Henry Frinzand, and Kenneth Burns. "Video Games Are Harmful to a Child's Development." *Parents* 4.3 (2011): 56-69. Web.

Paulson, Brian. "The Effects of Second-Hand Smoke." *Healthy Living*. Health Institute Publications, 16 Oct. 2009. Web. 19 Nov. 2011.

Second and subsequent lines are indented.

LO 2, 3   # 12.6   *CHICAGO* STYLE OF FORMATTING

The *Chicago* style of formatting is most commonly used for essays that are written in the discipline of history, though it is also used, occasionally, for essays that are written in other disciplines in the humanities. The *Chicago* style uses footnotes and endnotes, and records the list of references in a bibliography. One of the conventions of the *Chicago* style is the opportunity for you to comment extra-textually (i.e., in a footnote or endnote) on the sources that you've cited.

When you write an essay using the *Chicago* style of formatting, you include a note (endnote or footnote) each time you cite a source, whether the citation is a direct quotation or a paraphrase. Footnotes are recorded at the bottom of the page on which the source is referenced, and endnotes are put at the end of chapters or at the end of the entire document. In either case, a superscript number corresponding to a note with the bibliographic information for that source should be placed in the text, following the end of the sentence in which the source is referenced. *Chicago* style gives you the option of omitting a bibliography, if the first note for each source includes all relevant information about the source. If you cite the same source again, the second note will include only the surname of the author, the title (or a shortened form of the title), and page number(s) cited. If you cite the same source and page number(s) from a single source on more than one occasion, the corresponding note will use the word "Ibid." If you use the same source but make reference to information on a different page, the corresponding note should use "Ibid.", followed by a comma and the new page number(s). If you do include a bibliography, as most instructors prefer, even your first note for a source may include only the author's surname and title (often shortened), and the page number(s). Most citations will include the following three components: (1) author's name, (2) title or source, and (3) publication information.

12.6.1   General Principles to Guide You as You Write Your Paper in *Chicago* Style

Here are some guidelines to keep in mind as you write your essay using the *Chicago*-style format.

- Generally, first or third person is used in *Chicago*.
- Record your reference citations in footnotes or endnotes.
- Record references in a "Bibliography" at the end of the essay.
- Type the essay, double-spaced, using standard-sized paper (8.5" × 11") with 1" margins on all sides. Writers are expected to use 10- to 12-point Times New Roman font.
- You can format page numbers two different ways, according to the function of the page. On the pages that begin a major section, the page numbers appear at the bottom centre of the page, ¾ inch from the edge. Other pages include the page number in the upper-right corner, double-spaced above the text.

12.6.2 Guidelines for Referencing Using the *Chicago*-Style Format

Use the chart below to familiarize yourself with some of the more obvious features of *Chicago*-style referencing. (The full style is in *The Chicago Manual of Style*.)

Six Characteristics of Referencing Using *Chicago*-Style Format
1. In a bibliography, italicize the titles of books and journals. Place titles of articles and chapters in quotation marks.
2. In a bibliography, separate all major elements with a period.
3. For the bibliography, use the author's full name. Arrange alphabetically by the first author's last name. First line is flush left, then each subsequent line is indented five spaces. Each source is listed separately.
4. List the year of publication after the publisher or journal name.
5. For footnotes and endnotes, indent the first line by five spaces. The note number is not raised, and it's followed by a period. Authors' names are not inverted, but use the last name only to refer to an earlier note by the same author. Publication information is placed inside parentheses.

Examples of *Chicago*-Style Formatting of Citations and Bibliography Entries

Text (*double-spaced*):

The Gettysburg Address, delivered by Abraham Lincoln, came to be regarded as one of the "greatest speeches in American history." [10]

- ■ **Footnote or Endnote** (*double-spaced*)
- ■ 10. John William Booth, *The Battle of Gettysburg: The Whole Story* (New York: HarperCollins, 2001), 124.

Bibliography Entry (*double-spaced*)

Booth, John William. *The Battle of Gettysburg: The Whole Story*. New York: HarperCollins, 2001.

- ■ A *Chicago*-style bibliography, which appears at the end of your paper, lists every work you've cited in your notes. In addition, however, it may include works that you consulted but did not cite.

12.6.3 *Chicago*-Style Formatting for Articles with One Author

In the following exercises, you will find examples of articles with one author. Try to format the information for a bibliography entry using the correct *Chicago*-style format for articles written by a single author. You can use the first example as a guide.

George Brown. The Dangers of Cigarette Smoking. Journal of Medicine. July 2010. Volume 6, issue 4. Pages 36–60.

Correct *Chicago*-Style Format

Brown, George. "The Dangers of Smoking." *Journal of Medicine* 6, no. 4 (2010): 36–60.

⌐ Indent second and
⌊ subsequent lines.

In the *Chicago* style, you record the author's last name first, followed by a comma, followed by the full first name, followed by a period. The name of the article is noted in quotation marks. Notice that the period goes inside the quotation marks. This is followed by the name of the journal in italics, followed by the volume, a comma, and the issue of the journal (use the abbreviation "no." to indicate number), followed by the year in parentheses, then a colon and the page numbers. Notice that the page numbers appear without a page designation like "p.," "pp.," "page."

12.6.4 *Chicago*-Style Formatting Examples for Articles with One Author

*Format the following citations as bibliography entries using the correct **Chicago-style format.***

The Fall of the Euro by Bernard Gordonson. Journal of Economics, 2009. Volume 4, issue 2. Pages 40–50.

_____

_____

The Left Brain versus the Right Brain by Howard Strumboli. Educational Psychology, 2012. Volume 5, issue 6. Pages 34–46.

_____

_____

Video Games Are Harmful to a Child's Development by Henry Fordman. Gaming for Amateurs, 2011. Volume 1, issue 1. Pages 60–75.

_____

_____

Too Much Fast Food Is Bad for You by Ronald Kinship. The Journal of Healthy Living, 2012. Volume 7, issue 2. Pages 90–120.

_____

_____

The Link Between Heart Attacks and Smoking by Jennifer Cartwright. Journal of Medical Science, 2010. Volume 9, issue 1. Pages 29–49.

_____

_____

What Are the Risk Factors Associated with a Shorter Life-Span? By Kendra Quigley. Healthy Living, 2008. Volume 2, issue 2. Pages 45–60.

_____

_____

Fast Food Make-Over by Linda Garden. Journal of Healthy Lifestyle, 2010. Volume 4, issue 5. Pages 56–69.

_____

_____

The Dangers of Processed Food by Hannah Oak. Farm Life, 2011. Volume 3, issue 5. Pages 67–79.

_____

_____

Cell Phones Are a Hazard When Driving by Carter Ford. Car and Truck, 2010. Volume 6, issue 1. Pages 10–25.

_____

_____

The Dangers of Drinking and Driving by Georgina Stiff. Journal of Health, 2008. Volume 2, issue 4. Pages 15–30.

_____

_____

12.6.5 *Chicago*-Style Formatting for Articles with Two or More Authors

In the exercises below, we've provided you with examples of articles written by two or more authors. Record the information using the correct *Chicago*-style format for two or more authors.

George Brown and Brad Black. The Dangers of Smoking. Journal of Medicine. July 2010. Volume 6, issue 4. Pages 36–60.

Correct *Chicago*-Style Format for Two Authors

Brown, George, and Brad Black. "The Dangers of Smoking." *Journal of Medicine* 6, no. 4 (2010): 36–60.

Correct *Chicago*-Style Format for Three Authors

Brown, George, Brad Black, and Bob Green. "The Dangers of Smoking." *Journal of Medicine* 6, no. 4 (2010): 36–60.

Indent the second line.

When you cite books in *Chicago* style that have two authors, you list the first author's last name first, followed by a comma, followed by the author's first full name, followed by "and." This is followed by the full first name of the second author, which is followed by the last name of the second author. With three authors, only a comma follows the first author's given name, and a comma and "and" follow the second author's last name. The name of the article is identified by quotation marks. Notice that the period goes inside the quotation. This is followed by the name of the journal in italics, followed by the volume and issue of the journal, followed by the year of publication, followed by a colon. The page numbers are recorded next, followed by a period. Notice that the page numbers appear without a page designation such as "p.," or "pp.," or "page."

12.6.6 *Chicago*-Style Formatting Example for Articles with Two Authors

Format the following citations as bibliography entries using the correct **Chicago-style format.**

The Fall of the Euro by Bernard Gordonson and Brian Good. Journal of Economics, 2009. Volume 4, issue 2. Pages 40–50.

_____

_____

The Left Brain versus the Right Brain by Howard Strumboli and Hans Jorgensen. Educational Psychology, 2012. Volume 5, issue 6. Pages 34–46.

_____

_____

Video Games Are Harmful to a Child's Development by Henry Fordman and John Hollow. Gaming for Amateurs, 2011. Volume 1, issue 1. Pages 60–75.

_____

_____

Too Much Fast Food Is Bad for You by Ronald Kinship and Linda Collins. The Journal of Healthy Living, 2012. Volume 7, issue 2. Pages 90–120.

_____

_____

The Link Between Heart Attacks and Smoking by Jennifer Cartwright and Stephanie Jones. Journal of Medical Science, 2010. Volume 9, issue 1. Pages 29–49.

_____

_____

What Are the Risk Factors Associated with a Shorter Life-Span? By Kendra Quigley and Hannah Lost. Healthy Living, 2008. Volume 2, issue 2. Pages 45–60.

_____

_____

Fast Food Make-Over by Linda Garden and Jack Fromson. Journal of Healthy Lifestyle, 2010. Volume 4, issue 5. Pages 56–69.

_____

_____

The Dangers of Processed Food by Hannah Oak and Nicole Elm. Farm Life, 2011. Volume 3, issue 5. Pages 67–79.

_____

_____

Cell Phones Are a Hazard When Driving by Carter Ford and Henry Buick. Car and Truck, 2010. Volume 6, issue 1. Pages 10–25.

The Dangers of Drinking and Driving by Georgina Stiff and Kelsey Abstainer. Journal of Health, 2008. Volume 2, issue 4. Pages 15–30.

12.6.7 *Chicago*-Style Formatting for Books with One Author

In the following exercises, you will practise formatting a citation for a book with one author. Use the example below as a guide.

The Rise and Fall of Aspartame by Hugh Jordon. 2009. Rander Publishing, New York.
Correct *Chicago*-Style Format for Books
Jordon, Hugh. *The Rise and Fall of Aspartame.* New York: Rander Publishing, 2009.

When you cite books in *Chicago* style, you begin by recording the last name of author, followed by a comma, followed by the full first name of the author, followed by a period. This is followed by the title of the book, written in italics, with the first letter of every major word capitalized. The title is followed by a period. This is followed by the name of the city in which the book was published and the province or state (abbreviated) if the city is ambiguous or not well known, followed by a colon, followed by the name of the publisher, followed by a comma, followed by the year.

12.6.8 *Chicago*-Style Formatting Examples for Books with One Author

Format the following citations as bibliography entries using the correct **Chicago-style format.**

Diet Foods That Prolong Life by Jerry Pacemaker. 2012. Houghtin Publishing, San Francisco.

Smoking Can Cause Cancer by Bob Cigar. 2007. Goone House, Atlanta, Georgia.

The Prime Suspect in Death by Eating by Bill McMurtry. 2006. Polson Incorporated, Philadelphia, Pennsylvania.

Romantic Movies and the Connection to Real Life Relationships by Susie Smart. 2011. House of Marvin. Georgetown, New Jersey.

_____

_____

Factory Farms versus Organic Farms by Jessie Track. 2010. Windswept Publishers. Savannah, Georgia.

_____

_____

Death by Pesticides by Lowell Fields. 2011. Tree Top Publishers. Columbus, Ohio.

_____

_____

Video Games Kill Brain Cells by Peter Edge. 2009. Overland Publishers. Minneapolis, Minnesota.

_____

_____

In Moderation Fast Food Is Not Harmful by Burt King. 2012. House of Honour. Boston, Massachusetts.

_____

_____

Factory Farmers Are Not the Bad Guys by Jim Cussins. 2008. Static Publishing. Seattle, Washington.

_____

_____

Cars Pollute the Atmosphere by Josie Developer. 2009. House of Iron. Los Angeles, California.

_____

_____

12.6.9 *Chicago*-Style Formatting for Books with Two or More Authors

In the following exercises, you will practise formatting a book with two authors in the *Chicago*-style format. Use the example below to guide you.

The Rise and Fall of Aspartame by Hugh Jordon and Bob Hendrick. 2009. Rander Publishing, New York.

Correct *Chicago*-Style Format for Books with Two Authors

Jordon, Hugh, and Bob Hendrick. *The Rise and Fall of Aspartame*. New York: Rander Publishing, 2009.

Notice that we have indented the second line.

For Three Authors

Jordon, Hugh, Bob Hendrick, and Jessica Brown. *The Rise and Fall of Aspartame*. New York: Rander Publishing, 2009.

When you cite books with two or more authors in *Chicago* style, you format the citation in the following way. You begin by noting the last name of the first author, followed by a comma, followed the full first name of the author, followed by a comma, followed by "and." This is followed by the full first name of the second author and the last name of the author. The title of the book is written in italics and the first letter of every major word is capitalized. The title is followed by a period. This is followed by the name of the city in which the book was published and the province or state (abbreviated) if the city is ambiguous or not well known, followed by a colon, followed by the name of the publisher, followed by a comma, followed by the year of publication.

12.6.10 *Chicago*-Style Formatting Examples for Books with Two or More Authors

Diet Foods That Prolong Life by Jerry Pacemaker and Gerda Shunt. 2012. Houghtin Publishing, San Francisco.

Smoking Can Cause Cancer by Bob Cigar and Felicia Snuff. 2007. Goone House, Atlanta, Georgia.

The Prime Suspect in Death by Eating by Bill McMurtry and Gord Hefty. 2006. Polson Incorporated, Philadelphia, Pennsylvania.

Romantic Movies and the Connection to Real Life Relationships by Susie Smart and Nancy Sharp . 2011. House of Marvin. Georgetown, New Jersey.

Factory Farms versus Organic Farms by Jessie Track and Felicia Fields. 2010. Windswept Publishers. Savannah, Georgia.

Death by Pesticides by Lowell Fields and Kevin Grain. 2011. Tree Top Publishers. Columbus, Ohio.

Video Games Kill Brain Cells by Peter Edge and Travis Green. 2009. Overland Publishers. Minneapolis, Minnesota.

In Moderation Fast Food Is Not Harmful by Burt King and Harry Prince. 2012. House of Honour. Boston, Massachusetts.

_____

_____

Factory Farmers Are Not the Bad Guys by Jim Cussins and Howard Johnson. 2008. Static Publishing. Seattle, Washington.

_____

_____

Cars Pollute the Atmosphere by Josie Developer and Sabrina Comfort. 2009. House of Iron. Los Angeles, California.

_____

_____

In *Chicago* style, you include the author's last name and the date of publication.

When using a direct quotation, you include the author's last name, the year of publication, and the page number, but there is no page designation.

When using a direct quotation, you include the author's last name, the year of publication, and the page number, but there is no page designation.

In *Chicago* style you include the author's first name and the year of publication.

In *Chicago* style you include the author's last name and the date of publication.

12.6.11 Example of Paragraphs Written in *Chicago* Style

Notice the way in which the authors are cited in the text.

There was a time when smoking was not recognized as a danger to people or their health. Smoking was accepted as the norm and many adults smoked as a form of relaxation.[1] Smoking was a "part of popular culture as was evidenced by the number of television shows, game shows, and talk shows that showed people smoking."[2] Since the 1970s, however, government regulations in the United States and Canada have prohibited the depiction of characters on television shows or guests who appear on game shows or talk shows. The change in attitude has arisen due to scientific studies that have demonstrated that "smoking cigarettes is dangerous to people and their health."[3] Smoking cigarettes is harmful to people because smoking can lead to health problems, can affect people who are around smokers, and can lead to premature death.

Cigarette smoke contains more than four thousand different chemicals and at least four hundred of these are considered toxic or poisonous.[4] Brad Black (2009) reported that the chemicals found in cigarettes include not only nicotine and tar but also substances like DDT, carbon monoxide, formaldehyde, hydrogen cyanide, ammonia, and arsenic. These toxins can be found in items such as rat poison, nail polish remover, and some types of wood varnish. Despite the widespread warnings about chemicals in cigarette smoke, people continue to smoke. This is a testament to the addictive nature of nicotine.[5]

Footnotes
1. Blue, Andrew. "Smoking Kills." Journal of Healthy Living 15.1 (2008): 30–43.
2. Ibid, 34.
3. Brown, Gregory. "Harmful Effects of Smoking." Journal of Health 4.2 (2011): 20–34.
4. Black, Brad. "What's in a Cigarette?" Journal of Health and Wellness 3.2 (2009): 45–58.
5. Blue, "Smoking Kills."

12.6.12 References Page in *Chicago* Style

In *Chicago* style, the page of references is always placed on its own page and is labelled "Bibliography." The word is centred, but not underlined or bold. The individual reference entries are double-spaced, with the first line of the entry flush against the left margin and the second and subsequent lines indented. All authors are listed alphabetically by the first author's last name.

Use the model below to guide you when constructing a references page in *Chicago* style.

Sample *Chicago*-Style References Page

Bibliography

Brown, Jessica. "The Fast Food Diet." *Journal of Healthy Eating* 6, no. 4 (2010): 547–60.

Camelot, Arthur. *Legends of King Arthur*. Boston: Howard Publishing, 2012.

Hockman, Tannis. "Dangers of Smoking." *Healthy Lifestyles* 4, no. 4 (2009): 27–37.

Jordon, Hugh, and Bob Hendrick. *The Rise and Fall of Aspartame*. New York: Rander Publishing, 2009.

Mandrick, George, Henry Frinzand, and Kenneth Burns. "Video Games are Harmful to a Child's Development." *Parents* 4, no. 1 (2011): 56–69.

Paulson, Brian. "The Effects of Second-hand Smoke." *Healthy Living* 27 (2010): 48–54. http://www.healthyliving.com/articles.pdf.

> Second and subsequent lines are indented.

> In *Chicago* style, you include the author's last name and the date of publication.

12.7   CONCLUSION

In this chapter, we have reviewed the most prominent features of the the three most common writing conventions.. The focus on prominent features, rather than a provision of more extensive lists of the respective features, is intentional. As with other writing skills, using formatting conventions is a memory-intensive process for writers who have not yet internalized the rules. By concentrating on the specific features you're likely to use most often, you will acquire a working knowledge of the conventions more easily. This is not meant to suggest that other conventions are unimportant. Instead, it's intended to bring you closer to the practice of the experienced writer, who internalizes knowledge of frequently used writing conventions but refers to a style manual for information regarding conventions that are used less often.

MyCompLab®

How Do I Get a Better Grade?

Go to MyCompLab for additional help with your grammar, writing, and research skills. You will have access to a variety of exercises, instruction, and videos that will help you improve your basic skills and help you get a better grade.

✓•─Practice   **General Checklist for Formatting Style**

1. Do you know which formatting style you are expected to follow? If not, ask your instructor or consult the class syllabus.

2. Does your essay require a title page?

3. Do you need a running head?

4. Do you need page numbers?

5. Are you aware of the way to properly cite the sources you used in the essay?

6. Have you used the correct title for the references page (e.g., References, Works Cited, Bibliography)?

7. Have you double-spaced your entire essay?

8. Have you used a 12-point Times New Roman font?

✓•─Practice   **Peer-Review Worksheet for APA Formatting**

Essay Written By: _____

Peer Reviewer: _____

1. Is the title page correct? Does it have a running head that is flush left? Does it include the title of the paper? The name of the author (first name, middle initial, final name)? Is the institutional affiliation below the author's name?

_____

_____

_____

_____

2. Does the essay have page numbers in the right-hand corner?

_____

_____

_____

_____

3. **Are the in-text citations in the correct format? In APA formatting the following is correct:**

When citing a direct quotation at the end of the quote, APA follows the author, year of publication, page number format (e.g., Brown, 2001, p. 234).

When citing a direct quotation before the quote, APA uses the author and year of publication, and the page number goes at the end of the quote (e.g., Brown [2001] argued that "second-hand smoke is harmful to other people" [p. 25]).

When not citing a direct quotation, follow the format of author, and year of publication (e.g., Brown, 2001).

_____

_____

_____

_____

4. **Is the references list on a separate page? Are the authors listed alphabetically by last name? Are the second and subsequent lines indented?**

For Books:

Last name, first-name initial. (Year of publication). *Name of book.* City of Publication, Province or State (abbreviated): Publisher.

For Articles:

Last name, first-name initial. (Year of publication). Name of article. *Name of Journal, volume, issue number,* page numbers.

5. **Is each paragraph indented?**

_____

_____

_____

_____

6. **Is the paper double-spaced, 12-point Times New Roman?**

_____

_____

_____

_____

(*continued*)

(*continued*)

7. Is the essay written using the past tense to describe past events and the present tense to describe current events?

   _____

   _____

   _____

8. Is the essay written using the appropriate voice?

   _____

   _____

   _____

✓• Practice   Peer-Review Worksheet for MLA Formatting

Essay Written By: _____

Peer Reviewer: _____

1. Is there a title page? If so, there shouldn't be one unless your instructor requires one. On the first page of the essay, ensure that:

The name, the instructor's name, the course, and the date are in the upper left-hand corner of the page. Is it double-spaced?

   _____

   _____

Is the title of the paper double-spaced from the date?

   _____

   _____

Is the title centred? Is the title underlined, italicized, or placed in quotation marks? If it is, it shouldn't be.

   _____

   _____

Does the paper have a header in the upper right-hand corner that includes the author's last name, followed by a space with a page number?

   _____

   _____

2. **Are the in-text citations in the correct format? In MLA formatting the following is correct:**

When citing a direct quotation or when paraphrasing, MLA follows the author, page, number format (e.g., Brown, 234). If the author's name is used in the text, then only the page number is included in the parentheses (e.g., Brown found that ... [3]). Notice, that, unlike APA, there is no designation for page.

_____

_____

_____

3. **Is the Works Cited or Bibliography list on a separate page? Are the authors listed alphabetically by last name? Are the second and subsequent lines indented?**

For Books:

Last name, First name. *Title of Book*. City of Publication: Publisher, Year of Publication. Medium of Publication.

For Articles:

Last name, First name. "Title of Article." *Title of Journal, Volume and issue number (year)* pages. Medium of publication.

_____

_____

_____

4. **Is each paragraph indented?**

_____

_____

_____

5. **Is the paper double-spaced, 12-point Times New Roman?**

_____

_____

_____

6. **Are the use of tense and voice consistent?**

_____

_____

_____

✔•⌐**Practice**   **Peer-Review Worksheet for** *Chicago*-**Style Formatting**

Essay Written By: _____

Peer Reviewer: _____

1. Does the essay have a title page? Is the title centred a third of the way down the page?

   Is the name and class information centred a few lines below the title?

   _____

   _____

2. Does the essay have page numbers?

   _____

   _____

   Does every page that starts a major section have a page number?

   _____

   _____

   Are page numbers at the bottom centre of the page ¾ inch from the edge?

   _____

   _____

   Do other pages include the page number on the upper-right corner, double-spaced above the text?

   _____

   _____

3. Are the in-text citations in the correct format? In *Chicago*-style formatting, the following is correct:

   Footnotes or endnotes are used for citations. Footnotes in *Chicago* style generally include the author's name, the publication title, publication date, and publisher information (if being cited for the first time), and a page number, although a shortened form may also be used with any citation, if there is a bibliography.

   _____

   _____

4. Is the Bibliography on its own page? Are the authors listed alphabetically by last name? Are the second and subsequent lines indented?

For Books:

Last name, first name. *Title of Book.* **City of Publication and Province or State (abbreviated) if the city is ambiguous or not well known: Publisher, Year of publication.**

For Articles:

Last name, first name. "Name of Article." *Name of Journal* **volume, issue number (year): page numbers.**

_____

_____

_____

5. Is each paragraph indented?

_____

_____

_____

6. Is the paper double-spaced, 12-point Times New Roman?

_____

_____

_____

7. Are the use of tense and voice both appropriate and consistent?

_____

_____

_____

CHAPTER 13

Editing

Learning Objectives

At the completion of this chapter, you will be able to:

1. Identify the differences between the ways in which novice and experienced writers edit their essays.

2. Identify the ways in which the process of editing differs from the process of revising.

3. Edit your own essay strategically.

13.1   INTRODUCTION

In this chapter, we review the practice of editing, drawing a distinction again between editing and revision. We identify the significant differences between the editing practices that novice writers generally follow and those that more experienced writers follow. Novice writers often think they've finished the writing process when they add a period to the final sentence of the conclusion.

Not exactly.

Close, yes, but not finished.

An unedited essay, however wondrous, is a raw piece of genius, rich with insight and alive with promise. In some cases, if it's brilliant enough in its execution, it may even be good enough that it causes readers to overlook certain surface flaws. Imagine, however, the impact that same essay might have if it took the time to wash off and clean up. Proficiency in editing allows you to turn a good essay into a better essay. The editing process provides the opportunity to revisit your paper with an eye to surface details. This chapter will include a brief discussion of the strategies you might want to adopt when editing for (1) grammar, spelling, and punctuation, (2) formatting, and (3) citations and references.

13.2 UNDERSTANDING THE DIFFERENCE BETWEEN THE PRACTICE OF THE NOVICE WRITER AND THE PRACTICE OF THE EXPERIENCED WRITER IN EDITING

In order to understand the editing process that experienced writers follow, it's useful again to identify the differences between the writing practices of novice writers and those of experienced writers. You've seen the following chart in previous chapters. In this instance, you should notice that novice writers *focus on error avoidance rather than meaning; require thought for procedural, or "mechanical," writing functions;* and *begin writing without planning, and edit, if at all, for grammatical errors.* In contrast, experienced writers *focus on developing or refining meaning; have, to a significant degree, automated procedural functions;* and *invest time and energy in planning and reviewing.*

Novice Writers	**Experienced Writers**
■ *Require thought for procedural, or "mechanical," writing functions.*	■ *Have, to a significant degree, automated procedural functions.*
■ *Focus on error avoidance rather than meaning.*	■ *Focus on developing or refining meaning.*
■ *Begin writing without planning, and edit, if at all, for grammatical errors.*	■ *Invest time and energy in planning and reviewing.*
■ Focus on "knowledge telling" (i.e., relating all the information they have and can find on a topic, rather than exercising critical judgment to determine relevance).	■ Organize, and reorganize, essay structure to allow individual ideas to serve the overall purpose of the essay.

Throughout this text, we've encouraged you to focus on the development of meaning while you're engaged in the writing process. By waiting until the editing stage to begin the process of proofreading, you're able to concentrate on the larger questions of meaning and greater coherence in your writing.

At the editing stage, on the other hand, you want to turn your attention to housekeeping, attending to the departures from standard writing practice that might obscure your meaning or diminish your authority. For a number of reasons, novice writers occasionally skip this stage of the writing process. Sometimes they run out of time. Sometimes they believe it to be unnecessary, because they think that electronic programs have taken care of that for them (don't fall for it; software looks at what you wrote, not at what you meant).

Editing Is Important, But . . .

Editing is important. It will make a good essay better by rendering the text more readable and familiar to the reader. It's important to remember, however, that the ultimate purpose of writing is not avoidance of mechanical errors but the representation of meaning. In the end, the best advice is that you should assign editing its due. While it's important to set time aside to review and edit your essay, it's perhaps more important that you don't allow obsessions with formal correctness to distract you from your writing purpose while you're drafting the essay.

LO 1, 2, 3

13.3   EDITING VS. REVISION

In Chapter 11, we reviewed the practice of revision. We identified it as an integral and ongoing part of the writing process, designed to ensure that the emerging essay continues to correspond with the writer's intention. It's guided by an understanding that writing is sometimes a messy business, with ideas manifesting themselves on the page in ways that the writer had never intended. By circling back and revising the emerging text, the writer is able to shepherd the ideas back into line, ensuring that they serve the overall purpose of the essay. Revision is driven by the writer's concern with the development of meaning.

Editing, on the other hand, is like housekeeping. It's meant to render your draft respectable. Proofreading and editing increase the likelihood that the essay that you send out into the world will have its hair combed and a clean shirt on. It's generally easier to compose if you allow yourself to write for meaning without worrying excessively about mechanical errors. You do, however, need to return to the text at the end of the writing process to ensure that your essay is free of errors (which means, of course, that you should budget time for the editing process).

As you have, perhaps, noticed, editing your own work can be difficult. Writers are often so familiar with their own work that they read what the text ought to say rather than what it does say. In order to improve the efficiency of your editing process, you might try one of the following strategies:

1. Have a friend or classmate review your paper. Because this person is not aware of what you meant to say, he or she is more likely to notice errors.
2. Read individual paragraphs backwards. This was a common practice in the days of manual typesetting. Reading backwards forces you to pay attention to the individual words. Often, writers become so familiar with their text that they read words that aren't there, or miss errors that are there, because they see what they expect to see. The exercise of reading each word individually increases the likelihood that you will catch your mistakes.
3. Identify your own error pattern. Most writers tend to make the same errors over and over again. If you discover that you have a specific error pattern, pay particular attention to those errors when proofreading. It may, in fact, be useful to keep a record of the types of errors you make consistently and refer to that record when editing.

13.4   STRATEGIES FOR EDITING

LO 1, 2, 3

In the charts that follow, you will find strategies for undertaking the editing process at various points in the essay. Though the charts are far from exhaustive, you may find editing easier when you engage in the process systematically. If you're careful about catching these errors, your instructor will thank you (that gratitude is often represented by a higher grade).

13.4.1   Strategies for Reviewing Common Problems in Grammar, Spelling and Word Usage, and Punctuation

The first chart is one that focuses on strategies you can use to edit your essay for common problems in grammar, spelling and word usage, and punctuation. You'll notice that the chart doesn't list every mistake that a writer might make, but, rather, identifies specific strategies for identifying those difficulties. It's much easier to work through the essay when you're working with strategies and identifying categories of potential problems.

Ten Strategies for Reviewing Common Problems in Grammar, Spelling, and Punctuation
1. Turn on the spell-checker in your word processor. It's the twenty-first century. Use the technology Bill Gates gave you. At this point in history, failing to use the editing devices included in your word processor makes no more sense than writing a 1200-page treatise using a quill and ink.
2. Reflect critically on the advice the computer program offers. The computer does not know what you mean to say. You may have spelled the *wrong* word correctly (e.g., homonyms like *flour* instead of *flower; would* instead of *wood; your* instead of *you're*) and the spell-checker will give it a pass. On the other hand, the grammar-checker in many programs frequently suggests revisions that are unnecessary or incorrect. The program means well, but it's sometimes wrong.
3. Though your word processor will usually identify repeated words, it sometimes fails to note missing words. A second reader, like a friend or a classmate, will usually notice the mistake.

4. Review your sentences to ensure that you have, in all cases, expressed a complete thought.
  a. Every sentence should have a subject (e.g., in the sentence "The instructor marked the essays," the subject is *instructor*).
  b. Every sentence needs a verb. You also want to ensure that the verb you have used is correct (e.g., some verb forms require a second verb. In the sentence "The student was trying to write her essay but it was too noisy," the verb *trying* cannot stand without the verb *was*). Your ear will often catch an error if you read the text aloud.
  c. Every sentence needs an independent clause. A dependent clause cannot stand on its own (e.g., the fragment "Which is why the instructor docked marks on the essay" is incomplete. It desperately wants to modify or qualify an independent clause, but there is no independent clause with which to work).

(continued)

(continued)

5. Sadly, the practice of constructing sentences that begin on page 11 and continue through page 23 is no more effective than the practice of using sentence fragments. Writers often lose control of long sentences, crafting long strings of ideas that are joined by *and, but,* and *or.* Though there is a value to the complex sentence (i.e., it often permits the writer to explore a complex idea more effectively), it's often just as effective to break the long sentence into a number of shorter ones. In any case, if you're using long complex or compound sentences, you need to ensure that you have the punctuation in place to keep them under control.

6. Using commas to endlessly extend a sentence doesn't fool anyone. Comma splices occur when you try to link two, or more, main clauses in a single sentence using a comma but no conjunction (e.g., *and, but, or*).

7. When you're editing, you need to pay particular attention to agreement. Agreement between related elements in the text is largely unnoticeable when you've done it correctly and glaringly obvious when you haven't. Below we have identified three areas of particular concern:
   a. Subject/Verb Agreement: The subject and the verb need to agree in number, which means that if the subject is plural, the verb should also be plural (e.g., "When one of a group of students writes a paper, he or she does so individually and so the singular verb 'writes' is correct").
   b. Agreement in Tense: This is a common mistake, and one that is relatively easy to make, particularly in longer documents. As you become more familiar with a particular writing format, you tend to adopt the right tense automatically. However, even experienced writers find that managing tense can be a challenge. While you're editing, watch to ensure that tense does not shift (e.g., "The instructor *took* essays home to mark, but instead *watched* the ballgame. The instructor *ignores* the essays for the afternoon." The verbs *took* and *watched* are in the past tense. The verb *ignores* is present tense. The tense needs to agree, e.g., "The instructor *ignored* the essays for the afternoon").
   c. Agreement between Pronoun and Referent (i.e., the noun to which the pronoun refers): A pronoun allows you to refer to a noun without continually naming it (repeating the noun endlessly can become tiresome). It's important to ensure that the pronoun you use agrees in number and gender with the noun (e.g., "When *a student* writes a paper, *they* have to attend to agreement between noun and pronoun" could be modified in one of the following ways: "When *a student* writes a paper, *he or she* has to attend to agreement between noun and pronoun," or "When *students* write papers, *they* have to attend to agreement between noun and pronoun").

8. Parallelism is a writing practice that contributes to coherence by organizing ideas into patterns. The use of a common pattern for a series of related ideas identifies the relationship. In the following example, the writer has created a list of attributes that attach to a particular instructor; the parallel structure connects the ideas, with the noun *instructor* as the subject for three related predicates: "A good instructor knows his subject, is helpful outside of class, and makes class interesting."

9. Apostrophes: Plurals vs. Possessives. This is another common error. In general, apostrophes are used to indicate possession (or contractions, which are generally avoided in formal writing). Plurals, on the other hand, take an *s* without the apostrophe.
   a. Read your paper, stopping at only those words that end in an s. If the s is used to indicate possession, there should be an apostrophe, as in "Greg's football."
   b. Check the contractions, like you're for "you are" and it's for "it is." Each of these contractions should include an apostrophe.

   c. Remember that apostrophes are not used to indicate that a word is plural. When making a word a plural, only an *s* is necessary.

10. Colons and semicolons are sadly abused and misused. Each has a specific purpose and each is capable of great things. Each, however, needs to be used with care.
    a. Colon:
       - You can use a colon to join two clauses when you wish to emphasize the second clause (e.g., "In the summer, road construction causes problems for motorists: parts of Roblin, Grant, and Portage are closed during the construction").
       - You can also use a colon to point to a list that follows (e.g., "There are two primary uses for the colon: [1] to point to an idea you wish to emphasize, and [2] to begin a list").
    b. Semicolon:
       - You can use a semicolon to join two independent clauses when the second clause restates the first or when the two clauses are of equal emphasis (e.g., "In the summer, road construction causes problems for motorists; streets are closed and littered with machinery").
       - You also use a semicolon to separate items in a list when other punctuation in the sentence could be confusing (e.g., "In the summer, road construction causes a number of problems: roads are closed and littered with large, ungainly machinery; road crews hold up traffic interminably; and detours are generally so busy that the traffic grinds to an abrupt, unexpected halt").

13.5 PARAGRAPH WITH GRAMMATICAL MISTAKES

LO 2, 3

The paragraph below includes a number of errors in grammar, spelling or word usage, and punctuation. Though it is difficult to master the mechanics of language simply by hunting for mistakes, it is possible to improve your editing practice by learning to proofread systematically.

Young drivers, between the ages of sixteen and [1]twenty, do not have the maturity or experience to be able to make quick driving decisions at the best of times. When alcohol is factored in, the rate of fatal accidents in this age [2]group, rises, regardless of the amount of alcohol that is consumed. Even when alcohol is not involved, the lack of maturity and experience in [3]driving remain the major causes of vehicle accidents in this age group. When driving, the human brain has to deal with a large variety of tasks that do not only involve [4]driving. There is not only the operation of the vehicle, but also outside factors that can impact the driver's reaction time. Drivers have to be alert to other cars, pedestrians, road-repair [5]crews and bicycle riders. If any amount of alcohol is consumed, a [6]drivers reaction time is compromised. When a driver consumes alcohol, he becomes impaired. In order to operate a vehicle safely, [7]drivers must remain attentive to [8]there environment at all times. Any lapse in focus [9]could result in an accident. [10]The driver has slower reflexes, vision is impaired, visual perception is compromised and the amount of time needed to process information increases. [11]They're is no safe amount of alcohol to drink before driving. [12]Just say no. Is it worthwhile killing yourself or your friends, by drinking and driving[13]. [14]Don't drink and drive. [15]It can save a life: yours, or someone else's.

1 There is no need for the commas. Ask yourself what purpose these commas might serve.

2 Again, there is no need for a comma here.

3 This may be more effective with attention to the parallel structure (e.g., "the lack of maturity and lack of experience").

4 It is important to pay attention to the relationship between parts of a sentence. In this section of the sentence, the writer has "the human brain" driving. It could be modified like this: "When people are driving, their brains have to deal...."

5 Commas (or, occasionally, semicolons) are generally required to separate items in a list.

6 "Driver's" is a possessive. It requires an apostrophe.

7 In the previous sentence, the driver was singular. In this sentence, "drivers" are plural. It is best to be consistent when using the sentence subject to link sentences.

8 "There" is the wrong word (although it has been spelled correctly). The writer means "their."

9 "Could" is a shift from present tense.

10 This sentence would be more successful with a parallel construction (e.g., "The driver suffers slower reflexes, impaired vision, and compromised visual perception") and a sentence break (e.g., "In addition, the amount of time necessary to process information increases"— i.e., because the last item in the list cannot be easily modified to the same form as the other items in the list, it might be more effective to break the thought into two sentences).

11 This is both a contraction, which ought to be avoided in formal writing, and the wrong word (i.e., it is a homonym for "There").

12 The voice has shifted to second person (i.e., the "you should" is implied).

13 The use of this rhetorical question is a stylistic decision that might need to be reconsidered (rhetorical questions generally ought to be avoided). But as it stands, it requires a question mark.

14 Again, this represents a voice shift to the second person.

15 "It" is a pronoun with no referent. The sentence could be rewritten like this: "Taking this advice can save a life: yours, or someone else's."

LO, 3   13.6   EDITING FOR GRAMMAR, SPELLING, AND PUNCTUATION IN YOUR OWN ESSAY

Use the chart below to guide the way in which you edit for grammatical correctness when you're editing your own essay.

Making Writing Decisions — About Editing for Grammar, Spelling, and Punctuation in Your Own Essay Writing

What is the purpose of this writing decision?

Editing for errors in grammar, spelling, and punctuation serves two purposes: (1) it improves the readability of the text by rendering it in a form that corresponds to reader expectations, and (2) it increases the authority of the text by demonstrating your facility with the conventions of language.

What is the effect of this writing decision?

Strangely, grammatical correctness does not make a bad essay good. It does, however, make a good essay better. That is, editing for adherence to standard English form will improve an essay that is already successful in its organization and development of ideas, but will not rescue an essay that is not.

What considerations inform this decision?

Grammar serves writing. It is not served by writing. Ensure that you are editing with meaning in mind.

Suggested strategies for making this decision.

Use the chart "Ten Strategies for Reviewing Common Problems..." earlier in this chapter to organize your editing process. Editing is much more efficient when it is intentional and focused. For obvious reasons, you don't want to edit when you are tired. Let's face it. You will forgive yourself more readily when all you want to do is sleep.

Questions to guide decision making in your own essay.

1. Review the essay you are working on. It is generally a good idea, if possible, to return to the essay after a short period of time. Edit one page at a time.
2. Has the spell-checker identified misspelled words? Though it is generally correct in its analysis, the spell-checker is fallible. Check the words to make sure that the spell-checker has not incorrectly identified a word as being spelled wrong just because it is not in the word bank.
3. Has the spell-checker failed to identify a word that is spelled correctly but used incorrectly?
4. Are there words missing?
5. Does the punctuation serve your meaning? For instance, commas are usually used in English to isolate phrases that must be read separately. The purpose of punctuation is not, despite what you may have been told, to identify breath pauses.
6. Are there sentence fragments? Remember that a sentence expresses a complete thought. Are there sentences that run on forever?
7. Is the tense correct and consistent?
8. Have you checked for agreement between subject and verb? Is there agreement between pronoun and referent?

Writing Exercise I

Each of the following sentences contains one or more errors in grammar, punctuation, or spelling. Rewrite each sentence to correct the errors.

1. The man came to canada from italy to start a new life with his family.

_____

_____

2. The horse run away into the field when the boy wanted to catch it and ride it.

_____

_____

3.   The students wanted to raise money for there school field trip so they sold hotdogs, drinks and potato chips during the lunchhour.

_____

_____

4.   Jasons mom wanted to bake some cookies but she did not have any flower.

_____

_____

5.   Bob was try to get his motorcycle to work but there was something wrong with it and no matter what he did it would not start so he give up and went inside to watch television.

_____

_____

_____

6.   The boxer was continually hiting his opponent in the kidneys and the referee warned him that he would be disqualified if he did not stop.

_____

_____

_____

7.   It is hard to no when to stop runing if a bare is chasing you down a forest path.

_____

_____

8.   He went over board to rescue a small child, who had fallen into the water, in front of his horrified parents.

_____

_____

9.   Amanda remarked that "the water in the lake is so cold that my toes were frozen just from puting them into the water for a second."

_____

_____

_____

10. The coffee is cold by the time he drink it.

_____

_____

Look at the following answer key to evaluate your editing.

Answer Key

Each of the following sentences contains one or more errors. Rewrite each sentence to correct the errors.

1. The man came to canada from italy to start a new life with his family.
   The man came to <u>Canada</u> from <u>Italy</u> to start a new life with his family.

   In English, names of countries are always capitalized.

2. The horse run away into the field when the boy try to catch and ride it.
   The horse <u>ran</u> away into the field when the boy <u>tried</u> to catch it and ride it.

   This sense of the sentence seems to suggest that it ought to have been written in the past tense.

3. The students wanted to raise money for there school field trip so they sold hot dogs, drinks and potato chips during the lunchhour.
   The students wanted to raise money for <u>their</u> school field trip so they sold hot dogs, <u>drinks,</u> and potato chips during the lunch hour.

   their: The wrong homonym was used in this sentence.

   drinks: A list of three or more items generally requires a comma before the word "and" that precedes the last item.

4. Jasons mom wanted to bake some cookies but she did not have any flower.
   <u>Jason's</u> mom wanted to bake some cookies but she did not have any <u>flour</u>.

   Jason's: Need to show possession. The mother in the sentence is Jason's.

   flour: Wrong homonym used.

5. Bob was try to get his motorcycle to work but there was something wrong with it and no matter what he did it would not start so he give up and went inside to watch television.
   Bob was <u>trying</u> to get his motorcycle to work, but there was something wrong with it and, no matter what he did, it would not <u>start. He</u> gave up and <u>went</u> inside to watch television.

   trying: Needed to fix the verb so that it agreed with the action.

   start. He: Sentence needs to be broken into two.

   went: Verb tense was incorrect.

6. The boxer was continually hiting his opponent in the kidneys and the referee warned him that he would be disqualified if he did not stop.
   The boxer was continually <u>hitting</u> his opponent in the kidneys and the referee warned him that he would be disqualified if he did not stop.

   Incorrect spelling of the word. The spell-check program would have identified this as an error.

7. It is hard to no when to stop runing if a bare is chasing you down a forest path.
   It is hard to <u>know</u> when to stop <u>running</u> when a <u>bear</u> is chasing you down a forest path.

   know, running: Incorrect spelling of the word. The spell-check program would have identified this as an error.

   bear: Incorrect homonym.

8. He went over board to rescue a small child, who had fallen into the water, in front of his horrified parents.

   He went <u>overboard</u> to rescue a small child who had fallen into the water in front of the <u>child's</u> horrified parents.

   overboard: One word rather than two separate words.

   child's: You need to indicate the individual to whom the parents belonged. Was it the rescuer's parents or the child's parents?

9. Amanda remarked that the water in the lake is so cold that her toes were frozen just from puting them into the water for a second.

   Amanda remarked that the water in the lake <u>was</u> so cold that her toes were frozen just from <u>putting</u> them into the water for a second.

   was: Watch for verb tense.

   putting: Incorrect spelling of the word. The spell-check program would have identified this as an error.

10. The coffee is cold by the time he drink it.

    The coffee <u>was</u> cold by the time he <u>drank</u> it.

    was: Need correct tense.

    drank: Need correct tense

LO 3

13.7   EDITING FOR FORMATTING ERRORS

This chart provides strategies for proofreading for common problems in formatting. Because you may be asked to write using any one of a number of different formatting conventions, the chart identifies categories of difficulties rather than the specific problems themselves.

Five Strategies for Reviewing Common Problems in Formatting
1. Ensure that you are using the prescribed formatting style. Your instructor will have advised you of the format he or she expects for assignments. This is a common problem for novice writers, who often find that they have learned to use one formatting style only to discover that different disciplines and different courses use different formatting conventions. In Chapter 12, we identified some of the principal differences between the formatting styles. Review that chapter to see that your work corresponds to the expectations.
2. Ensure that margins, line spacing, page numbers, title pages, etc., correspond to the formatting protocol prescribed by your instructor. The easiest way to determine whether you have adhered to the format is by comparing it to an example. Looking at a visual model will usually reveal the differences more clearly than referring to a written list of rules.
3. Ensure that every direct quotation has been properly cited. A quotation is another writer's ideas expressed in that writer's own words. A direct quotation always requires

> either quotation marks or, if the quotation is a lengthy one, a marginal indentation without quotation marks.

4. Ensure that you have recorded in-text citations, or footnotes or endnotes, properly.

5. Ensure that you are writing in the voice and tense that are appropriate for the prescribed format. In some instances, instructors may permit you to write in the first person (e.g., *I, we, our*). In other cases, you will be required to use the third person (e.g., *he, she, they, the students*).

13.8 COMMON CITATION MISTAKES: A SAMPLE ESSAY

LO 3

The paragraph below includes a number of citations that have been formatted incorrectly. We have used the APA format to make corrections. There may be subtle differences between these examples of corrections and the way you would correct the citation in MLA and *Chicago* style. We discuss those formats at greater length both later in this chapter and in Chapter 12.

Young drivers between the ages of sixteen and twenty do not have the maturity or the experience to make quick driving decisions at the best of times [1](Brown, P.6). When alcohol is factored in, [2]Allen found that "the rate of fatal accidents in this age group rises regardless of the amount of alcohol that is consumed" ([3]2009, Allen, pp. 8). Even when alcohol is not involved, the lack of maturity and experience in driving remain the major causes of vehicle accidents in this age group. When an individual is driving, "the human brain has to deal with a large variety of tasks" [4](Brown, 2011, P.10). There is not only the operation of the vehicle but also outside factors that can impact the driver's reaction time. Drivers have to be alert to other cars, pedestrians, road-repair crews, and bicycle riders. If any amount of alcohol is consumed, driver's reaction time is compromised [5](from"Dangers of Drinking and Driving"). In order to operate a vehicle safely, the driver must remain attentive to their environment at all times. Any lapse in focus could result in an accident. When a driver consumes alcohol, he or she becomes impaired. If a driver reaches a blood alcohol level of 0.05, which is still below the legal limit of 0.08, a driver's ability to attend to events on the road is impaired ([6]from "Dangers of Drinking and Driving"). The driver has slower reflexes, vision is impaired, visual perception is compromised, and the amount of time needed to process information slows down ([7]see Brown, 2008). There is no safe amount of alcohol to drink before driving ([8]from "Dangers of Drinking and Driving").

1 When citing authors in the text, you must cite the year of publication as well as the author's last name. In this instance, no year of publication is indicated. In addition, there is a page number provided. This is not needed because this is not a direct quotation. This citation should be: "(Brown, 2011)."

2 The last name of the author does not stand alone. The year of publication needs to be included in brackets behind the author's last name. e.g., "Allen (2009)."

3 For this particular citation, there is no need to include the author's last name or the year of publication again at the end of the quote. The author's last name has already

been indicated at the start of the quote, as has the year of publication. In this case, the only information needed at the end of the direct quotation is the page number. There is also no need to use two *p*'s in the citation because only one page is listed. If the quote is on two pages then you would use double *pp*. The correct way to cite this is: "(p. 8)."

4 For this citation, the *P* for the page number is capitalized. It shouldn't be. When indicating a page number use a lowercase *p*.

5 When citing sources that have no author, it is correct to use the name of the article. The citation does not need to have the word *from* listed. The name of the article should be put inside quotation marks. The citation should also include the year of publication. For example, "("Dangers of Drinking and Driving," 2002)."

6 See previous comment.

7 There is no need to include the word *see* when quoting an author.

8 When citing sources that have no author, it is correct to use the name of the article. The citation does not need to have the word *from* listed.

LO 3 13.9   EDITING FOR CORRECTNESS IN FORMATTING IN YOUR OWN ESSAY

Use the following chart to guide the way in which you edit for adherence to formatting conventions when you are working on your own essay.

Making Writing Decisions	About Editing for Formatting in Your Own Essay Writing

What is the purpose of this writing decision?

The purpose of adhering to a prescribed format is, in part, to create a familiar textual environment, and, in part, to demonstrate that you belong to a particular intellectual community. Just as it would seem odd to write a formal letter to a close friend, so would it seem odd to write a familiar essay to an academic audience.

What is the effect of this writing decision?

Though decisions about format may seem arbitrary, they contribute to the success of an essay by providing a familiar textual environment to the reader. They also add to your authority as a writer by identifying you as a person who is knowledgeable of, and conversant with, the conventions of a particular discourse or field of study.

What considerations inform this decision?

In many ways, the adoption of a new format for writing can seem as difficult as acquiring a new language (it's not, but it might seem so). Understanding the purpose for the conventions of a particular format might allow you to internalize them more easily.

Suggested strategies for making this decision.

Identify five or six features of the format to focus on. These should be the obvious features of the format. For instance, look at the conventions for the title page and follow them exactly. Look at the conventions for the page layout. Again, follow those conventions exactly. Look at the conventions for in-text citations (in general), for tense, for evidence, and for pages labelled References, Works Cited, or Bibliography. Master the most import-ant features of the format first, and then, as necessary, turn to a reference text for the information that is needed less frequently (e.g., the appropriate way to cite a lecture or ways to cite an embedded quotation).

Questions to guide decision making in your own essay.

1. Turn to your completed essay. Identify the five or six features of the formatting con-vention that you are going to focus on. Make notes of more obscure formatting ques-tions as you work through the text.
2. Is the title page formatted correctly? Have you included the information that is pre-scribed by the writing reference guide and/or your instructor?
3. Are you required to include an abstract? Have you done so?
4. Look at the formatting of the page. Are the margins correct? Are you using the cor-rect font and font size? Should you double-space, and, if so, have you done so? Should you have a running head on the page? Are the page numbers formatted correctly?
5. Are you writing in the tense that is prescribed by the format guide?
6. Are the in-text citations formatted correctly? Have you used footnotes when you were meant to use parenthetical citations or endnotes when you were meant to use footnotes?
7. Return to the beginning to work on the more obscure formatting questions that arose during the first round of editing.

13.10 STRATEGIES FOR EDITING FOR CORRECTNESS IN REFERENCES LISTS

LO 2, 3

The following chart is meant to provide general strategies for identifying problems with your references list. As was the case with the chart identifying strategies for proofreading for correctness in formatting in general, this chart addresses categor-ies of problems, regardless of the formatting convention you are using in your essay.

Six Strategies for Reviewing Common Problems in Citations and References
1. Understand that there are subtle differences between the protocols for References pages, Works Cited, and Bibliographies. For instance, on both a References and Works Cited page, you list only the sources that you cited in your paper. In a Bibli-ography, on the other hand, you list the sources you used in your paper and also the sources you consulted but did not cite.
2. Alphabetize the list according to the last names of authors. Regardless of the format-ting style, you need to list all references alphabetically, according to the last name of the first author. If there is more than one author, in APA style list each author by his/her last name first (e.g., Brown, J., and Grey, D.).

(*continued*)

(*continued*)

3. Ensure that you are following the prescribed format when listing authors' names. In APA style, you don't write the full first name of the author in the references list. You only use the initial of the first name, such as "Brown, P. (2011)." On the other hand, in both MLA style and *Chicago*, the author's first name is included, such as "Brown, Peter. (2011)."

4. Ensure that you are including all publication information. Remember that one of the purposes of a References list, Works Cited list, or Bibliography is to provide enough information that your reader can go out and find the source you used.

5. Take care to format the page in accordance with the directions of the preferred formatting style. For instance, most styles use a hanging indent (i.e., the second and subsequent lines are indented). There are also punctuation protocols. Check a style guide to ensure that you've inserted colons, commas, and periods correctly.

6. Ensure that you've followed the correct protocol for recording online citations. For instance, in APA and *Chicago* styles, you must include the URL or DOI for any source you've retrieved off the internet.

LO 2, 3   13.11 REFERENCES AND BIBLIOGRAPHY ERRORS

The references list below contains a number of common errors. Though we have used the APA format to make corrections, many of the general principles for references lists are similar in MLA and *Chicago* style. There is a longer discussion of the differences between the formatting conventions both at the end of this chapter and in Chapter 12.

The title word, "References," should not be italicized or bold. It should be centred on the page, and it should be written in uppercase and lowercase letters. The second line needs to be indented. The word "accessed" needs to be replaced with "retrieved" and the date that it was retrieved is not necessary. Therefore it should read: "Retrieved from URL . . . (and include the link to the URL)."

Once again, the second line needs to be indented. The citation also needs to be moved since the letter *A* comes before *B*. Remember to always alphabetize your references.

References

Brown, J. (2008). Young drivers are more careless when drinking and driving. Accessed from www.dangersofdrinkinganddriving.com October 20, 2011.

Allen, G. (2009). The dangers of drinking and driving. In *Car and Truck Magazine, 30*, 2–10. www.drinkinganddriving.com retrieved on October 20, 2011.

Brown, John. (2011). Why do we still drink and drive? Random House Publishers: New York, New York.

www.drinkinganddriving.com: You cannot just list the URL without the title of the article. If there is no author, list the reference by the name of the article, e.g., Young drivers and the dangers of driving and driving (2010). Then list the URL. There is no need to record the date. The words "Retrieved from" go before the URL.

Brown, John: Once again the name is out of order. It's not alphabetized. Also, you do not need to list the complete first name of the author; use the initial only. Since there are now two Browns who are being cited, you have to put the oldest citation first, followed by the most recent. In this instance Brown (2008) would go before Brown (2011). Again, the second line needs to be indented. In addition, the name of the city in which the book was published comes before the name of the publisher. Include "Books" and "Press" but not "Publishers" or "Co.," etc., with the publisher's name. It should look like this: "New York, NY: Random House."

13.12 EDITING REFERENCES PAGES, WORKS CITED PAGES, AND BIBLIOGRAPHIES IN YOUR OWN ESSAY

LO 2, 3

Use the following chart to guide the way in which you edit References pages, Works Cited pages, and Bibliographies when you are editing your own essay.

Making Writing Decisions	About Proofreading the References Page, Works Cited Page, or Bibliography in Your Own Essay

What is the purpose of this writing decision?

Though there are subtle differences among the format conventions, the purpose of the References page, Works Cited page, and the Bibliography is the same: lists of references are intended to provide your reader with access to the works that you consulted while writing your essay.

What is the effect of this writing decision?

Again, despite the subtle differences in the format conventions, lists of references have a similar effect: (1) they acknowledge your debt to other sources, (2) they allow your reader to find the works you consulted and to access the ideas you've used in their original context, and (3) they provide your work with the authority of those sources you referenced. In addition, adhering to the conventions of a particular discipline enhances your own authority.

What considerations inform this decision?

Unfortunately, the conventions in formatting in any discipline tend to change fairly frequently. You ought to find access to an online formatting resource to ensure that the conventions you're following are current. Ultimately, however, you ought to remember this principle: you want to provide the information necessary for your reader to access the material you have cited and you want to do so in a manner that is consistent with the reader's expectations.

Suggested strategies for making this decision.

In the chart in Chapter 12 on editing for general correctness in format, we suggested that you identify five or six features of the format to focus on. This is also a useful strategy when editing the References page, Works Cited page, or Bibliography. By looking at the most important features of the list of references first, you will find the most common errors and the errors that are most obvious. These are the features that you want to learn to recognize easily. As always, you can turn to a reference text for the information that you need less frequently.

Questions to guide decision making in your own essay.

1. Turn to the list of references in the paper you are working on currently. What format are you meant to be using? Is it a References page? A Works Cited page? A Bibliography?
2. Have you checked the formatting style you're using (e.g., APA, MLA, *Chicago* style) for the specific protocols you are meant to follow?

3. Have you put the References, Works Cited, or Bibliography on a separate page?
4. Is the title of the References page centred? Remember that it should not be italicized, bold, underlined, or within quotation marks.
5. Have you listed the entries in alphabetical order by the author's last name?
6. Are the second and subsequent lines indented?
7. Have you double-spaced your entries?
8. Have you included the date of publication for each entry?
9. Have you entered the publication information (e.g., the name of the journal, the city and state or province in which the document was published, or the URL of a website)?

LO 2, 3 ## 13.13 EVALUATION CHECKLIST FOR EDITING

The following chart provides a series of general questions to use while editing your essay. Use the worksheet to ensure that you are editing in a systematic manner.

An Evaluation Worksheet to Guide Your Decision Making When Editing Your Own Essay
1. Turn to the essay on which you're currently working. Identify the section you are preparing to edit. In order to be successful in the process, you need to read actively.
2. Have you checked for missing words, homonyms, and spelling mistakes?
3. Read your sentences critically. Do they make sense? If not, have you checked the punctuation to ensure that it's correct? Have you used periods, question marks, commas, colons, and other punctuation marks correctly?
4. As you read the text, cross-check with your notes and reference materials to ensure that you have acknowledged anything that has come from an outside source. Have you cited ideas that have come from outside sources?
5. Have you clarified the formatting conventions you are meant to use (e.g., APA, MLA, *Chicago*)? Do you know whether you are meant to use in-text parenthetical citations? Footnotes? Endnotes?
6. Have you indentified direct quotations with quotation marks (for short quotations) or indented margins (for longer quotations), as prescribed by your research and citation style guide?
7. Have you determined whether you are meant to use a References page, a Works Cited page, or a Bibliography? Have you consulted your research and citation style guide to ensure that you're following the appropriate conventions?

13.14 PRACTICE ESSAY TO GUIDE EDITING IN APA

Read over the following paragraph checking for editing errors. See how many errors you can spot before moving on to compare your answers to those in the answer key. When you are editing, ask yourself both whether you can identify the specific errors and whether you understand why each is an error.

The use of firearms to participate in an annual fall ritual of killing wild animals is not without danger (Conrad Bright, 2008). Anyone who ventures out into the woods or fields has to take safety precautions. Jordan Call said that "one of the ways to safeguard not only yourself but other people who are hunting with you is to always make sure that you are wearing a safety vest." The vest that is recommended by the Government of Manitoba is one that is orange in colour (Government of Manitoba, 2009). Orange is bright enough that everyone who is hunting in a party can see one another (Government of Manitoba, 2009). The second thing one has to worry about is hunting on private property (Gordon, 1998, pp. 8). Some farmers get angry at the hunters who come on their lands without permission. The farmers are worried that the hunters will shoot domestic animals while they are looking for wild animals. Finally, when hunting in the fall, it is important that hunters be aware that the weather can get cold very quickly. They must be certain that they dress warmly and "have good footwear" (1999, Bob Donald, p. 667). As Donald says, they might have to outrun a bear when hunting for quail.

13.14.1 Answer Key to Editing Exercise

The use of firearms to participate in an annual fall ritual of killing wild animals is not without danger [1](Conrad Bright, 2008). Anyone who ventures out into the woods or fields has to take safety precautions. [2]Jordan Call said that "one of the ways to safeguard, not only yourself, but other people who are hunting with you, is to make sure that you are wearing a safety vest." The vest that is recommended by the province of Manitoba is one that is orange in colour [3](Gov't of Manitoba, 2009). Orange is bright enough that everyone hunting in a party can see one another (Government of Manitoba, 2009). The second thing one has to worry about is hunting on private property [4](Gordon, 1998, pp. 8). Some farmers get angry with hunters who come on their lands without permission. The farmers are worried that the hunters will shoot their domestic animals while looking for wild animals. Finally, when hunting in the fall, it is important that hunters be aware that the weather can get cold very quickly. They must be certain that they dress warmly and "have good footwear" [5](1999, Bob Donald, p. 667). As Donald says, they might have to outrun a bear when hunting for quail.

1 You do not need to include the first name of the author. You would need to cite the following: "(Bright, 2008)."

2 Again, you do not need to use the first name of the author, but you do need to include the year. So it should look like this: "Call (2007)."

3 Use the full name of the author, as shown in the following citation: "Government of Manitoba."

4 You do not need to have two p's to indicate one page.

5 The citation is all wrong. You want to use the last name only; there is no need to use the first name. The author's last name comes before the year of publication. The correct citation is: "(Donald, 1999, p. 667)."

How did you do? Did you catch all the errors in the paragraph? If you didn't, go back and review the ones you missed. Ask yourself what process you need to follow to catch those kinds of errors in the future.

13.15 PRACTICE ESSAY TO GUIDE EDITING IN MLA

Read over the following paragraph checking for editing errors. See how many errors you can spot before moving on to compare your answers to those in the answer key. When you are editing, ask yourself both whether you can identify the specific errors and whether you understand why each is an error.

> The use of firearms to participate in an annual fall ritual of killing wild animals is not without danger (Conrad Bright, 2008). Anyone who ventures out into the woods or fields has to take safety precautions. Jordan Call said that "one of the ways to safeguard not only yourself but other people who are hunting with you is to always make sure that you are wearing a safety vest." The vest that is recommended by the province of Manitoba is one that is orange in colour (Government of Manitoba, 2009). Orange is bright enough that everyone who is hunting in a party can see one another (Government of Manitoba, 2009). The second thing one has to worry about is hunting on private property (Gordon, 1998, pp. 8). Some farmers get angry at the hunters who come on their lands without permission. The farmers are worried that the hunters will shoot domestic animals while they are looking for wild animals. Finally, when hunting in the fall, it is important that hunters be aware that the weather can get cold very quickly. They must be certain that they dress warmly and "have good footwear" (1999, Bob Donald, p. 667). As Donald says, they might have to outrun a bear when hunting for quail.

13.15.1 Answer Key to Editing Exercise

> The use of firearms to participate, in an annual fall ritual, of killing animals, is not without danger [1](Conrad Bright, 2008). Anyone who ventures out into the woods or fields has to take safety precautions. Jordan Call [2]said "that one of the ways to safeguard, not only yourself, but other people who are hunting with you, is to always make sure that you are wearing a safety vest". The vest that is recommended by the [4]province of Manitoba is one that is orange in colour [3](Government of Manitoba, 2009). Orange is bright enough that everyone who is hunting with you can see you (Government of Manitoba, 2009). The second thing one has to worry about is hunting on private property [4](Gordon, 1998, pp. 8). Some farmers get angry with hunters who come on their lands without permission. The farmers are worried that the hunters will shoot their domestic animals while looking for wild animals. Finally, when hunting in the fall, it is important that hunters be aware that the weather can get cold very quickly. They must be certain that they dress warmly and "have good footwear" [5](1999, Bob Donald, p. 667). As Donald says, they might have to outrun a bear when hunting for quail.

1 You do not need to include the first name or the year in MLA. MLA style prefers that you use the author's name in your own sentence: "Bright writes that the use of firearms...." The year is not used in parenthetical citations; if the same author is cited for two or more works, include a shortened version of the titles. In a parenthetical citation, this would be "(Bright)."

2 State a source's opinions and conclusions in the present tense. This citation to quoted words needs a page reference: ". . . safety vest' (233)."

3 You do not need to include the year in MLA.

4 The page number follows the author's last name without a comma or the abbreviation for "page": "(Gordon 8)."

5 In this instance you just need the last name of the author and the page number, so: "(Donald 667)."

13.16 PRACTICE ESSAY TO GUIDE EDITING IN *CHICAGO* STYLE

Read over the following paragraph checking for editing errors. See how many errors you can spot before moving on to compare your answers to those in the answer key that follows. When you're editing, ask yourself both whether you can identify the specific errors and whether you understand why each is an error.

The use of firearms to participate in an annual fall ritual of killing wild animals is not without danger (Conrad Bright, 2008). Anyone who ventures out into the woods or fields has to take safety precautions. Jordan Call said that "one of the ways to safeguard not only yourself but other people who are hunting with you is to always make sure that you are wearing a safety vest." The vest that is recommended by the Government of Manitoba is one that is orange in colour (*Government of Manitoba*, 2009). Orange is bright enough that everyone who is hunting in a party can see one another (*Government of Manitoba*, 2009). The second thing one has to worry about is hunting on private property (Gordon, 1998, pp. 8). Some farmers get angry at the hunters who come on their lands without permission. The farmers are worried that the hunters will shoot domestic animals while they are looking for wild animals. Finally, when hunting in the fall, it is important that hunters be aware that the weather can get cold very quickly. They must be certain that they dress warmly and "have good footwear" (1999, Bob Donald, p. 667). As Donald says, they might have to outrun a bear when hunting for quail.

13.16.1 Answer Key to Editing Exercise

The use of firearms to participate, in an annual fall ritual, of killing wild animals, is not without danger [1](Conrad Bright, 2008). Anyone who ventures out into the woods or fields has to take safety precautions. Jordan Call [2]said that "one of the ways to safeguard, not only yourself, but other people who are hunting with you, is to always make sure that you are wearing a safety vest." The vest that is recommended by the province of Manitoba is one that is orange in colour [3](*Government of Manitoba,* 2009). Orange is bright enough that everyone who is hunting in a party can see one another (*Government of Manitoba,* 2009). The second thing one has to worry about is hunting on private property [4](Gordon, 1998, pp. 8). Some farmers get mad at hunters who come on their lands without permission. The farmers are worried that the hunters will shoot their domestic animals while looking for wild animals. Finally, when hunting in the fall, it is important that hunters be aware that the weather can get cold very quickly. They must be certain that they dress warmly and "have good footwear" [5](1999, Bob Donald, p. 667). As Donald says, they might have to outrun a bear when hunting for quail.

1. Bright, Conrad. "Firearm Safety" Journal of Hunter's Guidebook 2.1 (2008): 45–67.

2. Call, Jordan. "Shooting Safely" Journal of Wildlife 4.5 (2012): 56–87.

3. Government of Manitoba Journal of Archives 2009. Winnipeg, MB.

4. Gordon, Gregory. "Privacy Laws When Hunting" Journal of the Laws of Canada 5.2 (1998): 8.

5. Donald, Bob. "Dressing for Hunting" The Wildlife Federation 6.1 (1999): 667.

13.17 CONCLUSION

You've worked hard on your essay, carefully crafting your argument, explaining and defending your ideas, artfully weaving in supporting ideas from respected reference documents. You have every reason to be proud of yourself. Before you submit the document, however, you need to give it every chance to succeed. Editing ensures that you're tailoring the essay to meet the expectations of your reader.

In this chapter, we've introduced you to a number of strategies for editing. For most writers, developing a systematic approach will make the process of editing more effective. By identifying specific sections on which to work, and the strategies that are applicable to those sections, you are better able to concentrate on the process. Similarly, by identifying the key features of both in-text citation and the list of references, you are more likely to focus on matters of substance.

MyCompLab®

How Do I Get a Better Grade?

Go to MyCompLab for additional help with your grammar, writing, and research skills. You will have access to a variety of exercises, instruction, and videos that will help you improve your basic skills and help you get a better grade.

✓• Practice   **Peer-Evaluation Worksheet for Editing**

Title of the Essay _____

Draft of Essay Submitted By: _____

Peer Evaluator: _____

Are there words that are consistently misspelled in the essay?

_____

_____

Are there problems in sentence structure that persist throughout the essay?

_____

_____

Are there particular errors in punctuation that persist throughout the essay?

_____

_____

_____

Is the tense appropriate to the format the writer is using and is it consistent throughout the essay (i.e., does the tense shift back and forth in the essay)?

_____

_____

_____

Has the writer used the same words repeatedly throughout the essay? If so, which words?

_____

_____

_____

Has the author chosen words that convey the meaning of ideas clearly? What words are ambiguous (not clear)?

_____

_____

_____

Has the writer followed the assigned formatting style for the essay?

_____

_____

_____

What aspects of the formatting need to be changed to ensure that the essay adheres to the formatting style?

_____

_____

_____

Has the writer indented the first sentence of each paragraph?

_____

_____

_____

(*continued*)

(continued)

Is the essay double-spaced?

_____

_____

_____

Do the in-text citations adhere to the required format? If not, how should they be changed?

_____

_____

_____

Is the title page formatted correctly? Should the essay have running heads? Are the page numbers formatted correctly?

_____

_____

_____

Is the references page correct? Have the authors been listed alphabetically by the last name of the first author?

_____

_____

_____

What further information, if any, do you think should be brought to the attention of the writer?

_____

_____

_____

Templates for Common Academic Writing Styles

14.1   INTRODUCTION

One of the more common difficulties for novice writers is in managing the difference between the conventions of writing in one course and the conventions of writing in another. Unfortunately for novice writers, it seems that learning to write academic papers in colleges and universities is a two-step process: (1) writers must first acquire the general skills necessary to craft a coherent essay, and (2) they must then learn to adapt to the specific conventions of each particular discipline. In this chapter, we provide writing templates for some of the more common essay styles you will encounter in your courses. Because the differences between essay styles are more profound than they sometimes appear, we also provide you with writing strategies for each major section of the respective essay, identifying the ways in which those sections might be different from the generic academic essay we discussed earlier in this text. Regardless of the essay style, of course, you'll use a similar *process* of writing (i.e., you will go through the stages of planning, writing, and revising). In this chapter, you will learn to tailor your understanding of the generic essay to a specific writing style that is appropriate to the writing circumstances.

LO 1 14.2   UNDERSTANDING THE DIFFERENCE BETWEEN THE PRACTICE OF THE NOVICE WRITER AND THE PRACTICE OF THE EXPERIENCED WRITER

In this particular instance, the difference between the novice and the experienced writer becomes a little more complicated. While it's true that there continue to be differences between the two even as writers begin to write across the curriculum (i.e., even when writers begin to write in a field in which they are unfamiliar), it is also true that each of us becomes a novice again when we venture into an unfamiliar writing environment. There is always a period of adjustment as we learn to adapt to new writing purposes, new audiences, and new reader expectations. As is usually the case, however, there are differences in the way that novice writers and experienced writers make those adjustments. In the following chart, we've noted that novice writers who find themselves in unfamiliar writing situations *focus on error avoidance rather than meaning; begin writing without planning, and edit, if at all, for grammatical errors; and focus on "knowledge telling" (i.e., relating all knowledge they have and can find on a topic rather than exercising critical judgment to determine relevance).* Experienced writers, on the other hand, *focus on developing or refining meaning; invest time and energy in planning and reviewing; and organize, and reorganize, essay structure to allow individual ideas to serve the overall purpose of the essay.*

Novice Writers	Experienced Writers
■ Require thought for procedural, or "mechanical," writing functions.	■ Have, to a significant degree, automated procedural functions.
■ *Focus on error avoidance rather than meaning.*	■ *Focus on developing or refining meaning.*
■ *Begin writing without planning, and edit, if at all, for grammatical errors.*	■ *Invest time and energy in planning and reviewing.*
■ *Focus on "knowledge telling" (i.e., relating all the information they have and can find on a topic, rather than exercising critical judgment to determine relevance).*	■ *Organize, and reorganize, essay structure to allow individual ideas to serve the overall purpose of the essay.*

The principal difference between novice and experienced writers is that experienced writers continue to operate by focusing on the development of meaning. While their procedural knowledge (i.e., knowledge of the rules of writing) may not provide its usual advantage in unfamiliar disciplines, their knowledge of structure and coherence do. Experienced writers tend to apply many of the strategies they know (e.g., strategies for determining purpose and audience, and strategies for developing effective patterns of organization) in the new situation. In the planning stage, they may reflect on important differences between the new environment and the one they know but, having made adjustments for those differences, they write for meaning. They know that they will later have to revise and edit to ensure conformity with the expectations of the readers in each of the different subject areas.

In many cases, novice writers also return to the practices they know when they find themselves in unfamiliar writing situations. Their difficulty is that the practices are not very effective. Novices generally don't plan well (in part, because they don't reflect on the differences in purpose and audience in the new environment) and they usually return to the practice of *knowledge telling*, hoping perhaps that information might carry their essays. Sadly, it won't. What might work, on the other hand, is a return to principles that have guided us in this text: an understanding of the goal you're trying to achieve (i.e., one of the fundamental principles of metacognition) and a reflection on the decisions that will allow you to achieve that goal.

14.3 RESEARCH ESSAYS ACROSS THE CURRICULUM

LO 2, 3

Why do instructors assign research essays in courses that don't usually include writing assignments? You're not the first student to ask that question and you won't be the last. However much you may cling to the suspicion that it's a conspiracy to make your life miserable, there may be a handful of competing explanations. Instructors assign essays for a variety of reasons, including:

- Writing assignments foster critical thinking about, and deeper understanding of, the various concepts students are studying in the courses. When students write essays about course content, they are more likely to engage with the material actively. This leads to a greater degree of understanding of the content.
- Research for writing assignments provides students with the opportunity to explore different views on a particular subject and come to their own conclusions on the basis of the evidence presented in the articles or textbooks they read.
- Writing assignments provide students with the opportunity to research a project in their own way.
- Writing assignments that require research of some kind offer students the opportunity to become familiar with the most important journals in the field. Knowledge of the research journals also provides students with an

understanding of research methodologies typically used in the area and the writing conventions used in each discipline.

- Writing assignments give students both experience in writing in different disciplines and the opportunity to make informed decisions about the possibility of conducting further study in those areas.

- Writing assignments help students to develop their writing skills. Students generally become better readers, thinkers, and learners in courses in which they've had the opportunity to explore ideas through writing.

Writing to learn is widely recognized as an effective educational strategy and writing about course content allows you to engage with the material in a deeper and more critical way. It also helps you to develop a personal understanding of the material that you're studying.

LO 4   14.4   USING THE IDDL MODEL TO ORGANIZE ESSAYS IN DIFFERENT DISCIPLINES

In Chapter 1, we discussed the difficulties that some students experience in adjusting to the different rules that apply to written assignments in different disciplines. Those difficulties reflect a real challenge. There are, however, strategies that might allow you to manage the problem to some degree. Despite the differences that exist between the disciplines, there are certain similarities as well. Regardless of the discipline in which you're writing, the process of writing an essay will generally reflect many of the principles we have already discussed. You will write with a clear purpose, you will identify your audience, and you will offer some kind of evidence to establish the validity of your claims. You will also write with an understanding that you're leading your reader from the beginning of the written work to the end, making logical connections between the various elements.

In this chapter, we provide instruction that will help you adapt the IDDL writing model to make essay writing easier in the different categories of academic disciplines you may face. The benefit of using a general writing strategy like the IDDL model is that, once you develop some proficiency in using it, you will find that the processes of planning and organizing become automatized to some degree. In turn, this allows you to devote more of your working memory to critically analyzing the content you're investigating. By using the model as a general guide to draft your essays, you may also begin to internalize some of the embedded questions that guide your decision making in the writing process.

LO 4   14.5   USING TEMPLATES

One of the criticisms of templates, or writing models, is that they have the potential to reduce complex questions to simplistic formulas. That doesn't have to be the case. Templates are not meant to be fill-in-the-blank formats. They are meant to provide you with guidelines for preparing essays in the different discourse communities you will encounter. By attending to the specific features that characterize essays in the respective discipline, and by addressing the questions that each template provides, you should find it easier to concentrate on the content of the essays rather than the form. Keep in mind, however, that these are examples only. Your instructor may have more specific guidelines that he or she wants you to adhere to.

The advantage of templates, particularly for undergraduate students in college and university, is that they permit students to move from one discourse community to another relatively easily. The templates offer a general overview of the writing conventions that the individual disciplines follow. Though the templates can't write the essay for you, or even anticipate all the challenges you might meet in your writing process, they do allow you to more easily recognize the various elements that are generally required in the respective disciplines. These should prove useful in helping you adapt to the different discourses that you will be required to write in. It's important to remember, however, that a template is not a blueprint. It's only a guide.

14.6   THE TEMPLATE DEBATE   LO 4

Most students arrive at college or university with some template experience. The five-paragraph essay, a model that is often used in high school instruction, is a template. That template directs students to organize their essays into five units (i.e., introduction, body paragraph 1, body paragraph 2, body paragraph 3, and conclusion). According to many of its critics, structured models (like the five-paragraph essay) instruct students in the shape of the finished product, providing them with a sense of what they are meant to produce, but also lead them to believe that they can simply fill in the blanks and still produce good writing. In short, according to these critics, templates result in unimaginative writers who fail to explore ideas fully or to question their own assumptions and beliefs.

On the other hand, there are many who argue that, because templates provide students with a quick guide to form and format, they help students' explorations of ideas. Who is right? Probably a little bit of column A and a little bit of column B. Many of us find it useful to see formatting conventions represented visually, complete with embedded questions that direct our attention to important writing decisions. At the very least, the templates that follow will allow you to quickly identify the significant differences between the writing styles that characterize different disciplines.

14.7   GENERIC ESSAY FORM   LO 2, 3, 4
AND DISCIPLINE-SPECIFIC
WRITING STYLES

Throughout this text, we use a relatively generic model for argumentative essays. As we explained previously, the IDDL model is meant to allow you to concentrate on developing your ideas without simultaneously having to attend to concerns about structure and coherence. The model works by providing a visual representation of the relationship between the various parts of the essay and the larger structure—focusing on the logical connection between ideas—and by embedding questions that guide you to think critically about both content and form.

Though some writing assignments may require you to write in a genre other than the argumentative essay, most research into academic writing at colleges and universities suggests that argumentation, implicitly at least, is the most common organizing principle for essays. However much essays in the different disciplines may differ, they generally share that principle.

14.7.1 Characteristics of the Different Writing Styles

Discipline	Epistemological Assumptions	Typical Type of Evidence Required	Typical Formatting Conventions
Humanities in general (e.g., English, philosophy)	The world can be known objectively and subjectively. There is generally an expectation that writers will explore a theme or idea using reason, but, in some cases, interpretations of texts, philosophical positions, or phenomena can be arrived at subjectively.	Evidence will derive from journal articles or books that provide in-depth research into a topic or from the text. The articles you choose should be written by scholars who are experts in the area you're researching.	MLA (Modern Language Association)
Humanities—history	The study of history is informed with two assumptions that, at first glance, are diametrically opposed: the evidence for historical events is objectively verifiable, but the interpretation of that evidence is, to some degree at least, subjective.	History papers usually derive their evidence from fact-based papers, articles, and books. The important thing to remember is that each paper, article, or book may be biased by the author's personal point of view, thereby requiring a careful reading of more than one source on the topic.	*Chicago*
Social sciences (e.g., psychology, sociology)	In the social sciences, research might be undertaken using either objective or subjective methodologies, but essays in these fields are meant to reflect an objective analysis of evidence.	When writing a social science paper, you will generally be looking for evidence from articles in academic journals. These articles will usually cite either quantitative or qualitative studies.	APA (American Psychological Association)
Natural sciences (e.g., biology, physics)	In the natural sciences, writing is expected to reflect an objective stance.	For the most part you will use quantitative evidence. This means you will stick to factual information. The natural science essay is not a place to give your personal opinion.	CSE (Council of Biology Editors), AMA (American Medical Association), or Harvard Method. Occasionally, some instructors will ask that you use APA.

14.8　WRITING AN ESSAY IN THE HUMANITIES (E.G., ENGLISH, PHILOSOPHY)

LO 2, 3, 4

Writing in the humanities requires a curious balance of subjectivity and objectivity. However deeply you might believe that analysis of a text or philosophical question are simply a matter of opinion, successful essays in the humanities generally display both insightful analysis of a particular text or question and evidence in support of that position. In some disciplines in the humanities, writers might be expected to make their arguments more artfully, and less explicitly, than the case would be in other disciplines, but the underlying structure of the essay is nonetheless logical.

Essays in the humanities are generally intended to provide an opportunity for you to demonstrate your ability to analyze arguments, events, or texts critically, and to explain your analysis clearly. It's important, therefore, that you shake off that widely held suspicion that the best grades go to long, rambling essays that are cluttered with polysyllabic and incoherent rants, and instead embrace this liberating axiom: however complex a question might be in the humanities, your analysis of it ought to be clear, coherent, and relevant. It is important to note that, though essays in the humanities might occasionally employ evidence that appears subjective (e.g., the writer's own analysis of a theory, phenomenon, or text), the writer is still obliged to demonstrate that that evidence is compelling and appropriate. For instance, in the case of an English paper that is exploring the symbolic use of flowers in the poetry of Emily Dickinson, it's not enough to say that the symbols are there: you need to provide examples that demonstrate the strength of your claim.

14.8.1　Specific Features of Essays in the Humanities

The principal characteristic that distinguishes essays in the humanities from essays in the sciences or social sciences is the way in which writers from different disciplines approach the question they are addressing. In the humanities, writers tend to focus on *interpreting* or *understanding* a social, aesthetic, or historical phenomenon. The chart below identifies some of the general characteristics of academic writing in the humanities.

Ways in Which an Essay in the Humanities Corresponds to the Generic Essay Model	Ways in Which an Essay in the Humanities Might Differ from the Generic Essay Model
Like other academic essays, essays in the humanities are generally guided, implicitly or explicitly, by logic.	In some disciplines in the humanities, the reasoning of an essay may be subtle and implicit. The underlying argument of an essay, however, generally reflects a logical pattern of ideas.

(*continued*)

(continued)

Assertions are supported by evidence.	The evidence used in essays in the humanities tends be textual (i.e., drawn from the text you're analyzing), rely on reference to authority (i.e., drawn from the work of scholars), or factual (i.e., a matter of history or public record).
Introduction of supporting evidence follows a specific convention.	In the humanities, evidence is generally woven into the text, serving the argument without bringing attention to itself. All ideas that do not originate with the writer of the essay are identified with textual citations.
Formatting corresponds to a specific format convention.	Most writers in the humanities use MLA, APA, or *Chicago* formatting conventions for academic essays.

14.8.2 Writing a Paper in the Humanities

The charts below identify a process for writing essays in the humanities. The first chart identifies some of the things you need to consider prior to beginning the essay.

Things to Think about before Beginning to Write Your Paper in the Humanities
■ Analyze the assignment carefully. Whatever you believe you already know about writing essays, and whatever we have suggested in this text, you are writing first for a specific audience. Understand what is expected of you and ensure, even in the planning stage, that you are meeting that expectation. Review the requirements for the essay. If you don't understand those requirements, schedule an appointment with your instructor to ask.
■ Articulate a provisional thesis statement and draft a tentative outline using the IDDL model. For many novice writers, essays in the humanities pose a greater risk of aimless meandering than other essays.
■ Use the tentative outline to focus your research. Determine the specific questions that need to be answered.
■ Use the questions to identify the resources you will need. Be thorough but selective. Though it is important to consult the resources necessary to develop a balanced view of the question you're exploring, it's also important to limit your search to materials that are relevant.
■ If your research causes you to reconsider specific aspects of your provisional thesis or outline, revise the thesis or outline to correspond to your new understanding. Remember that both the thesis and the outline ought to be specific enough to guide you through the writing process.

You can use the IDDL model to generate the structure of an essay in the humanities. It's important, however, that your essay reflect the features that characterize writing in these fields. Use the chart below to guide you.

Introduction
Structure your introduction around a clear and specific thesis statement, remembering that the purpose of the introduction is to guide your reader to, and through, the essay. One of the most common problems for novice writers in the humanities is a lack of focus. While you may have been taught to begin your essay with an interesting anecdote or wide-ranging observation about the world in general, academic writing is generally characterized by precision. You want to orient your reader to your essay and provide enough information to allow him or her to anticipate the direction the essay will take.

Questions to Guide Composition:

- Have you organized your essay around a clear and specific thesis statement?
- Have you limited the scope of the essay?
- Have you clearly identified the principal themes around which you will structure the essay?

Body of the Essay

The body of the essay is where you will expand upon the key themes and arguments that you established in the introduction, supporting them with relevant evidence. These themes will be directly related to the questions you're exploring. The number of ideas you discuss depends on the length of the essay you're writing, and the number of paragraphs you include depends on the number of ideas you wish to explore. Organize key ideas into discrete paragraphs, ensuring that each paragraph is governed by a single controlling idea.

Questions to Guide Composition:

- Have you organized the important themes of the essay into discrete units (i.e., either paragraphs or a series of related paragraphs)?
- Are the paragraphs linked by a single controlling idea?
- Is the order of the paragraphs logical? Does the order permit the reader to follow your chain of thought?
- Do the paragraphs, or groups of paragraphs, link back to the controlling thesis of the essay?

Supporting Evidence

In the humanities, your argument might be supported by reference to scholarly articles or other authoritative sources, or to the text itself. Speaking generally about vague ideas or drawing broad conclusions without any supporting evidence is not enough. Analysis in the humanities is not merely a matter of opinion, but rather a carefully argued interpretation that is justified by reference to evidence.

Questions to Guide Composition:

- Have you provided evidence to support the assertions you've made?
- Have you documented the evidence you've used?

Conclusion

Your conclusion should draw the elements of the essay together to demonstrate the validity of your position. The nature of the subject matter in essays in the humanities sometimes leads writers to indulge in rhetorical excess, overstating the significance of the case that has been made. Fight that temptation. Your purpose is to summarize the case you've made in the essay.

Questions to Guide Composition:

- Have you introduced new ideas in the conclusion? If so, you ought to explore those ideas prior to the conclusion or edit them out of the essay.
- Have you provided a clear synopsis of the argument you've made? Have you demonstrated the way in which the individual elements of the essay are meant to serve the overall purpose of the essay?

14.8.3 Using the IDDL Model in the Humanities

In the following example, we've provided a topic and modelled the way you would use the IDDL model to organize your essay. Notice the way in which the thesis statement provides the initial guidelines for structuring your essay.

Topic: Discuss the Traditional Assessment of Hamlet as an Indecisive Youth Whose Inability to Act Results in Tragedy

Thesis Statement: Though Hamlet has often been regarded as the author of his own misfortune, indecisive in a time that demands action, his hesitation may in fact reflect the triumph of reason over passion. Throughout Shakespeare's play, Hamlet demonstrates distaste for ungoverned passion, a predisposition for critical inquiry, and the ability to act when the time is right.

- ■ **Is the thesis clear?**
- ■ **Is it focused?**
- ■ **Is it measurable?**

Subthesis 1: Hamlet's preference for reason over passion is demonstrated by his general distaste for passion.

- ■ **What is the relationship to the main thesis?**
  - • This is the first of the principal claims of the main thesis.
- ■ **What information is needed to explore or substantiate the claim of subthesis 1?**
  - • In this section of the essay, you will need to find textual evidence supporting the claim that Hamlet's hesitation reflects his disdain for unbridled passion.
  - • You will generally use quotations from the text to establish the validity of the argument.
    - • Evidence: For instance, you might cite the scene in which Hamlet mocks his mother for her unseemly haste in remarrying.
    - • Evidence: You also might cite his treatment of Ophelia, whose principal failing appears to be her love for him.
    - • Evidence: You might choose to find evidence of Hamlet's own self-deprecation, moments at which he wonders whether he is only pretending to be reasonable to hide his cowardice.
  - • Having gathered the evidence you need, you would cite it, explain it, and organize it around the subthesis.

Subthesis 2: Hamlet's preference for reason over passion is demonstrated by his predisposition to critical inquiry.

- ■ **What is the relationship to the main thesis?**
  - • This is the second of the principal claims of the main thesis.
- ■ **What information is needed to explore or substantiate the claim of subthesis 2?**
  - • In this section of the essay, you will need to find textual evidence supporting the claim that Hamlet's hesitation reflects his predisposition for critical inquiry.
  - • You will generally use quotations from the text to establish the validity of this aspect of the argument.
    - • Evidence: In support of this subthesis, you might cite the scene in which Hamlet demonstrates his philosophical nature while speaking with his friend Horatio.
    - • Evidence: You also might cite the play Hamlet arranges in which he stages a recreation of the murder of his father to determine whether his treacherous uncle might betray himself by reacting.
    - • Evidence: You might choose textual evidence that demonstrates the dispassionate way in which Hamlet sends Rosencrantz and Guildenstern to their deaths for betraying him
  - • Having gathered the evidence you need, you would cite it, explain it, and organize it around the subthesis.

Subthesis 3: Hamlet's preference for reason over passion is demonstrated by his willingness to act when circumstances declare action to be appropriate.

- ■ **What is the relationship to the main thesis?**
  - • This is the third of the principal claims of the main thesis.

■ **What information is needed to explore or substantiate the claim of subthesis 3?**
- In this section of the essay, you will need to find textual evidence supporting the claim that Hamlet's hesitation reflects his willingness to act when it's reasonable to do so.
- You will generally use quotations from the text to establish the validity of this aspect of the argument.
  - Evidence: In support of this subthesis, you might note that Hamlet has no difficulty in slaying the man behind the drape (Polonius) when he believes he has been spied upon.
  - Evidence: You could also cite the duel with Laertes, when Hamlet, however reluctantly, kills the man in self-defence.
  - Evidence: You might choose evidence from Act V, when Hamlet, finally convinced of the justice of his position, kills Claudius in an act of vengeance.
- Having gathered the evidence you need, you would cite it, explain it, and organize it around the subthesis.

Counter-argument:
■ **Why would a reasonable person disagree with the proposition that Hamlet is more rational than indecisive?**
- Despite his original misgivings about the death of his father, Hamlet is not persuaded to act until the ghost of his dead father tells him to do so. That's right. The champion of reason and caution is acting on the word of a ghost.
  - Evidence: You would probably refer to the scene in which Hamlet talks to a dead man.

Conclusion:
Traditional criticism of Shakespeare's character Hamlet has generally suggested that the young Dane is a victim of his own indecision. Such a reading requires accepting that one ought to go about murdering relatives on the word of a ghost. If, on the contrary, one believes that it is prudent to verify the ghost's claims with some sort of confirming evidence, it becomes easier to accept that Hamlet's greatest shortcoming is the volume of evidence he requires. Otherwise, his distaste for ungoverned passion, predisposition to critical inquiry, and ability to act when the time is right recommends him as a role model for the youth of the present day.

14.9 WRITING A PAPER IN THE SOCIAL SCIENCES (E.G., PSYCHOLOGY, SOCIOLOGY)

LO 2, 3, 4

Though the process of writing an essay in the social sciences is not significantly different from the process of writing an academic essay in the humanities (i.e., writers go through the same process of planning, writing, and revising), there are some fundamental differences in epistemology (or study of knowledge). In the social sciences, writers are generally presumed to be presenting a position on the basis of objectively verifiable evidence. Research papers in the social sciences are designed to allow you to demonstrate that you can explore the existing research literature, critically examining the best sources available, and arrive at a conclusion that is supported by scientific evidence. Essays in the social sciences are generally expected to be more objective in process and tone, and your personal experience with a phenomenon is usually not relevant to the discussion. The format for research papers in the social sciences reflects this epistemological position: in the formatting convention of choice for the social sciences (i.e., APA), you generally allow your evidence to testify for you (though you still have an obligation to contextualize, and explain the significance of, the evidence) and essays are generally written in third person (e.g., he, she, they). Reports of one's own research should be written in first person. By foregrounding the evidence, you are implicitly arguing that your conclusion is not a matter of interpretation but a matter of fact.

An essay written in the social sciences also requires you to analyze the evidence you're putting forward. It's not enough to merely summarize the information you find in other sources. If you're writing a social science paper, you have to be able to think critically about the information you're presenting. Have you demonstrated that the evidence is representative of the prevailing thought in the field? Does an article represent a position that is at odds with the orthodox view? You also have to ensure that the information is relevant to the argument you're making. One of the common failings of novice writers is the attempt to make evidence fit the thesis rather than basing conclusions on the evidence they find.

14.9.1   Specific Features of Essays in the Social Sciences

The following chart identifies some of the specific characteristics of essays in the social sciences. Of particular importance to novice writers is the expectation that all assertions will be supported by reference to authority.

Ways in Which a Social Sciences Essay Corresponds to the Generic Essay Model	Ways in Which a Social Sciences Essay Differs from the Generic Essay Model
Essays in the social sciences are generally guided, implicitly or explicitly, by logic.	The essay format normally used in the social sciences (i.e., APA) prescribes that information be organized in a particular way. Therefore, the structure of the essay is predetermined. Within each of the sections, however, the organization of ideas and information ought to be governed by logic.
Assertions are supported by evidence.	In social sciences, all assertions and claims are underwritten by reference to evidence in the research literature.
Introduction of supporting evidence follows specific convention.	In the social sciences, evidence is usually explored generally in a literature review, then introduced as necessary to support assertions and identified with citations.
Formatting corresponds to a specific format convention.	It is almost always the case that writers in the social sciences will use APA.

14.9.2 Writing a Paper in the Social Sciences

The following charts identify a process for writing essays in the social sciences. The first chart identifies some of the features of essay writing in the social sciences that you should consider prior to beginning the essay.

Things to Think about before Beginning to Write Your Social Sciences Paper
■ As we suggested in the introduction to writing papers in the humanities, you should analyze the assignment carefully. Disciplines in the social sciences are rarely asking that you provide an opinion on a phenomenon. In most cases, you will be writing a research paper. Review the requirements for the essay. If you don't understand those requirements, schedule an appointment with your instructor to ask.
■ Articulate a provisional thesis statement. The format of research papers in the social sciences is usually prescribed by the instructor and/or the conventions of APA. The IDDL writing model can still be helpful, however, in organizing an outline for your essay. It's important to remember that information is being gathered for a purpose. It's not uncommon for students who are writing in the social sciences to list endless pages of quotations and paraphrases without ever explaining the significance of the information.
■ Use the tentative outline to focus your research. Determine the specific questions that need to be answered.
■ Use the questions to identify the resources you will need. Be thorough but selective. Though it is important to consult the resources necessary to develop a balanced view of the question you are exploring, it's also important to limit your search to materials that are relevant.
■ Identify the resources that you need. Use your library portal to access academic psychology databases such as PSYCHNET or PSYCHInfo. You can also use Google Scholar. These sites provide access to authoritative articles and/or abstracts published in peer-reviewed journals.
■ Highlight pertinent sections or phrases in the articles, colour-coding them to correspond with the principal themes of your essay. This will make it easier to transfer the information when you're writing the essay.
■ Once you're finished with the research, revise your outline. The outline will provide structure to the essay. It will also ensure that the content you develop is relevant to your topic.

When writing an essay in the social sciences, it's important to remember that you will argue from the evidence, clearly demonstrating that the claims you make are supported by research. It's necessary, therefore, that your writing be sufficiently precise that the relationship between the claims you make and the evidence that supports those claims is clear and unambiguous.

Introduction
The introduction needs to articulate the thesis of your essay, clearly identifying its scope and significance. Resist the temptation to enliven the introduction with interesting anecdotes or thought-provoking quotations.

(continued)

(*continued*)

Questions to Guide Composition:

- Have you organized your essay around a clear and specific thesis?
- Have you limited the scope of the essay?
- Have you identified the key ideas that you will explore in the essay?

Research Question

After you have identified your topic area, state your research question explicitly. Since you are likely writing an essay that is making an argument on the basis of a literature review (as distinct from an essay that is reporting original research), your research question is one that will be answered in your paper.

Questions to Guide Composition:

- Have you identified a research question?
- Is the question expressed in a clear and unambiguous manner?
- Is the question measurable?

Literature Review

The literature that you will use in your paper should provide insight into the topic or research question that you've identified. When writing the literature review you will need to provide a critical analysis of the current academic literature in the field. There are two pitfalls to avoid: (1) the temptation to argue on the basis of opinion or anecdote rather than evidence, and (2) the temptation to list information without identifying its significance.

Questions to Guide Composition:

- Have you organized the literature review coherently? Are the articles that are linked thematically discussed in a common section of the review?
- Are the various sections of the review organized logically? Does the order in which the information is presented make sense?
- Have you provided analysis and discussion of the articles you've listed?

Discussion

The discussion section of a social sciences essay provides an opportunity for critical analysis of the ideas that were introduced in the literature review. This is also the point at which you will identify the relevance of the studies to the research question.

Questions to Guide Composition:

- Does your discussion follow the logic of your argument?
- Have you demonstrated the significance of the literature you reviewed?
- Has the evidence you provided clearly addressed your research question?

Conclusion

The conclusion in a social sciences essay will generally provide a brief review of the essay's main themes, with a critical discussion of the relative merits of competing ideas and theories. Though it's not necessary to impose greater certainty than the evidence warrants, the conclusion should ensure that the reader is not left with unanswered questions.

Questions to Guide Composition:

- Has the conclusion answered the questions raised in the essay?
- Have you provided a clear and succinct encapsulation of your position?
- Have you limited your conclusion to that which was demonstrated by the evidence you provided?
- Have you identified the significance of your argument?

14.9.3 Using the IDDL Model in the Social Sciences

In the example below, we've provided a topic and modelled the way in which you could use the IDDL model to organize your essay. Notice how the provisional thesis statement serves to provide a guiding structure for the essay.

Topic: What Is the Impact of the Media on Human Behaviour?

Thesis Statement: Recent studies appear to confirm Marshall McLuhan's insight that individuals are formed by the media rather than informed by it. These studies suggest that individuals adopt behaviours that they would otherwise avoid because mass media destabilizes the normal sense of self, normalizes new exotic behaviours, and recasts those behaviours as socially desirable rather than anti-social.
- ■ **Is the thesis clear?**
- ■ **Is it focused?**
- ■ **Is it measurable?**

Subthesis 1: Individuals adopt behaviours that they would otherwise avoid because mass media destabilizes the normal sense of self.
- ■ **What is the relationship to the main thesis?**
  - • This is the first of the principal claims of the main thesis.
- ■ **What information is needed to explore or substantiate the claim of subthesis 1?**
  - • In this section of the essay you will need to find studies verifying that, because of the influence of mass media, individuals are more inclined to adopt behaviours that they would otherwise avoid.
  - • You will generally use studies from social science journals to establish the validity of the argument.
    - • Evidence: For instance, you might cite a study that demonstrates the effect that mass media has on self-identity.
    - • Evidence: You might find a study that demonstrates that certain dissociative disorders (psychological conditions in which individuals respond to crisis by creating a new identity) are more common among those who have greater exposure to the media.
  - • Having gathered the evidence you need, you would cite it, explain it, and organize it around the subthesis.

Subthesis 2: Individuals adopt behaviours they would otherwise avoid because mass media normalizes new exotic behaviours.
- ■ **What is the relationship to the main thesis?**
  - • This is the second of the principal claims of the main thesis.
- ■ **What information is needed to explore or substantiate the claim of subthesis 2?**
  - • In this section of the essay you will need to find studies verifying that, because mass media normalizes new exotic behaviours, individuals adopt behaviours they would otherwise avoid.
  - • You will generally use studies from social science journals to establish the validity of the argument.
    - • Evidence: You might cite a study that demonstrates the effect mass media has on a community's tolerance for unusual behaviour.
    - • Evidence: You might look for studies that demonstrate that there is an increase in high-risk sports following their repeated appearance on television programs.
  - • Having gathered the evidence you need, you would cite it, explain it, and organize it around the subthesis.

(*continued*)

(*continued*)

Subthesis 3: Individuals adopt behaviours they would otherwise avoid because mass media recasts these behaviours as socially desirable rather than anti-social.
- ■ **What is the relationship to the main thesis?**
  - • This is the third of the principal claims of the main thesis.
- ■ **What information is needed to explore or substantiate the claim of subthesis 3?**
  - • In this section of the essay, you will need to find studies verifying that individuals adopt behaviours they would otherwise avoid because mass media normalizes new exotic behaviours.
  - • You will generally use studies from social science journals to establish the validity of the argument.
    - • Evidence: You might cite studies identifying changes in attitude regarding a behaviour following its adoption by celebrities.
    - • Evidence: You might look for studies demonstrating a change in social mores that is associated with television programs depicting a lax moral code.
  - • Having gathered the evidence you need, you would cite it, explain it, and organize it around the subthesis.

Counter-argument:
- ■ Why would a reasonable person disagree with the proposition that individuals adopt behaviours that they would otherwise avoid because mass media destabilizes the normal sense of self, normalizes new exotic behaviours, and recasts those behaviours as socially desirable rather than anti-social?
  - • There appear to be limits to the effect that mass media will have on the behaviour of healthy individuals. Though most individuals are influenced to some degree by exposure to mass media, very few lose the sensibilities and values of their local social groups.
- ■ In this instance, you would probably seek evidence from research studies that identify the extent to which healthy individuals are influenced by the mass media.

Conclusion:
The normalizing effect of mass media has been documented in a number of studies, many of which suggest that individuals adopt behaviours that they would otherwise avoid because mass media affects an individual's sense of self in the same way that events in the immediate environment might do. Mass media also appears to have the effect of diminishing anxiety about previously taboo or exotic behaviours, sometimes rendering those behaviours as socially desirable rather than different and anti-social. Though there are limits to the effect that mass media might have on healthy individuals, it appears that it does play a role in determining the way in which individuals construct themselves as social beings.

LO 2, 3, 4

14.10 WRITING IN THE NATURAL SCIENCES (E.G., BIOLOGY, CHEMISTRY, PHYSICS)

Like writers in the humanities and the social sciences, writers of essays in the natural sciences go through a process of planning, writing, and revising. However, there are some features of writing in the natural sciences that tend to be particular to these disciplines. Writing in the natural sciences usually reflects a tendency toward plain prose, subordinating the desire for evocative expression to the need for clarity and precision. Essays in science may deal with complex theories, but they also operate from objectively verifiable data. Language is not meant to get in the way. For the most part, science speaks through hard evidence, using facts and statistics to make a case, and editorializing is usually discouraged. Unless your instructor specifically asks that you offer an opinion in an essay, it's best to restrict yourself to an unambiguous delivery of information.

Writing in the sciences might take a number of forms: there will be occasions in which you are asked simply to record information in a prescribed manner (e.g., lab reports), to report on your own experimental study (these tend to follow a specified format that is particular to the field of study and the purpose of the article), or research papers. In the example included at the end of this section, we walk through the steps of writing a research paper in the sciences using the IDDL model. While the ability to write a lab report or an article on experimental research is a skill of considerable importance, it tends to be guided by protocols that are too specific to be covered in a general discussion. We have, however, provided three charts (the next three) identifying, respectively, the general characteristics of writing in the natural sciences; some of the varieties of writing modes in the natural sciences; and the usual steps of the writing process you would use for writing a report or article in the natural sciences.

14.10.1 General Characteristics of Writing in the Natural Sciences

Ways in Which a Natural Sciences Essay Corresponds to the Generic Essay Model	Ways in Which a Natural Sciences Essay Differs from the Generic Essay Model
Essays in the natural sciences are generally guided explicitly by logic.	As is the case with structures for essays in the social sciences, essay structures for essays in the natural sciences are usually prescribed by the respective formatting conventions (e.g., AMA, Harvard Method, or CSE). Within each of the sections, however, the organization of ideas and information ought to be governed by logic.
Assertions are supported by evidence.	In the natural sciences, all assertions and claims are underwritten by reference to evidence in the research literature or by reference to experimental data.
Introduction of supporting evidence follows specific conventions.	As is the case with evidence in essays in the social sciences, evidence in essays in the natural sciences is usually explored generally in a literature review, then introduced as necessary to support assertions and identified with citations.
Formatting corresponds to a specific formatting convention.	It is almost always the case that writers in the natural sciences will use AMA, Harvard Method, or CSE.

14.10.2 Different Modes of Writing in the Natural Sciences

This chart identifies some of the different modes of writing you may encounter in the natural sciences.

Varieties of Writing in the Natural Sciences
■ Writing in the natural sciences takes a number of forms, ranging from lab notebooks—which include data records—to essays, scientific articles, and reports.
■ Lab notebooks are written records of experiments, materials used, and the results obtained. A lab notebook ought to provide enough information for another individual to reconstruct your experiment. Charts and drawings are acceptable to use in a lab notebook.
■ Data records are often part of a lab notebook. Scientists often record their observations in table format when they are observing an experiment or collecting data in the field. Data records often contain only numbers and short phrases.
■ When writing scientific articles or reports, you have to follow a strict format. The reader generally anticipates that information will be delivered in a specific order and in a particular format. Most reports include the following seven sections: title, abstract, introduction, methods and materials, results, discussion, literature cited.

14.10.3 Writing a Report or Article in the Sciences

As noted above, the variety of writing protocols in the sciences makes it difficult to identify a single protocol for writing reports or articles in the sciences. The suggestions below are a guide only.

Preparing to Write Your Natural Science Report
■ As always, analyze the assignment carefully. Reports in the natural sciences generally focus on the description of processes or phenomena, identification of cause and effect, or analysis of current theories. Review the requirements for the report.
■ If you don't understand the requirements, schedule an appointment with your instructor to ask questions.
■ Determine the format that is expected for the work. Based on that format, construct a tentative outline.
■ Use the tentative outline to focus your research. Determine the specific questions that need to be answered.
■ Use the questions to identify the resources you will need. As always, be thorough but selective. Though it's important to consult the resources necessary to develop a balanced view of the question you're exploring, it's also important to limit your search to materials that are relevant.
■ Identify the resources that you need and the research methodology you're expected to follow. Use your library resources to access academic databases, or Google Scholar. These resources provide access to authoritative articles and/or abstracts.
■ If your preliminary research has changed your understanding of the topic, revise the outline to correspond to that new understanding.

Introduction

The introduction to a report in the natural sciences will answer the questions what, why, and how. You're expected to define your purpose, identifying the subject under investigation and the characteristics of the subject. In the introduction, you will also briefly cite the literature that supports your choices and identify the question or controversy that led to your investigation. You're generally expected to identify the purpose of your report, and explain the way in which your research or investigation serves to address some aspect of the question or controversy you identified above. Usually, you will briefly state the findings of your report (in one sentence if possible).

Questions to Guide Composition:

- Have you identified a purpose for your report?
- Have you contextualized the subject of the report within the current scientific literature?
- Have you explained the way in which the report you're writing addresses an important question or controversy within the field of study?

Materials and Method

This section is meant to recount the steps that you, or others, have followed in undertaking a particular investigation. You need to provide enough information that your reader could repeat the experiment.

- Identify, and explain the source of, chemicals and/or animals used.
- Explain your experimental design, including the number and types of animals, quantities, and concentrations of chemicals.
- Explain the types of equipment used.
- Explain under what conditions the experiment was carried out.
- Explain the procedures used to measure the effects you studied.

Questions to Guide Composition:

- Have you identified the materials, equipment, and conditions of the experiment?
- Have you listed, and explained, the specific procedures of the study? Have those procedures been listed in a logical order?

Results

Normally, in a report in the natural sciences, you will use the results section to report the specific effects that were anticipated in the materials and method section. You don't usually undertake a discussion or draw conclusions at this point. Instead, you report what you have found, dividing results of complicated experiments into types and reporting on each in a separate paragraph.

In this section, you generally itemize relevant results, specifying both qualities and quantities, and use language that clearly specifies physical effect or character. When the volume of data becomes so extensive as to be too difficult for a reader to process, or too burdensome for you to record, you might choose to report the information in a table or in graph form.

Questions to Guide Composition:

- Have you listed all significant results?
- If the study is complex, have you organized the results into categories?
- Is the data too dense to be comprehensible? Would it be more effective to report data in a table or graph?
- Does your word choice clearly indicate the effects you observed?

Discussion

The "Discussion" section of a report in the natural sciences is often the final section of the paper. This is where you provide an explanation and/or an interpretation of your results. You might choose to begin the section by restating the question you posed in the introduction.

(continued)

(continued)

You will generally report each of the results from the results section in its own paragraph, beginning the paragraph with a one-sentence summary of the procedure used and result obtained. That sentence will be followed with the conclusion, speculative or otherwise, that can be drawn from the result. Because you're usually reporting on a causal relationship, you might choose to use language that reflects causality (e.g., "therefore, this result shows that," "this result suggests that," "this result supports the conclusion"). For each result, you're also expected to identify the scientific literature that supports or contradicts your findings, and discuss the way in which your conclusions fit within the larger context of the existing literature.

Use your final paragraph to identify the way in which your study and findings may relate to a larger issue or to the existing understanding of the phenomenon. As always in academic writing, it's important to be measured and precise in your summation. If you've found that electric automobiles might marginally diminish the North American dependence on fossil fuels, report that. Don't lose yourself in claims that exceed your findings.

Questions to Guide Composition:

- Have you organized your discussion around the results you observed?
- Does your discussion follow the logic of your argument?
- Are you using language that identifies the causal relationship between the elements?
- Have you demonstrated the significance of the literature you reviewed?
- Have you clearly demonstrated the way in which your research question has been addressed by the evidence you provided?

14.10.4 Using the IDDL Model to Draft an Essay in the Sciences

In the example below, we've provided a topic and modelled the way in which you might use the IDDL model to organize your essay. As was the case with essays in the social sciences, essays in the natural sciences are expected to argue from the evidence, demonstrating clearly that the claims being made can be substantiated, or to report facts. In addition to an objective stance, therefore, it's particularly important that your writing be precise and unambiguous.

Topic: Climate Change

Thesis: Climate change is both a climatological and sociological phenomenon, affecting the ecosystem in ways that will have a profound impact on human populations. The degree of social change can be expected to correspond, roughly, to the degree of climatic change with impacts being felt in food supplies, water supplies, and shelter.

- **Is it clear?**
- **Is it focused?**
- **Is it measurable?**

Subthesis 1: Climate change will affect human populations due to its effect on food supplies.

- **What is the relationship to the main thesis?**
  - This is the first of the principal claims of the main thesis.

- ■ **What information is needed to explore or substantiate the claim of subthesis 1?**
  - In this section of the essay, you will need to find studies that verify climate change will have an effect on agriculture and that the effect will profoundly influence human populations.
  - In this essay, you will probably require two sources of information. The first, which you will use to establish a connection between climate change and agriculture, could come from journals in a number of sciences (e.g., climatology and environmental science). The second, which you will use to explain the effect of changes in agriculture on human populations, might come from journals in anthropology, sociology, or human geography.
    - Evidence: You might begin by citing evidence that identifies the effect of environmental change on agriculture in general.
    - Evidence: You might also cite evidence to demonstrate the degree of the effect of the change and the range of effects in different areas.
    - Evidence: You will probably need to cite some evidence of the effect that agricultural changes have on societies (e.g., human settlement patterns or social interactions).
  - Having gathered the evidence you need, you would cite it, explain it, and organize it around the subthesis.

Subthesis 2: Climate change will affect human populations due to its effect on water supplies.
- ■ **What is the relationship to the main thesis?**
  - This is the second of the principal claims of the main thesis.
- ■ **What information is needed to explore or substantiate the claim of subthesis 2?**
  - In this section of the essay, you will need to find studies that verify that climate change will have an effect on water supplies and that the effect will profoundly influence human populations.
  - Again, you will probably require two sources of information. The first, which you will use to establish a connection between climate change and water supplies, could come from journals in a number of sciences (e.g., climatology and environmental science). The second, which you will use to explain the effect of changes in water supplies on human populations, might come from journals in anthropology, sociology, or human geography.
    - Evidence: You might begin by citing evidence that identifies the effect of environmental change on water supplies in general.
    - Evidence: You might also cite evidence to demonstrate the degree of the effect of the change and the range of the effects in different areas.
    - Evidence: Again, you will need to cite some evidence of the effect that water shortages have on societies (e.g., human settlement patterns or social interactions).
  - Having gathered the evidence you need, you would cite it, explain it, and organize it around the subthesis.

Subthesis 3: Climate change will affect human populations by precipitating changes in settlement patterns.
- ■ **What is the relationship to the main thesis?**
  - This is the third of the principal claims of the main thesis.
- ■ **What information is needed to explore or substantiate the claim of subthesis 3?**
  - In this section of the essay, you will need to find studies verifying both that climate change affects human settlement patterns and that changes in settlement patterns in industrialized societies tend to be problematic.

(continued)

(*continued*)

- In this case, you may need information on the effect of agricultural changes and water shortages on human populations; the general effect of societies having to migrate to find new sources of food and water; and the specific difficulties that industrial societies face when natural resources are lost. This information will probably come from journals in anthropology, sociology, or human geography.
  - Evidence: You might begin by citing evidence that identifies the effect of large-scale moves of societies in response to diminishing food and water supplies.
  - Evidence: You might also cite evidence to demonstrate the degree of the effect of the change and the range of the effects in different areas.
  - Evidence: You may also choose to search for research on the differing effects of relocation on nomadic populations and industrial or fixed populations.
- Having gathered the evidence you need, you would cite it, explain it, and organize it around the subthesis.

Counter-argument:
- ■ Why would a reasonable person disagree?
  - The extent of climatic change has been exaggerated.
  - Humans have dealt with climate change before.
  - As it always has, human ingenuity will uncover a solution.
- ■ You might cite evidence of previous changes in climate and human adaptation to those changes.

Conclusion:
The changes in climate that are currently being experienced will have a profound effect on human societies. Despite the fact that human responses to climatic change are a sociological phenomenon, and therefore might be expected to vary, the social changes are predictable. Existing information allows researchers to develop an algorithm to predict the future on the basis of the relationship between predicted changes to the environment, corresponding changes to agricultural practices and water supplies, and historical data about previous social responses to climate change. Using that algorithm, it is safe to predict that life will soon be very unpleasant.

14.11 CONCLUSION

One of the difficulties that novice writers in academic settings report most often is the problem of adapting to the shifting standards and formats of discourse across the disciplines. Though the advice offered in this chapter will not resolve that difficulty completely, it's meant to foreground some of the fundamental differences between common academic writing styles. The principle that emerges in each of the different writing protocols is that form serves a purpose. Writers in the humanities seek to establish the validity of their positions through reasoned analysis or interpretation of primary works, theories, or phenomena, and/or by reference to authority. Writers in the social sciences, on the other hand, generally argue for a particular conclusion on the basis of experimentation or by reference to existing studies. Finally, writers in the natural sciences, who usually write to report an observed effect or to explore theoretical positions, tend to argue on the basis of their own observations or by reference to the reported observations of other scientists. There is a commonality between the three forms: in each case, writers seek to establish that a particular conclusion is reasonable by citing relevant evidence. The difference between the forms lies in the manner in which the argument is structured and in the nature of the evidence offered.

MyCompLab®

How Do I Get a Better Grade?

Go to MyCompLab for additional help with your
grammar, writing, and research skills. You will have access to a variety of
exercises, instruction, and videos that will help you improve your basic
skills and help you get a better grade.

The Reviewing Stage

In the final section of this text, you've been attending to questions of format and editing. Though you've focused throughout the writing process on the development of meaning (as you ought to have done), you're aware that the essay you've written belongs to a specific discourse or writing community. You want to ensure, therefore, that it doesn't embarrass itself by behaving in an inappropriate manner when you send it out into the world.

Each of the chapters in this section addressed a specific category of writing conventions. The first, Chapter 12, spoke to the conventions that belong to a particular formatting style. With those conventions in mind, you review your essay to determine whether you've followed the principles that govern the format of the page, the expected authorial stance (i.e., the voice), the writing tense, the format for citations, and the format for lists of references. Chapter 13 introduced strategies for editing your essay for adherence to common language usage. Using those strategies, you edit your essay systematically, identifying and correcting errors in spelling, punctuation, and word usage. The templates of Chapter 14 identified some of the discipline-specific conventions of essay writing that operate in different subject areas, including the types of evidence that are expected, the degree of subjectivity that is permitted, and the pattern of organization that essays usually follow. You use those templates to ensure that your essay conforms to the expectations of readers in a respective discipline.

CHAPTER 12: THE IMPORTANCE OF FORMATTING

In Chapter 12, we began with a discussion of the purpose of adhering to formatting conventions. We acknowledged that decisions about formatting conventions might appear arbitrary, with seemingly unimportant questions about the placement of commas or line spacing growing to assume a disproportionate significance in the final evaluation of your essay, but also argued that decisions about formatting have a greater effect than you might imagine.

Understanding the Effect of Following Formatting Conventions
1. What is the effect of using the appropriate formatting convention?
2. How does your adherence to the prescribed formatting convention affect your reader?
3. What kinds of decisions are affected by formatting conventions?

Understanding the Difference between Formatting Conventions (e.g., APA, MLA, *Chicago*)
1. Is a title page required in APA? MLA? *Chicago?*
2. Which font is used in APA? MLA? *Chicago?*
3. Which line-spacing convention is used in APA? MLA? *Chicago?*
4. What voice is used in APA? MLA? *Chicago?*
5. What tense is used in APA? MLA? *Chicago?*
6. How are page numbers formatted in APA? MLA? *Chicago?*
7. How are in-text citations formatted in APA? MLA? *Chicago?*
8. Are footnotes/endnotes used in APA? MLA? *Chicago?* How are they formatted?
9. How are references formatted in APA? MLA? *Chicago?*
Thinking Strategically about Managing Multiple Formatting Conventions
1. Which formatting convention will you use most often in your courses?
2. What are the five most important features of that formatting convention?
3. How can you memorize, or internalize, those five features?
4. What are the next five important features, in order of the frequency with which they will occur in your writing?
5. How can you memorize, or internalize, those five features?
6. Compare the ten features of the formatting convention that you will use most often to the formatting convention(s) that you will use infrequently. What are the important similarities? What are the important differences?

CHAPTER 13: EDITING

Chapter 13 introduced a strategy for editing your essay systematically. Editing is important. It ensures that you will deliver a readable essay. Editing also increases your authority as a writer, demonstrating to the reader that you're conversant with the rules of standard usage (e.g., grammar, punctuation, diction), and that you care enough about the essay you're presenting to follow those rules carefully. By reviewing your essay for mechanical errors, you make a good essay better.

However, as we noted in the chapter, novice writers often concentrate on error avoidance, worrying about mechanical errors to the extent that they are not able to attend to their primary purpose of developing and refining their respective thesis. Therefore, it's important that you develop strategies for editing that permit you to focus on the process of writing first, and the process of editing later. It's easier to undertake a systematic review of errors when you are not, simultaneously, concentrating on developing and organizing your major themes.

Understanding the Effect of Editing for Standard Usage
1. What is the difference between the process of revision and the process of editing?
2. What is the effect of careful editing?
3. What effect does editing have on the clarity of your essay?
4. How does editing affect the readability of your essay?
5. How does editing affect your credibility with the reader?
6. Why is it more effective to review your sentences after you've completed a paragraph, or series of related paragraphs, than during the process of their composition?

Editing Strategically
1. Think about the formatting style you're expected to use (e.g., APA, MLA, *Chicago*). Identify the five most significant features of that formatting style (e.g., page layout, citations, tense). Does your essay adhere to those requirements?
2. Review your list of references, comparing it to a style guide. Does the references list correspond to the references list in the style guide?
3. Review the first page of your essay, looking for mechanical errors (e.g., mistakes in spelling, word choice, word usage, punctuation, etc). What are the five most common mistakes you find? Use that list to edit your essay.
4. Read the essay again. Are you still finding a pattern of common mistakes? Create a second list of common mistakes and use it to guide a second round of editing.

CHAPTER 14: TEMPLATES FOR COMMON ACADEMIC WRITING STYLES

The conventions that we discussed in Chapter 12 referred to cross-discipline formatting protocols. In Chapter 14, we reviewed discipline-specific writing conventions. While there is a certain degree of overlap in the principles that inform the two types of conventions (e.g., disciplines that employ the APA format tend to have similar expectations in terms of the kind of evidence that will be used to support an argument), there are also differences that derive from the traditions of scholarship in each respective discipline. As was the case with the management of multiple formatting conventions, it's important to recognize that you don't need to acquire an equal proficiency in all discipline-specific writing conventions. Concentrate first on the conventions you will use most often (i.e., the ones that apply to the greatest number of your courses).

Thinking about the Effect of Discipline-Specific Writing Conventions
1. What are the important differences among writing conventions in the different disciplines?
2. What are the general differences in the patterns of organization in the different disciplines?
3. How does the difference in the nature of evidence affect your writing decisions?
4. How does the difference in the degree of subjectivity permitted affect your writing decisions?
5. What effects do those differences have on your understanding of writing?

Thinking Strategically about Using Discipline-Specific Writing Conventions
1. What is the category to which the majority of your courses belong (e.g., humanities, social sciences, or natural sciences)?
2. What is the discipline to which the majority of your courses belong (e.g., English, history, sociology, anthropology, biology)?
3. What are the most significant features of the conventions in that discipline?
a. What is the usual pattern of organization for essays in that discipline?
b. What voice (first, second, or third person) is usually used in writing essays in the discipline?

     c. What does that suggest about the relationship between the writer and the kind of evidence that will be offered?

     d. What kind of evidence is usually required in essays in that discipline?

4. What specific decisions do you have to approach differently to write effectively in this discipline?

5. How are you going to change your decision-making processes to effect that change?

6. What are the significant differences between writing in the discipline you identified above and writing in the disciplines of your other courses?

7. What specific decisions do you have to approach differently to write effectively in these other disciplines?

8. How are you going to change your decision-making processes to effect those changes?

INDEX